STUDIES IN THE UPANIṢADS

STUDIES IN THE UPANIṢADS

By
GOVINDAGOPAL MUKHOPADHYAYA

PILGRIMS BOOK PVT. LTD.
DELHI - 110033

STUDIES IN THE UPANIṢADS

Pilgrims first edition - August, 1999

Published by
PILGRIMS BOOK PVT. LTD.
416, Express Tower, Azadpur Commercial
Complex, Delhi-110 033
Phone: 7132459 Fax: 91-11-7249674
E-mail: pilgrim@ndb.vsnl.net.in

Distributed by
PILGRIMS BOOK HOUSE
P.O. Box 3872, Kathmandu, Nepal
Tel.: 424942, 425919
Fax: 977-1-424943
E-mail: pilgrims@wlink.com.np
Web Site: http://gfas.com/pilgrims

Varanasi Branch
PILGRIMS BOOK HOUSE
P.O. Box 38, Durga Kund,
Nababganj, Varanasi
Phones : 314059, 314060

Cover design & Typesetting by Samey Singh

ISBN 81-7624-068-0
Price : Rs. 300/-

Printed at :
Excel Prints
WZ 559B, Naraina Village
New Delhi-110028.

IN MEMORIAM

PRANGOPAL MUKHOPĀDHYĀYA

Father and Fount of Light

वक्ता चास्य त्वादृगन्यो न लभ्यः।

यत्ते मरीचीः प्रवतो मनो जगाम दूरकम्।
तत्त आ वर्तयामसीह क्षयाय जीवसे।।

Ṛgveda.
10.58.6

PREFACE

The present work is the outcome of a prolonged intensive study in the sacred lore of the Upaniṣads. The study was mainly taken up with the object of finding out the unique nature of the Absolute or Brahman directly from the Upaniṣadic texts and also to investigate into the methods of approach to that Absolute as propounded in the Upaniṣads and finally to enquire into the characteristics of the final realization. I was initiated into these studies by my late lamented father, who was to me the living embodiment of Upaniṣadic wisdom. I feel that I have been the most ineffective instrument for transmitting his luminous realizations.

I was singularly fortunate in having the privilege of studying the sacred texts at the feet of two eminent masters of Indian wisdom, Dr Sarvepalli Radhakrishnan and Mahamahopadhyaya Dr. Gopinath Kaviraj, while I was a research scholar in the Benares Hindu University. I cannot adequately express my gratitude to them and especially to the latter for having graced my book with a foreword from his pen. What I owe to Srimat Pratyagātmānanda Saraswati and Sri Krishna Prem is more than a matter for acknowledgement. Sri Krishna Prem, though living the life of a recluse in the lonely heights of the Himalayas, took a brotherly interest in my work and made valuable suggestions and corrections.

I gratefully acknowledge my indebtedness to Dr. Satkari Mookerjee, the then Asutosh Professor of Sanskrit in the Calcutta University, Dr. N. K. Brahma, the then Head of the Department of Philosophy in the Presidency College, Calcutta, the late Dr. Subodh Chandra Mukherjee, Mayurbhanj Professor of Sanskrit in the Benares Hindu University and Dr. P.L. Vaidya, who succeeded the latter—all of whom guided me in my researches at different periods.

The first edition of this work has long been out of print and friends from India and abroad have been pressing me to bring out a second edition of it. I am happy that the renowned publisher of Indological studies and books, PILGRIMS BOOK PVT. LTD., have come forward to fulfil that demand. I have thoroughly revised the book and have also added one chapter on the OMKĀRA, for the two distinct ways which the Upaniṣads delineate, viz. the analytic and the synthetic, converge and coalesce in the OMKĀRA, from which both these ways stem out. This Chapter, therefore, has been a fulfilment of the two ways, making the circle complete and truly integral. The secret of the OMKĀRA has been sought to be unveiled in all aspects as far as possible.

My revered father as well as my respected teachers and illuminating guides like Mahāmahopādhyaya Padma-Vibhūṣana Dr. Gopinath Kaviraj, Dr. Sarvepalli Radha Krishnan, who had originally inspired me to undertake these studies in the Upaniṣads, have all left me since. I have also lost the wayfarer to the same goal, my sole friend and companion, the incomparable saint and devotee, Sri Krishna Prem, who guided me affectionately at ever step and personally revised the entire writing. But their lights still shine as brightly as ever to guide me in my intellectual pursuits and spiritual journey. May this second edition of the book, which owes everything to them alone, be an humble offering of homage to them all.

I earnestly hope that the perennial wisdom of India, as enshrined in the Upaniṣads, will be studied by all earnest seekers of truth all over the world in the coming century and millenium, for the Upaniṣads are the eternal solace of life as well the solace in death. The Upaniṣads yield a new sense at every reading, for they contain the eternal fount of wisdom.

GOVINDA GOPAL MUKHOPADHYAYA

Calcutta
August 1999

CONTENTS

Page

PREFACE .... vii-viii

ABBREVIATIONS .... xv-xviii

FOREWORD .... ix-xx

Prolegomena 1-37

Part I

THE GOAL

CHAPTER I

The Problem of Reality 41-96

The goal—the problem—two forms of Brahman—transcendence and immanence—their true significance—true meaning of *'mithyā'*—degrees of Reality—negative description—its real significance—view of Royce examined—the true picture of the goal—the false ideas pointed out—Immanence—Iśvara—Rāmānuja's views—Bhartṛprapañca—Śaṅkara—nature of *Jīva*—Is it eternal or evanescent—*Māyā*—the solution of the original problem—the true Vedāntic vision—Western views of Reality examined—Descartes—Leibniz—Spinoza—Kant—Hegel—Bergson—Alexandcr—Jeans and Eddington—the uniqueness of the Upaniṣadic view.

CHAPTER II

The Problem of Knowledge 97-126

The nature ot the Upaniṣadic knowledge—thc problem—thc Atman not the object of knowledge—Perception—Inference —Intuition—*Sākṣat aparokṣāt*—Vedāntic view of *pramāṇas*—the discourse of Yājñavalkya on *Jyotis*—the significance of *vākya* and *śravaṇa*—the nature of *tattvajñāna*—the relation of *Jñāna* and *karman*—the value and utility of synthesis—the misrepresentation of transcendental knowledge—different views of Brahmadatta, Maṇḍana, Bhartṛprapañca—their reconciliation—the Western theories of truth examined—Correspondence—Coherence—their inadequacy—the Upaniṣadic of an unique type of knowledge.

Part II

THE WAY

CHAPTER III

The Preparation 129-157

The three paths—primary necessity of a teacher—the method of approach to the teacher and significance—*Brahmacarya-Sattvaśuddhi—Āhāraśuddhi—Yajña—Śreyas* and *Preyas—Kratu-Satya—Dharma—Yajña, Adhyayana* and *Dāna—Śraddhā—Pitā, Ācārya* and *Atithi*—Absence of stress on *Ahiṁsā* and *Īśvarapraṇidhāna*—the three '*da*'—condemnation of immoral acts—Summary—the Western critics' imputation of disregard for morality in the Upaniṣads—reply to the charges.

CHAPTER IV

Contemplation 158-182

The second step—its necessity—its distinction from the first step—the utility of the first step—the role of *Mukhya Prāṇa*—the meaning of *upāsanā*—its purposes—its constituents—the place of feeling or *bhakti* in it—the need of an *ālambana*—features of *Upāsanā*—grades of *Upāsanā—Pratīka* and *Ahaṁgraha—Sampat, Āropa, Saṁvarga, Adhyāsa—Saguṇa* and *Nirguṇa Upāsanā*—the principle of classification—varieties of approach in the Upaniṣads—mystic elements—*nādā—prāṇāyāma—jyotis* the two broad methods of *yoga* and *viveka*—synthesis and analysis.

CHAPTER V

The Synthetic Way 183-205

The three centres of synthesis and the three *Vidyās* corresponding to them illustrated—the *Dahara—vidyā—Udgītha—vidyā—Madhu-vidyā.*

ABBREVIATIONS

SANSKRIT

AU	Aitareya Upaniṣad.
AŚU	Atharva Śikha Upaniṣad.
ASU	Atharvaśira Upaniṣad.
ARR	Advitaratnarakṣaṇam. Bombay Edition.
AP	Anubhūtiprakāśa.
ATU	Atharvaśira Upaniṣad.
BH	Bhāgavatam. (with Śrīdhara's Commentary).
BU	Bṛhadāraṇyaka Upaniṣad. (with Śāṅkara Bhāṣya).
BS	Brahma-Siddhi. Madras Edition.
CU	Chāndogya Upaniṣad (with Śāṅkara Bhāṣya).
DVP	Daharavidyāprakāśikā.
DS	Durgāsaptaśatī.
GPK	Gaudapādakārīkā.
GRIJ	Ganganath Jha Research Institute Journal.
IU	Īśa Upaniṣad.
JMV	Jīvanmuktiviveka.
KTU	Kaṭha Upaniṣad.
KSU	Kauṣītaki Upaniṣad.
KU	Kena Upaniṣad.
KH	Khaṇḍanakhaṇḍakhādya. (Introduction by Śaṅkara Bhāratī).
PMB	Mahābhāṣya of Patañjali. Keilhorn's Edition.
Mai.	Maitrī Upaniṣad.
Ma.	Māṇḍūkya Upaniṣad.
MS	Manusaṁhitā.
MU	Muṇḍaka Upaniṣad.

NS	Naiṣkarmya Siddhi.
NBS	Nārada Bhakti Sūtra.
Nir.	Nirukta (Yāska).
NSU	Nyāya Sūtra.
PD	Pañcadaśī.
PK	Praṇavakalpa.
PGV	Parapakṣagirivajra.
PP	Pañcapādikā.
PPB	Praśastapādabhāṣya (with Setuṭīkā and Vyomavatī vṛtti).
PRU	Praśna Upaniṣad.
RS	Rudrasaṃhitā.
RT	Ratnatraya.
RV	Ṛgveda.
RVS	Raghuvamśam.
ŚB	Śāṅkara-Bhāṣya (on Brahmasūtra, Bṛhadāraṇyaka & Chāndogya etc.)
SK	Sāṅkhya-Kārikā.
SP	Śiva Purāṅa.
SS	Sāṅkhya Sūtra.
ST	Sāradatilaka.
SA	Samvidullāsa.
SBH	Śrībhāṣya. Madras Edition.
SDS	Sarvadarśanasaṁgraha.
SD	Śatadūṣaṇī. Conjeeveram Edition.
SG	Śivagītā.
SK	Spandakārikā.
SLS	Siddhāntaleśasaṁgraha. Chowkhamba Edition.
STA	Svachhanda Tantra.
ŚU	Śvetāśvatara Upaniṣad.
TU	Taittirīya Upaniṣad.
TL	Tantrāloka.
TS	Tantrasāra.
Vār.	Vārttika.
VPD	Vākyapadīya.

VVR Vārivasyārahasya.
VAS Vedārthasaṅgraha.
VKL. Vedāntakalpalatikā.
VPB Vedāntaparibhāṣā. Edited by Sarat Chandra Ghosal Calcutta.
VS Vārttikasāra.
YMD Yatīndramatadīpikā. Poona Edition.
YS Yoga-Sūtra.

ENGLISH

STD Alexander—Space Time and Deity.
IU Aurobindo—(i) Isha Upanishad.
LD (ii) Life Divine.
CE Bergson —Creative Evolution.
SIV Bhattacharya K.C.—Studies in Vedantism.
VD Bosanquet—Value and Destiny of the Individual.
AR Bradley —Appearance and Reality.
PHS Brahma N.K.—Philosophy of Hindu Sadhana.
ER Caird, E. —Evolution of Religion.
PHR Caird, J. —Philosophy of Religion.
NAV Coomaraswamy, A.—A New Approach to the Vedas.
SWK Datta, D.M.—The Six Ways of Knowing.
PU Deussen —Philosophy of the Upaniṣads.
NPW Éddington—The Nature of the Physical World.
PR Edwards —Philosophy of Religion.
NRDR Falk, Maryla—Nāma-Rūpa and Dharma-Rūpa.
PU Gough —Philosophy of the Upaniṣads.
PTE Green, T.H.—Prolegomena to Ethics.
IHD Guenon, Rene—(i) Introduction to Hindu Doctrines.
MBV (ii) Man and his becoming according to the Vedanta.
TOP Hocking —Types of Philosophy.
TUP Hume —Thirteen Principal Upaniṣads.
EM Huxley, Aldous—Ends and Means.
PP Inge, W. —Philosophy of Plotinus.

Pr.	James, W.—(i) Pragmatism.
VRE	—(ii) Varieties of Religious Experience.
PHP	Jeans, J. —Physics and Philosophy.
NT	Joachim, H.—(i) Nature of Truth.
SES	—(ii) A study of Ethics of Spinoza.
GP	Joad, C.E.M.—Guide to Philosophy.
KM	Keith, A.B.—(i) Karma-Mīmāmsā.
PVU	(ii) Philosphy of the Veda and the Upaniṣads.
STV	Kirtikar —Studies in Vedanta.
YK	Krishna Prem—The Yoga of the Kaṭhopaniṣad.
IH	Otto, R. —The Idea of the Holy.
IG	Pringle-Pattison—The Idea of God.
EWT	Radhakrishnan, S.—(i) Eastern Religions & Western Thought.
IVL	(ii) An Idealist View of Life.
RPU	(iii) Philosophy of the Upaniṣads.
CSU	Ranade —A Constructive Survey of the Upaniṣads.
AG	Roy, D.K.—Among the Great.
WI	Royce —The World and the Individual.
HWP	Russel, Bertrand—History of Western Philosophy.
HPH	Schwegler—History of Philosophy.
HM	Sircar, M.N.—Hindu Mysticism.
TDI	Spinoza—Tractatus de Intellectus.
CIL	Underhill, Evelyn—Concerning the Inner Life.
UL	Urquhart, W.S.—The Upaniṣads and Life.
HOP	History of Pantheism.
CIP	Contemporary Indian Philosophy.

JOURNALS

CR	Calcutta Review.
HG	Hibbert Journal.
IA	Indian Antiquary.
IHQ	Indian Historical Quarterly.

FOREWORD

The Upaniṣads occupy a unique place in the history of spiritual and philosophical thought of India, nay of the whole world. Their value is to be assessed, not simply as a storehouse of wise sayings and parables which influenced the life of old people detached from the world, but as a living fountain of Divine Wisdom capable of quenching the thirst of ardent souls hankering after Peace and Blissful Existence. We all know that the different schools of orthodox philosophical thought in early medieval India had their origin in the Upaniṣads and most of the practical lines of approach towards the Goal of Life had their first inspiration from them. And in the cryptic utterances and obscure cult traditions found scattered in this literature we can easily detect traces of great mystic wisdom which do not easily lend themselves to the understanding of average and superficial intellect. A study of the Upaniṣads from every angle of vision is, therefore, essential for a proper appreciation of the spirit of Indian Culture.

I, therefore, heartily welcome the publication of the present Upaniṣadic studies of Dr. Govindagopal Mukhopādhyāya as a valuable contribution in the field of orthodox scholarship. The value of these studies consists mainly, I believe, in the way in which the writer has approached the subject. First of all, he has attempted to present the conception of the Supreme Reality and Knowledge which the Upaniṣads hold up as the highest ideal to our vision. Then he has described the path and has shown the pilgrim starting on this path under the guidance of the Master (*Guru*) (or of the Inner Monitor within, the *Antaryāmī*). But before the actual journey commences there is, as he has shown, a stage of preparation. Progress in the journey is evidently marked by the degrees of clarity in contemplation reached by the *sādhaka*. The Path is both synthetic and analytic. When the Goal is reached—not certainly as a result of the continued progress of the pilgrim's movement (which, of course, is the expression of his personal effort) but as the effect of the spontaneous outflow of Grace descending on the soul out of the Supreme Height or from the Deepest Abyss, as an act of super-abounding Freedom or Election (*Varaṇa*),—what happens is not simply the restoration of the soul's lost freedom but its establishment in the self-aware unity of Supreme Reality and Knowledge.

I commend the book, as coming from a young erudite scholar who had the benefit of close association in his earlier years with a man of singular spiritual insight in the person of his illustrious father, to the reading public interested in spiritual studies.

But I have one personal request to make to the writer, I should like to ask him to present us, if possible, with a *critical and comprehensive study* of that aspect of ancient Indian Wisdom which is reflected in the Upanisads. To be thorough and penetrating it should have in its background a living assimilation of the mystic traditions of the earlier Vedic age represented by the *mantras* and *brāhmanas* as a whole. There is no doubt that the so-called *karmakānḍa* finds its true significance only when it is accepted as a symbolical presentation to the uninitiated mind of the deeper mysteries of the esoteric Vedic *sādhanā*. It is also expected that valuable light might be thrown on this study, with special reference to several obscure issues involved, if it included within its scope a careful consideration of the contemporary religious thought-currents outside the Upaniṣadic pale in the esoteric circles of Buddhism and Jainism, in the earlier *Pañcarātra* and *Ekāyana* thought and in the ancient Āgamic traditions of various schools. In the last place, if it is true that every school of subsequent religious thought in India traces its descent, directly or incidentally, from the Upaniṣads, we should be prepared to find in them the signs of its first adumbration. A comprehensive study of this kind, which should have an integral view-point and look upon different cultural traditions with equal respect as being divergent expressions of the same basic Indian pattern, has long been a desideratum.

Dr. Mukhopadhyaya has my best wishes for success in this proposed literary enterprise.

GOPINATH KAVIRAJ

2A, Sigra,
Varanasi.

PROLEGOMENA

I

The need for a fresh approach and its aim

The propriety of a fresh enquiry into the ancient texts of the Upaniṣads may be easily questioned. For there is a general impression that they have been explored to the full, both historically and philosophically, from various aspects by eminent scholars of the East and the West and very little remains to be said or done about them any more. Yet we have been prompted to make an intensive study of them anew because we have felt that the true essence of the Upaniṣadic teaching has hardly been revealed so far and still requires to be grasped in all its bearings. That the real significance has been missed is evident from the lamentable confusions and deliberate distortions made about this sacred teaching by almost all of the Western scholars and philosophers even upto the present day. Though scholars like Radhakrishnan have tried their best to present the true spirit of the Upaniṣadic teaching and ably replied to the criticisms levelled against it by Western scholars like Gough, Deussen etc., yet Keith persists in maintaining that "Radhakrishnan ignores the fundamental moral indifference of the Upaniṣads by reinterpreting them in the light of absolute idealism". So we have felt the need of quoting Upaniṣadic texts freely and of presenting the views of the Upaniṣads through their texts alone to meet the charges levelled against them. The 'moral indifference' which Keith and others read into the text of the Upaniṣads is due to their total lack of apprehension of the transcendental nature of the Upaniṣadic knowledge. The failure to understand the true nature of this knowledge has led in the field of metaphysics to a colossal misconception about the nature of the Absolute or Brahman as presented in the Upaniṣads, which in its turn has produced in the sphere of ethics the idea of 'moral indifference'. Thus our aim in the following pages will be twofold: firstly, to clear the metaphysical confusion by presenting a true picture of the Reality as depicted in the Upaniṣads and secondly, to remove the illusion of 'moral indifference' or the misconception about the absence of ethical content by bringing into light the true method of the Upaniṣadic approach to that Reality and the consummation reached thereby.

It is not at all surprising, that a true apprehension of this ancient wisdom has not been possible at all in the West and has ultimately led to such conclusions as 'contradictions *in adjecto* are the normal characteristic of the Upaniṣads', for verily the Upaniṣads contain a secret which is not easy to explore or unravel. The term 'Upaniṣad' essentially means the 'secret' or *rabasyam*. As Deussen puts it: "Certain mysterious words, expressions and formulas, which are only intelligible to the initiated, are described as Upaniṣad". The expressions or formulas look mysterious because of their cryptic nature and they were put in such a form with a double purpose: firstly, to conceal the supreme teaching from the uninitiated and non-believers and secondly, by exciting the curiosity and wonder of the true secker to bring his mental faculties to their full stretch as he contemplates over the symbol or expression. One who secks enlightenment or knowledge must exert himself to the utmost, and apply himself to the finding of the solution of the puzzle with unremitting labour. But a flat and explicit statement hardly stimulates our intellectual faculties because its plainness is patent and needs no further clarification. It is only a pithy saying, carrying a latent import behind it, that forces the intellect to actively engage itself in finding the hidden and true significance or meaning. The sacred texts of the Upaniṣads are thus full of such secret expressions or formulas and this fact is borne out by the very basic meaning of the term `Upaniṣad.' Hence wonder is the first and the last word about the Reality, the realiser of that Reality, as well as the method of that realisation as contained in the Upaniṣads. It is wonderfully beheld, it is wonderfully spoken and it is wonderfully heard. There is something amazing about it all.

A protest may be raised here by the rationalist mind that we are being led to mysticism, to a sphere beyond all reason and logic and so we must hasten to assure that nowhere does the Upaniṣadic teaching flout the reason or run contrary to it but on the contrary unequivocally affirm that the Reality is revealed only to the highest reason, the subtlest one-pointed intellect.[4] Hence to the surface mind and the unrefined intellect the truth no doubt remains hidden and so, if by the term 'mysticism' one understands that which is secret or hidden, it can very well be said of the Upaniṣads that they are full of mysticism, because they contain nothing but secret teachings (*guhya-ādeśāḥ*) which is the very basic meaning of the term 'Upaniṣad'. And it must also be noted that the secret teachings are not set forth in a haphazard fashion without any principle of reason running behind them. They are the embodiments of the highest reason, being the essence of the Veda, the repository of all wisdom. If one devotes his thoughts in finding out the process of reason which is at work behind all the teachings of the Upaniṣads, he is sure to be struck by the amazing logical precision and supreme harmony of thought running throughout the whole Upaniṣadic literature. It is *Vidyā* or Supreme Knowledge that is imparted here and hence there is nothing irrational or illogical in these teachings. It should not be mistakenly thought that the Upaniṣads contain only idle intellectual speculations of primitive mankind about the nature of the world and the soul, which are mostly crude and vague. By thrusting mere intellectualism into the Upaniṣads and by reading the texts in that light alone, the Western scholars have all been deprived of the true wisdom they contain. By confusing *Vidyā* or *Jñāna* with mere intellectual knowledge, even Deussen, the only ardent and sympathetic student and interpreter of the Upaniṣads in the West, makes a gross misrepresentation of the essential teachings contained therein. As he puts it in his introduction to the *Philosophy of the Upanisds:* 'Why then do we need a release from this existence? Because it is the realm of sin, is the reply of the Bible. The Veda answers : Because it is the realm of ignorance. The former sees depravity in the volitional, the latter in the intellectual side of human nature. The Bible demands a change of the will, the Veda of the understanding'.[5] After thus pitting the intellect against the will he gives his verdict in favour of the latter and then suddenly comes to the conclusion that the will happens to be the more fundamental of the two, as Schopenhauer views it and hence as 'the will and not the intellect is the centre of a man's nature, so surely must the pre-eminence be assigned to Christianity, in that its demand for a renewal of the will, is peculiarly vital and essential'.[6] From this as a natural corollary or an easy deduction is made patent the fact that the Upaniṣads are definitely anti-ethical, inasmuch as they totally neglect the will which is the spring of all moral actions. This view thus tries to represent the Upaniṣads as embodying a one-sided approach to the Reality, viz. through the intellect alone. The basis of all such misrepresentations lies in the failure to conceive the transcendental nature of the knowledge that the Upaniṣads impart.

It is no mere intellectual acquaintance with the nature of the Ātman or Brahman or a mere theoretical knowledge about it that is aimed at anywhere in the Upaniṣads, but a living and concrete experience of the Brahman or Ātman is sought everywhere. This is unmistakably clear from the story of Nārada in the Chāndogya Upaniṣad,[7] where he gives a long list of the sciences he had mastered and thereafter laments that he is merely a knower of hymns (i.e. sacred texts or books) and not a knower yet of the Ātman. That he still lacked the knowledge of the Ātman was evident to him from the fact of the persistence of grief or sorrow in him. Only the knower of the Ātman transcends all grief and hence he prays to the teacher to take him to the other shore beyond all darkness. Had mere intellectual knowledge been the aim of the Upaniṣads Nārada would not have begged of his teacher to impart to him the knowledge of the Ātman, for he was already well-versed in all the Vedas and Purānas, which contain complete descriptions about the Ātman. It is thus for *'Vijñāna'* or thorough knowledge and living experience that the teacher is approached and not for mere intellectual discipline.[8]

An approach to the teacher was considered indispensably necessary to have the knowledge, and its significancc lies in the fact that only an experienced soul can generate the experience in another soul—only a burning candle can light another. This also hints at the transcendental nature of the Upaniṣadic knowledge, because it is not generated through a process of intellectual reasoning but comes as a flash and breaks upon the soul with the uniqueness of a revelation through the ringing and revealing words of the teacher which penetrate into the very core of being and rend the veil of ignorance. But we must add that this revelation comes only after a most arduous intellectual discipline and rigorous moral training. The light no doubt comes from above but it must be received and retained below. This receptivity has to be cultured and cultivated and it depends on one's own making. Givenness is no doubt the essential mark of knowledge but the receptivity is never given, it has to be achieved through intense self-effort. The one is *vastutantra,* i.e., dependent on the object, the other is *kartṛtantra* i.e. dependent on the subject, devolving upon the doer. We shall find throughout our study of the Upaniṣads how they give equal scope to both in their respective spheres and thereby achieve a wonderful harmony and reconciliation of a problem that has proved baffling and insoluble to many.

That there was no lack of stress on the volitional aspect in the Upaniṣadic approach to the Reality will be evident from the innumerable passages in the Upaniṣads which we have collected together under a section called 'The Preparation'. We have devoted a whole section to it in order to show the utter hollowness of the charge of 'moral indifference' which has been laid at the door of'the Upaniṣads times without number by all Western interpreters, without a single exception. We have already pointed out that the fatal delusion has been caused by the inability to grasp the true nature of the transcendental knowledge that the Upaniṣads contain and teach. The aim of the Upaniṣads is not merely to be freed from the taints of sin like that of the Bible, but to be freed from the fetters of finitude which is the root cause of all sin. Release from the realm of sin is only the first prayer of the Upaniṣads, merely the initial step in the onward march-*Asato mā sad gamaya.* We have shown in the delineation of the way how they move on and on till the final and total freedom is gained. Merely the removal of animality does not bring perfection and complete freedom, for the seed of imperfection still remains and the chain of bondage still clings to the feet. Not even the attainment of divinity, in the sense of assimilation of one's being to that of the luminous but still finite gods, brings the fullness of freedom, the completeness of perfection. It is only on the achievement of infinity that the utter release, the total freedom, the absolute bliss is gained. Hence the Upaniṣads do not seek a relative freedom or a partial autonomy and never rest content till the final cause of all sin and suffering is removed root and branch and hence their significant name, the 'Upaniṣad'. Śaṅkara while clarifying the etymological meaning of the term 'Upaniṣad' points out : 'This Brahmavidyā is signified by the term 'Upaniṣad' because the whole 'Saṁsāra' or creation along with its cause is absolutely uprooted and removed by those who are engaged in it (i.e. this Brahmavidyā). The root *sad* preceded by *upa* and *ni* carry this meaning'[9]. Again he says : 'Those who take recourse to this Brahmavidyā with faith and devotion and in a spirit of identification, for them it removes all the evils of birth, old age, illness etc., brings the realisation of the Supreme Brahman and totally extinguishes ignorance which is the cause of the 'saṃsāra'. It is therefore termed 'Upaniṣad' because the meaning of *Sad* preceded *by upa and ni* is known to be such'[10].

Thus the very basic meaning of the term 'Upaniṣad' throws a clear hint about the nature of the teaching which the scriptures known by that name contain. The Upaniṣads strive after a complete recasting of the whole man, a total transformation of his entire personality. All the elements that constitute a human being-will, intellect and feeling-are each and all involved in this process of Upaniṣadic Brahmavidyā. We have traced the different phases through which the Upaniṣads proceed step by step in purifying the will, the intellect and the feeling-all the constituents of personality-without neglecting the physical too and finally concern themselves with the removal of the last film of finitude, thereby leading to the attainment of the Infinite or Brahman. From the outcome of this attainment, too, it is clear beyond doubt that the Upaniṣads did not seek a partial realisation through the intellect alone. What happens when this supreme vision dawns? The Upaniṣad replies: 'The knots of the heart are unloosened, all doubts arc removed, the actions too are annihilated on the Supreme being seen'.[11] Desires vanish, doubts are banished and actions are dissolved. In other words, with the removal of desire all feelings are fulfilled, with the dispelling of doubt the intellect is at rest, and with the dissolution of *karman* or action the will too becomes unfettered. Thus the vision brings fulfilment in all the aspects of life. Hence it is clear that Brahmavidyā does not signify a mere intellectual apprehension of the Brahman. 'By knowing the Brahman one becomes the Brahman'-is the most emphatic assertion of the Upaniṣads. We know of no other scripture in the world in which we may find a statement of similar nature. But does mere intellectual knowledge about a thing make one identical in being with the thing itself? One must ponder deeply over the implications of such a knowledge, which bears the promise of a total metamorphosis of the ordinary creature of ignorance into the All-Knowing Brahman, immediately, as it dawns upon the individual soul. To skip over it as mere intellectual knowledge is to miss the whole spirit and teaching of the Upaniṣads.

That mere intellectualism was not meant by this knowledge is clear from a categorical statement in the Upaniṣad:, 'This knowledge can be achieved neither through reasoning nor by a shining intellect, not even through repeated hearing'[11]. These methods are all discarded summarily because they do not touch the core of being, as they spring from a superficial curiosity of the surface self. The Upaniṣads want to get to the very ground of the soul, to the foundational consciousness itself which underlies all the faculties of understanding,—thinking, feeling and willing, cognition, affection and conation. That foundation being touched, all others are transformed automatically. And so the only way of attaining this knowledge, the Upaniṣad states, is to get wedded unto it, to choose or court it (*Vṛṇute*) as the sole pursuit of one's whole being. Only then the Reality reveals its form to such a seeker.

We have dealt at length with the question of mere intellectualism in the Upaniṣadic teaching because not only in the West but unfortunately in this country too there has been a lamentable distortion and confusion of it with mere intellectual knowledge. This has led to an utter stagnation in the spiritual life and a total absence of true illumination. The degeneration has set in from as far back as the time of the great Vedāntist, Vidyāraṇya, who in his *'Jīvanmuktiviveka'* frankly admits,[12] rather laments that the modern seekers after knowledge (*idānīntanāḥ*) without going in for the primary purification and contemplation engage themselves through mere curiosity (*autsukyamātrāt*) in this quest for knowledge all at once. They only make a show of purification for the time being, (*tātkālika*) and rush for the knowledge directly. Thus what was sought with the urge of the whole being in the Upaniṣadic times, henceforward became a matter for mere idle curiosity and speculation. This was responsible for the delusion which made the intellectual knowledge pass for *tattvajñāna* or metaphysical illumination. The key to realisation was thus lost and only arid abstraction filled the mind which sheds no light on the gloomy path of life nor takes the lamenting self to the other shore beyond all darkness, for which we saw Nārada prayed, and which is the true aim of the Upaniṣadic knowledge everywhere. So the inner man remained untouched, buried in the ignorance as before and subject to all the vicissitudes and distractions of life. Hence the necessity was felt to supplement this so-called *tattvajñāna* with yogic practices for controlling the mind and extinguishing the desires. But we have seen that the Upaniṣads promise immediate extinction of all desires and actions with the very dawning of this knowledge and this markedly points out the fatal misrepresentation of the true nature of the *tattvajñāna*. The true *tattvajñāna* once generated stands in no need of supplementation through other auxiliary methods or processes, because it is not a compartmental thing, not exclusively a mental or intellectual product but springs from the very essence of being or the core of the self. It is the 'foundational consciousness' as Haldane calls it, and as such underlies all the phases of consciousness. Hence the fulfilment which it brings is not partial but total and complete.

II

The basic teaching of the Upaniṣads & its uniformity

The misrepresentation of the true nature of the Upaniṣadic knowledge has been due to a total failure to grasp the essential spirit of the entire Upaniṣadic teaching. The whole edifice of Brahmavidyā, we have tried to depict, rests on two fundamental concepts, viz. that of the Agni and the Ātman, and hence the whole Brahmavidyā may be classed under two broad categories, one the Agnividyā, the other the Atmavidyā. Almost all the Upaniṣads without a single exception point out the two phases unfailingly. Agni is the principle of change or transformation, the supreme Cosmic Energy which is at work behind this whole world of manifestation. It is sometimes called Āditya, sometimes Prāṇa and sometimes again Agni. That all the different names signify the same thing is expressly stated by the Upaniṣad itself: 'This is Prāṇa, Agni, which is rising as Surya or the Sun'.[14] The same text calls it *Viśvarūpa,* of a universal form, which rightly reveals its true nature, because it is the universal principle underlying all the particular manifestations that is signified by these terms. As Yama points out to Naciketas: 'This Fire is the Creative Power which brings about the manifestation of all worlds, of which it is thus the root or basis'.[15] The created things are thus directly connected with this principle and only through it can lift themselves to the sphere of the Uncreated. From the particular to the Universal and thence to the Transcendent is always the method of Upaniṣadic approach to the Reality.

The Iśa Upaniṣad

Thus the *Iśa,* opening with the proposition of covering the whole existence by the Lord i.e. of seeing the Uncreated behind all created things, ends with a fervent prayer to Agni to lead forward towards the goal. *Iśā vāsyam* is no doubt the final goal but the initial movement towards it lies with Agni. Thus he who wants *Iśā vāsyam* must pray first of all, *Agne naya.*[16] This is the unmistakeable teaching of all the Upaniṣads and not of the Īśa alone.

But where does Agni lead? It leads to its own home, its native abode which is 'the fulfilment of all desire, the foundation of the world, the infinity of creative will, the fearless other Shore, the Great One mantra-bodied (*stomam*), the Wide-extended, that in which all is established'.[17] But to stop here will be fatal for the seeker because it will be delusive to mistake the attainment of some relatively lofty stage for the final Goal and to rest content with that. Hence though Agni leads forward, yet on reaching its final limit it covers the face of the Truth or the Reality in the form of the resplendent Sun. Therefore, the seeker has to pray to it again, not this time to lead him on but to leave the scene altogether, thereby allowing him to see the Reality in its utter nakedness or true nature.[18] So the Sun is asked to retract its rays, withdraw its light because its lid, though golden, covers the Truth.[19]

The acceptance of Agni as the sole guide in the beginning and its abandonment in the final phase of the quest is the great secret and paradox of the whole Brahmavidyā. The failure to comprehend this secret has led to two forms of illusion. Some have clung to the Agnividyā which in the *Īśa Upaniṣad* is termed 'avidyā' because of its concern with the multiplicity, not realising that mere knowledge of the many, however luminous, can never lead to that one 'Sun beyond the darkness'. Others have gone to the other extreme of not accepting its guidance at all, thinking that, since it is to be finally abandoned, it is wiser to abandon it from the very beginning, or rather not to accept it at all. It need hardly be mentioned that the latter go into a deeper darkness than the former. Because the former though falling short of the final vision, still obtain a relatively high sphere of illumination while the latter indulge in mere speculation and grope in darkness with a false pretension to the supreme knowledge, presuming to have known the final truth. This is what has happened with modern Vedāntists, who have totally ignored the Fire and have made a haughty pretension to know the Reality directly without its aid. But 'the secret of the Fire must be known if we would desire to cross the dark and evil swamp. Without it, mere intellectual study, whether dignified by the title Vedanta or by another such name, is but the building of a mental tower of Babel, an aspiration to a Heaven that no bricks of words or thought can ever reach, a thing whose useless ruins remain to view as one more 'philosopher's folly'. How many are there not who spend their whole life in the study of Vedānta and kindred philosophies and yet confess in the end that nothing has happened. The world has remained the same world, their senses have remained the same vicious and unruly horses, the Light that was to have shone forth has remained hidden and the Unitive Knowledge of which they have read and argued so much has remained a metaphysical theory, something the experience of which must be postponed till after death. All this is through the ignorance of the Fire'.[20]

In our times there has set in a reaction to this neglect of the Fire but this is also leading to a swing to the other polar extreme. In the attempt to stress the importance of the Fire, some modern exponents are almost placing it on the altar of the Absolute and worshipping it as such, thereby exposing themselves to the equally fatal danger of missing the supreme goal. The unerring vision of the Upaniṣads steers clear of all such one-sided grasp of truth and makes the right use of Agni in its own sphere yet with a full knowledge of its final limit. Agni, as we have pointed out, is the principle of growth or transformation and this growth naturally has a limit. It leads towards the supreme felicity (*rāye*)[21], which has its end in the state of Prajāpati, who is the source of all creation, but beyond is the sphere of the Uncreated which can only be attained by the uncreated principle in us, viz. the Ātman. Only the Ātman can realise the Ātman or Brahman. The clear demarcation of the two spheres and their mutual relation has been depicted all through the various Upaniṣads and it is only this outlook that has guided them everywhere in solving all sorts of problems, metaphysical, epistemological, ethical etc.

The Kena Upaniṣad

Like the *Īśa Upaniṣad, the Kena,* too, after indicating the true nature of the Supreme Reality by such statements as 'That is other than the known as well as beyond the unknown' and showing that neither anyone of the senses nor the mind can comprehend it but rather, on the contrary, they function only through it, goes on to make the paradoxical statement that it is known to the unknowing and is unknown to the knowing! In this way the Upaniṣad tries to impress upon the seeker the incomprehensible and unfathomable nature of the Supreme Reality. The Upaniṣad also knows full well that it is impossible to attain to this dizzy height all at once and so immediately brings in the myth of the gods' quest for the knowledge of the Brahman. Here the failure of each of the gods, one after another, in their attempt to comprehend the nature of the strange phenomenon or apparition (*yakṣam*) standing before them, illustrates the inscrutable nature of it. They all rushed towards it (*abhyadravat*) with proud pretensions but had to return baffled and bewildered. Then finally to Indra, the lord of gods, appeared the divine resplendent Mother Umā Haimavatī who communicated to him the fact that the *yakṣa* was none else but the Brahman. Thus through the medium of the Mother could the gods come to learn about the nature of the Brahman." Here the figure of Umā or the Mother represents the Creative Principle, which we have termed Agni and its importance as a medium for the supreme knowledge has been made all too clear to need further elucidation.

The Kaṭhopaniṣad

In the *Kaṭhopaniṣad* Naciketas before enquiring about the Ātman, seeks enlightenment about the true nature of the celestial Fire (*svargyam agnim*) by his second boon and this explicitly makes clear the order and sequence of the two knowledges. The effect of this knowledge is also sung in glorious terms. 'He who has thrice kindled the Naciketas Fire, has united with the Three and performed the three Acts, crosses over beyond birth and death. Having known and thoroughly realised that Shining Power, the Knower who is born of the Brahman and (who is the one) Power deserving of worship, one goes to the ever-lasting Peace'[23]. 'The wise man who having kindled the triple Naciketas Fire and known this Triad, builds up that Fire in meditation, he having already destroyed the bonds of death and gone beyond sorrow enjoys the bliss of the Heavenly world'[24]. But Naciketas, the true seeker, does not rest content with this relatively high and glorious attainment. He next puts the supreme question to Yama about the ultimate nature of the Self or Ātman and Yama tries to dissuade him from making this final enquiry by offering again and again the most alluring gifts for enjoyment. But Naciketas spurns them all, seeking nothing else but the complete enlightenment or the saving knowledge. This unerringly points out that only one with the supremest detachment in him can press forward to the ultimate goal, while others get involved in various relatively high states of achievement. This is the true '*vairāgya*', which views all else but the Absolute as relative and perishable[23] and therefore does not rest content with anything less than the Supreme Reality. Even the sublime attainment of the Universal Being, which is made possible through the knowledge of the Fire, is cast aside as of relative value, and Yama rightly praises Naciketas eloquently for his spirit of supreme detachment.

But it must be remembered that this detachment or renunciation or rather the casting off (*atyasrākṣīḥ*) of even the grand achievement of the vastness of the Universal Being can come only after one has actually realised the state and seen it for himself. That is why the text runs: 'Thou hast with firmness cast aside after having *seen* it'[26]. The *'atyasrākṣīḥ'* came after *'dṛṣṭvā'*, a point which should not be missed, for otherwise the casting off or rejection has no meaning at all. Rejection presupposes possession, but a false idea of *vairāgya* ignores this fundamental fact and rushes for an empty rejection, which is no rejection at all. The Upaniṣad everywhere prompts the seeker to realise higher and higher states of being, and thereby first attain the highest stature which again is to be finally surpassed by even another forward movement. There is nothing unnatural or rash in the Upaniṣadic conception of detachment. It is not through a violent effort that a severance is effected here but it is achieved in as natural a way as the youth outgrows the child. Hence it is nowhere the teaching of the Upaniṣads that 'it is not exertion, but inertion and a perfect inertion, that is the path to liberation' as Gough states[27]. On the contrary, it is the path of extremest exertion, which leads to the completest expansion that is indicated by the Upaniṣads. 'Arise, awake' is always the soul-stirritig call of the Upaniṣads which banishes all 'inertion' whatsoever and infuses a spirit of enthusiasm which is unequalled. The slightest 'inertion' or lack of alertness may bring about a total ruin, a complete destruction, because the path is not a rosy one but sharp as the edge of the sword, as the Upaniṣad warns, adding that the seers call it a hazardous path[28]. The Reality is also described as the Mighty Fear, the Upraised Thunderbolt[29] to impress upon the seeker the necessity of a supreme boldness and extreme alertness in facing it. Thus 'inertion' is foreign to the very spirit of of the Upaniṣads, as will be shown from the actual statements in all the Upaniṣadic texts.

The Praśna Upaniṣad

Again, in the Praśnopaniṣad, the first two *praśnas* or questions are essentially about Prāna and only later in the subsequent four questions an enquiry is made about the nature of the Ātman. Prāna is also expressly identified with Agni and its universal nature too is asserted in a categorical statement we have already quoted[30]. The

Praśna Upaniṣad also incidentally throws interesting light on the principle inherent in the creation of all beings. It says that when Prajāpati desired to create he first took recourse to Tapas and thereafter generated a twin principle or *mithuna.* This twin principle is comprised of what are termed here as Prāna and Rayi, the Sun and the Moon and it is their commingling which leads to the exuberance of creation. That this twin principle is at work everywhere and in all phases of time is further shown and described in detail. Thus the month is conceived as Prajāpati, of which the dark fortnight is Rayi and the bright one Prāṇa. Similarly of the day and the night the former is conceived as Prāna, the latter as Rayi. This dark and the bright are the two movements which signify the basic law of creation and pervade all through. Life and death, waking and sleep, work and rest, youth and age, day and night—everywhere we find this law in action. These two principles take the form of Siva and Sakti in the Tantras and there the symbol of the Sun and the Moon has been worked out in greater detail with which we need not concern ourselves here. We must only take note of the fact that the Upaniṣads recognise a principle of unity-in-difference at the basis of creation, of which Prāṇa happens to be one chief component.

The importance of Prāṇa in sustaining the creation is further stressed and elucidated in the second question through a legend where it is shown that with the attempt on the part of Prāṇa to depart, all other functions of different senses began to cease automatically and only with its return their functions too were restored, which proved beyond doubt the all-sustaining universal nature of Prāṇa, that everything rested in Prāṇa[31]. Hence in order to have a full knowledge of the workings of the universe, one must try first to comprehend the true nature of Prāṇa, for the whole secret of creation lies with it. So the Upaniṣad states: 'All this and whatever is in the heaven is under the control or dominion of Prāṇa'[32]. As we found in the Īśa that Agni was humbly approached for leading the seekers towards felicity (*rāye*), so here too the second question closes with a fervent prayer to Prāna to bestow on them prosperity and wisdom and protect them like a mother protecting her sons[33].

This remarkable similarity of thought proves beyond doubt that the same strain runs throughout the whole texture of the Upaniṣadic teaching. The aim is everywhere the attainment of the highest stature, the achievement of the completest development through the instrument or medium of Prāṇa and then to pass beyond to the immeasurable and the unfathomable out of whose depth even this glorious Prāṇa has its emergence. Thus there is nowhere a spirit of escapism traceable in the Upaniṣads but instead there is a bold attempt to grapple with all the pressing problems of life in order to find their supreme solution. Existence is not shunned as a mere illusion or phantasmagoria but its secret is sought to be unravelled and mastered through a thorough knowledge of Prāṇa or Agni which is the one active principle behind all existence.

The much misunderstood socalled *māyāvāda* or illusionism is contrary to the very spirit of the Upaniṣads and also to the writings of its original founder, the great Śaṅkarācārya, as we have tried to show in our exposition of the goal. The common criticisms levelled against Śaṅkara are absolutely beside the mark and betray a lamentable ignorance on the part of the critics of his profound doctrine, which tries to bring out the true spirit of the Upaniṣadic teaching in terms of a strictly logical system. Gough, for example, has completely misrepresented the Vedānta and the spirit of the Upaniṣadic teaching through his all too superficial presentation of it. Speaking about the Upaniṣadic period he says: 'There were now virtually two religions, the Karmamārga or path of rites for the people of the villages, living as if life with its pleasures and pains were real and the Jñānamārga or path of knowledge, for the sages that had quitted the world and sought the quiet of the jungle, renouncing the false ends and empty fictions of common life and intent upon reunion with the sole reality, the Self that is one in all things living'.[34] He also asserts that, 'the sum and substance, it may almost be said, of Indian philosophy, is from first to last the misery of metempsychosis and the mode of extrication from it,'[35] and that 'in every state there is nothing to expect but vanity, vexation and misery'.[36] The absurdity of such statements will be manifest from what we have already pointed out as the central core of the Upaniṣadic teaching. Nowhere in the Upaniṣads is to be found any spirit to 'quit the world' or 'seek the quiet of the jungle'; but on the contrary, all the great exponents of Brahmavidyā were essentially men of the world and their supreme injunction too was that 'one should wish to live a hundred years doing verily works in this world'.[37] Hence the Jñānamārga which they propounded was not one which was set in opposition to the Karmamārga but it was a path which transcended all oppositions and contradictions, giving equal scope to all in their respective spheres, neither neglecting some nor rejecting any. Neither is there any attempt in the Upaniṣads to seek 'the mode of extrication from the misery of metempsychosis' but rather they seek the mode of expansion from *ānanda to ānanda,* through the development of Prāṇa, the Cosmic Energy, which makes everything grow and expand.

But, again, they do not stop merely with this expansion; the enquiry and the search is pursued further, as here, in the *Praśnopaniṣad,* where immediately at the end of the second question, the third question seeks enlightenment about the origin of this Prāṇa too. On this question being put, the Ṛṣi is rightly struck by the genius of the questioner and remarks: 'you are putting a question which is beyond all questions' (*atipraśnān pṛcchasi*) and eulogises him as the most proficient enquirer about Brahman (*brahmiṣṭhosi*) and as such consents to tell him the secret of the origination of Prāṇa.[38] 'From the Ātman is the Prāṇa born',[39] and thus it is clear that Prāna is the first emanation from the Ātman, out of which again emanates the whole of existence. Hence in the return movement too, one has first to resolve the existence in Prāṇa and thence resolve that too in the Ātman.

To skip over this order is to run the risk of missing the true goal. 'One must not wish to leave out the steps between and penetrate directly'. It is not easy to get back the true status of the Ātman all at once and the sages of the Upaniṣads were very well aware of this fact. Speculation about it from a distance only leads to a deeper darknesss and will never generate the true illumination. Without the supreme refinement of the intellect, without the complete growth of our personality in all its parts, this supreme majesty of the Ātman or Brahman can never be apprehended or grasped. 'If we would transcend personality, we must first take the trouble to become persons.'[40] After the completest development comes the fulfilment and realisation and never before that. Nature is a cautious and careful mother and will never allow us to get out of her arms and walk our own way until she finds us completely mature and developed. Unless we complete the cycle of development there is no hope of getting out of it. To know the greatest thing that is the Brahman, we too must grow great. This is the indisputable and unequivocal teaching of the Upaniṣads. That is why the Praśna Upaniṣad, while concluding its discourse, makes a reference to the Purusa with sixteen parts or *kalās,* and says that only after the development of all *kalās* or parts of the being, one can hope to merge in the Absolute, as the river merges in the ocean losing its name and form and becomes partless and immortal.[41] One must first grow whole if he wants to reach the sole reality. The whole is in the Prāna and beyond it is the Ātman, the sole reality. From the part to the whole and thence to the sole reality, is everywhere the eternal order mapped out in the Upaniṣads.

The Muṇḍaka Upaniṣad

In the very opening of the *Muṇḍakopanisad,* a clear distinction between two forms of knowledge is specifically made by the following statement: 'There are two vidyās to be learnt' thus say the knowers of the Brahman; one is *Parā*, the other *Aparā*'[42]. In the category of Aparā is included all the Vedas as well as the Vedāṅgas and of the Parā it is simply stated that it is that through which the Immutable is attained or realised This definition of Parā Vidyā makes it clear beyond doubt that it does not signify a method of mere intellectual apprehension but indicates the science of a direct realisation of the Supreme Reality. Another point to be noted here is that both the forms of knowledge viz. Parā as well as Aparā, are prescribed to be learnt and mastered (*veditavye*) and not the Parā alone. Without proficiency in the Aparā, which makes the intellectual development complete, it is impossible to gain an access to the realm of the Parā Vidyā, and this point is unfailingly stressed all through the Upaniṣads.

Next the *Muṇḍaka* gives a picture of the Immutable which is to be apprehended through the Parā Vidyā. But, as we have pointed out, the Upaniṣad knows that it is impossible to grasp the Supreme all at once and so immediately the process of creation is described to make the Absolute seizable. The second part, as is usual with all the Upaniṣads, brings in the topic of the Fire.[44] The kindling of the flame to the full (*samiddhe havyavāhane*) and the offering or sacrifice of all unto it through faith (*Śraddhayā*) is enjoined and the Upaniṣad warns that he who fails in this duty of sacrifice loses all the seven spheres of existence,[45] i.e. faces utter extinction. The seven tongues of the Fire are also described in detail and it is stated that he who makes the offerings at the right time with all these tongues of the flame ablaze is borne to the supreme sphere of the lord of the gods by the rays of the sun. The final limit of the expansion to which Agni leads is also set forth very clearly here. It is the sacred Brahmaloka, the highest of all spheres, to which the rays of the Sun carry the sacrificer.[46] But immediately, in accordance with the true spirit of the Upaniṣads, which have as their final goal only the Supreme Reality, the unstable nature of even this grand achievement through the medium of Agni is emphasised. These sacrifices or cults of fire are insecure boats[47] and as such cannot carry one beyond to the other shore. Hence those who cling to the fire alone have to move round and round in the cycle of birth and death because nothing but the supreme knowledge can get one out of that cycle, and bring about the final deliverance. To gain this supreme knowledge one must be filled with a spirit of total detachment and self-abandonment and that is why the Upaniṣad says here that those who reside in the forest with alms-begging as their vocation, the utterly calm and enlightened souls, move through the door of the Sun to the eternal sphere where is the Immortal Puruṣa, the Immutable Ātman.

We have already spoken about the true ideal of detachment or *vairāgya* and have tried to distinguish it from its other false and spurious forms. But here we must again sound a note of warning to those who take this text here as an unmistakeable proof of the fact that the Upaniṣads extol the ideal of *sannyāsa* or going to the forest and preach the 'cult of beggars' as well as condemn loudly the way of karman. The conflict and opposition between the ways of karman and jñāna or sannyāsa is a creation of our ignorance. To the clear eye of the Upaniṣadic sages no such conflict appears, for they definitely delimit the spheres of the two, clearly mark out their respective boundaries. They give full scope to karman, or to its presiding deity or source of inspiration, Agni, in the sphere of creation but they equally know that the Uncreated cannot be gained through anything created,[48] and hence they abandon it altogether when the time for approaching the Uncreated comes. But this abandonment of karman is never taken recourse to unless and until one has seen for himself the final limit of development attainable through karman. Here lies the crux of the whole Upaniṣadic wisdom, which is stated once more in the *Muṇḍaka* most emphatically : 'The Brāhmin should attain the spirit of renunciation only *after having examined the spheres earned or achieved through karman*'.[49]

Thus this Upaniṣadic spirit of renunciation is not born out of any spirit of disgust or annoyance nor is it prompted by the desire to get away from the pressing cares of life to enjoy the bliss of solitude in the forest. It is born of a unique vision before which all else, however glorious, becomes dimmed into insignificance and hence is cast aside. Though possessing the vastness of a Universal Being, though actually enjoying the glories of the great Brahmaloka, one is seized yet with a divine discontent, which does not allow him to rest there but goads him on still. The promise of a still higher achievement dawns on him and so he has to cast off all that he had earned or gained so far, in order to move on. But one catches glimpse of the supreme height of the vision only when he has reached the last summit of Kārmic achievement. Hence as we found in the *Kaṭhopaniṣad* the statement, *dṛṣṭvā atysrākṣīḥ,* so here too the same point is stressed once more by the words *parīkṣya nirvedamāyāt,* and thus the true significance of sannyāsa is also brought out very clearly, which he who cares may grasp easily if deliberate distortion is not his aim.

The *Muṇḍaka* also gives the direct lie to the charge of inaction or 'inertion' attributed to the Upaniṣadic teaching. It specifically states that the best of the realised souls is he who has his play in the Ātman, who has his love or attachment for the Ātman as well as he who is full of action.[50] It also enjoins that the Brahmavidyā is to be imparted only to the active souls (*kriyāvantaḥ*)[51], which definitely shows that only the virile souls could venture to take up the quest and were initiated in this supreme vidyā and never the weaklings. 'This Ātman can never be realised by one who is devoid of strength',[52] is the most emphatic statement of the Upaniṣad here. Had 'inertion, a perfect inertion' been the path to liberation according to the Upaniṣad, as Gough takes it, then such statements would never have found any place in the Upaniṣadic texts. Only exertion demands strength and the Upaniṣadic demand for strength in the seeker is a demand for the utmost exertion which will be required to reach the final limit of the quest. We have shown in the section called *'The Preparation'* how the whole period of Brahmacarya was essentially devoted to gather the required strength before the actual quest was undertaken.

The *Muṇḍaka,* like the *Praśna,* finally refers to the *kalās* or parts of being and their final mergence in the unity of the Immutable.[53] But before speaking about this utter unity, where all name and form are lost as rivers in the ocean, the Upaniṣad speaks of the realisation of the All-pervading in all ways and also of the entering into the All.[54] This proves once more our thesis that the Upaniṣadic approach to the Reality is always through the universal to the transcendent and never otherwise.

The Māṇḍūkya Upaniṣad

This is brought out clearly once again in the *Māṇḍukyopaniṣad,* which though the shortest treatise in the whole Upaniṣadic literature, contains the profoundest wisdom. It deals with the four states of the Self as well as the four measures of Oṅkāra and traces their correspondence. In a section exclusively devoted to Oṅkāra we have tried to probe into its mystery. Here we must only take note of the fact that though the Turiya or the Fourth is the supreme and final goal, yet it can be apprehended only after passing through the third. Of this third status the Upaniṣad says : 'This is the Lord of all, this the Knower of all, this the Indweller, this the Source or Womb, out of which spring all created things and to which they return'.[55] This sounds strikingly similar to the passage of the *Muṇḍaka,* we have just quoted above, which speaks of the realisation of the All-pervading in all its facets or aspects. Hence one must trace back the whole manifestation first to its source or cause, and only thereafter move to the sphere beyond all causality. Neither should one stop merely at the source, and rest content with the discovery of the cause of all manifestation alone but must pass beyond. That is why even this overlordship, even this omniscience does not satisfy the Upaniṣadic sage for he feels that it is still a stage of sleep or utter inconsciencc when compared with the true status, the transcendental majesty of the Self. Nothing short of this final awakening which breaks even this blissful cosmic sleep will satisfy him. But we must reinind ourselves once again that, according to the Upaniṣads, as it is imperative to leave behind this state of the glorious majesty of the Universal in order to reach the ultimate goal of the Transcendent, so it is equally imperative to achieve the former state first, to actually possess the overlordship before aspiring to reach the ultimate end.

This truth is revealed again by the analysis of the three measures of Oṅkāra, *a, u* and *m*. The first mora *'a'* stands for *āpti* or attainment. The attainment of higher and higher states of being and fulfilment thereof is the basic note of OM, and hence the Upaniṣad says that one attains all that he desires and also becomes the foremost if he gains a knowledge of only this first mora.[56] Then the second, '*u*', signifies the rising to the zenith of glory or supreme excellence (*utkarṣāt*) and as the Upaniṣad says, to the knower of this second mora the stream of knowledge goes on moving higher and higher.[57] Lastly, in '*m*' this movement towards higher and higher development attains its culmination or end (*apiti*). But these three form only one arc of the great circle of OM, the arc that is visible in manifcstation. But in order to complete the circle a further movement is necessary towards the other arc, the invisible arc which is beyond all manifestations, the apparently dark arc of the Transcendent, which is called the Immeasurable, the Fourth, the Unusable, the End of all existence, the Good, the Non-Dual.[58] Thus only with the joining of the two arcs is the circle completed and the movement which was initiated with '*a*' then finds its fulfilment again in '*a*', the whole cycle having been completed. Hence '*a*' is the '*ādi*' or the starting point of the movement and again '*a*' is the '*āpti*' or the attainment or fulfilment of the movement.

Of this unique synthesis of the Upaniṣads, the Onkāra stands as the supreme symbol. It eternally signifies the great fact that in the Upaniṣadic wisdom or view of the Reality nothing was left out or rejected but everything was given its due place or scope and thereby an unique synthesis was evolved which is the fruit of a comprehensive and inherent unity. Of this final state of absolute harmony the Upaniṣad says: 'The Self alone enters into the Self through the Self'.[59] The *mātrās* or measures of OM lead step by step to this supreme end and this is everywhere the invariable method of the Upaniṣads.

The Taittirīya Upaniṣad

The Taittirīya Upaniṣad, through the very sub-division of its book, broadly indicates the relation of the Universal and the Transcendent, the need of the highest development and the subsequent surpassing of it. It therefore opens with the *Śikṣāvallī,* literally the section for training, which is exclusively devoted to the one supreme task of impressing upon the seeker the necessity of an all round developement, beginning from the physical right upto the intellectual. No other Upaniṣad can match the Taittiriya in this respect, viz. in its attempt to bring home the extreme importance of this development to the seeker through the use of the strongest imperatives as well as the most fervent prayers.

In the very opening it signifies that its first aim is the attainment of *yaśaḥ and brahmavarcasam,*[69] glory and divine power. Then Indra, the master of rhythms[61] is invoked to sprinkle or shower *medhā* or the power of apprehension and retention of the supreme wisdom. The seeker prays that may he be made fit for holding the immortal essence[62] and hence he also prays that his body be made invulnerable or immaculate.[63] He also prays: 'May my tongue be made the sweetest, my ears fit for profuse hearing (of instructions)'." The next thing prayed for is *śri* or prosperity all around." These two things must be combined, viz. *śrī* and *medhā or prajñā,* for an affluence without the sobering effect of intelligence is likely to lead to degeneration and an intelligence or wisdom shorn of plenitude or prosperity remains barren and fruitless. So the ideal that the Upaniṣads uphold is not of a beggar but of a king, full of all majesty and prosperity, plenitude and splendour. It must also be noted here that this prayer for *śrī* and *medhā* is strikingly akin to an almost identical prayer found in the *Praśnopaniṣad,* where Prāṇa is propitiated and asked to bestow *śrī* and *prajñā.*[66] What was addressed to Prāṇa there is being repeated here to Indra who stands as the highest embodiment of the Creative Energy or Prāna.

Even the physical necessities are not neglected. *Śrī* is conceived as carrying to the seeker clothings as well as food and drink for all times.[67] The Upaniṣads knew full well that want in the material plane hampers the soul in its spiritual flight and so they first sought all-round security in the material level before commencing the higher quest. They sought all these provisions not for their own enjoyment but for others only, who may gather round them for getting the knowledge or seeking enlightenment. That is why they immediately send a call around, praying that Brahmacārins or seekers after knowledge may flock to them from all quarters like the flowing waters which rush downwards all around.[68] Thus it is only for the dissemination of knowledge that the prosperity is sought and not for personal enjoyment. The seeker plunges himself in prosperity which swells in its thousand streams (*sahasraśākhe),* and prays: 'I enter into thee, O Prosperity, do thou also enter into me'.[69] The invocation of prosperity leads finally to the state of complete self-autonomy or the attainment of the kingdom of the Self (*svārājyam).*[79] In other words, one then becomes the full man, the master of himself with the complete flowering of his personality and the fulfilment of all his desires.

It may be noted here that it passes our comprehension how in spite of such specific statements strewn all over the Upaniṣads, statements which fervently call upon the seeker to develop and grow through the fulfilment of all his wants and desires, scholars like Keith could say that 'the aim of the self turns out to be the annihilation of every human desire and activity, an ideal which renders all active philanthropy idle and which has caused the chief virtues of India to take the form of resignation, passive compassion and charity'.[71]

But we must again remind ourselves that the Upaniṣad does not merely stop with the attainment of lordship or *svārājyam.* It still moves on till it attains the Supreme. Hence after *'āpnoti svārājyam'* comes in the next section *'āpnoti param'*.[72] Even in the attainment of this *'param'* or Supreme, the Upaniṣad shows that the way is through a gradual evolution of the personality beginning from the *annamaya* and ending with the *ānandamaya.* Only then one reaches the ultimate support, the tail end of the whole cosmos, the Brahman.[73] The implications of this method we have tried to make clear in a separate section, called the 'Analytic Way' and we need not dwell on it any further here.

The Aitareya Upaniṣad

The Aitareya Upaniṣad is exclusively devoted to the exposition of the process of creation, which proves once again that creation was not dismissed as a mere nothing or shunned as an inexplicable evil but its mysterious nature was sought to be explored in order to find out the truth that sustains it. Explaining the process of creation as far as possible the *Aitareya* finally concludes that the whole creation, beginning from Brahmā down to the solid earth, with all its infinite varieties, is finally established or rooted in the Supreme Consciousness *or Prajñāna* and this *Prajñāna* is verily the Brahman[74].

The Chāndogya Upaniṣad

Next the *Chāndogya Upaniṣad,* the vast repository of all the *vidyās* or various methods and techniques of knowledge, opens with the worship of the *Udgītha* which literally means contemplation through the uplifting music. Thus the call for upliftment or growth is the very basic note of the *Chandogya.* It says that one who worships the *Udgītha* gets the fulfilment of all his desires as well as expands or enriches the streams of desire.[75] It also enjoins upon the seeker to worship with knowledge and faith, which will infuse more vigour in the act of contemplation and thereby make it really potent.[76] Is this all a call for inertion or inaction? In an analysis of the true nature of contemplation, we have tried to show how all the elements of one's personality are involved in it according to the Upaniṣadic view of it, and so we need not go into the details of it here.

As the *Chāndogya* begins its series of *vidyās* with the *Udgithavidyā* so it ends the series with the *Daharavidyā.* Its first call is for an expansion towards the heights through the uplifting instrument of rhythm and harmony and its final call is for a plunge into the depths of the heart, into the very core of being to find out the supremely subtle thing inherent therein. Hence after describing numerous ways of contemplation or the innumerable *vidyās,* which lead to expansion and illumination, the *Chāndogya* finally concludes with *the Indra-Virocana Saṁvāda,*[77] where the quest of the Ātman is described as the sole aim. But here again, the true nature of the Self is not revealed all at once but only by a gradual elimination of the false notions of the lower selves, through a progressive growth in consciousness. It also shows how an ignorant and unrefined soul like Virocana sticks to a false or partial notion, taking it to be the final truth and thus remains in eternal delusion. Indra, on the contrary, moved higher without remaining satisfied with a relative truth because he went through long periods of more and more rigorous *tapas,* which purified his vision and enabled him to perceive the inadequacy of the knowledge which had been imparted to him previously. The clarification of vision comes only through *tapas,* otherwise anyone with an average intelligence could have had the knowledge of the Ātman. This stress on *tapas* proves once more that the nature of the Upaniṣadic knowledge was not at all merely intellectual. Had it been so, Prajāpati would not have deferred the imparting of the instruction every time for such long periods of thirty-two years. An adequate growth, an appropriate intellectual development in the seeker was needed before true enlightenment could be generated in him. Hence throughout the whole Upaniṣadic literature one finds the insistent demand for *tapas* before the actual instruction is imparted.

Thus the *Chāndogya* lends complete support to our contention that the knowledge of the Ātman cannot be had or rather the very enquiry about it cannot commence unless one has explored the *Prāṇavidyā* or *Agnividyā* to the full in all its numerous phases. Through *vidyā* or *upāsanā* to *jñāna* was always the eternal order indicated by the Upaniṣads. The breaking of this order has led to the tendency to discredit *upāsanā* or *vidyā* as of relative and insignificant value and to the total misconception of the *jñāna*, which always dawns only after the completion and perfection of the being through the *vidyās.* In order to have a grasp of the real bearing of the Upaniṣadic teaching, the true order of and relation between *vidyâ* or *upāsanā* and *jñāna* must always be kept in view and this is what we have been tracing out through all the different Upaniṣads.

The Bṛhadāraṇyaka Upaniṣad

Finally, the great *Bṛhadāraṇyaka Upaniṣad,* great in bulk as well as in profundity of thought, also unerringly points out the mutual inter-relation of *Prāṇavidyā* and *Ātmavidyā,* though its main aim is to give a correct exposition of the nature of the Ātman alone. It opens with the topic of the Aśvamedha[75] or the highest sacrifice which here symbolizes the sacrifice of the animal in us and a consequent achievement of purification of being. Thus *yajña* purifies one's being and it is, therefore, the first step in the approach to Reality which we have termed 'Preparation'. After the attainment of the culmination or the highest point of *yajña,* there begins *yoga* or *upāsanā.* That is why the *Bṛhadāraṇyaka* after finishing the topic of Aśvamedha or the highest sacrifice, brings in the *Udgītha upāsanā* once again, which is depicted as the supreme science of *Mukhya Prāṇa* or the central Cosmic Energy. The final culmination of this *upāsanā* is in *'abhyāroha,*[79] or higher and higher ascent, a progressive growth from the unreal to the real, from darkness to light and from death to immortality. The attainment of the highest development of being is the fruit of this *Prāṇavidyā* and its whole aim is voiced through that famous verse : *'Asato mā sad gamaya, tamaso mā jyotir gamaya, mṛtyor mā amṛtam gamaya'.*[80]

But as usual even the attainment of this immortality does not satisfy the sages of the Upaniṣads, because it is a relative immortality, the immortality of Prāṇa or the universal principle. At every stage in the approach to Reality there is a taste of immortality, which follows as a consequence of the removal of certain limitations. This limitation is termed 'death' in different contexts. Thus at the end of the description of the Aśvamedha here it is said that one who performs this sacrifice conquers death; death never gets hold of him, rather it becomes his very self.[81] Similarly we found in the *Kaṭha,* statements about the attainment of *Agnividyā,* which also refer to the conquest of death, such as 'crosses over beyond birth and death,'[82] 'having already destroyed the bonds of death,[83] etc. Here also the effect of the *Udgītha* is described in similar terms with regard to all the senses, which were freed from death through the *Mukhya Prāṇa.* The refrain is : *'mṛtyum atikrānto,'*[84] having crossed beyond death. Thus the term *'mṛtyu'* signifies different things at different levels and as such immortality, too, has its variations accordingly, and one must always take note of this fact before assessing the value of any achievement whatsoever.

The *Bṛhadāraṇyaka* here throws some light on the term *'mṛtyu'*. It says: 'Hunger is Death'[85] and this hunger is nothing but a synonym of desire. It also says at the end of the *Udgītha upāsanā, 'pāpmānam mṛtyum apahatya'* i.e. having killed or conquered death which is sin. This sin or *pāpman* has been clearly depicted in the *Udgītha* as the sin of attachment, which makes the senses cling to what is attractive to them i.e. pleasant and avoid what is unattractive or unpleasant. This like and dislike born of attachment or desire is the sin and also the death, which is conquered here through the instrument of *Mukhya Prāṇa,* which is free from all such attachments for particular aspects, being universal in its nature. Thus the immortality attained here is the immortality of the Universal achieved through a release from the sphere of the particular. As the *Chāndogya* spoke of the fulfilment of all desires through the *Udgītha,* so here, too, it is said that a singer of the *Udgītha* (*udgātā*) can bring for himself or for the *yajamāna* or the man for whom he sings, anything that is desired, as it were, through a mere song (*āgāyati*).[86] Hence one gains the fulfilment of all desires on being freed from the clutches of death here, and on attaining the immortality of the universal. This is the '*kāmasyā'ptim*'[87] referred to by Yama in the *Kaṭha.*

But even beyond this is the true and absolute freedom, the utter freedom of the Transcendent. There the fetters of finitude are cast off totally because one passes altogether beyond the category of the finite to the supreme category of the Infinite. This supreme category is that of the Ātman and hence the *Bṛhadāraṇyaka* immediately after recounting the nature of the immortality of the universal brings in the topic of the Ātman.[88] The beauty of the *Bṛhadāraṇyaka* and its greatness lies in this that it does not leave any of the steps undescribed but proceeds step by step in the proper sequence, leading the seeker through a gradual refinement towards the final enlightenment. This is everywhere the method adopted by the Upaniṣads and nowhere is it more clearly presented than in the *Bṛhadāraṇyaka.* Those who take the *Bṛhadāraṇyaka* as a mere treatise on the nature of the Ātman and fail to take note of the other antecedent topics dealt with here, miss the entire teaching and its deeper implications.

Thus our long analysis of all the ten principal Upaniṣads has revealed the remarkable unity of thought running through them all depicting the unique synthesis of the Universal and the Transcendent through the two broad concepts of Prāṇa or Agni and Ātman. The later Upaniṣads we need not explore here any further.

III

Upaniṣad & 'Brahmavidyā

The term 'Upaniṣad'

We have indicated that the basic meaning of the term 'Upaniṣad' is *'rahasyam'* or the supreme secret. As Deussen also concludes after giving the numerous possible meanings of the term : 'If the passages collected in my index to the Upanishads under the word Upanishad are examined, it will be at once evident that, taken together, they involve the meaning, "secret sign, secret name, secret import, secret word, secret formula, secret instruction," and that therefore to all the meanings the note of secrecy is attached. Hence we may conclude that the explanation offered by the Indians of the word *Upanishad* as *rahasyam,* "Secret," is correct.'[89] In fact, this is the sole meaning of the term indicated by the Upaniṣads themselves and it carries this import all through the Upaniṣadic literature. Now the secrecy of the doctrine embodied in the Upaniṣads consists in this that it teaches something which is not taught or learnt anywhere else. Hence it is distinguished from other secular sciences or branches of knowledge in that it deals with something which does not come within the scope of any other branch of knowledge. This something is the biggest thing, the fundamental basis of all things, viz. Brahman.

The Upaniṣads thus contain or embody the science of the Ultimate Truth and that is why the doctrine of the Upaniṣads has come to be known as *Brahmavidyā.* In fact, the two terms 'Upaniṣad' and *'Brahmavidyā'* have come to signify the same thing and are used as synonyms as Śaṅkara explicitly says : 'This *Brahmavidyā* connoted by the term Upaniṣad.'[90] In fact, the *Muṇḍaka Upaniṣad* itself in its very opening verse mentions this term, *'Brahmavidyā'* and calls it as the basis of all *vidyās* or sciences.[91] Thus there is no doubt about the fact that the literature passing by the name 'Upaniṣad' is concerned with nothing else but Brahman. Not only does it concern itself merely with the exposition of the true nature of Brahman but being a *vidyā* or spiritual science it also shows the way to Its realization and also recounts the effects that follow from such realization i.e. the nature of the consummation attained.

Guru or the Teacher

Now, *Brahmavidyā* has a long tradition behind it. As traced by the *Muṇḍakopaniṣad,* its first originator is Brahmā himself, the Prajāpati or the Creator of the world. the sustainer of the universe, the first of the gods.[92] It is thus as old as creation itself and hence its eternal nature. From Brahmā it was transmitted to his eldest son Atharvan, who in his turn gave it to Angirā and Angirā gave it to Bharadvāja Satyavaha and finally Bharadvāja narrated it to Angiras. To this Angiras came Śaunaka for enlightenment about *Brahmavidyā.*[93] *Brahmavidyā,* being essentially a spiritual science, needed a transmission from the teacher, who had mastered it fully and it was not a thing which all could handle as they wished or master without the aid of a guide. Here lies the supreme importance of the approach to the Guru in the proper way, the *'gurūpasadana'* with which *Brahmavidyā* begins, for unless the teacher condescends to reveal the secret wisdom there is no other way of gaining it. That is why the Upaniṣad enjoins that one must approach the Guru or the Teacher for this knowledge.[94]

Another reason, as to why the knowledge could not be had without the aid of a Guru, was this that most of the varieties of *Brahmavidyā* were exclusive experiences of particular sages and as such absolutely under their custodianship. To learn that particular technique of *Brahmavidyā* was impossible without the guidance of that particular teacher proficient in it. Hence one had to come in touch with the particular line of tradition through which a particular *vidyā* was handed down. As the *Muṇḍaka* traces a particular line, so the *Chāndogya* mentions another in connexion with the *Madhu-vidyā.* This *Madhuvidyā* was first revealed by Brahmā to Prajāpati and Prajāpati narrated it to Manu, who in his turn gave it to the created beings and in the particular context, Uddālaka Āruni got it from his father.[95] Similarly in connexion with the *Udgītha-vidyā* it is mentioned that three persons became proficient, rather specialists in Udgītha, viz. Śilaka Śālāvatya, Caikitāyana Dālvya and Pravāhana Jaivali.[96] In the case of the ethical virtues, too, we find one particular sage devoting himself exclusively to the cultivation of one moral virtue, as Rāthitara, who was truthful in speech, took to truth as the one supreme virtue, a second, Pauruśiṣṭi, eternally engaged in *tapas,* declared *tapas* to be the one primary thing, and a third Nāka Maudgalya holds that study and exposition, *svādhyāyapravacana,* alone constitute the whole ethical life.[97] So in the matter of *vidyās,* different sages were experts in different lines and they exclusively possessed the secret of their respective lines of approach. The *Śāṇḍilya-vidyā,* for instance, was a *vidyā* or technique exclusively evolved and perfected by the sage Śāṇḍilya. Similar is the case with *Upakosala-vidyā* and others of a similar type. Hence we find frequently the picture in the Upaniṣads of one sage going to another, or a group of them visiting another for further enlightenment about a particular method, or *vidyā.*

The family tradition of Brahmavidyā

The tradition of *Brahmavidyā* was also generally maintained through the family line, i.e. as a general rule it was transmitted from the father to the son. The *Chāndogya* specifically enjoins that the father should communicate it only to the eldest son or to the most devoted student residing with him.[98] That this was the general custom is also evident from numerous instances in the Upaniṣads. Thus in the passage in the *Muṇḍaka* already referred to, it is mentioned that Brahmā gave the *Brahmavidyā* to his eldest son Atharvā.[99] So Uddālaka Āruṇi got it from his father. Similarly, in the *Taittirīya,* it is said that Bhṛgu approached his father Varuṇa for being instructed about Brahman.[100] It is also mentioned in connexion with the *Udgītha-vidyā* in the *Chāndogya* that the sage Kauṣitaki asked his son to expand and develop the knowledge gained by the father.[101] So Śvetaketu also had his enlightenment from his father Gautama.[102] It is also recounted how the gods, the demons and men, all the offsprings of Prajāpati, approached their father for enlightenment after observing the period of *brahmacarya* with him.[103] That it was everywhere expected as a general rule that the son should inherit the wisdom from his father is also proved by the story of Śvetaketu, where the father rather chides his son for going off the right track and reminds him of the glory of his family, in which none is ever expected to remain ignorant in the Vedas and thereby to turn out into a false degenerate Brāhmaṇa. Hence he asks the son to observe *brahmacarya* for gaining the supreme knowledge.[104] In the recounting of the effects of various *vidyās* too we find frequently mentioned that in the family of one who gains this knowledge none is born who is not a knower of Brahman and thus it is clear that it was earnestly desired and prayed for that the knowledge should be preserved in unbroken continuity through the line of the family.

Features of the tradition

Another interesting feature emerges from this importance of the family tradition in *Brahmavidyā* as we have discussed it. It is clear beyond doubt that the men who possessed and transmitted the *Brahmavidyā* were men of the world, *gṛhasthas* and not world-renouncing ascetics (*sannyāsins*). The term *'mahāśāla'*, too, is frequently used as a qualifying adjective of the men who were engaged in *Brahmavidyā,* which unmistakably proves that only those men who had achieved eminence in the worldly life were thought fit to have the knowledge. Only the full-statured, the completely developed men were entitled to enter the arena of *Brahmavidyā* and this proves once again our thesis that only after the highest development or growth could this transcendental knowledge be grasped and retained and never otherwise. Thus we hear that Śaunaka was a *'mahāśāla'*, a great householder, who approached Āṅgirasa for getting the knowledge.[195] Similarly it is described that Pracīnaśāla, Satyayajña, Indradyumna, Jana and Buḍila, all *'mahāśāla'* and *'mahāśrotriya'*, great householders and great scholars in Veda, gathered together to discuss about the nature of Ātman and Brahman.[196]

That only men of the first rank, eminent and distinguished in the world and full of prosperity as such, were the possessors of this knowledge is also proved by the fact that many of the teachers in *Brahmavidyā* are found to be kings, like Ajātaśatru, Aśvapati, Pravāhaṇa Jaivali etc. Even among the seekers of *Brahmavidyā* the name of king Janaka shines in its own majesty. It is also clear from the instance of Janaka how the kings used to encourage the study of *Brahmavidyā* by offering great wealth and provision to a truly enlightened man.

Thus *Brahmavidyā* was not confined to a class of ascetics alone but had a wide range of adherents in which were included the people and the kings alike, men as well as women, Brāhmins as well as Kṣattriyas. Women were also not debarred from having any access to *Brahmavidyā,* as is evident from the picture of Yājñavalkya instructing his wife Maitreyī, as well as another woman of eminence, Gārgī.

We must here note in passing that we cannot agree with Deussen when, from the fact that in some cases kings happened to be the instructors in *Brahmavidyā,* he draws the inference that, 'the conceptions of the Upaniṣads, though they may have originated with the Brāhmans, were fostered primarily among the Kṣattriyas and not within Brāhman circles, engrossed as those were with the ritual',[197] or again that 'the doctrine of the Ātman, standing as it did in such sharp contrast to all the principles of the Vedic ritual, though the original conception may have been due to Brahmans, was taken up and cultivated primarily not in Brāhman but in Kṣattriya circles, and was first adopted by the former in later times'.[198] He even goes so far as to state that this teaching with regard to the Ātman was studiously withheld from them, that 'it was transmitted in a narrow circle among the Kṣattriyas to the exclusion of the Brāhmans'.[109] All these wrong inferences are drawn because of the confirmed prejudice and biased view about the antagonism between the so-called Vedic ritual and the Upaniṣadic *Brahmavidyā.* We have already pointed out how Agni and Ātman form the warp and woof of the whole texture of the Upaniṣadic *Brahmavidyā,* and this Agni is the central principle round which grows up the elaborate Vedic ritual. The Upaniṣadic doctrine never sets itself against the cult of the fire in a spirit of hostility and opposition. On the contrary, it gives full and adequate scope to Agni and only completes the movement initiated by it by moving still further in the region of the Ātman. *Yajña* is no doubt described as a leaky boat,[110] but that is because it is not strong enough to lead one to the sphere of the Ātman, which is beyond its reach. The doctrine of the Ātman or *Ātmavidyā* does not signify the rejection of the doctrine of Agni or the Vedic ritual but only signifies the fulfilment and transcendence of the latter by the former. *Ātmavidyā* can never dispense with *Āgnividyā,* for without the purification through Agni or *Yajña* the enquiry about the Ātman can never come, and hence it is impossible for the *Ātmāvidyā* to decry the latter but it only points out the limitation of the Agni, having itself moved further on.

That Deussen's assertion about the fostering of *Brahmavidyā* among the Kṣattriyas alone and not within Brāhmin circles is absolutely unfounded is proved by a specific statement in the *Bṛhadāraṇyaka* which he too quotes incidentally while totally ignoring its real import. When Gārgya Bālāki after expounding the nature of Brahman to King Ajātaśatru remained silent, having exhausted the whole range of his experience, the latter made the historic statement that Brahman is not truly apprehended by this much knowledge. At this Gārgya prayed like a disciple to the King to enlighten him further, to which the King replied : 'that is a reversal of the rule, for a Brāhmaṇa to betake himself as a pupil to a Kṣattriya in order to have the Brahman expounded to him'.[111] This proves beyond doubt that the general rule was that Brāhmanas used to impart *Brahmavidyā* to others and this was an exception to the general rule, so the King felt awkward, he being a Kṣattriya at the request of Gārgya, a Brāhmaṇa, to teach him. Had *Brahmavidyā* been limited 'in a narrow circle among the Kṣattriyas to the exclusion of the Brāhmans', who were supposed to be 'engrossed with the ritual', how could such a statement be made that as a general rule the Brāhmaṇas transmitted it? Such narrowing down of the circle was absolutely unknown in the Upaniṣadic times.

On the contrary, the *Brahmavidyā* was freely exchanged among all the higher classes and sexes, without any restriction whatsoever. For the sake of gaining this supreme knowledge, even a haughty Brāhmaṇa never hesitated to bow down before a Kṣattriya as an humble seeker, as illustrated by the proud Gārgya Bālāki (*dṛptabāḷāki*), though that was contrary to the general law or custom. None was debarred from having this knowledge because it was verily universal in nature and in the *Vārttikasāra* it has rightly been said : 'All men are certainly entitled to have this knowledge'.[112] What was true, however, as we have pointed out, is the fact that certain *vidyās* or methods of approach belonged to certain families or classes alone, were, in fact, their exclusive monopolies; hence we find the picture in the Upaniṣads frequently of one particular man being approached for a particular knowledge. As for instance, when Uddālaka Āruṇi was approached by the five Ṛṣis, viz. Prācīnaśāla, Satyayajña, Indradyumna, Jana and Buḍila for enlightenment about the *Vaiśvānara vidyā* or *Agnividyā,* he realized his incompetence to teach them about it and hence directed them to King Aśvapati Kaikaya, who was considered proficient in that particular *vidyā.*[113] Similarly, Gautama being asked by his son Svetaketu to teach him about the *Pañcāgni-vidyā,* failed to say anything and promptly admitted his ignorance about it. 'Had I known it why should not have I told it to you?', he said to his son. Then both the father and the son went to King Pravāhaṇa Jaivali, who had originally put the question about the five fires to Śvetaketu, and sought enlightenment from him. Upon this the King told him that this particular *vidyā* had never gone to any Brāhmana before him i.e. he was the first Brāhmaṇa who was going to have this knowledge, and because of it, i.e. of the possession of this particular *vidyā,* the Kṣattriyas had ruled all over the world[114]. We have already pointed out that the *Agnividyā* leads to unending prosperity and fulfilment of all desires, to a state of overlordship, and as such it is no wonder that the Kṣattriyas or the ruling classes possessed this knowledge to the exclusion of other classes and thereby maintained their superior position and glory of eminence. Thus it is plain that one particular class sometimes used to have the exclusive monopoly of a certain form of *vidyā* but there was no bar to a free exchange of the *vidyā* between the different classes. Only one had to betake himself to the man, particularly expert in that *vidyā* and approach him in the proper way, and, if the teacher thought him fit for holding the knowledge, he ungrudging imparted it to him without any scruple or hesitation.

Adhikāra or Eligibility for Brahmavidyā

This fitness for holding the knowledge is known as *adbikāra.* Of the true *adhikārin* of *Brahmavidyā* it is said that he must be of a calm disposition and possess self-control[115]. To attain this calm disposition one had to go through a rigorous discipline of celibacy, *brahmacarya* before the actual *vidyā* was imparted to him. The details of this discipline and its implications we have disscussed in the section called 'The Preparation'. It is also strictly enjoined that one should not read about this *Brahmavidyā* who has not carried out the vow i.e. has not gone through the proper discipline.[116] The *Brahmavidyā* is to be revealed only to those who are men of action, versed in the Vedas, devoted to Brahman, and who have propitiated with devotion the Fire as well, having carried out in the proper way the vow of carrying the Fire in the head[117]. This proves once again the close connection of the cult of Fire with *Brahmavidyā.* Only at the culmination of the worship of the Fire, only after the attainment of mastery in the cult of Fire, the *Brahmavidyā* used to be revealed. A spirit of absolute devotion to the Teacher is also demanded, as in the *Śvetāśvatara:* 'The highly-souled men reveal all these truths to one who has supreme devotion to God and an equal devotion to the Guru'[118]. As we have already indicated that the *Brahmavidyā* was generally revealed to the son or the most devoted pupil, so the *Śvetāśvatara* and *Maitrī* Upaniṣads strictly forbid its transmission to others : 'Impart it to no one, who is not tranquil, who is not a son or a pupil'[119]. This profoundest mystery of all is to be revealed to no one, who is not a son or a pupil and who has not yet become tranquil'.[120] Thus of all the conditions of a true *adhikārin,* tranquillity is one which is most insistently demanded. The Guru was also to be a man not only of great learning but a man of experience, whose sole devotion is in Brahman, who is literally 'stationed' in Brahman (*śrotriyam brahmaniṣṭham*)[121].

The Value of Brahmavidyā

The importance and value which was attached to *Brahmavidyā* and how it was prized above everything else is also clear from a passage in the *Chāndogya,* where it is said that 'though he (the knower of *Brahmavidyā*) were to be offered in return for it all the kingdoms of the ocean-girdled earth, yet should he bethink himself 'the other is of greater value'[122]. All earthly gains are insignificant when compared to this priceless treasure. That is why Naciketas, the true seeker, rejected all the tempting offers of earthly enjoyments and even heavenly ones, held out before him by Yama and sought nothing else but the supreme knowledge. This also shows that it was not mere intellectual knowledge on which such a high price was set that even all the earthly gains could not be exchanged for it, but it was the saving wisdom, which completely lifted one out of the realm of finitude. The failure to comprehend the true nature of this knowledge has led to the bewilderment of Keith, who says that 'it is simply inconceivable why on the ground of such theoretic knowledge, men should abandon the desire for children, should give up their property and wander about like beggars, practising a foolish asceticism'.[123] The absurdity of such remarks will be evident to any one who has had even a glimpse of the true Upaniṣadic wisdom.

Absence of Dogmatism & Varieties of Approach

Another marked characteristic in the culture of *Brahmavidyā* in the Upaniṣadic times is the free spirit and open-mindedness with which it was cultivated throughout. No bias or prejudice ever dominated the mind of any seer nor did anyone cling to his own realisation taking it to be final and supreme. On the other hand, the general method was always a mutual discussion of respective viewpoints and the correction and supplementation of one by the other. The seers used to meet together, forming a council of friends, as it were, to compare the notes of the journey towards the Reality.

Not vain argumentation was the method but the reporting of concrete realisation of each was always sought. So it is told that the three experts in *Udgītha,* viz. Śilaka Śālāvatya, Caikitāyana Dālbhya and Pravāhaṇa Jaivali all met together and said: 'We are all specialists in *Udgītha,* so let us mutually discuss about the *Udgītha'.*[124] Similarly, the five seers already referred to, Prācīnaśāla and others, met together for coming to a decision about the nature of Ātman and Brahman.[125] Instances need not be multiplied, for this was the invariable method followed in the cultivation of *Brahmavidyā.* Sometimes, having failed to come to a final solution of their difficulties, they used to go in a body to a man of higher enlightenment, as in the above case the five seers later approached Uddālaka Āruṇi, who in his turn directed them to Aśvapati. Under the patronage of Kings too such councils of wise men used to meet from time to time as is evident from the story of Janaka.[126]

About the innumerable variety of methods through which *Brahmavidyā* used to be imparted, we need not concern ourselves here, for they have all been comprehensively traced and analyzed by Ranadc in his *'Constructive Survey of Upaniṣhadic Philosophy'.*[127] We beg to close our introduction with an approximate list of the various *vidyās* found in the Upaniṣads, out of which we have tried to deal with three prominent ones, viz., the *Dahara-vidyā,* the *Madhu-vidyā* and the *Udgītha-vidyā* in details. The main principle behind all the *vidyās* is the same, though the techniques differ, and the approaches are diverse.

(1) *Agnividyā*	— Kaṭha. 1.1.13-19.
(2) *Ātmavidyā*	— BU. 1.4.7-8, 15, 2, 4.5. Muṇḍ. 2.2.5 Māṇḍ. Kaṭha. 1.2. ff.
(3) *Udgīthavidyā*	— CU. 1.3-9. BU. 1.3.
(4) *Upakosalavidyā*	— CU. 4.10-15.
(5) *Omkāravidyā*	— CU. 1.1.1-7, Kaṭha 1.2.15.16. Māṇḍ. Tai. 1.8, Muṇḍ. 2.2.4-6. Praśna 5.
(6) *Gāyatrividyā*	— CU. 3.12.
(7) *Daharavidya*	— CU. 8.1.1-2.
(8) *Dirghāuṣyavidyā*	— CU. 3.16.
(9) *Pancāgnividyā*	— BU. 6.2.9-13. CU. 5.4.8.
(10) *Prāṇavidyā*	— BU. 5.13. 1-4.
(11) *Bhūmavidyā*	— CU. 7.23.1.

(12) *Madhuvidyā* — CU. 3.1-5. BU. 2.5-6.
(13) *Manthavidyā* — BU. 6.3.1-13. CU. 5.2.4.
(14) *Sāṇḍilyavidyā* — CU. 3.14.
(15) *Samvargavidyā* — CU. 4.3.
(16) *Satyakāmavidyā* — CU. 4.4-9.
(17) *Sāmavidyā* — CU. 2.1-22. BU. 1.3.25-27.

Besides these we have reference to other secular *vidyās* like the following: *Devavidyā, Bhūtavidyā, Kṣatravidyā, Nakṣatravidyā, Sarpadevajanavidyā*[128] etc.

References

1. PVU, p. 587.
2. PVU, p. 587.
3. PU, p. 16.
4. dṛśyate tvagrayā buddhyā. KTUI, iii. 12.
5. PU, p. 48.
6. Ibid, p. 49.
7. CU, 7.1.
8. tadvijñānārtham sa gurumevābhigachhet. MuU. 1.2.12.
9. ŚB, IU. 1.
10. Ibid, TU. 1.
11. MuU, 2.2.8.
12. JY, p. 234.
14. PR, 1.7-8.
15. YK, p. 35.
16. IU, 18.
17. KTU, 1.2, 11.
18. satyadharmāya dṛṣṭaye. ĪU. 15.
19. vyūha raśmīn samūha tejo. IU, 16.
20. YK, pp. 128-129.
21. ĪU, 18.
22. tato haiva vidāñcakāra brahmeti. KU, 26.
23. KTU, 1.1.17.
24. Ibid. 1.1.18.
25. ś v o b h ā v ā . . . s a r v a m jīvitamalpameva. Ibid., 1.1.26.
26. KTU, 1.2.11.
27. PU, p. 65.
28. KTU, 1.3.14.
29. Ibid. 2.6.2.
30. PR, 1.7.
31. prāṇe sarvam pratiṣṭhitam, Ibid, 2.6.
32. PR, 2.13.
33. Ibid.
34. PU, p. 17.
35. Ibid., pp. 20-21.
36. Ibid., p. 23.
37. IU, 2.
38. PR, 3.2.
39. PR, 3.3.
40. EM, p. 325.
41. akalo amṛto bhavati. PR, 6.5.
42. MU, 1.1.4.
43. yayā tadakṣaram adhigamyate. Ibid. 1.1.5.
44. MU, 1.2.
45. ā saptamānstasya lokān hinastī,

Ibid. 1.2.3.
46. yajamānam vahanti. MU, 1.2.6.
47. plavā hyete adṛḍhāḥ. Ibid., 1.2.7.
48. nāstyakṛtah kṛtena. Ibid, 1.2.12.
49. MU, 1.2.12.
50. Kriyāvān eṣa brahmavidām variṣthaḥ. Ibid., 3.1.4.
51. Ibid, 3.2.10.
52. Ibid. 3.2.4.
53. pare avyaye sarva ekībhavanti. MU. 3.2.7.
54. Sarvagam sarvataḥ prāpya sarvamevāviśanti, Ibid., 3.2.5.
55. Mā, 6.
56. Mā. 9.
57. Ibid, 10.
58. Ibid, 12.
59. Mā, 12.
60. Saha nau yaśah saha nau brahmavarcasam. TU. 1.3.1.
61. Chandasām ṛṣabho. Ibid.
62. Amṛtasya devadhāraṇo bhūyāsam, Ibid.
63. śarīraṁ me vicarṣaṇam. TU, 1.3.3.
64. Ibid.
65. tato me śriyam āvaha. Ibid, 1.4.2.
66. Śrīś ca prajñāñ ca vidhehi naḥ. PR. 2.13.
67. annapāne ca sarvadā. TU. 1.4.2.
68. Ibid. 1.4.3.
69. Ibid.
70. āpnoti svārājyam. TU, 1.6.2.
71. PVU, p. 598.
72. TU, 2.1.
73. brahma puccham pratiṣṭhā. Ibid. 2.5.
74. prajnānaṁ Brahma. AU. 3.3.
75. āpayita ha vai kāmānām.....sambardhaitā ha vai kāmānām. CU. 1.1.7-8.
76. vīryavattaram bhavati. Ibid. 1.1.10.
77. CU. 8.7. ff.
78. BU. 1.1.
79. BU. 1.3.28.
80. Ibid.
81. apa punar mṛtyum jayati nai'nam mṛtyur āpnoti mṛtyur asyā 'tmā. BU, 1.2.7.
82. tarati janmamṛtyū. KTU, 1.1.17.
83. mṛtyupāśān purataḥ praṅodya. Ibid. 1.1.18.
84. BU, 1.3.12.16.
85. aśanāyā hi mṛtyuḥ. BU, 1.2.1.
86. Ibid. 1.3.28.
87. KTU, 1.2.11.
88. BU, 1.4. ff.
89. PU, p. 15.
90. se 'yam brahmavidyā upaniṣacchabdavācyā. ŚB, Intr. to BU, p. 2.
91. sarvavidyāpratiṣṭhām, MU, 1.1.1.
92. Ibid.
93. Ibid.
94. tadvijnānārtham sa gurum evā 'bhigacchet. MU, 1.2.12.
95. CU, 3.11.4.
96. CU, 1.8.1.
97. TU, 1.9.
98. jyeṣṭhāya putrāya pitā brahma prabrūyāt praṇāyyāya vā 'ntevāsine. CU, 3.11.5.
99. atharvāya jyeṣṭhaputrāya prāha. MU, 1.1.1.
100. bhṛgur vai vāruṇir varuṇam pitaram upasasāra, TU. 3.1.

101. CU, 1.5.2.
102. Ibid. 6,1.1.
103. BU, 5.2.1
104. CU, 5.1.1.
105. MU, 1.1.3.
106. CU, 5.11.1.
107. PU. p. 17.
108. Ibid. p. 19.
109. Ibid.
110. plavā hyete adṛdhāḥ yajñarūpāh. MU, 1.2.7.
111. BU, 2.1.15.
112. manuṣyamātro vidyāyām adhikāri bhaved dhruvam. VS, 1.884.
113. CU, 5.11.
114. Ibid, 5.3.
115. praśāntacittāya śamānvitāya. MU, 1.2.13.
116. nai 'tad acirṇavrato adhīte. MU, 3.2.11.
117. MU, -3.2.10.
118. ŚU, 6.23.
119. nā 'putrāya aśiṣyāya vā. ŚU, 6.22.
120. nā 'putrāya nā 'śiṣyāya.... nā 'śāntāya. Maitrī, 6.29.
121. MU, 1.1.1.
122. CU, 3.11.6.
123. PVU, p. 594.
124. CU, 1.8.1.
125. sametya mimāṁsāṁcakruḥ. CU, 5.11.1.
126. Kurupāñcālānām brāhmaṇā abhisametā babhūvuḥ. BU, 3.1.1.
127. pp. 34-40.
128. CU, 7.1.2.

PART I

THE GOAL

CHAPTER I

THE PROBLEM OF REALITY

It has been the invariable custom with all the Indian systems of philosophy to enunciate the goal first, before exploring the way to attain it. They all feel that before the actual quest begins, the goal must be set forth as clearly as possible, because ignorance about the goal often leads to a half-way halt or an abrupt termination of the movement, originally initiated with a view to reaching the final truth of things. The danger of mistaking a relative truth for the final one is always there for one who makes the hazard of moving forward without a definite end or aim. The map must be drawn first of all, setting out the limit of the journey as well as marking off the boundaries. Of course, the map or picture differs one from another, according to the divergences of the minds that draw it. Thus the Sāṅkhya picture presents in broad relief the twin principle of Prakrti and Purusa, the true knowledge of which is the whole end and aim of its seeking. The Yoga picture while agreeing in essentials with the Sāṅkhya one, adds the concept of an Īśvara who is, however, only the first of all puruṣas. The Nyāya prefers to draw the picture in a wealth of details and hence the ultimate things or *padārthas,* whose knowledge it seeks, are enumerated as sixteen. The Vaiśeṣika, though sharing an identical ideology with Nyāya, is a lover of brevity and so cuts down the figure from sixteen to six or seven. The whole picture of Purva Mīmāṁsā is devoted to the portrayal of the one essential thing, that matters most according to it, viz., Dharma. Finally, the Uttara Mīmāṁsā or Vedānta tries to picture the unpicturable, to map the unmappable, through the help of the suggestions and symbols thrown out by the Upaniṣads about the nature of that supreme object, the Vast and the Infinite, viz. Brahman. Being the greatest universal thing, Brahman naturally includes within it all the innumerable fragments of the particular and so the conception of it too is, by its very nature, so comprehensive as to include all partial view-points in its all-embracing harmony. We must try to gather from the Upaniṣads themselves the picture, which they present, about the final goal and then judge its merits.

The Goal of the Upaniṣads

Now, what is the goal of the Upaniṣads? The *Īśopaniṣad,* one of the oldest in verse, in its very opening line gives tbc answer thus: *'Īśā vāsyam idam sarvam'*. On one side is *Īśa* or the Lord, while on the other is *'idam sarvam',* all this, and they are to be joined together by the term *'vāsyam'*. But immediately a problem arises in connexion with the meaning of the term *'vāsyam',* which plunges us straight into the heart of the hardest metaphysical problem. As Sri Aurobindo in his book on the *Īśopaniṣad* points out : 'there are three possible senses of *'vāsyam', "to be clothed",* "to be worn as a garment", and "to be *inhabited"*[1]. Śaṅkara adopts the first sense, while Sri Aurobindo prefers the last one. The adoption of one sense or the other fundamentally determines the outlook of the chooser in regard to the nature of the relation he thinks to be subsisting between *'Īśa'* and *'idam'*. In terms of modern philosophy, these two entities may be termed as the subject and the object and the whole aim and endeavour of philosophy, upto the present day, has been to determine the exact relation between these two terms. And the attempt to determine it has led to the division of the world of philosophy into two warring camps, each of which tries to assign superiority to one of the terms over the other. One denies the independent existence of the object apart from the subject and turns out an idealist, while the other vehemently denounces the reality of the subject and pins its falth in the reality of the objcct alone, calling itself a realist. Some, of a compromising nature, have thought it wise to stand in the middle and effect a synthesis by giving scopc to both, as well as admitting the reality of each of them. The whole history of philosophy is the story of this swing of human thought from one pole to the other and its occasional stop in the middle to effect a compromise.

Thus, being caught up in the net of division, wc are seeking to bridge the gulf of the apparent division between '*Īśa*' and *'idam'*. Their mutual opposition is undeniable; otherwise, there would have been no need to seek a reconciliation between the two through *'vāsyam'*. Now, this reconciliation may be effected in various ways, as the difference in the interpretation of the term *'vāsyam'* itself indicates.

Firstly, a reconciliation may be effected by denying the one and affirming the other; secondly, by denying both; thirdly, by affirming both; and, fourthly, by transcending both. Does the Upaniṣad seek to obliterate or efface '*idam*' altogether by enjoining that it should be *clothed* or covered totally by *Īśa* or does it ask the seeker to instal the *Īśa* in the bosom of *'idam'* as the *inhabitant* without covering its existence altogether? In other words, is the world to be swallowed up by the Lord or inhabited by Him?

Before seeking the answer to this fundamental question it will be wiser to determine, first of all, the connotations of the two terms, whose reconciliation is to be sought, because the clearing up of the concepts will go a long way in helping the final solution of the problem. To determine the nature of the *Īśa* is the one main pre-occupation of all the Upaniṣads. It is variously termed as *Brahman, Ātman, Puruṣa, Ąkṣara, Īśa* etc., from different points of view. Of these the most common appellations are Brahman and Ātman and their identity too is specifically stated by the Upaniṣad itself: *'ayam ātmā brahma'*[2]. The Brahman or the Ātman is the sole pursuit of the whole *Brahmavidyā* in the Upaniṣads. 'Brahman is called the goal'[3], 'That Immutable is the goal'[4], 'That Ātman is to be seen'[5], 'He is to be searched, He is to be enquired about'[6], thus the Upaniṣads speak again and again.

Definition of Brahman or Ātman

The next question that comes to the mind is: What is signified by the term Brahman or the term Ātman? Here again we are confronted with a difficulty, for various passages in the Upaniṣads describe the Brahman or the Ātman in numerous ways, which seem conflicting and often inconsistent with one another. The two broad features of the conflicting nature of the statements are (i) affirmation and (ii) negation, i.e. in some places it is described as identified with all existence, while in other places it is pointed out solely by the stripping off of all identifications whatsoever, by a drastic and relentless denial. 'All this is the Ātman',[7] 'All this is verily Brahman'[8] and such other statements unequivocally affirm the identification of all this with Brahman or Ātman, Again, 'He however, the Ātman, is not so, not so (*ne 'ti, ne 'ti*). 'He is incomprehensible, for he is not comprehended; indestructible, for he is not destroyed; unaffected, for nothing affects him; he is not fettered, he is not disturbed, he suffers no harm'[9], or 'That it is, O Gārgi, which the wise call the Imperishable (*akṣaram*);

it is neither thick nor thin, neither short nor long, neither red (like fire) nor fluid (like water), neither shadowy nor dark, neither wind nor ether (space), not touched, without taste or smell, without eye or ear, without speech, without understanding, without vital force and without breath, without mouth or size, without inside or outside; never consuming anything nor consumed by any'[10] and such other statements vehemently deny all identification, with any aspect of existence. Shall we then say with Keith that "contradictions 'in adjecto' are the normal characteristic of the Upaniṣads"[11] or that "the hopeless inconsistencies of the view of Yājñavalkya become painfully obvious"?[12] Contradictions and inconsistencies no doubt confront us at every step but that is no reason why one shoutd leave things at that after pronouncing a mere hasty condemnation. If one seeks the solution of the contradictions patiently from the Upaniṣad itself, then there is no reason why it should not be forthcoming with the clearness of the morning light, dispelling all darkness whatsoever. It is our own bias and prejudice that always deprive us from getting the true solution. 'Spiritual books are written in the language of the Spirit and must be spiritually discerned. They yield a new sense at every reading and it is only after many years that most of us begin to realize the colossal nature of our own initial mistakes'[13]. The real spirit can never be taught, it must be caught through an attitude of sympathy with the true essence of the Upaniṣadic teaching. And so let us try our best to get in touch with it.

Two forms of Brahman

One Upaniṣad mentions that there are two forms of Brahman, the manifest as well as the unmanifest'.[14] Another Upaniṣad speaks of the *Para* and the *Apara-Brahman.*[15] The *Maitrī Upaniṣad* says: 'There are two *Para-Brahmans* to be contemplated, the *Śabda* as well as the *Aśabda,* the *Śabdabrahman* and that also which is *Para'.*[16] Thus the two descriptions which appeared manifestly contradictory point in reality to two distinct forms of the same Brahman. The *mūrta* or the manifest is the form identified with manifestation, the *amūrta* or the unmanifest form is by its nature distinct from all manifestation. That form which is the active principle in all manifestation is called the *Sabdabrahman* or in the technical terminology of the later Vedānta, the *Īśvara.* The other which is not so engaged or connected with manifestation is the *Aśabda* or the *Para Brahman.* In terms of Western philosophy, the one may be called the God, the other the Absolute.

But the problem of problems remains: what is the relation between the *mūrta* and the *amūrta,* the *Śabda* and the *Aśabda,* the God and the Absolute? Are they identical or distinct? 'We are thus face to face with the ultimate problem which may be variously described as the problem of the Absolute and God, of the One and the Many, of Transcendence and Immanence, of Eternity and Time, of the Infinite and the Finite, of the Universal and the Particular'.[17] It is an ancient problem but it still remains as acute as in the days of Plato and Śaṅkara.

Brahman and Creation

The Upaniṣads are emphatic that at the root of the whole manifestation is Brahman. That out of which all these things are born, by which they live and unto which they return and merge, that is Brahman'.[18] Nay, the very root meaning of the term 'Brahman' signifies its creative nature. That which grows or swells is literally Brahman, and hence, as Dr. Maryla Falk rightly points out, originally the term Brahman signified the female principle and did not convey the neuter conception that is now assigned to it.[19] 'The vast Brahman is my womb' says the Lord in the Gītā.[20] But manifestation or creation essentially implies a change or a movement and if Brahman is the cause of it then that too must be changeful in its nature or at least must be affected somehow or other by the changes in the effect. If the immutability of Brahman is to be preserved, change must be denied or Brahman must be conceived as itself changing or moving.

The Upaniṣads steer clear of this dilemma. We have pointed out in the introduction that all the Upaniṣads unfailingly point out the two broad features of Reality viz., Agni and Ātman. The whole structure of the Upaniṣadic wisdom rests on these two conceptions, and it is through the instrument of these two principles that the Upaniṣads solve all problems, however hard. with an ease that is striking and remarkable. Now, as Agni or Prāna the Supreme Reality produces and sustains the whole existence. 'Whatever is, all this world issues forth from the moving Prāṇa',[21] 'All that is here and in the heavens are under the control of Prāṇa'.[22] Agni is, therefore, significantly called *'Jātavedas'* the knower of all that is created and as the *Nirukta* points out, in giving its various etymological meanings, it also signifies that all created things know it[23] because it is the source of them all and as such in direct touch with them. It also exists eternally in every cycle of creation, it is behind each and every manifestation[24]. It is again the *Śabda Brahman,* the root of all creations, the Supreme Logos, the Creative Word. It is also *Śāvitrī,* the Divine Mother, who gives birth to the universe, and *Gāyatrī,* the redeeming Mother, who guides all movements in the hearts of beings as well as in the heavens. Its very nature is composed of two principles, *Jñāna* and *Kriyā,* Reason and Action, as Śaṅkara rightly points out[25] and hence creativity is its fundamental feature. Here, 'Reality is undoubtedly creative, productive of effects in which it transcends and expands its own being',[26] as Bergson states it. But this Prāṇa is a richer principle than Bergson's *elan vital,* for it is not a blind urge or a pointless movement alone like the latter, moving on and on without knowing an end, but a luminous conscious force that knowingly creates and creatively knows. Here knowledge and movement go hand in hand and what the vision directs the movement executes. Thus direction and execution proceed from the same source here and therefore Prāṇa is at once the '*anujñā*'[27] or the command, as well as the '*saṁvardhaitā*',[28] the executor of the exuberant flow of creation. Hence, *'mithuna'* or the mixture of two, i.e. unity-in-difference, is the very basic nature of Prāṇa. The world with its differences and diversities is here taken up within the unit of the single organism of Prāṇa, the parts meet in the whole, the subject and the object are found to be complementary parts of the same whole.

Hegel's Absolute Idea thus comes very near this conception of Prāṇa in the Upaniṣads. His idea of the principle of differentiation within the unity of the Absolute bears close resemblance to the similar Upaniṣadic conception about Prāṇa. Hegel's view appears very fascinating to our mind and still holds its sway over us because 'what our intellect really aims at is neither variety nor unity taken singly but *totality*',[29] as James rightly points out. Our intellect is confronted with a bewildering variety and its sole effort is directed towards the construction of a system or a coherent whole out of this chaotic mass. It endeavours to create a perfect world in the sense of a rounded whole, 'a spherical system with no loose ends hanging out for foreignness to get a hold upon'. Hence our intellect conceives that the Absolute is the entire system of internal discords transmuted into ever richer harmonies and into the harmonious unity of the whole. Organic unity is the highest unity that our intellect can comprehend or envisage.

But still there is a higher unity beyond it as pointed out by the Upaniṣads. We were confronted with the dilemma that if Brahman is the cause of the universe or the manifestation, it must be conceived as itself changing, or change must be denied if the immutability of Brahman is to be preserved. Through the conception of Prāṇa, we have found, the Upaniṣads do not deny or explain away change or manifestation, but rather exhibit that the whole wealth of creativity is in the very heart of Reality. But how then is the immutability of Brahman preserved if change or movement happens to issue out of its very centre? It is preserved through the conception of transcendence, which is the quintessence of the whole Upaniṣadic wisdom. As Agni or Prāṇa, Reality is immanent, as Ātman it is transcendent. '*Asaṅgo hy ayaṁ puruṣaḥ*'[30] is the supreme truth indicated about the nature of the Ātman. The Ātman is absolutely untouched or untainted by all the colourful changes wrought over it and retains its pure majesty unsullied all through.

Then, does transcendence imply that the Ātman or Brahman is outside the sphere of existence, far above the noise and tumult enjoying a blessed solitude? We must warn readers here that the Upaniṣadic conception of transcendence and immanence should never be confused with the conceptions passing by those names in the West. In the West, transcendence has always signified the exclusive aspect of Reality, which is outside and above the process of creation and this has given the inspiration to Deism or Theism which worships Reality from a venerable distance, adoring its tremendous majesty and extolling its utter unapproachability. Immanence stands for the opposite conception, which signifies a total identification of existence or creation with Reality, which equates God and the world and as such leads to Pantheism, which finds God as an intimate companion, no longer above and beyond but close to the heart and here in the dust. Between these two extremes stands the so-called Panentheism which tries to cut a middle path by putting forth the view that the nature of Reality is all immanence and some transcendence. It holds that the Supreme Reality is completely immanent in the universe but this does not exhaust its entire nature and so it is something more and hence partly transcendent.

The Indian view or the Upaniṣadic conception of Reality is everywhere represented and condemned in the West as sheer pantheism, which strikes at the root of all morality and obliterates the distinction between good and evil, virtue and vice. Pantheism is defined as the doctrine which 'identifies God with the entire universe, which beholds him in the movement of the tiniest insect or in the lustre of the brilliant gem, in the mind of a Socrates or in the brain of a Newton.'[31] But if this pantheism be the doctrine of the Hindus, how the latter can be condemned in the same breath as a theory of illusion passes our comprehension. In order to condemn the Indian theory of so-called illusion, the Western scholars would represent it as sheer transcendentalism and again just to represent the Indian doctrine as the most obnoxious and abominable, in which there is 'unbridled license of a sensuous idolatry', in which 'the grossest impurities are not only permitted, but perpetuated under the sanction of religion,'[32] they would call it mere pantheism. All this is the result of a bias or prejudice which is regrettable in every true scholar.

The Upaniṣadic Conception of Transcendence & Immanence

The Indian or Upaniṣadic conception of transcendence and immanence is totally different and distinct from the Western view. Here transcendence never signifies an aloofness or exclusion, because the Brahman of the Upaniṣads is not a unitary principle which is opposed to the multiplicity of creation. Not only has it created the whole of existence, not only has it brought all this into being, but, having created this all, has veritably entered into it as the Upaniṣad expressly declares (*tat sṛṣṭvā tadēvā 'nuprāviśat*).[33] Not only is it the efficient cause, the *nimitta-kāraṇa,* of the creation but the material cause, the *upādāna-kāraṇa,* too. The *anupraveśa,* the entering into creation, the very fact of immanence signifies its transcendence. Here the entering or *anupraveśa* does not indicate something like the entering of one thing into another but simply points to the fact that by the act of creation the Supreme Reality has made itself accessible to the intellect (*buddhi*). This access to the intellect is the true meaning and significance of *'anupraveśa'*. But the intellect is the subtlest thing, being the very first and foremost principle in creation, and naturally that which can enter, even into this subtlest thing must be subtler still. Only the subtle can enter into the gross and not vice versa. Hence the Brahman surpasses even the intellect in subtleness and thus easily enters into it; and being subtler than the intellect it is not touched or tainted by any of the blemishes of the intellect. By the very fact of its entering, it proves its transcending nature. Transcendence thus, in our sense, always signifies the uniqueness, the *vilakṣaṇatā,* the distinctness of Brahman, and never any exclusiveness or apartness. 'Other than known, and more than the unknown is that'[34] declares the Upaniṣad, while signifying the transcendent nature of Brahman.

Here the two terms '*anyat*' and '*adhi*' peculiarly suggest the uniqueness of the nature of Reality and signify its transcendence of all categories of thought.

Similarly the '*ne 'ti ne 'ti*' of Yājñavalkya simply signifies the distinctness of the Ātman from all this that is here and does not convey any sense of excluding everything from it, as is ordinarily supposed. The Brahman of the Upaniṣads has no opposition whatsoever to anything and as such need not exclude anything in order to maintain its reality or purity. Thus '*ne 'ti ne 'ti*' does not deny the reality of existence, it 'denies all the empirical characterization of reality'.[35] It just signifies that Reality is something unique and distinct from the empirical. If we keep this sense of denial in mind, then it will be clear that 'the denial of attributes and qualifications to Brahman does not reduce it to a void'[36] but on the contrary, points to its inexhaustible fullness, which remains absolutely undiminished even after the whole of creation streams out of it, because it is not touched by this process of continuous ebb and flow at all, being absolutely distinct from all this. Here by a strange mathematics even after the subtraction of the full from the full, the remainder still remains the full![37]

How does this miracle happen? It happens because Brahman creates not in the ordinary way of a cause and effect series, but in a unique non-causal way. This is the much misunderstood theory of *vivartavāda* in Vedānta. In all the creations we find in the world, the effect is produced through a transformation of the cause into something else. The cause dies in order to give birth to the effect. Whether we agree with the view of *ārambhavāda* and say that the effect is something new and novel, which has just come into being and was previously non-existent, or concur with *pariṇāmavāda* that it was already there in the cause in a latent form and has only been made patent through the process of so-called creation, a change in the cause, some form of alteration in it, has somehow or other to be admitted, in either case, in order to account for the emergence of the effect. Is it possible in any way to keep the cause absolutely unaltered, and yet have the effect produced? The *vivartavāda* makes a bold attempt in this line. It tries to show that even in this world there are illustrations of an effect being produced without any change or modification whatsoever in the cause. and here are brought in the classic examples of illusions, like the rope-snake etc. The examples or illustrations have been taken in the wrong way everywhere and their true significance has been missed. It is generally assumed that by these illustrations the Vedānta has sought to explain away the world as a mere illusion or phantasmagoria, whereas the illustrations have quite another bearing. They only seek to show the unsullied nature of the cause, which is not touched in any way by the effect imposed upon it. As Śaṅkara puts it: 'Not by the fact that a water-snake is taken to be a snake does it become full of poison nor a snake being taken for a water-snake becomes poisonless'.[38] Similarly all the imperfections and limitations in creation do not touch Brahman at all, its eternal substratum, though Brahman is taken to be the world mistakenly. The illustration only goes upto this point and should not be pressed further.

The Vedānta, being a system of philosophy, tries to bring home the supra-rational truth in terms of rational concepts to the human mind. Without twisting or flouting human logic, it attempts to systematize the ineffable experience of the Absolute or Brahman. Here it almost sets an impossible task before it, for how can the supra-rational be presented through the methods of the rational intellect? Either the supra-rationality suffers or has to be sacrificed, or rationality has to go. But the unique achievement of the Vedānta lies in this that it never brings down the supra-rational even an inch from its glorious height and yet presents a rational account of the whole manifestation out of it. It keeps the cause absolutely unmodified and yet accounts for the effect. It does not again say that a part of the cause is modified and a part of it remains unmodified, for that is contrary to all logic and will make the one indivisible reality a mere combined product of different parts and as such destroy its true unity. It keeps the whole cause unmodified and yet explains the modification or effect. This is not an explaining away of things but the only real attempt at explanation. The explaining away is, on the contrary, resorted to by those who merely accept the contradictory nature of Reality as presented to our intellect and experience and pronounce that this contradiction is the fundamental nature of it. To state that the Absolute or Brahman itself is modified as well as unmodified i.e. contradictory in nature is to equate Reality with the merely empirical.

It will not be out of point here to refer to the criticism of Hegel by Herbart. 'Inherent contradiction, says Hegel, is the very nature of these notions, as of all things in general; becoming, for example, is essentially unity of being and non-being etc. That, rejoins Herbart, is impossible so long as the principle of contradiction still retains its authority. That the notions of experience present contradictions is no fault of the objective world but of subjective perception, which must redress its erroneous construction by a transformation of these notions and an elimination of their contradictions. Herbart accuses the philosophy of Hegel of empiricism, in that it accepts from experience these contradictory notions unaltered; and notwithstanding discernment of their contradictory nature, regards them, just because they are empirically given, as justified and even on their account, transforms the science of logic itself'.[39] Hegel thus not only accepts the contradiction and attributes the contradictory nature to Reality, without attempting any solution but he also flouts the ordinary logic by inventing a logic of the Absolute. In other words, he frankly admits that to the ordinary logic the contradiction is inexplicable, and insoluble. The Vedānta, on the contrary, boldly accepts the fact of experience, acknowledges the contradiction and finally solves it in a unique way. It brings in the classic examples of illusion, because on the intellectual plane there is no other analogy through which the unmodified nature of the cause along with the production of the effect can be illustrated, The plane of the intellect is accustomed to *'Pariṇāma'*, i.e. creation through modification, it never knows creation without modification save in the cases of illusion, and that is why these illustrations are cited.

Unreality of Existence

But it may be objected here that this definitely takes away the reality of the created things and reduces the world to a mere illusory appearance, and though it may be the view of Saṅkara, yet it may not be acceptable to us, concerned as we are here solely with the Upaniṣads. The question then comes: Do the Upaniṣads pronounce the world to be unreal? Certainly there are passages which definitely state all existence to be of a fleeting nature,[40] pronounce it to be of very little worth[41] and contrast the little with the Vast or *Bhūman* and condemn it as perishable[42] and even go so far as to declare the many to be non-existent.[43], So the doctrine of illusoriness of created things is not an invention of Śaṅkara but has its roots in the Upaniṣads. All these "are covered by falsehood" declares the Upaniṣad.[44] But the whole confusion arises from the use of the word *'anṛta'* or *'mithyā'* in connection with the existence of the world. Words always create a confusion because of their association with a certain definite import beyond which we cannot go. *'Mithyā'* has always come to mean, in ordinary parlance, the unreal or non-existing. But the term *mithyā* is never applied in this sense to the world, and one must therefore carefully distinguish between the *'asat'* and the *'mithyā'*, the non-existent and the untrue. The world is not *asat,* non-existent because it is verily a fact of experience, as the *Vedānta-Sūtra* expressly declares: *nābhāva upalabdheḥ.*[45] It is *mithyā* only in the sense that it has got a spurious reality. Its reality is not genuine, because it does not belong to it but is only delegated to it by something else. Hence its reality is a dependent reality and not an independent one, which can stand on its own grounds. Dependent reality, borrowed reality, spurious reality is called *mithyā,* false, i.e. not genuine. The Upaniṣads have no objection if any one feels satisfied by using the term *satyam* with regard to the world or existence but then the Absolute or Reality must be called *Satyasya Satyam,*[48] the Truth of the Truth, i.e. one must then distinguish between two orders of truth, in which the lower truth is sustained by the higher.

Thus we find that it matters little whether we call the world *Satya* or *mithyā*, if we rightly understand the connotations of these two terms. Even those who advocate the reality of the world can never assert that the world is of the same order of reality as the Absolute, but there are some who will raise a storm if it is called unreal or *mithyā*. It is only strict logic which forces one to use the term *'mithyā'*, for Truth is one and undivided, and it is logically absurd to speak of a more true or less true. If it is true, it is wholly true, if it is not true then it is false, that is the imperative demand of logic.

Degrees of Reality

The question immediately comes: Do the Upaniṣads not recognise degrees of reality? Certainly they do but at the same time they know its limitations. This less and more, or the degrees are essentially a product of the intellect or the mind and do not apply to Reality itself. The intellect, while apprehending Reality, apprehends less or more of it according to its power of apprehension and attributes the degrees to Reality, while actually they belong to the intellect itself. Thus there are no degrees *in* Reality, though the degrees are *of* Reality. The Upaniṣads present Reality as a value from this point of view and they draw a hierarchy of values too : 'Higher than the senses are the (subtle) objects of sense; higher than those objects is the mind, higher than the mind is the intellect or *buddhi*; higher than the intellect is the Great Self or *Mahān Ātmā;* higher than the *Mahat* is the Unmanifest; higher than the Unmanifest is the Supreme Self or the *Puruṣa.* That is the End, that the Ultimate Goal',[47] or again, 'Higher than the senses is the mind; above the mind is the intellect; beyond the intellect is the Great Self; above the Great Self is the Unmanifest; higher than the Unmanifest is the Self or *Puruṣa,* all-pervading and devoid of any characteristic mark, having known which, every living being is liberated and goes to the immortal state'."

Thus as we rise in the ladder of consciousness we get a clearer and clearer view of Reality but that does not signify that Reality itself is graded in nature. We have pointed out that it is only the power of apprehension that creates the degrees, and power always signifies a movement, and movement is essentially a function of Prāṇa. Thus degrees of reality hold very true in the sphere of Prāṇa, which is graded in its very nature but they do not apply to the Ātman, which is single and simple in its being. Even the so-called illusionist Saṅkara admits degrees of reality on the plane of the mind as when he says in his commentary on the *Vedānta Sūtra* that 'although *one and the same* self is hidden in all beings, movable as well as immovable, yet owing to the gradual rise of excellence of the minds which form the limiting conditions of the Self, Scripture declares that the self, *although eternally unchanging and uniform* reveals itself in a *graduated series* of beings and so appears in forms of various dignity and power'.[49] Thus the axiological and the logical views of Reality are both placed side by side in the Upaniṣads and do not contradict each other because they refer to two distinct spheres altogether. Axiologically, Reality exhibits higher and higher values, appears richer and richer in content and being, while logically it remains the same one unchanging Reality. The Upaniṣads give equal scope to both *pariṇāmavāda and vivartavāda.* What is *pariṇāma* on the plane of the *prāṇa* and *buddhi* is *vivarta* on the plane of the Ātman or Brahman.

Purpose and value of Creation

Still our intellect protests. Being accustomed to *pariṇāma* or evolution, which is a fact of experience to it and hence very true, it refuses to acknowledge any plane or sphere, where this law of evolution or *pariṇāma* does not hold good. It questions: 'Even if this experience of ourselves is illusory, the illusoriness itself is part and parcel of the experience and cannot be conjured away. For, since we are parts of the Reality, our experience—illusoriness and all—is in the end a portion of God's experience. But the God, who is timeless, complete and positive Reality cannot be conceived as the ground of evil, error or illusion. *As we experience them* they are in respect to such a God 'mere negations'; and yet *as we experience them* they have a distinctive character and are in some sense real'.[50] But the Upaniṣads nowhere conjure away the fact of experience. On the contrary, they show the extreme importance and utility of the so-called illusory world. It is this dual, this unreal, this finite which suggests the non-dual, the Real, the Infinite. All these forms of diversity are assumed by the Infinite itself in order to make its true nature revealed. 'Indra assumes these diverse forms through *māyā* in order to make known his own form'.[51] The *'pururūpa'* or diverse forms are thus meant to point towards the *"svarūpa'* or the true form. As Śaṅkara rightly points out here: 'Had this name and form not been manifested then the unconditioned form of this Ātman, called the *prajñānaghana,* would not have been revealed.'[52] There is thus a deep purpose behind the manifestation and hence it is not to be rejected or conjured away as a mere nothing. It is only by contrast with the unreality of the world that the reality of Brahman is realized, and here lies its supreme value and utility. That is why Reality creates this opposition between knowledge and ignorance, good and evil, virtue and sin etc. In itself, Reality, does not stand in need of an opposite principle in order to makc itself real, but it is only to make its *apprehension* possible that the creation of an opposite principle is needed. To make itself *known* (*praticakṣaṇāya*) it has created the diversity and not to make itself real. It is real by its own inherent nature and is not dependent on anything else to make itself real.

Hegel and his followers make Reality itself composed of these two opposite principles, unity and diversity, and they think that these two constitute the very nature of Reality, which makes their Absolute a spurious one, because, according to them, appearance without reality would be impossible, for what then could appear? And reality without appearance would be nothing, for there certainly is nothing outside appearances.'[53] Such a relativity of the Absolute and the world takes away the very absoluteness of the Absolute because it militates against the intrinsic self-sufficiency of the Absolute. The Upaniṣads never make this mistake of making the Absolute dependent on something else and thereby reducing it to a relative entity. They know that 'while a grin required a cat, a cat need not always have a grin',[54] i.e. though the world always stands in need of Brahman in order to exist, yet Brahman never looks towards the world for its *existence.*

The mind in order to apprehend the existence of Brahman no doubt needs the world, for, as we have pointed out, it is only through the immanence that the transcendence is apprehended or realized, but that is no reason for attributing to Reality itself the necessity that is indispensable to the mind. The Upaniṣadic conception thus gives full scope and value to the appearances and yet never makes them a part and parcel of Reality. Reality is always established in its own majesty, declare the Upaniṣads: 'In what is the *Bhūman* or the Vast established? In its own majesty or not even in its own majesty'[55].

It is so very self-sufficient that the Upaniṣads even feel diffident to state that it is established in *its* own majesty, and retracts its own statement, for that may give the impression that the *Bhūman* has to look to its own majesty in order to have its existence. Utter freedom, complete self-sufficiency is the mark of the Absolute, and the Upaniṣads never compromise it for the sake of our inability to grasp it.

Contradictions Reconciled

The Upaniṣads thus feel no difficulty whatsoever in asserting the complete immanence of Brahman in the world, as well as, in the same breath, declaring its complete transcendence. Everywhere they say that it is from the *Akṣara* or the Immutable that all the mutations proceed.[56] They even speak in the same line of a verse of the two aspects: 'It is without life, without mind, pure, higher than the supremely Immutable. From this is born life, mind, as well as all the senses; the sky, the wind, the fire, the waters, the earth, the sustainer of the universe'.[57] Similarly, the *Īśa* speaks of the two functions in the same verse, the *'paryagāt'* and the *'vyadadhāt',* the spreading all around and the making or ordering of things. As Sri Aurobindo translates it: 'It is He that has gone abroad—That which is bright, bodiless, without scar of imperfection, without sinews, pure, unpierced by evil. The Seer, the Thinker, the One who becomes everywhere, the Self-existent has ordered objects perfectly according to their natures from years sempiternal'.[58] As Rabindranath Tagore has pointed out[59] in his brilliant exposition of this verse, that the first two lines describe Reality only in the neuter, while the concluding two lines use the masculine, which is very significant. In the first part again, Reality is described simply through negatives, like *akāya, avraṇa, asnāvira, apāpaviddha* etc., while in the second it is represented positively as the *kavi, manīṣī, paribhū, svayambhū* etc. To the Upaniṣadic eye it is the same Reality viewed from two aspects, now from within and now from without. The two pictures do not make Reality dual but leave its unity unimpaired. The difference is in the points of view and not in Reality itself. Seen from within, the divine nature is Being resting in itself, centred in itself, and, viewed from without, it is the source from which streams out the exuberant flow of creation, and unto which it returns. The absolute God thus becomes the creator God, when we look at it from the end of the world. Here Reality streams down into the world it has created, and penetrates, sustains and controls it. Here it is described as the 'Lord of all, the knower of all, the Indweller, the Source, the (principle of) generation and dissolution of all created things.'[60] But there it is all pure Being and nothing else. "Neither inwardly conscious, nor outwardly conscious, nor in both ways conscious, nor conscious all through, neither knowing nor unknowing, invisible, intangible, incomprehensible, indescribable, unthinkable, inexpressible, founded solely on the certainty of its own self, the end of all existence, tranquil, blissful, timeless, that is the fourth, that is the Ātman, that is to be known."[61]

This description wholly through negative terms creates in our mind the idea that the Reality is going to be depleted of all contents, it is being deprived of all richness and we are being led towards an utter blank, a vain abstraction, a void, a zero. This has led to the idea in the West that the Brahman of Indian philosophy is a characterless nothing, an empty abstraction, a purposeless empty power without wisdom and activity, a unity into which all existences pass as into a dark and eternal night. That is why Caird describes the Indian Brahman as "an abyss of a negative infinitude......a unity which has no principle of order in the manifold differences of things but merely a gulf in which all difference was lost."[62] In the same strain, Pfleiderer describes Brahman as "an indeterminate abstract Being, which is hardly distinguished from nothing; an abyss which produces and maintains the finite; it is like the cave of the lion into which all the footsteps lead and none lead out again".[63] Instances need not be multiplied, for they are all too common in each and every book of the Western scholars and philosphcrs. But these writers and critics do really deserve our sympathy, for it is not usually possible for the human mind to conceive of this transcendent sphere of Advaita, accustomed as it is to grow and know through a relation of duality. The Upaniṣads are very well aware of this fact; they state clearly the possibility of confusion in many of the discussions about Brahman. Thus this fear seized the heart of Maitreyī, when Yājñavalkya, describing to her the nature of Brahman, said that there was no consciousness thereafter[64] i.e. after the realization of Brahman. To this Maitreyi protested, saying, that she was being utterly confused, because she felt that she was being led to a state of utter unconsciousness, an absolute Void, and Yājñavalkya immediately reassured her, saying that, he did not mean to confuse her, the Ātman is truly immortal, and its nature or being is beyond annihilation.[65] Similarly Indra, when instructed by Prajāpati that the nature of the Ātman was akin to the state of sleep, felt disconcerted on thinking that then everything would face utter extinction, and the state would not be an enjoyable one at all.[66] So he returned to Prajapati, who appreciated his difficulty and clearly distinguished the true nature of the Ātman from the state of sleep or unconsciousness. He assured him that one did not lose everything there but rather got back his own true form,[67] became the Supreme Puruṣa, full of all enjoyments. It is a state where all is lost, yet all is found.

True Significance of Negative Descriptions

Hence, as we have already pointed out, the negative particle *ne'ti* which is so frequently used in describing Brahman, does not signify an annulment or rejection of all, as we commonly suppose, but everywhere suggests the uniqueness of Brahman or Ātman. The supreme experience of the Ātman or Brahman has no parallel in our common world of experience; it is something of a 'wholly other' nature and therefore those who refuse to move beyond the common experience of thought or those who try to push the analogy of this our experience to the sphere of the Absolute will certainly miss it.

Fortunately, there are some in the West who have lately realized the true significance of the negative approach and seem to appreciate it, finding its parallel in some of the Western mystics' approach to Reality. Dr Otto, in his remarkable book, *'The Idea of the Holy'* rightly remarks: "This aspiration for the 'void' and for becoming void and for becoming nothing, must seem a kind of lunacy to any one who has no inner sympathy for the esoteric language and ideograms of Mysticism and lacks the matrix from which these come necessarily to birth. To such one, Buddhism will be simply a morbid sort of pessimism. But, in fact, the 'void' of the Eastern, like the 'nothing' of the Western mystic, is a numinous ideogram of the 'wholly other'."[68] James too in his *'Varieties of Religious Experience'* gives a correct appreciation of the Upaniṣadic approach through negatives thus: 'Their very denial of every adjective you may propose as applicable to the ultimate truth,—He, the Self, the Ātman, is to be described by "No! no!" only, say the Upaniṣhads—though it seems, on the surface, to be a no-function, is a denial made on behalf of a deeper Yes. Whoso calls the Absolute anything in particular, or says that it is *this,* seems implicitly to shut it off from being *that*—it is, as if, he lessened it. So we deny the 'this', negating the negation which it seems to us to imply, in the interest of the higher affirmative attitude by which we are possessed".[69] Coomaraswamy, the great scholar and art-critic, hence rightly observes that "such a negative manner of speaking is inevitable for here negation, *ne' ti ne 'ti,* 'not so, not thus' is a denial of limiting conditions, a double negative; not as with us who 'make innate denial' that we are other than ourselves, an affirmation of limiting conditions. So Godhead is 'void', light and darkness, it is rid of both, 'poised in itself in sable stillness', it is 'idle', 'effects neither this nor that', is 'as poor, as naked and as empty as though it were not; it has not, wills not, wants not, 'motionless dark'."[70]

Royce's view examined

There are, again, some eminent philosophers, who, while deeply appreciating the true significance of this negative approach, yet do not feel quite at home in this dizzy height of the transcendent and hence recoil back to the safe level of synthesis of the intellect. The case of Royce is an instance to the point. We believe that no other philosopher in the West has presented the view of the Upaniṣads more faithfully and sympathetically, yet ultimately, somehow or other, he fails to truly appreciate the supreme Upaniṣadic wisdom, and perhaps his Hegelianism proved stronger than his spirit of appreciation. He raises the problem very nicely: "Absolute immediacy, perfect peace, fulfilment of meaning by a simple and final presence—when do we finite beings come nearest to that? On the border-lands of unconsciousness, when we are closest to dreamless slumber. The Absolute, then, although the Knower, must be in truth Unconscious. But if this is so, wherein does the Absolute Being differ from pure Nothingness?"[71] He himself states further that "the seers of the Upaniṣads are fully alive to this problem. It is a mistake to imagine that they ignore it. More than once they discuss it with the keenest dialectic."[72] He then repeats the question: "Is the Absolute verily a *mere* nothing,''?[73] and answers it as follows: "The Hindoo's answer to this last question is, in one sense, precise enough. The Absolute is the very opposite of a mere Nothing. For it is fulfilment, attainment, peace, the goal of life, the object of desire, the end of knowledge. Why then does it stubbornly appear as indistinguishable from mere nothing? The answer is: *That is a part of our very illusion itself.* The light above the light is, to our deluded vision, darkness. It is our finite realm that is the falsity, the mere nothing. The Absolute is All Truth."[74] There can not be a more faithful and illuminating presentation of the Upaniṣadic view than this. But from this he goes to conclude that "this mystic Absolute gets, for the Hindoo, its very perfection from a Contrast-Effect,"[75] and here he definitely errs, for as we have already pointed out the perfection or existence of the Absolute never depends on the contrast with the illusory world but its *apprehension by us,* no doubt, does depend on this contrast alone. So it is not true to state that "this contrast-effect and this alone, gives the zero, that is the limit of the finite process, its value, its truth, its absolutcness".[76] Taking his stand on this Contrast-Effect, Royce goes on to show the inherent inconsistency of the Upaniṣadic view of the Absolute thus: "But a zero that is contrasted with nothing at all, has so far not even any contrasting character, and remains thus a genuine and absolute nothing. Hence, if the Absolute of the Mystic is really different from.nothing, it is so by virtue of the fact that it stands in real contrast with our own real but impcrfect Being. We too then are. If our life behind the veil is, as the mystic says, our goal, if already, even as we are, we are one with the Knower, then the absolute meaning does not ignore, but so far recognizes as real, even by virtue of the contrast, our present impcrfect meaning.[77] .... But to suppose, as the mystic does, that the finite search has of itself no Being at all, is illusory, is *māyā,* is itself nothing, this is also to deprive the Absolute of even its poor value as a contrasting goal. For a nothing that is merely other than another nothing, a goal that is a goal of no real process, a zero that merely differs from another zero, has as little value as it has content, as little Being as it has finitude".[78]

The whole misapprehension arises from the failure on Royce's part to appreciate truly the significance of the socalled unreality or illusoriness or *māyā*, as he calls it. The Upaniṣads nowhere deny that 'we too then are', but we are, not in virtue of ourselves, but we exist only through the existence of the Absolute or Brahman. Royce would feel comforted and reassured if some reality is conceded to the finite, if it is said that 'it is *real in its own way*'[79], and the Upaniṣads never object to conceding this sort of reality to the finite. The finite is certainly real in its own way, but it is not real in the way the Absolute is Real. The Reality of the Absolute is of a different category altogether, because It is Real on its own merit, while all else is real by virtue of its reality and has no intrinsic reality of its own. Hence, as we have already pointed out, it is only strict logic which forces Saṅkara to call the finite unreal, when contrasted with the Absolute Reality, while he himself admits degrees of reality *within the realm of the finite.* Thus, it is not a contrast between two degrees of reality here, between the less real and the more real, but between two different *orders* of reality. The contrast is not between one nothing and another nothing, between one zero and another zero, but between the only true thing and the nothing, between the only one integer and the infinite zeros. Remove the integer and all the zeros become mere nothing, while attached to it, they acquire infinite value.

Royce wants to picture the Infinite as only a magnified finite, because he thinks "it is not only the goal but thc whole series of stages on the way to this goal that is the Reality."[80] But, as Joachim puts it, "the Infinite cannot be regarded as merely a bigger or a more lasting, or a numerically greater finite: its nature is in no sense made up of finite parts. It must be conceived in a manner *toto genere* different from that in which we conceive the finite."[81] This is what the Upaniṣads think about the nature of the Infinite. The Upaniṣads never try. to effect a hollow compromise between the finite and the infinite. "The finite has not somehow to be retained in the Absolute. The Vedānta does not pull up the finite to the level of the Absolute nor does it bring down the Absolute to the level of the finite. It gives us another solution of the problem. The Absolute is all in all of the finite, it is its *adhiṣṭhāna* and *āśraya,* its ground and support. The finite cannot and does not live for a moment without the Absolute. But what from the standpoint of true knowledge is the Absolute appears as the finite from the standpoint of ignorance or ordinary empirical knowledge."[82] Thus it is the finite which points towards its ground or substratum by the very fact of its dependence on the Infinite and the contrast-cffect is enhanced and not diminished by the so-called unreality or rather dependent reality of the finite.

Hocking's view examined

We have quoted Royce at length and have engaged ourselves so long with him, just to show how a great mind, even on approaching the very border of the Supreme Reality ultimately recoils to its own safe harbour of the intellect. Royce's is not the only case, but most of the great thinkers and philosophers suffer from this 'last infirmity of the noble mind'. Being accustomed to move on the crutches of the intellect, they get afraid finally to dispense with them and move unaided straight into the heart of Reality to perceive the soul through the soul. They timidly knock at the door of Reality but remain wavering even when the door is ajar and miss the opportunity of entering into the *sanctum sanctorum.* Hocking's illuminating book, "Types of Philosophy" is another illustration to the point. He nicely states the difference between Realism, Idealism and Mysticism, thus : 'Realism separates object and knower, idealism holds that all objects belong to some knower; mysticism holds that the objects and the knowers belong to each other-they are the same reality, they are one'.[83] He deals exhaustively with each of the three views, adding his own critical comments at the end of each. He begins with Realism and finishes with Mysticism and it apparently seems that he realizes that the true consummation or the final solution lies in Mysticism, but he really purports to show that Realism and Mysticism are two extremes, the one favouring total separation, the other total union, and the wisdom lies in the middle, in the views of Idealism. He admits, while introducing the topic of Mysticism that "ldealism—even with the intuitions which lead to it—leave us unsatisfied, suffering 'with the wound of Absence.' There is, so to speak, another stage of intuition, in which the sense of otherness drops away and the knower realises that he is identical with the inner being of his object."[84] But, he again gets alarmed at this total dropping away of otherness, the entire identity of the knower and the known. He apprehends that "pure unity, unless it were understood to be the unity of something plural, would be a non-descript unity indistinguishable from nothing".[85] This apprehension again and again haunts our mind and prevents us from viewing the Reality in its utter truth and nakedness. It is again this bias which represents the transcendence as an exclusion or aloofness, which is never its real sense, as we have already pointed out. Hocking therefore recoils back from the position of the mystic, refusing to proceed to the farthest limit along with him and feels secure in the mid-position, swinging or alternating between the one and the many. His sense of the practical predominates over his sense of the real and hence he concludes : "The law of alternation is a practical principle, perhaps the chief of practical principles. It declares that we cannot make out a good life either by exclusive contemplation of the One or by intelligent management of the Many; but we must have both, in the form of a rhythm, like the rhythm of work and play, or of sleep and waking."[86]

We have already pointed out how all these misapprehensions arise due to the failure to comprehend the true nature of transcendence. We have mentioned Hocking's case, because both he and Royce refer to the Upainsadic view as belonging to the type of mysticism. But we must here warn that the Upaniṣadic doctrine is too great to be contained in any single 'ism'. If mysticism signifies an 'exclusive contemplation of the One' then the Upaniṣadic teaching is most emphatically not mystic in character. There is no spirit of exclusiveness in the Upainsadic teaching; on the other hand, it exceeds even the supreme inclusiveness. The Upaniṣadic or the Vedāntic doctrine is hence significantly termed *'advaita'* or non-dualism. It does not exclusively seek the One, nor lean towards the many, neither does it somehow work up a compromise between the two but transcends both. "It is no 'nearer' 1 than 2 and we may also note that the term *advaita,* usually loosely tendered as monism, means actually non-dualistn, which is not quite the same thing."[87] The Upaniṣads are very well aware of the synthesis, which Hocking and Royce and thinkers of the same line put forward. They know how to 'have both, in the form of a rhythm' and this rhythm is the Prāṇa or Agni, as we shall try to show in dealing with the diffcrent *vidyās.* This law of rhythm is truly 'the chief of practical principles'. nay, the very basic principle behind all manifestation. But that does not mean that this law is the final truth of things, though it may be 'the chief of practical principles'. There is still behind it a source from which even this supreme law emanates, and the Upaniṣads never rest content till they reach that final source, the Light of all lights (*jyotiṣāṃ jyotiḥ*),[88] the Truth of all truths (*satyasya satyam*).[89] They never deny the value of the practical principle, but rather give the fullest scope to it and yet pass on to view things from the standpoint of the Real. There is thus no conflict between the practical and the real from the Upaniṣadic point of view, and the Upaniṣads never try to bring down the real and completely identify it with the practical in order to make it suit our taste and temperament.

The True Nature of Reality

What then is the picture of Reality or the Absolute as we can finally draw it from the Upaniṣads? We have seen that the texts speak of both forms, *Para* and *Apara,* the Transcendent as well as the Immanent. Is it then a composite picture, of which the one half represents transcendence and the other half immanence? The Upaniṣads never try to join up somehow the two contradictory aspects or get them placed together on the same canvas. They never try to effect a *'samuccaya'* or synthesis or getting together of the two, nor do they cause a sundering between them. A *samuccaya* or synthesis is necessary where there is an opposition between two terms, which stand in the relation of thesis and antithesis. But the transcendence of Brahman which we have tried to depict, has no opposition to immanence if we rightly comprehend its nature. The Western conception, as we have pointed out, takes them in opposite senses and hence, there are some who posit a third entity, which is represented as neutral in its nature and of which both transcendence and immanence are two equally real aspects, and in this way, they try to effect a reconciliation between the two and yet keep the Absolute above the conflict. But the Upaniṣads, we have found, speak of two Brahmans and not of a third beyond both, because, according to them, there is no relation of opposition between immanence and transcendence which are to be reconciled in a third neutral entity. Here the transcendence itself signifies the real nature of the Absolute or Brahman and the very same transcendent Reality is viewed as immanent when looked at from the end of the world. 'Spirit-in-itsclf is transcendent, Spirit is immanent in reference to the order of expression'.[90] 'The transcendent alone is truth, the dynamic divine is the transcendent presented in the aspect of relation'.[91] The relation or the absence of relation leaves the transcendence unimpaired. The transcendent is called *'para',* the supreme or the higher, and the immanent *'apara'* or the 'not-supreme' or the lower, not to depreciate the one and exalt the other, but the immanent is *'apara'* in the scnse.that it is the view of Reality through a medium or relation and hence not direct and intimate, while the transcendent is the view of Reality in and through itself, and hence *'Para'*. But one must pass through this immanent to the transcendent, because every one of us happens to be a denizen of the world of relations and, as such, must view Reality through the relation first, before hoping to pass beyond all relations. The attempt to view the transcendent from the end of the world will always lead, as it has led everywhere up till now, to a vague abstraction. The Neo-Vedāntists, in their zeal to extol the *Nirguṇa Brahman,* have almost reduced it to a mere nothing, an empty contentless being. Hence Vidyāraṇya rightly reminds us that only those who have meditated on the *Saguṇa Brahman* are fit to know the *Para Brahman,* and learn this supreme *Brahmavidyā.*[92]

We must also note here that the true has always its counterfeit and thus there is a false transcendence, as well as a false immanence which imitate the originals and thereby cause a deception. The false transcendence is achieved by cutting oneself off altogether from all manifestation and through the ushering in of a blissful silence. This is the path of Sāṅkhya, which seeks an aloneness or *kaivalya,* away from the diverse mutations of *prakṛti.* The true transcendence, too, is a state *above* all manifestation, but *not aloof* or *away* from manifestation. Neither is it *in* all manifestation and yet somehow *above* it. It has no in or out, within or beyond, below or above. It is *'anantara', 'avāhya.'* It is, what it is, in its own majesty, preserving its uniqueness amidst all contradictions. It is also the silence, but not the silence that is opposed to movement or change. It is called the Silence, because its inherent nature or uniqueness is never disturbed or moved in any place or time. There is always a risk of misunderstanding this supreme silence as the silence of death, which benumbs all the creative flow of life but in fact it is the silence of which both death and immortality are equally shadows.[93] The world is thus not cast off in this true transcendence, as in Śāṅkhya, for that would mean a lapse into dualism and an abandonment of the true *advaita* position. The true *advaita* never needs the excision of a second in order to achieve its non-duality, for that very sundered or excised part will remain as an eternal challenge to its genuine non-duality, and falsify it. The *Vārttikasāra,* therefore, rightly points out that if the world is denied in Brahman and is conceived as existing apart from it, then it will lead to the view of the Sāṅkhya and therefore the all-inclusiveness is being stated.[94] To know the transcendent, then, is not to lose the immanental richness but to surpass it through a fullness that is over-flowing. To know it, is to comprehend it in its own being or essence, as well as, in the details of all relations, because having transcended all relations, it knows how all relations work and arrange themselves. Having reached that Light of all lights, one not only knows it in its pure white radiance, but also comes to know how, through what curvatures and colours, it appears manifold in the world of manifestations. It will not do merely to know that all this is the play of that one Light but one must also know the *how* or the details of the process through which the Light appears in diverse colours. To state in the terms of the classical example of Vedānta, it will not do merely to know that the snake is nothing but the rope, but one must fully know how, through what process of misapprehension, the rope had appeared as the snake. Till then the illusion will not be dispelled, the fear will not be removed, the truth will not be revealed. True transcendence thus implies a knowledge in details of the entire process of manifestation.

The Conception of Immanence of Īśvara

Having distinguished the spurious or pseudo-transcendence from the true one, let us now proceed to have an acquaintance with the aspect of immanence. Immanence, again, does not mean merely a pervasiveness through all space and time. Rather it signifies the principle of sustenance, which makes things exist and appear. It is that aspect of Reality which is in identification with existence. We have already pointed out that the immanent is nothing but the transcendent seen from the aspect of the world. It is thus Brahman itself which becomes the Īśvara, when taken or viewed in reference to the world or creation. As the *Pañcadaśī* expressly says : 'It is Brahman itself which appears as Iśvara, when in contact with the *upādhi* of its Śakti'.[95] This *Śakti* is termed as *māyā* or *prakṛti* by the *Śvetāśvatara,* the nature of which we shall have to discuss presently. He who is in touch with this *māyā* is the *Maheśvara* or the Supreme Lord.[96] "Īśvara then is the self as shining on and in *māyā* which has the three gunas (attributes or elements) of *sattva, rajas* and *tamas,* and is, accordingly, both *triguṇātīta* (transcending these gunas) and *śuddha-sattva-upādhi* (invested with a transparent body of *sattva*)"[97]. 'That one God covered himself of his own nature by the net born of the *pradhāna* or *prakṛti,* like the spider enveloping itself by the web'[98]. One thing which is to be marked here is that he covered himself of his own accord (*svabhāvataḥ*), and not by any compulsion. This is what makes him *Īśa* or the Lord, while the *jīva* becomes *anīśa,* because his covering is not conscious or self-willcd, but rather imposed or thrust upon him. Hence the *jīvas* cannot lift the veil or remove the net whenever they wish, while Īśvara is always free to do so. Therefore the *jīvas* look towards Īśvara for help in the matter of the removal of this veil.

Here the close connexion between the Īśvara and the Guru becomes patent. Not only is he the Creator but also the Redeemer. The *Pātañjala Yoga-Sūtra,* therefore, rightly calls him the eternal and most supreme Guru.[99] Vyāsa, in his commentary, points out that though he has no personal benefit to gain yet his sole concern is to favour the created beings (*bhūtānugrahaḥ prayojanam*).[100] This function of *'anugraha'* is something like a divine prerogative with him. The *Kaṭha Upaniṣad* expressly mentions this latter function: 'The Self-manifested has pierced the apertures of the senses outwards, therefore creatures look outwards and do not see the inner self'.[101] The *Bṛhadāraṇyaka* and the *Kauṣītaki* also state it more explicitly: 'It is he who makes that man perform good deeds whom he wants to uplift, and again it is he who makes that man perform evil actions whom he wants to thrust downwards'.[102] Thus the creatures or *jīvas* are absolutely at the mercy of Īśvara. This, however, does not make the Īśvara a mere despot, or reduce the *jīvas* into mere automata, for the *jīvas* are, in reality, his own images or reflections. He becomes the benefactor or oppressor, not of some entities which are apart from him, but he oppresses or molests himself by himself and again favours himself through himself. This is what is called his play or sport or *līlā* (*lokavattu līlākaivalyam*).[103] The Tantras rightly lay stress on these functions of *'nigraha'* and *'anugraha',* and emphasize, that not even a thousand effort on the part of the *paśu* or the *jīva* can remove the original ncsciencc, the limitation or 'dirt of smallness' or finitude, the *āṇava mala*. It is only *Paśupati,* the Lord, who has deliberately put on this veil, that can lift it once more through his act of grace. Here lies the significance of *dīkṣā* or initiation, which symbolises the removal of the original veil by an act of grace from above.

Thus the conception of Īśvara provides a great hope and affords a sustenance to all created beings, who are plunged in ignorance.

Brahman does not sit aloof having plunged the world in ignorance but is eternally engaged as Īśvara in taking it once more out of the mire or darkness. Īśvara is actively interested in every bit of creation, though as Brahman he remains absolutely untouched and unconcerned. As Īśvara he is the vast refuge of all,[104] the adorable beneficent Lord.[105] He sits in the heart of all creatures as the Ruler,[106] the Great Soul lords over all.[107] He is the Controller of all, the Ruler of all, the Lord of all.[108] He is the Overlord, the Sustainer of all creatures, the Lord of all creatures, the Bridge, which sustains and prevents the separation of all these spheres.[109] He is the Mighty Fear, the Upraised Thunderbolt.[110] 'Out of its fear the wind blows, out of its fear rises the Sun as well as the Fire and the Moon, and the fifth, Death flies';[111] or, as another Upaniṣad puts it, 'out of its fear the fire burns, out of its fear burns the Sun, out of its fear move or run Indra, Vāyu and the fifth Mṛtyu or Death'.[112] He is again called the Immutable, the *Akṣara,* and 'by the ruling or ordaining of this *Akṣara,* O Gārgī, the Sun and the Moon are sustained, by the ruling of this *Akṣara* the heaven and the earth are sustained, by the ruling of this *Akṣara* the seconds, moments, days, nights, fortnights, months, seasons and years are sustained, by the ruling of this *Akṣara* flow the rivers towards the east from the white mountains and similarly other rivers to their respective directions'[113] and so on. Again, it is he who pervades everywhere: 'His eyes are all the world over, his mouth all around, his hands and feet everywhere. He is also called the *Antaryāmi* or the Indweller: 'This is the Lord of all, the Knower of all, this the Indweller.'[115] 'This your Ātman, the Indweller is Immortal'[116] and Yājñavalkya goes to point him out in details as the indwelling principle in all the elements, quarters, planets as well as in the creatures, in their lives, minds and the senses.[117] He is also represented as of golden colour, the effulgent Puruṣa, the Creator, the Lord, the progenitor of Brahmā.[118] It is rare to find so rich and beautiful a description of God in any religious literature of the world. The whole Upaniṣadic literature resounds with the glory of this personal God or Īśvara, and his glowing description is strewn all over. Thus, this Īśvara is not a 'myth', as Gough and other writers similarly disposed, have ventured to describe, in their ignorance of the true bearing of the Upaniṣadic teaching. And we must also here point out another very erroneous conception which is very much current: "Brahman and Īśvara have sometimes been called the higher god and the lower god. The distinction is, to say the least, misleading, and probably the overdefinite language of some of the systematizing scholiasts is responsible for it. No doubt there is a distinction between the *conceptions.* Yet Īśvara is not *in reality* different from Brahman."[119] Īśvara is nothing but Brahman viewed with reference to the world, as we have already pointed out, and hence they are the same Reality.

That this Īśvara is the same as Prāṇa is expressly stated in the *Kauiṣītaki;* 'It is this Prāṇa itself which is the *Prajñātmā,* or Conscious Self, the Delight, the Undecaying, the Immortal', and the passage concludes, 'this is the Sustainer of the spheres, the Lord of the spheres, this the Lord of all'.[120] Thus this Prāṇa represents the Concrete Absolute, of which Hegel and his followers are so staunch advocates. Hence, the synthesis of which Hegel speaks was not unknown to the Upaniṣads, but they passed on further in order to find a still higher solution, of which Hegel had no idea. The *Śvetāśvatara,* evidently a later Upaniṣad with a definite theistic note, almost anticipates the Hegelian dialectic through the positing of three terms. We have previously pointed out that the earlier Upaniṣads all speak of two Brahmans and do not feel the need of positing a third, but here in the *Śvetāśvatara* we find a reference to three forms of Brahman (*trividham brahman etat*)[121], viz. the Enjoyer, the Enjoyed and the Director. It, again, says that *vidyā* and *avidyā* are concealed in the Supreme Infinite Brahman, of which *avidyā* is fleeting and *vidyā* is immortal and He who controls both is another[122]. This reminds one of a similar solution given in the *Gītā* through the three concepts of *Kṣara, Akṣara* and *Puruṣottama.* The earlier Upaniṣads, when they speak of the Īśvara as the third status, rcfer to the Supreme or Para Brahman as the fourth or *turīya,* in order to distinguish it from the former.

Rāmānuja's view

The vast Upaniṣadic wisdom contains all forms of solutions and that is why it has been possible for different and divergent systems to quote the Upaniṣadic texts in support of their respective views. Śaṅkara's is not the only system which goes by the name of Vedānta, but there are other schools like that of Rāmānuja, which are equally affiliated to the Vedāntic system of thought, i.e. spring from the Upaniṣads. Rāmānuja is an advocate of the Concrete Absolute, and to him, the Ultimate Reality is the repository of all beneficent qualities, one who sustains all by a fraction of his own power and is full of power, majesty, knowledge, great strength etc.[123] The teachings of the Vedānta, according to him, are, that there are three ultimate entities known to philosophy: the intelligent individual soul, the non-intelligent matter and God; that God is the Supreme Brahman, and is the cause of the universe, matter and soul constituting his body or modes, *'prakāra';* that the soul enters into matter and thereby makes it live and similarly God enters into matter and soul and guides them from within;[124] that Brahman is not devoid of attributes[125] but endowed with all the imaginable auspicious qualities;[126] that the world, as we see it, is not illusory but real, only its reality is not independent of or apart from Brahman;[127] that these three entities are naturally distinct from each other;[128] that there is no essential oneness of the individual self with the supreme self;[129] that salvation means not that the individual soul becomes identical, in essence, with the Supreme Self, but that it acquires most of the divine qualities of that Self, and, in that sense, becomes one with Him.[130] Brahman, according to Rāmānuja, thus comprises within itself, distinct elements of plurality, which all lay claim to reality. It is a Personal God, who is all-powerful, all-knowing and all-merciful. Thus, to use the usual terminology of Hegelian philosophers, we have in Rāmānuja's system God, man and nature, man transcending nature, and both man and nature finding their ultimate reconciliation in God—a unity-in-diversity.

Bhartṛprapañca's view

Even before Śaṅkara, a great Vedāntin thinker, named Bhartṛprapañca, was the upholder of the conception of the Concrete Universal. Unfortunately, Bhartṛprapañca's original works are not available and one has to collect his views only from other's references to him. Śaṅkara refers to him again and again in his *bhāṣya,* and Sureśvara, in his great *Vārttika,* presents the latter's views somewhat fully and clearly. The credit goes to Professor Hiriyanna for collecting the views of this old Vedāntin from the fragments and presenting them beautifully in a nutshell[131]. Hiriyanna points out that, Brahman, according to Bhartṛprapañca, is *'saprapañca'*—not robbed of its manifestations but possessing all of them, and, he adds, that this conception resembles that of the 'concrete universal' in modern philosophy. 'Bhartṛ maintained like Śaṅkara that monism was the ultimate teaching of the Upaniṣads. A conspicuous feature of the latter's doctrine is the distinction between a *'para'* or higher and an *'apara'* or lower Brahman. Bhartṛ also appears to have recognized this distinction; but while Saṅkara explains the lower Brahman as an appearance (*vivarta*) of the higher and therefore not of the same order of reality, Bhartṛ regards them both as real in the same sense. According to Śaṅkara, the two Brahmans form, as it is put, a non-duality (*a-dvaita*). The relation between them (*tādātmya*) is unreal, it being a relation between things of different orders of being. In Bhartr's doctrine, on the other hand, the two things related being equally real, the relation also is real. But the things are not altogether disparate, so that the relation is not one of entire distinction (*bheda*) as between a pot and a piece of cloth. It is rather *bhedābheda* and the Ultimate Reality may, therefore, be described as an 'identity-in-difference'[132].

We have referred here to Rāmānuja and Bhartṛprapañca to show that the Indian philosophic thought is not unaware of the conception of the Absolute as an identity-in-difference, as is generally supposed. Śaṅkara, too, knows it fully well and gives it an honoured place in his scheme of things. He also sings the glory of the Īśvara and says that this grand creation, which it is impossible even to conceive through the mind, can be brought into being by the supreme Īśvara alone and never even by all the great gods and angels or other divine powers. The Advalta Vedāntin, too, has to look to this Īśvara for favour in order to have the desire for *advaita* and so it has been rightly said that it is only through the favour of Īśvara that men have the desire for the non-duality.[133] Śaṅkara unfailingly points out and emphatically states that the knowledge of this Apara Brahman is the door to the knowledge of the Para Brahman,[134] and so it cannot be skipped over or dispensed with as a mere 'myth' or 'fiction'. The difference between Bhartṛ and Śaṅkara is, therefore, only a difference in emphasis and not in essentials, and it is very curious and interesting to find that Sureśvara tries to explain Bhartṛ's viewpoint as *in effect* the same as Śaṅkara's and represents Bhartṛ as a *vivartavādin* instead of a *pariṇāmavādin*[135].

As a matter of fact, if one judges the whole of Indian thought impartially, remembering the true significance of transcendence as we have put it, then it will be found that each and every system points ultimately towards this unique state, though sometimes the emphasis is put on one aspect and sometimes on the other. Thus, the Yoga system, which is represented as an 'isolationist' school of thought, really hints at this transcendent state because it does not speak of *kaivalya* all at once but only after the *vibhūtipāda,* where one attains omniscience and omnipotence.[136] This great achievement, too, is cast off ultimately in order to attain *kaivalya.*[137] Here the stress is on *kaivalya,* but the *vibhūti* is not ignored. Similarly, the Tāntric thought, which is represented simply as evolutionary or dynamic in character, has also this transcendental aspect everywhere. Contrary to the Sāṅkhya, here the stress is no doubt on *Śakti* or Power, but the final goal is the supreme *Śiva,* which is beautifully described thus: "(Though) full of activity (it looks) idle, (though) light in its sole nature (yet) dark, not a void (yet) like the void, such is the inscrutable nature of *Śambhu or Śiva*".[138] Similarly of this final state of realization the Tantras speak thus: "Then in that supreme sky, with the sun and moon having set, one remains, as it were, unconscious as in the state of sleep, yet wide awake, (with his consciousness) uncovered''.[139] The Upaniṣads, we have pointed out, lay equal stress on both the aspects through the two concepts of Prāṇa or Agni and Ātman, and thereby work out an unique synthesis.

The Concept of Jīva or the Individual Soul

The conception of Iśvara has taken us too far. Closely allied to this concept is the other one of *Jīva.* In fact, the two are represented in the Upaniṣad as close friends, an eternal pair of birds occupying the same tree.[140] Of the two birds one eats the tasteful fruits, while the other merely looks on, without eating anything.[141] In other words, the one is the enjoyer, the other is the seer. Now this enjoyment is the enjoyment of the fruits of action, and it is the *jīva* who becomes attached to or bound by the actions and hence comes under bondage. Therefore it laments from the loss of its lordship or freedom and is downcast, plunged in sorrow.[142] Only when he views the other, the Lord, and realizes his greatness, then alone is he freed from all lamentations.[143] The *jīva* is then a projected image of *Iśa,* which is sent forth into the lower world of birth and death. These images are our personal selves and hence the *Kaṭha* speaks of the one as the light and the other as the shadow.[144] These shadows or images 'are thrown down into the sea of physical matter like a fisher's net, and, when their 'catch' of experience is full, they are withdrawn once more by the fisher'. Hence the *Śvetāśvatara* significantly calls the Īśvara *'jālavān',* the netter or the fisher. He himself does not descend into the sea but 'sits above in his boat throughout the long ages of the Cosmic Day, knowing in himself neither birth nor death nor sorrow'.

There is a lot of discussion and divergent opinions as to whether the *jīva* is a projection or image of Īśvara, or whether both of them are images of the one Supreme Brahman.[145] We prefer to hold with the author of *Vivaraṇa* that the *jīva* is an image of Īśvara, for, this explains more clearly the necessity of the dependence of the former on the latter, as well as their close mutual connexion. This also satisfactorily accounts for the *svātantrya* or the independence of the Īśvara and dependence of *jīva*. The difference between *jīva* and Īśvara is sometimes accounted for by saying that when the pure consciousness becomes reflected in māyā it becomes Īśvara, while when reflected in *avidyā* it becomes *jīva*. *Māyā* is represented as made up of pure *sattva,* untainted by *rajas and tamas,* and *avidyā* is said to be of darkened *sattva,* overpowered by *rajas* and *tamas.*

There are, again, others who distinguish between the two by saying that in *māyā*, the *vikṣepa* or distraction element predominates, while in *avidyā,* the *āvaraṇa* or covering, or concealment is the main element. Hence Īśvara being connected with the diffusive or distractive aspect goes on creating the diversity, without being covered or enveloped by nescience, while the *jīva* is completely in darkness being totally overpowered by the covering function. This also explains why the one is all-knowing and the other absolutely ignorant. Others again hold that Īśvara is the reflection of the consciousness in *avidyā,* while *jīva* is the reflection in the *antaḥkaraṇa* or mind. However divergent may be the views, it is clear that somehow or other, the one and the same light has been split into two, and the difference is only the difference of the medium which reflects the light and not of the light Itself.

A very vexed question remains about the status of *jīva*. Is it permanent and eternal or a mere fiction and evanescent? There is a passage in the *Kaṭha* and *Śvetāśvatara* which seems to support the eternal nature of *jīva*. It describes the Īśvara thus: 'He who is eternal among eternals, conscious among conscious entities, who, as one, distributes or allocates the desired things to many'.[146] This passage asserts that Īśvara and *jīva* have these aspects in common, viz, that they are both eternal and conscious, while they differ in this that the one is singular, the other is plural and the one lacks the objects of desire, while the other supplies them to the other. This last feature reveals that the *jīvas* lack *ānanda,* while they share the nature of *sat* and *cit* with Īśvara. We shall have occasion to show that the *ānandamaya* is verily Īśvara, as expressly stated in the *Māṇḍukya*[147] and hence bliss is the marked feature of Īśvara which distinguishes him from *jīvas*. This bliss signifies fullness, and as the Īśvara is not limited within the bounds of finitude, his fullness and bliss are inherent in his very nature, while the *jīvas* being essentially limited and imprisoned in finitude suffer from a lack of fullness and are deprived of bliss.

But the crux of the question is: what happens when the bonds of finitude are shaken off? Does the *jīva* still retain his entity or does he become absorbed in the vastness of the infinitude? In Western philosophical thought, even Bosanquet, who solely concerns himself with the destiny of the individual, has to admit that in the Absolute the content of the imperfect individual, has to be 'transmuted and rearranged',[148] and there is an 'expansion and *absorption* of the self'.[149] Bradley also speaks of the perfection and harmony which the individual attains in the Absolute as 'the complete gift and dissipation of his personality', in which 'he, as such, must vanish'. 'The finite, as such, disappears in being accomplished'.[150]

To the Upaniṣads the problem does not appear as a baffling one. The Upaniṣads everywhere emphatically affirm the complete identity of *jīva* and Brahman: 'As pure water dropped in another pure water becomes absolutely like that, similar is the state of the self of the knowing sage'.[151] 'As all these flowing rivers, moving towards the ocean, on reaching the ocean lose themselves, removed are their name and form, and they are called the ocean itself, similarly the sixteen parts of this realiser or knower, on getting the Puruṣa are lost, gone are their name and form and are called as Purusa itself';[152] The term *'astam gacchanti'*. literally '*sets*' or '*gets lost*',. may cause an alarm to many, who believe that the loss of individuality is a loss of all consciousness. But one must remember that 'to be rid of the ego is not to be rid of life'. Here, one rather loses to find, dies to live. From the point of view of the Supreme, the question of the persistence of individuality is superfluous, and from the standpoint of Īśvara, the question is readily taken up and it is specifically stated that the individual who gets this realisation, 'on rising from this body', i.e. casting off the false or spurious individuality and on attaining the Supreme Light, is endowed with his own true form (*svena rūpeṇā' bhiniṣpadyate*),[153] he becomes the Supreme Puruṣa (*sa uttamaḥ puruṣaḥ*).[154] It is always our finite consciousness that gets alarmed at the very idea of its merging in the Infinite, but, in fact, the moment one sheds his individuality, he is endowed with a super-individuality, which far surpasses our comprehension.

The Upaniṣads, thus, do not make the Absolute a mere unity of persons, or a system of selves, related to each other as parts of a substance like a college and its members, as conceived by Mctaggart, but keep the absolute unity of the Absolute or Brahman intact and yet allow full scope and value to the individuals in the sphere of existence. *Jīva* is, empirically, not a fiction but a reality, and though he cannot be called *jiva,* as such, on attaining the supreme yet that does not in any way signify that he vanishes into nothingness. On the other hand, he attains a fullness, which was always his, on casting off the fetters of finitude. He becomes the true Purusa on ceasing to be a *jīva.* Hence it is not a loss but a regaining of the true personality.

The Concept of Māyā

But what really makes the one Supreme Consciousness split up into two, the *jīva* and the Īśvara? We have already seen that it is through the instrumentation of māyā that this division occurs. Not only does it create the twin selves, the higher and the lower, the wise and the ignorant, the happy and the miserable, the seer and the eater but it also makes a deeper division, the division between the subject and the object. As it brings forth the *jīva,* and the Īśvara, so it immediately provides them with a *jagat* or world to be enjoyed and ruled by each of them respectively. Thus the division between the subject and the object is within the womb of *māyā,* and beyond that is the undifferentiated unity.

Now, what is this supreme power called māyā, which is at the root of creation and behind all manifestation? The usual translation of the word as 'illusion' is entirely misleading, and has led to a complete misunderstanding of the whole Vedānta. *Māyā* is essentially that which measures (*mīyate anayā*). Hence it signifies that function which measures the Immeasurable, sets a limit to the limitless. From this comes its secondary sense of the power of concealment, for unless the vastness of the Infinite is concealed, it becomes impossible to represent it as small or finite. Its third sense of conjuring trick or deception also follows from this, in as much as it deceives all by presenting the Infinite as the finite, the Vast as the small, the Eternal as the fleeting, and also vice versa. It is, therefore, represented as having two functions, viz. veiling and distraction, *āvaraṇa* and *vikṣepa.* It first puts a veil on the face of Reality and this is its covering function; thereafter, it goes on to make some other things pass for the Truth or Reality and this is its distracting function. This concealment of Truth or Reality is referred to, again and again, in the Upaniṣads,[155] which evidently point to the *āvaraṇa* of *māyā,* and the second function is also referred to in the famous line: '*Indro māyābhiḥ pururūpa īyate,'*[56] where the assuming of many forms is attributed to *māyā,* and the term is used in the plural to make it tally with the plurality of forms assumed thereby.

There are some who are disposed to think that the doctrine of *māyā* is an invention of Śaṅkara and that it does not find any place in the Upaniṣads, but this is an absolutely wrong idea, as has been ably pointed out by Ranade.[157] Śaṅkara may have worked it out in detail but the idea lies rooted in the Upaniṣads themselves. Gough rightly refutes Colebrooke, who is wrong in imagining that it is a later graft upon the old Vedantic philosophy, and firmly asserts that "the tenet of *māya* is no modern invention; the thought, if not the word, is everywhere present in the Upaniṣads, as an inseparable element of the philosophy, and the word itself is of no infrequent occurence;...... there has been no addition from without, but only a development from within; no graft but only a growth".[158]

All the problems of philosophy, of immanence and transcendence, unity and diversity, finite and infinite arise because of the presence of this principle of *māyā*. *Māyā* represents the principle of non-Being, it is the matrix of all becoming. The problem immediately arises: what is the relation between this non-Being and the Being? If this non-Being or becoming is in a relation of identity with Being, then the immutability of Being ceases, and again, if the relation is a relation of difference, then there are two independent principles, which destroy the doctrine of *advaita.* To get out of this dilemma, the Vedantins call it *'anirvacanīya'* or inexplicable, but it must be remembered that this inexplicability is only to the human consciousness, from our point of view, because we, being a product of *māyā,* cannot know, as such, the nature of our origin. As the *Nāsadīya Sūkta* of the *Ṛgveda* points out: "Who knows and who shall say whence has it come, whence this creation? Even the gods came after it and hence who shall know whence did it come?"[159] Only He who is beyond the *māyā* and sits above it knows its nature, to all else who are below it, i.e. under *māyā*, the knowledge is hidden and it's nature remains inscrutable.

Those who complain that the Vedānta thus leaves things unexplained, evidently forget that the very attempt to explain this original mystery is self-stultifying, because it is something like an attempt to ride on one's own shoulders. As Green puts it: "The old question, why God made the world, has never been answered, nor will be. We know not why the world should be; we only know that there it is''.[160] Those who feel a satisfaction in attributing the becoming to the very nature of Being, thereby, make the Being, or the Absolute lose its very character. The Vedanta, on the contrary, accepts the mystery with veneration, acknowledges the becoming as a fact, and yet holds on with equal firmness, to the other great fact of the intrinsic self-sufficiency of the Absolute, its pure non-dual nature. Thus, *māyā* is not a fiction or an unreality, not '*asat',* to *us,* to our empirical consciousness, and again, it is not a reality or *'sat'* from the standpoint of the Absolute. Hence it is called neither *'sat'* nor *'asat'*. neither something nor a pure nothing. The Reality is one and indivisible, and yet that very Reality apparently splits itself somehow into two. A mirror comes, as it were, in the middle, and makes the one original face split in twain. The splitting is only apparent, for when the mirror breaks or is removed it is again the one single face. Hence *māyā* is not darkness, but shining and resplendent like a clean mirror, and so the Upaniṣad calls it the golden lid, which covers the face of Truth.[161] Again, it is sometimes called the truth and then the Reality is called the Immortal (*amṛta*),[162] which signifies that the one is the apparent truth and the other the abiding or immortal truth (*satyasya satyam*).

Māyā, in one sense, is the repository of all knowledge, and again, it is the very seat of ignorance, a bewildering paradox. The entire knowledge of the whole manifestation is here, because she holds within her womb the entire creation, and again it is here that the veil is cast over the face of Truth or Reality, and the plunge into the ignorance is taken. Īśvara, being the Creator, is in eternal union with *māyā,* which "is properly speaking the 'means whereby' the Great Magician (*māyin*) operates, viz. all the 'measure' (root *mā*, as in *nirmā,* 'to create') that belongs to the divine nature, *svabhāva, prakṛti* etc."[163] Hence the

Śvetāśvatara rightly calls this power as the *own* power of the Lord (*devātmaśaktim*).[164] It is not something ṣeparate and undivine in nature like the *prakṛti* of Sāṅkhya. In the words of Śaṅkara it is "the divine power, in which names and forms lie unevolved and which is the antecedent condition of names and forms."[165] The Lord is never separate from this power but in eternal conjunction with it. 'His supreme power is said to be of many kinds; knowledge, will and action are natural to Him.'[166] The Creator without his power of creativity is inconceivable. It is through the medium of this mirror of *māyā* that the supreme consciousness assumes self-consciousness, comes to know itself, as it were, in all its richness.

Thus Īśvara and *māyā* are in a relation of identity-in-difference, the power and the wielder of power being inseparable from each other, yet different somehow from each other. The division is, in other words, within the one and the same entity. "Hence comes the peculiarity that the *parā-prakṛti* is both different from Brahman and an aspect of Brahman." From the standpoint of the Supreme or the Absolute, the question of the relation between it and *māyā* does not arise at all, because there it is one undivided homogeneous Reality (*ekarasa*). Only when 'the pure Spirit becomes the subject' then immediately comes confronting it 'the non-subject or object' and 'interaction between the two sets in.' 'The cosmic process is the gradual realisation of values in its upward ascent from pure nothingness to the Kingdom of God, under the influence and inspiration of the living God.'[167] Thus the whole evolution is in *māyā,* and, within her is the polarity of subject and object. Īśvara or God is, no doubt, above maya and so is the Supreme or the Absolute, but the one is above it as a controller or ruler, while the other is above it as its support and substratum (*adhiṣṭhāna*). Hence the one is organically related with it, while the other is eternally unrelated because of its uniqueness. "While God is organically bound up with the universe, the Absolute is not."[168] So, "creation neither adds to nor takes away from the reality of the Absolute. Evolution may be a part of our cosmic process, but the Absolute is not subject to it. The Absolute is incapable of increase."[169] Thus this conception of *māyā* accounts for the evolution and yet preserves the perfection of the Absolute. It takes its reality from the Absolute, works out the diversity, and yet leaves the original unity unimpaired.

Māyā has been identified with *prakṛti* in the *Śvetāśvatara*[170] and the famous verse *'ajām ekām'* etc.[171], evidently represents it as composed of three *guṇas,* symbolised by the three colours, red, white and black. It should also be noted that it is *'ajā'* i.e. without birth or beginning because, as we have pointed out, nobody knows its origin. It is also sometimes identified with *avidyā,* but as we have pointed out, a distinction, too, is drawn between them. *Māyā* is represented to be composed of pure *sattva*, while *avidyā* is impure through the admixture of *rajas* and *tamas. Māyā* is a more general term which includes both *vidyā* and *avidyā.* It binds through *avidyā* and again releases through *vidyā.* So in the Tantras we find the propitiation of the Mother, for it is only she who can effect the release, because the bondage, too, is purely due to her. The Tantras have also, therefore, classified maya from different aspects, and named them differently as *mohamāyā, māyā, mahāmāyā, yogamāyā* etc. The Upaniṣad, through its legend in the *Kena* about the divine resplendent Mother Umā, evidently refers to this pure and divine form of *māyā,*[172] who alone, finally, reveals the nature of the Supreme Reality to Indra. Those who neglect this *vidyā* or divine aspect of *māyā* miss the whole significance of it. Again, "the term *avidyā,* as applied to her, means primarily the dark abyss of *non-being* (for *'vid'* means both to be and to know), and secondarily the mysterious darkness of the unmanifest state.''[173] It is in this sense that the *term 'asat'* is used to denote her in many places in the Upaniṣads, as well as the term *'avyākṛta'*. She has contraction and expansion in her very nature and so sometimes she is the mere potentiality of all things and sometimes the actuality.

Solution of the Problem

We now return to our original problem with which we started our enquiry, viz. *'Īśa vāsyaṁ idaṁ sarvam.'* We have surveyed so far the nature of *Īśa* and have just seen the nature of *'idam'* or non-Being as presented by *māyā.* In our ordinary consciousness the *'idam'* predominates, the world of objects prevails over the subject. The *Īśa* lies covered or concealed under the load of *'idam'*. Instead of the *Īśa* covering the *'idam'*, the *'idam'* has come to cover the *Īśa.* Now the process has to be reversed, the 'backward-flowing movement' has to be initiated, the gaze has to be turned back (*āvṛttacakṣuḥ*), the '*parāk*' or the outward must turn *'pratyak'* or inward. A return to pure subjectivity is demanded. Does it mean an annulment or negation of all objectivity?

No; the Upaniṣad itself goes on to show the stages through which this return to subjectivity is realized and points out its true nature. When the hold of the *'idam'* is first slackened, one begins to feel dimly the presence of the other element, viz., *Īśa* or Ātman along with it. Gradually the *'idam'* is integrated with the *Īśa,* the objects are found to inhere in the subject, like the beads strung together in a thread. As the vision grows, one comes to realize an organic unity between the two : there is no subject without the object, nor any object without the subject; all the *bhūtas* are in the Ātman and the Ātman is in all the *bhūtas.*[174] Here, one feels ,the existence of the one in the other and through the other'[175], as Pringle-Pattison puts it. But still there is a higher vision, where the objects (the *'bhūtas'*) are not seen *in* the Ātman but *as* the Ātman itself (*ātmai 'vā' bhūt*),[176] i.e., the objects are found to exist only in and through the Ātman. Here the term *'abhūt'* does not signify a 'becoming' of the Ātman, for that has already been indicated in the previous verse through the statement of the reciprocal relation of cause and effect subsisting between the *bhūtas* and the Ātman, and again between the Ātman and the *bhūtas.* Here what the Upaniṣad hints at is the transcendental relation subsisting between the objects and Ātman. In reality, the objects *are* the Ātman, and not mere products of the Ātman, for that would signify a relation of difference even in the midst of identity. It is to the deluded vision that the objects appear as independent entities. With the first dawning of knowledge and a partial removal of delusion, the objects appear as dependent on the Ātman and no longer separate and independent, but then the Ātman, too, has to be dependent on them. So in the final vision, the absolute freedom of the Ātman is once more realized; there is no relation of mutual dependence any more, for there are no two entities here, but the Ātman itself is all in all, all the objects or *bhūtas* have no separate existence. In the previous state, there was a 'seeing' (*anupaśyati*) as well as a seer (*yas tu*), but here it is a 'becoming' (*abhūt*) and there is, hence, no longer a seer, who observes through a relation of separation, but the observer or realizer becomes the very ground or substratum, the *'adhiṣṭhāna'* of all (*yasmin*).

The Upaniṣads, thus, solve the problem of the subject and the object not by a denial of the one and an affirmation of the other, neither by a denial of both, nor by an affirmation of both, but simply through a transcendence of both the terms. So, the '*vāsyam*' in the sense of 'inhabiting' may be realized in the stage of '*yas tu sarvāṇi bhūtāni'*, but in the next stage of *'yasmin'*, the *'vāsyam'* assumes a different meaning. It is not a 'clothing' or 'covering' in the sense that it makes the *'idam'* non-existent or invisible, but it is a 'clothing' through which the *'idam'* is still seen, but no longer as a separate reality but as the Ātman itself. The two senses will also differ according as one interprets the term, *'Īśa'*. If by *Īśa*, the Īśvara is taken, then he undoubtedly inhabits all the things created, he being organically related to the universe; but if by *Īśa*, one takes the Supreme or the Ātman, then the sense of inhabiting no longer fits, because the Ātman is all in all, there is nothing else to be inhabited by it. Thus the Upaniṣad itself beautifully explains the process or stages of *'vāsyam'* through the two successive verses.

As Coomaraswamy rightly points out, "it is, then, a fundamental error to assume that either Veda or Vedānta regards the world as a mistake; what is asserted is that in so far as its parts or principles are *separately* envisaged and not in their integrity, *sub specie aeternitatis* as God sees them all together, the vision is a sorry one. The unenlightened man has knowledge of (*avidyā*) each thing *independently* and runs in vain pursuit of particular goods (*pṛthakpaśyans tān evā 'nubidhāvati. Kaṭha 4. 14*), as Ulvich Engelberti expresses it, *ignoratia divisiva est errantium*. But whoever looks in the eternal mirror and that is the same thing as 'with eyes inverted' or 'thinking inversely' (*pratyakcetana* - *Yoga Sūtra* 1.29) or 'upstream' (*pratikūla* etc, *passim*) or with *daivyacakṣus* and not the *māṁsacakṣus* sees at once all things and God, as He sees Himself and so, far from losing anything, possesses all things in their incorruptible perfection. It is not the spectacle but the profane vision, that of the unrelated sciences or humanism for example, that the Vedānta calls an 'illusion' (*moha*)..... What Śaṅkara denies is the ultimate reality of things as they are known 'ignorantly' i.e. objectively and as they are in themselves, not that of things "as they are in God."[177] A modern Vedāntin beautifully points out the uniqueness of the Vedāntic vision thus: "The world as not separate from *Cit* or Consciousness is one vision. The *Cit* as not one with the world is the second. Now with the opening of the first (vision), the world is conceived as true or real; with the dawning of the second, the sense of unreality (comes), but with the opening of both comes the clear vision that the *Cit* alone is really true and all else apart from it is untrue. Thus, though the world is by its nature untrue, yet from the nature of the Ātman is verily true".[178] He also distinguishes clearly between the Buddhist, Tāntrik and Vedāntist visions thus: "The *Vijñānavādin* is predominantly of internal vision alone, the *Śūnyavādin* is predominantly of both visions (because he denies both the inner and the outer), the *Svātantryavādin* (Tāntrik) is predominantly of a divine vision alone, but the Vedāntins have all their three eyes wide open, they having plunged in that ocean of non-duality, without cancelling or negating the inner and outer existences".[179] Such is the uniqueness of the Vedāntic vision, which the Upaniṣads embody. It does not shut its eyes to existence but keeps them wide open looking simultaneously above and below. The final solution of things lies here alone; all other solutions are only partial because they do not heal the division but only cover it up. This will be evident from a cursory glance at the different solutions proposed by Western philosophers through the ages.

Descartes

In Western philosophic thought it was Descartes, who first felt acutely the existence of the division, or rather created it himself. So he is rightly looked upon as the father or originator of modern Western philosophy. He began with universal doubt and ultimately stumbled upon the great truth that the doubter could not be doubted, which he formulated in that famous proposition of his, *'Cogito ergo sum'*. Descartes then discovered that in complete distinctness from this principle of thought was the other principle of extension, and these two formed the warp and woof of our whole existence. He also found that 'thought and extension are not only different from each other but it is the very nature of these substances to negate each other; for spirit is not only cognizable without the attributes of body, but it is in itself the negation of the attributes of body'.[180] Spirit and body are essentially diverse and possess nothing in common. He understands both of these as 'substances', i.e., elements which stand on their own right, independently of each other. They stand opposed to each other like centrifugal and centripetal forces. Having, thus placed mind and matter, consciousness and the world , in complete separation from each other, Descartes fails to answer the question as to how they happen to get mutually connected and affected by each other. For every such act of connexion he has to bring in a third substance, God, as a *deus ex machina,* who effects the unity of the ego with the matter or extension.

Spinoza

The artificiality of this conception struck the thinkers that followed Descartes. Spinoza, who came next, realized that the inner contradiction of the philosophy of Descartes lies in his attribution of substantiality to the two entities, viz., matter and mind, both of which he takes as a substance. The remedy lies, Spinoza thought, in abandoning the conception of both as substances and instead, taking them as forms of the manifestation of a single substance. In the philosophy of Spinoza this one substance is named God. He says, that 'by Substance, I mean that which is in itself and is conceived through itself. In other words, that of which a conception can be formed independently of any other conception'.[181] This notion of substance being assumed, there can exist, according to Spinoza, only a single substance. What is through its own self alone is necessarily infinite, unconditioned and unlimited by anything else. A plurality of infinites, is, therefore, impossible, and hence the plurality of substances, as assumed by Descartes, is necessarily a manifest contradiction. It is possible for only one substance, and that an absolutely infinite substance, to exist. So, the two substances of Descartes, matter and mind, are taken by Spinoza as the two 'attributes', in which the single substance reveals itself to us. It is only the human understanding that invests substance with the two attributes, substance itself being unexhausted by any such specialities of form.

It is impossible to do justice to the sublime conception of Spinoza within a short compass. He made one of the boldest attempts, in the whole history of Western philosophic thought, to rise above the contradiction in order to view things *sub specie eternitatis.* But yet the complaint against him is that his substance is like the lion's den to which all footprints lead, but *nulla vestigia retrorsum.* As James puts it: "You cannot redescend into the world of particulars by the Absolute's aid or deduce necessary consequences of detail, important for your life, from idea of his nature".[182] So Joachim feels that "there is an inner contradiction in his conception of God, as at once excluding all determination and comprehending an infinite diversity of ultimate characters".[183] "There is nothing to explain why the unity should, even in appearance, be broken up into multiplicity, why the Infinite should appear in the guise of innumerable finites, why this world of illusion should be here at all''.[184] Thus Spinoza's lofty conception of substance failed to account for the dualism and contradiction here below, for his substance was much too aloof and indifferent to concern itself with these differences. Though he freed substance from all opposition and contradiction by conceiving it as one and infinite, and not two like Descartes, yet as attributes, thought remained only thought and extension as only extension and this makes it inevitable that the one will exclude the other. So the search for in inner principle of union between them had still to be pursued. The reconciliation must be found through the very two terms of opposition and this could be effected in two ways: either from the end of matter or from the end of the spirit. Either mind was to be subordinated to matter or matter was to be subsumed under mind. Descartes began with dualism, Spinoza summarily resolved it through his neutralism, but after him the philosophical world, abandoning his neutralism, definitely divided itself into two hostile camps, viz, of Idealism and Realism, the one taking the side of mind, the other that of matter. The conflict has remained eternally acute ever since, though there have been heroic attempts to effect a compromise every now and then.

Leibnitz

The first reaction to the views of Spinoza is noticed in Leibnitz, who set himself in sharp opposition to Spinoza's conception of substance. "Like Descartes and Spinoza, Leibniz based his philosophy on the notion of substance, but he differed radically from them as regards the relation of mind and matter, and as regards the number of substances. Descartes allowed three substances, God and mind and matter; Spinoza admitted God alone. For Descartes, extension is the essence of matter; for Spinoza, both extension and thought are attributes of God. Leibnlz held that extension cannot be an attribute of a substance. His reason was that extension involves plurality and can, therefore, only belong to an aggregate of substances; each single substance must be unextendcd. He believed, consequently, in an infinite number of substances, which he called "monads"."[185] Thus, in antithesis to the philosophy of Spinoza, the fundamental thesis of that of Liebniz is this: there is a plurality of monads which constitute the element of all reality, the fundamental being of the whole physical and spiritual universe. This is the Monadology of Leibniz which was the reaction from Spinoza's monism. For Spinoza's One Infinite Substance, Leibniz substituted a plurality of independent finite substances, meaning by "substance" not (as in Descartes and Spinoza) something static and inert, but that which is essentially dynamic and active. But Leibniz, by his conception of plurality of monads, created a fresh difficulty. As he expreses it : 'the monads have no windows through which anything may come in or go out', and thus, since each monad is independent and self-sufficient the question as to how they come to interact, as in the case of perception, remains unanswerable. To save the situation, Leibniz has to take recourse to a 'pre-established harmony' between the monads, which leads almost to a relapse to the position of Descartes, who had also conceived of God as effecting the tie between matter and mind. If the unity of the universe was to be saved, then the absolute independence of the monads had to go, or if the absolute independence of the monads was to be preserved, the unity was impossible of achievement. So the problem remained where it was.

Kant

The next great figure in Western philosophy was Kant, who tried to effect a compromise between the one-sided realistic and idealistic tendencies that preceded him. Before him, while on the one hand, empiricists, like Locke, Berkeley and Hume, assigned to the mind, in subordination to the world of sense, a role of pure passivity, the rationalists, on the other hand, like Descartes, Spinoza and Leibniz, assigned to it, in superiority to the world of sense and in its sufficiency for its own self, a role of pure activity. 'Kant, for his part, endeavoured to harmonize the pretensions of both. He proclaimed the mind or the ego, as practical ego, free and autonomous, the unconditioned arbiter of itself, but again as theoretical ego, absolutely receptive and conditioned by the world of sense.'[186] Kant began his enquiry with a critical scrutiny of the origin of human experience or cognition in man, and hence his philosophy is critical and known as criticism. Kant's famous *'Critique of Pure Reason'* is devoted to this scrutiny and he arrives at the following results. He finds, first of all, that all cognition involves two factors, the subject and the object, the cognizer and the cognized. Of them, the one factor, the external object, contributes the material of knowledge, while the other factor, the subject contributes the form,—those notions, viz, by virtue of which alone any connected knowledge, any synthesis of individual perceptions into a whole of experience, is possible. Both these factors are equally indispensable for all knowledge whatsoever; were there no external world, there were no perceptions; and were there no *a priori* notions, these perceptions were merely an indefinite plurality and maniness, a chaotic mass, without mutual combination, and without connexion the unity of a whole. In that case there would not be any such thing as experience. Therefore, Kant concludes, that while perceptions without notions are blind and notions without perceptions are empty, cognition is a union of both, in this way that it fills up the frames of notions with the matter of experience or rather disposes the matter of experience into the net of notions.

Thus, though Kant discovered the unity of subject and object in all human experience or knowledge, yet this healing of the division proved absolutely deceptive and of no value whatsoever. For along with the discovery of the fusion of the subject and the object, Kant also came to discover that it is impossible to know things as they are in themselves. The very unity of the subject and the object stood as a stumbling block to the knowledge of the thing-in-itself, because, in all cognitions the contribution of the subject produces some change in the object. The innate forms or categories mould or modify the object i.e., in other words, the object appears to us only as modified by categories. Secondly, no perceptions reach us pure and uncoloured, but only through the medium of time and space. Whatever is to be perceived, must be perceived in time and space; without them perception is impossible, because they are the universal forms of all objects of sense. Thus being an active contributor to the process of cognition, the subject makes it impossible for the object to reveal itself in its true being. The very fusion or unity of two elements destroys the purity of the cognition and turns it into a spurious one. It follows, then, that we only know appearances and not things themselves in their own true nature. So, 'unknown and unknowable' was the last word of Kant about the true nature of things, and the philosophical world remained in utter darkness as before. The light was still to be found.

Hegel

A light was kindled in Hegel, which seemed almost to be the final, that will dispel all darkness and provide a supreme solution to all the problems. In fact, the nineteenth century was wholly dominated by the philosophy of Hegel and it still holds its sway over a large section of philosophical thinkers. Hegel resolved the deadlock which Kant's thing-in-itself had brought about. The unity of subject and object, which Kant perceived as permeating all human cognitions, was to Hegel the very soul of Reality. Thought itself was to him the

Absolute and the very impact and opposition of being and non-being provided for him infinite richness to its conception. As he states it: "Being, as being, is nothing fixed or definite; it yields to a dialectic and sinks into its opposite, which also taken immediately is nothing (saying that God is only the supreme Being and nothing more is declaring Him to be so negatively also). The mere Being, as it is mere abstraction, is, therefore, the absolutely negative. To prevent one nullifying the other, man must first discover some field-predicate for Being, to mark it off from Nothing; this of necessity leads to the onward movement, and gives to Being a 'true or concrete significance' (and this significance consists in the idea of Becoming). Becoming is the unity of Being and Nothing. The unity has to be conceived in the diversity, which is all the while present and explicit. To become is the true expression for the resultant of 'to be' and not 'to be'. Becoming is the first concrete thought and therefore the first notion, whereas Being and Naught are empty abstractions''.[187]

Thus to Hegel the very process of thought reveals the dynamic self-evolution of the Absolute Idea. Hence he rejects his predecessor Schelling's bare principle of identity, on the ground that it reduced the Absolute into 'monotony and abstract universality', a kind of 'eternal night in which all cows are black'. Hegel, therefore, discards static categories and lays great stress on the idea of development. But yet the crux of the question remains: Is this development real or purely formal and logical? A close scrutiny of Hegel's philosophy reveals that he takes the development as purely logical. There is, at the heart of things, no real flux but the movement is purely dialectical. The Absolute has no history and from the point of view of the Eternal Being, time and history are illusions. This is stated by Hegel himself in a passage, which has become famous since Pringle-Pattison first pointed it out, in which Hegel repeats the word *Tauschung* four times, which literally means a 'deception'. He states thus : "Within the range of the finite we can never see or experience that the End has been really secured. The consummation of the infinite End, therefore, consists *merely in removing the illusion,* which makes it *seem* yet unaccomplished. The Good, the absolutely Good, is eternally accomplishing itself in the world and the result is that *it need not wait upon us, but is already* by implication, as well as *in full actuality, accomplished.* This *is the illusion under which we live.........* In the course of its process, *the Idea creates that illusion* by setting an antithesis to confront itself, and its action consists in *getting rid of the illusion,* which it has created".[188] Thus Hegel takes away with one hand the reality he had conceded to the process or movement with the other. His reconciliation is thus found to be far from satisfactory and Pringle-Pattison rightly complains against this view thus: "But can we hope to preserve the interest if we admit to ourselves-even though it be only in our speculative moments-that it is all a cleverly arranged deception? The view, as Hegel here presents it, seems to me, I confess, to paralyze our energies at their source".[189]

Hegel was thus forced to admit the illusory nature of the dynamic movement and yet he tried desperately to give a reality to the history through time. The contradiction between the timeless and the time thus remained unsolved. Hegel left unanswered the question, why should Absolute Perfection, to which there is nothing 'unaccomplished', delight in creating the illusion of imperfection? How is Perfection in general to be reconciled with even the appearance of many particular imperfections? Though the solution which Hegel offered was at first hailed as unique and supreme, yet ultimately, on a close analysis, it was found to have left the problem where it was, the chasm remaining as wide as ever. The root of the problem is that if one tries to assign reality to the process of change or movement, then the Absolute itself has to be conceived as changing and as yet imperfect, or if the Absolute is to be conceived as perfect and eternally self-complete, then the process of change becomes only apparent and turns out to be illusory.

Hegel's solution having proved deceptive, the twentieth century witnessed a reaction against the whole idealist mode of thought. It was felt that so long philosophy had been much too engrossed with the analysis of the mind, which in its turn had led to mere abstractions, without any touch with the concrete nature of life and the world. So the natural demand was that 'the centre of gravity of philosophy must, therefore, alter its place. The earth of things, long thrown into shadow by the glories of the upper ether, must resume its rights'.[190] The need of the modern man was 'a philosophy that will not only exercise the powers of intellectual abstraction but that will make some positive connextion with this actual world of finite human lives'.[191] The tremendous progress and achievement of modern science too contributed not a little to this orientation of outlook. Philosophy which was so long under the domination of psychology, hence forward came to be dominated by physics and biology. On the one hand, the analysis of matter by the physicist has led almost to a return to the views of Kant, because a principle of uncertainty, an unknowable X is baffling all scientists, and on the other hand, the study of life has revealed almost a bewildering richness, which is absolutely beyond the grasp of the intellect. This has also led to a revolution in the method of philosophy. Intellect has given place to intuition, reason to feeling.

Bergson

The chief protagonist of this new type of philosophy is Bergson, who raises the standard of revolt of the modern man of action against the cool intellectualism of all philosophers beginning from Plato. To Bergson, reality is a flux or change. The universe is conceived as one continuous flow, and the vital urge has neither beginning nor end, neither completeness nor finality. 'The world, then, is the embodiment of an immanent principle of living change, which, as it comes into existence, progressively creates the evolving universe. This principle is Bergson's celebrated *elan vital.*'[192] Bergson, thus, does not show any regard for a finished and eternally complete Absolute but even goes so far as to say that this idea of staticity is a mere illusion of the intellect. He says that 'we are at ease only in the discontinuous, in the immobile, in the dead. *The intellect is characterized by a natural inability to comprehend life.*[193] So he sets up intuition as the supreme method for grasping the living reality and discards the intellect altogether. The novelty of Bergson's views is no doubt striking but the drawback lies in the fact that there is no distant end or aim to direct the course of his creative evolution, and the final truth of things turns out to be cosmic pointlessness. Bergson has, no doubt, rendered a great service to philosophy by releasing it from the static prison-house of the intellect, but he has gone again to the other extreme, by making that very unfettered state of release an end in itself, which has made his philosophy a merely aimless wanderer. He has deeply felt the throb of creative impulse but has not been able to follow it to its ultimate source or end. Hence he fails to comprehend the 'whence' and 'whither' of the movement and so the riddle of existencc remains unsolved.

Alexander

Closely following Bergson, Alexander sets up a creative and living picture of his Absolute as Space-Time. His Absolute may be conceived as an infinite and continuous whole, of which Space may be described as the body and Time as the soul, and which is impregnated from the beginning with a creative nisus. "The real is Space-Time as a whole and every complex or part within it. Our consciousness of reality is the consciousness, that anything we apprehend belongs to Space-Time...... Reality is, then, experienced whether in enjoyment or contemplation as that which belongs to Space-Time or the character of reality is the character of so belonging."[194] And again, "within the all-embracing stuff of Space-Time, the universe exhibits an emergence in Time of successive levels of finite existences, each with its characteristic empirical quality'.[195]

But the main difficulty remains that it leaves unexplained how the higher evolves out of the lower. If the Absolute be bare SpaceTime, shorn of all contents that belong to our experience, what is the source of the qualities that we experience? Whence do the higher qualities come, if they are not somehow or other latent in the Absolute from the beginning? Hence, at every stage of evolution, one has to admit a complete miracle, and so Alexander feels that all are absolutely in the dark about the nature of the next higher quality that is to evolve, viz. Deity. "Our human altars still are raised to the unknown God. If we could know what deity is, how it feels to be divine, we should first have to have become as gods. What we know of it is but its relation to the other empirical qualities which precede it in time. Its nature we cannot penetrate."[196] Here his agnosticism is complete.

Jeans, Eddington

Similar is the case with the scientist-philosophers, like Jeans and Eddington. Through their approach to Reality with the aid of science they find that "most of our common impressions of substance, world-wide instants and so on, have turned out to be illusory, and the externality of the world might be equally untrustworthy."[197] The reality escapes the scientist, he is only left with illusions and so he frankly adinits that "the supposed approach through the physical world leads only into the cycle of physics, where we run round and round like a kitten chasing its tail and never reach the world-stuff at all".[198] Thus here, too, the unknowability looms large and the problem sits heavy on the soul. By exhausting both the ends, viz. of mind as well of matter, Western philosophy stands today perplexed, because everywhere a deadlock confronts it and an inner contradiction wholly falsifies all its solutions. One is forced ultimately to admit, like Russel, that "empiricism and idealism alike are faced with a problem, to which, so far, philosophy has found no satisfactory solution. This is the problem of showing how we have knowledge of other things than ourself and the operations of our own mind."[198] In other words, the problem is the old problem of the subject and the object: how they come to be connected if they are utterly disparate, and again, if they are really one what creates the division? Their unity as well as diversity is perplexing indeed. All solutions have been tried,—the equal affirmation of both, the outright denial of both, the affirmation of one and the denial of the other and so on—but all have been found wanting. Is there, then, no way out of the problem?

The unique nature of the Upaniṣadic solution

The Upaniṣads show us the way out of this insuperable difficulty by offering the supreme solution in the form of the unique conception of the Ātman or Brahman. Western philosophy, as all too briefly we have seen, through its long history is merely moving in a circle since the time of Descartes, and this has been the case because there is a fundamental error in the original conception of Descartes, which has escaped the notice of all so far. Descartes gave the primary place to thought; and it was thought which gave the clue to him to the existence of the 'I' or the ego. The 'I', thus, had a secondary and derived existence, and the original principle was taken to be thought, which, however, was confronted by its opposite, viz. extension or matter. The opposition between thought and matter has, therefore, continued to be fundamental, and though there have been heroic attempts to resolve the opposition either by a violent denial of one of the terms or by a worked-up compromise between the two, yet no attempt has been made to transcend the opposition through the conception of a still more fundamental thing than thought, which is the very pre-supposition of both thought and extension. The Upaniṣads do not posit the existence of the 'I' or the Self through thought, but the Ātman, according to them, is the most fundamental of all things, and hence self-revealed bv nature. As Radhakrishnan aptly puts it: 'Descartes' *cogito ergo* sum, "I think therefore I am" is not correctly expressed. I am not because I think, I think because I am. *Sum ergo cogito.* The self is primary and consciousness is inherent in it......... It is not a necessity of thought or an object of faith as Kant affirms, but is enjoyed as the content of spiritual consciousness. It is the felt awareness of transcendent reality".[200] Descartes' famous dictum has thus to be reversed if the final solution of the problem is to be found. The Upaniṣads give the clue to the reversal of the original wrong position taken up by Western philosophy, for, to the Upaniṣads, it is always the Ātman that is the most fundamental and primary of all things, the eternal prius of everything in the world. The whole enquiry of the Upaniṣads centres round this 'Ātman which is the inmost of all things' (*ya ātmā sarvāntaraḥ*),[201] and as the true nature of this Ātman is revealed nowhere else than in the texts of the Upaniṣads, hence it is significantly called the Puruṣa of the Upaniṣads (*aupaniṣadaṁ puruṣam*).[202] It is only by a true comprehension of this '*aupaniṣadam puruṣam*'that the final solution of all problems can be found.

We have seen that it is called the inmost of all things (*sarvāntaraḥ*), but does that mean that it is purely inward by nature? That it is not so is proved by other statements of the Upaniṣads which assert that all the outer manifestations, too, are this Ātman.[203] Then is it both inward and outward by nature? The famous statement of the *Māṇḍukya* about the true nature of the Ātman categorically states that 'it is neither inwardly conscious, nor outwardly conscious nor conscious both ways'.[204] We are always accustomed to think in terms of the outer and the inner. We only think of inclusion and exclusion, but the Ātman transcends both. It does not include as well as exclude all, but neither includes nor excludes anything. As Sureśvara states, again and again, about the nature of the Ātman: 'It is neither exclusive nor pervasive'.[205] If it is not exclusive, we immediately think that it must be all-pervasive, and if it is not all- pervasive we take it to be exclusive by nature, and hence, by denying both, the transcendental nature is sought to be indicated here. But does not this total denial of both amount almost to a denial of the very existence of the principle called Ātman? To guard against it Sureśvara immediately adds that it is 'full and stationed in itself' (*pūrṇaḥ svātmany avasthitaḥ*).[206] It is not a *'śūnya'* or a void that is conveyed by this absolute denial, but it is a *'pūrṇa'*, an immeasurable fulness which transcends all, that is sought to be grasped through this negation. The *Māṇḍukya,* too, after indulging in a relentless denial or absolute negation finally says that it is 'the very essence of the sole awareness of the Self' (*ekātmapratyayasāram*),[207] and is utterly 'calm, beneficent and non-dual' (*śāntaṁ śivam advaitam*).[308]

That there can be no question of exclusion in this conception of the Ātman is proved by the very term *'turīya'*, which is used to describe the supreme nature of the Ātman. *'Turīya'* means the 'fourth', and hence it does not exclude three, but not only includes but transcends it. The three are not cast off, nor taken in, but simply transcended. Again, we must remind that this transcendence merely means the uniqueness, by virtue of which the Ātman, though in touch with all the three states, remains untouched by them all. The ordinary dual conception of immanence and transcendence has no meaning here. 'The question of immanence and transcendence does not arise with reference to the Absolute. For immanence implies the existence of an other in which the Absolute is immanent. But the Absolute represents the totality of being and there is nothing other than it.'[209] The *Turīya,* therefore, does not represent a single aspect of being but stands for that which covers all, and because it covers all, it necessarily transcends all i.e. stands unique from all else. It is the simultaneous awareness of all the levels of existence or consciousness that is signified by the term *Turīya.* Hence, as we have seen, Śaṅkara Bhārati rightly represents the true Vedāntin as one with his three eyes wide open (*visphāritalocanatrayās tu vedāntinaḥ*). There is no sense of withdrawal in this conception of transcendence, there is no shutting of one's gaze or a refusal to see all existence. Through this vision, one comes to realize how the same Reality while remaining a non-dual pure unity or *'abbeda'* in its true nature, appears as a unity-in-difference or *'bhedābheda'* in the plane of Prāṇa or Buddhi, and again as complete difference or *'bheda'* in the still lower level of the ignorant mind. The Ātman or Brahman of the Upaniṣads is, accordingly, no abyss which swallows up all finite beings; it is no cave into which everything passes as into a kind of eternal night'; it is no 'lion's dcn into which all the footsteps go and none lead out again.' The final solution of all problems lies in this unique conception alone and it is by providing us with this solution that the Upaniṣads prove their unerring wisdom and shine in a singular blaze of glory.

References

1. IU, p. 1.
2. BU, 2.5. 19; 4.4.5.
3. brahma tallakṣyam ucyate. MU. 2.2.4.
4. lakṣyam tade vā 'kṣaram MU. 2.2.3.
5. ātmā vāre draṣṭavyaḥ. BU, 4.5.6.
6. so 'nvestavyas sa vijijñāsitavyaḥ. CU, 8.7.1.
7. idaṁ sarvaṁ yadayam ātmā, BU, 2.4.6.

8. sarvaṁ khalvidaṁ brahma. CU. 3.14.1.
9. BU, 4.2.4.
10. BU, 3.8.8.
11. PVU, p. 587.
12. Ibid. p. 594.
13. CIL, p. 88.
14. BU, 2.3.1.
15. ARU, 5.2.
16. Maitrī, 6.22.
17. PR, p. 265.
18. TU, 3.1.
19. NRDR, p. 8.
20. Gītā, 14.3.
21. KTU, 2.6.2.
22. PRU, 2.13.
23. jātāni vai 'nam viduh. Nir, 7.5.
24. jāte jāte vidyate. Ibid.
25. vijñānakriyāśaktidvaya-sammūrchitaḥ. ŚB, on CU, 3.14.2.
26. CE, pp. 49-50.
27. CU, 1.1.8.
28. Ibid.
29. Pr, p. 130.
30. BU, 4.3.16.
31. HP, vol. I, p. 252.
32. PR, pp. 321-23.
33. TU, 2.6.
34. anyad eva tad viditād atho aviditād adhi. KU, 3.
35. HM, p. 59.
36. Ibid. p. 60.
37. pūrṇasya pūrṇam ādāya pūrṇam evā 'vaśiṣyate. Śāntipāṭha. ĪU.
38. Na hi ḍuṇḍubhas sarpa ity etāvatā saviṣo bhavati na vā sarpo ḍuṇḍubha ity etāvatā nirviṣo bhavati. ŚB, on VS, 2.2.10.
39. HPH, p. 280.
40. śvobhāvā martasya. KTU, 1.1.26.
41. sarvaṁ jivitam alpam eva. Ibid.
42. yad alpaṁ tan martyam. CU, 7.24.1.
43. neha nānā 'sti kiñcana. KTU, 2.4.11.
44. Anṛtena hi pratyūḍhāḥ. CU, 8.3.2.
45. VS, 2.2.28.
46. BU, 2.1.20.
47. KTU, 1.3.10-11.
48. KTU, 2.6.7-8.
49. VS, 1.1.12.
50. SES, p. 254.
51. Indro māyābhiḥ pururūpa īyate. BU, 2.5.19.
52. yadi hi nāmarūpe na vyākriyete tadā 'syā 'tmano nirupādhikaṁ rūpaṁ prajñānaghanākhyaṁ na pratikhyāyeta. Ibid. ŚB.
53. AR, p. 467.
54. RPU, p. 30.
55. sve mahimnī 'ti yadi vā na mahimnī 'ti. CU, 7.24.1.
56. akṣarāt sambhavatī 'ha viśvam, Mu. 1.1.7.
57. MU, 2.1.3.
58. ĪU, 8.
59. Cf. his 'Śāntiniketana' in Bengali.
60. Māṇḍ, 6.
61. Māṇḍ, 7.
62. ER, vol. I, pp. 262-3.
63. "Lectures" I. 13-15.
64. na ca pretya saṁjñā' sti. BU, 4.5.13.
65. avināśi vā ayam ātmā anucchittidharmā, BU, 4.5.14.

66. vināśam evā 'pīto bhavati nā' ham atra bhogyaṁ paśyāmi. CU, 8. 11.1.
67. svena rūpeṇa abhiniṣpadyate. CU, 8. 12.3.
68. IH, p. 30.
69. VRE, p. 416.
70. NAV, p. 6.
71. WI, pp. 168-9.
72. Ibid.
73. Ibid. p. 170.
74. WI, p. 171.
75. Ibid.
76. WI, p, 174.
77. Ibid. pp. 181-2.
78. Ibid. p. 193.
79. Ibid. p. 194.
80. WI, p. 193.
81. SES, p. 34.
82. Brahma : VT, CR, Jan.' 42.
83. TP, p. 381.
84. Ibid. p. 380.
85. Ibid. p. 414.
86. TP, p. 415.
87. YK, p. 164.
88. MU, 2.2.9.
89. BU, 2.1.20.
90. HM, p. 49.
91. Ibid. p. 57.
92. AP, 6.98.
93. yasya chāyā amṛtaṁ yasya mṛtyuḥ. RV, 10.121.2.
94. apoditaṁ yadi jagad brahmaṇo'nyatayā sthitam. tadā sāṅkhyamataprāptir ataḥ sārvātmyam ucyate. VS, 2.42.
95. tac chaktyupādhisaṁyogād brahmai 've 'śvaratāṁ vrajet. PD. 3.40.
96. māyāṁ tu prakṛtiṁ vidyān māyinaṁ maheśvaram. SU. 4.10.
97. SIV, p. 33.
98. yastū 'rṇanābha iva tantubh pradhānajaiḥ deva ekaḥ svam āvṛṇot, Ś 6.10.
99. Sa pūrveṣām api guruḥ kāle 'navacchedāt. YS, 1.26.
100. VBH, YS, 1.25.
101. Parāñci khāni vyatṛṇat svayambhū, KT 2.1.1.
102. Kauṣ, 3.8.
103. VS, 2.1.23.
104. sarvasya śaraṇaṁ bṛhat. ŚU, 3.17.
105. varadaṁ devam īḍyam. Ibid. 4.11.
106. śāstā janānāṁ hṛdaye sanniviṣṭaḥ. Ibi 3.13.
107. sārvādhipatyaṁ kurute mahātmā. Ibi 5.3.
108. sarvasya vaśī sarvasya īśānaḥ sarvas 'dhipatiḥ. BU, 4.4.22.
109. eṣa sarveśvara eṣa bhūtapāla e bhūtā'dhipatir eṣa setur vidharaṇe eṣā lokānām asambhedāya. Ibid.
110. mahad bhayaṁ vajram udyatam. KTU 2.3.2.
111. TU, 2.8.
112. KTU, 2.33.
113. BU, 3.8.9.
114. ŚU, 3.3.
115. Māṇḍ, 6.
116. BU, 3.7.23.
117. BU, 3.7.
118. rukmavarṇaṁ kartāram īśa brahmayonim. MU, 3.1.3.
119. SIV, p. 34.
120. sa eṣa prāṇa eva prajñātmā ānando 'aja amṛtaḥ. Kaus. 3.8.
121. ŚU, 1.12.
122. Ibid. 5.1.

123. Samastakalyāṇaguṇātmako 'sau svaśaktileśād dhṛtabhūtavargaḥ/ tejobalaiśvaryamahāvalodhasu-vīryaśaktyādiguṇaikarāśiḥ. Śrī Bh, VS, 3.2.11.
124. Śrī Bh, Madras ed. p. 2.
125. Ibid.. pp. 156, 344-5.
126. Ibid. p. 232.
127. Śri Bh, p. 233.
128. Ibid. p. 235.
129. Ibid. p. 146.
130. Ibid. p. 148.
131. IA, Vol LIII.—1924, pp. 77-86.
132. IA. Vol. LIII+1924, p. 78.
133. Īśvarānugrahād eva puṁsām advaitavāsanā. AP, 6-85.
134. etāvad vijñānasya dvāratvāc ca parabrahmavijñānaṁ prati. ŚB, on BU, 2.1.14.
135. Vār, śl. 1164, p. 666.
136. sarvabhāvādhiṣṭhātṛtvaṁ sarvajñātṛtvaṁ ca. YS, 3.49.
137. tad vairāgyād api doṣalījakṣaye kaivalyam. Ibid. 3.50.
138. udyogamayam ālasyaṃ prakāśaikātmakaṁ tamaḥ/ aśūnyaṁ śūnyakalpaṁ ca tattvaṁ kim api śāmbhavam. SU, 3.9.
139. tadā tasmin mahāvyomni pralīnaśaśibhāskare/ sauṣuptapadavan mūḍhaḥ prabuddhaḥ syād anāvṛtaḥ. SK, 2.9.
140. dvā suparṇā etc. MU, 3.11.
141. Ibid.
142. MU, 3.1.2.
143. Ibid.
144. KTU, 1.31.
145. SLS, p. 79 ff.
146. ŚU, 6.13., KTU, 2.5.13.
147. prajñānaghana eva ānandamayo....eṣa sarveśvaraḥ etc. Māṇḍ, 5-6.
148. Logic Vol. ii, p. 258.
149. VD, p. 263.
150. AR, pp. 419-20.
151. KTU, 2.4.15.
152. PRU, 6.5.
153. CU, 8.12.3.
154. Ibid.
155. amṛtaṁ satyena channam. BU, 1.6.3., anṛtāpidhānā. CU. 8.3.2. etc.
156. BU, 2.5.19.
157. CSU, p. 223 ff.
158. PU, p. 248.
159. RV, 10.129.
160. PE. Sec. 100.
161. hiraṇmayeṇa pātreṇa satyasyā'pihitaṁ mukham. ĪU, 15.
162. BU, 1.6.3.
163. IHQ. Vol. XI, Sept. '35.
164. ŚU, 6.8.
165. daivī śaktiḥ avyākṛtanāmarūpā nāmarūpayoḥ prāgavasthā, ŚB, VS, 1.4.9.
166. svābhāvikī jñānabalakriyā ca. ŚU. 1.3.
167. HJ, Vol. XEIV, July, 46.
168. IVL, p. 343.
169. Ibid.
170. māyāṁ tu prakṛtiṁ vidyāt. ŚU, 4.10.
171. Ibid. 4.5.
172. bahuśobhamānāṁ umāṁ haimavatīm, KU, 24.
173. YK, p. 163.
174. yas tu sarvāṇi bhūtāni ātmany

evā 'nupaśyati sarvabhūteṣu cā 'tmānam. IU, 6.

175. IG, p. 254.
176. ĪU, 7.
177. IHQ vol. XI, Sept. '35.
178. viśvam cidabhinnam ity ekā dṛṣṭiḥ cin na viśvābhinne 'ti dvitīya. Tatrā'dyonmīlane jagati satyatvabuddhiḥ prarohati, dvitīyonmīlaṇe tu mithyātvamatiḥ, dvayor evo 'nmīlane tu cid evai 'kā paramārthasatī tadanyad asatyam iti nirmalā matir iti. Evañ ca svarūpeṇa mithyābhūto 'pi prapañcaś cidātmanā satya eva. KH, p. 39.
179. Kevalāntaradṛṣṭipradhāno vijñānavādī....ubhayadṛṣṭipradānas tu śūnyavādī, divyalocanamātrapradhānas tu svātantryavādī, visphāritalocanatrayās tu vedāntinaḥ āntaravāhyaprapañcam anavadhiryai 'va tādṛśādvaitasarasi nimajjanāt, Ibid. p. 30.
180. HP, p. 162.
181. Eth. Prop. VIII.
182. PT, pp. 70-71.
183. SE, p. 106.
184. PR, p. 266.
185. HWP, p. 606.
186. HP, p. 210.
187. LH, pp. 161-69.
188. LH, pp. 351-2.
189. IG, p. 412.
190. PT, pp. 122-23.
191. Ibid. p. 20.
192. GP. p. 542.
193. CE, p. 174.
194. STD, pp. 247-8.
195. STD, p. 345.
196. Ibid. p. 347.
197. NPW, p. 284.
198. Ibid. p. 280.
199. HWP, p. 635.
200. Hibb. Jl. vol. XLIV. July '49.
201. BU, 3.4.1.
202. BU, 3.9.26.
203. idaṁ sarvaṁ yad ayam ātmā. BU. 2.4
204. nāntaḥprajñaṁ na vahiḥprajñaṁ 'bhayataḥ prajñam, Māṇḍ. 7.
205. Vārt, 2.7. 55.
206. Vārt, 2.7.55.
207. Māṇḍ 7.
208. Ibid.
209. CIP, p. 285.

CHAPTER II

THE PROBLEM OF KNOWLEDGE

The Upaniṣads do not merely furnish us with a perfect picture of Reality but also enjoin us to know it and it alone to the exclusion of all else. "Know that alone and discard all other talks,"[1] is the injunction, the imperative command of the Upaniṣads. But why is this supreme stress on the necessity of knowing it? What is the value of knowing it? "This is the bridge of immortality"[2], "Only by knowing it one transcends death, and there is no other way of attaining, (immortality)"[3], answer the Upaniṣads. So it becomes imperative for us to enquire into the nature of this knowledge that promises immortality and carries one beyond the sphere of sorrow and suffering.

The Upaniṣads, in many places, signify this knowledge by the term 'seeing': "He who is free from desire *sees* or beholds it,"[4] "It is *seen* by the keen and subtle intellect"[5], "This Ātman is to be *seen"*[6] and so on. This specifically denotes that this knowledge is not mere idle speculation or intellectual theorising about the nature of the Ātman, but a direct vision, an immediate apprehension of it. As the ordinary man of ignorance *sees* the outer world of objects, so also the exceptionally gifted soul *beholds* the inner Ātman, having turned his gaze inwards.[7] As there is an outer perception through the senses, so there is an inner perception through the soul and it is this perception or beholding that the Upaniṣadic knowledge denotes.

But a problem immediately confronts us. The Upaniṣad no doubt enjoins that the Ātman is to be seen (*draṣṭavyaḥ*). But how can it be seen? Is it an object of perception? The Upaniṣads categorically deny the possibility of its apprehension through the senses. — "Not within the field of vision stands its form, nor with the eye can anyone see it."[8] Perception being thus ruled out, inference, too, automatically becomes nullified. For inference is never possible without a basis of perception; nor has it any mark or *linga* to serve as the middle term of a syllogism. Then remains testimony. But testimony can never give us a direct knowledge about a thing, it only brings an indircct acquaintance with the existence of a thing. Neither is analogy of any help here, for the Ātman, as we have seen, is distinct from all else, and hence there is nothing in the universe which can be cited as analogous to it. Hence all the ordinary means of knowledge *or pramāṇas* that are at our disposal fail us in bringing the intimation of the Ātman.

The problem however is deeper. At the root of the failure of all the *pramāṇas* to comprehend the Ātman lies the supreme fact that the Ātman never becomes the object of knowledge, it is the eternal subject. It is, therefore, that the Upaniṣad asks: 'How shall ye know the knower?". It is impossible to make the knower the object of knowledge, for that will need another knower and so on, leading to a *regressus ad infinitum.* As the Ātman never becomes the object of knowledge, the Upaniṣad paradoxically states that it is unknown to the knowing and known to the unknowing.[10] In other words, he who asserts that he has come to know the Ātman, signifies thereby that he has made the Ātman the object of his knowledge, which is a manifest absurdity. For, the object is always the not-self (*anātman*), the *idam* (it) as opposed to the Ātman (the Self), the *Īśa* (the Lord) or the *aham.* Therefore, so long as one knows 'another' as an object beside him, one does not know the self (Ātman), but only the not-self (*anātman*). On the contrary, he who states that he has not known the Ātman, rightly comprehends it, for he, thereby, asserts the great truth that the Ātman has not been the object of his knowledge.

But how then to distinguish between this not-knowing of the enlightened and the utter ignorance of the unenlightened ? Does not this not-knowing amount almost to agnosticism? Is the Ātman or Brahman of the Upaniṣads then similar to the Great Unknowable of Herbert Spencer or the Thing-in-itself of Kant which is always beyond the grasp of the human mind? The very next verse of the Upanisad removes this apprehension: 'It is known in every act of cognition and thus one attains immortality.'[11] It remains unknown (*avijnātam*) and yet is known in every act of cognition, *pratibodhaviditam,* that is the paradox. In other words, it is never the object of knowledge, and hence unknown, and yet the very ground of all knowledge, and hence is felt in each and every particular act of cognition. As in the problem of Reality we pointed out that the negative statements are made only for a deeper affirmation, so here in the problem of knowledge, the Upaniṣads deny the knowability of the Ātman in order to assert the foundational nature of its knowledge. As the Reality is unique, so the method, too, of knowing it is unique. Our ordinary consciousness fails to apprehend the nature of this knowledge, as it fails to realize the true nature of the transcendent Reality. It is necessary, therefore, to analyze the nature of our ordinary consciousness or modes of knowledge and then contrast it with the transcendental apprehension.

Perception

Our ordinary cognition always involves a dualism. It necessarily pre-supposes a knower and a known and the function of the *vṛtti* or the mode of the mind is to effect a union between the two. In fact, our whole life is an unconscious endeavour to establish a link with the outer world. In every act of our life we are trying to take in what lies outside of us, to make the outer object a part and parcel of our being. But yet we are never wholly successful. Though we can take in a portion of the outer world into ourselves, the real essence still lies outside us and so there is no complete fusion of our being with the world, no absolute coalescence between the knower and the known. It appears that our intellect merely touches the outer fringe of the object and never enters into the heart of it. This happens because our intellect is unaccustomed to this act of identification and it knows things only from a distance, through a relation of separation. A second characteristic of our mode of perception is that in it the object is never revealed in its true nature, because the subject always makes an active contribution to the act of perception; and so, in the very process of knowing an object, it modifies or colours the latter. The subjective tinge always disfigures the pure original form of the object. Thirdly, every act of perception is bound by space and time. We only perceive a thing here and now. We cannot look before and after, but our gaze is fixed on the immediate present. Similarly a thing which is at a distance or covered by barriers does not come within our view. These limitations are inherent in all perception. Again, it knows only the particular and never comprehends the general or the universal.

Inference

Inference goes ahead of perception in this that it frees the mind from the limitation of the senses and thereby widens the field of knowledge. Though the fire may not be within the ken of one's perceptual knowledge, yet one may be quite sure of its existence, if smoke is perceived. The faculty of Inference is, thus, not vain imagination, but a method of knowledge, a *pramāṇa,* and, in fact it is this power of inference which distinguishes man from the animal. Man, being essentially a thinking being, can never rest content merely with what the senses present and report to him. He constructs, out of that data or material supplied by the senses, a coherent system of thought. extending, thereby, this knowledge to the future and to the past. Man, therefore, can look before and after; he can apprehend the future as well as bring back the past. The antecedents and the consequents of an event are all before the gaze of the intellect that indulges in Inference. Inference also corrects perception and hence stands superior to it. The senses often prove to be false reporters and in many cases delude us by presenting the very opposite picture of truth. The senses tell us that the Sun moves round the earth and it is only reasoning which comes to correct this total misrepresentation of the actual fact, which is just the opposite of it.

Thus though reason or intellect helps greatly in the growth and correction of knowledge, yet this help is tendered only at the expense of the directness that the sense-perception contains. Inference or reasoning always brings an indirect awareness of things, it cannot make one *see* directly that the fire is there. Inference is always mediate, that being its intrinsic character and it never becomes immediate, for that will destroy its very nature. Bergson has beautifully pointed out that the intellect is essentially a 'tool-making faculty', or, in other words, it is a practical faculty evolved for the purpose of action in the world. The 'tool-making faculty' has no doubt helped man immensely in the management of the life in the world, but it has taken him away, at the same time, from the soul or heart of life. "It goes all round life, taking from outside the greatest possible number of views of it, drawing it into itself instead of entering into it."[12] Hence the intellect presents us only with a snapshot view of things or an infinite number of static pictures, which never brings us in touch with the original living reality. Thus, so far as the heart of the reality or life is concerned, the intellect has not helped man to get near it, but, on the contrary, has taken him far away from the true centre. The circumference has been widened no doubt but the touch with the centre has been lost. The horizon of knowledge has been extended at the cost of direct awareness.

Intuition

But there lies in man another faculty, far deeper and richer than the intellect, through which he gains back the directness of apprehension he had lost. The intellect has made him look outward, away from the centre of life, 'but it is to the very inwardness of life that intuition leads us'.[13] But what is this faculty called intuition'? As Bergson puts it : "By intuition, I mean, instinct that has become disinterested, self-conscious, capable of reflecting upon its object and of enlarging it indefinitely".[14] In the terminology of Yoga philosophy it is *prajñā.* It does not mean a hazy or indistinct knowledge of a thing but signifies the clear light of reason, which views things directly all at once.[15] *Prajñā* or intuition is, thus, not a faculty which is 'incapable of giving us anything else than simple being'. but it is a vision direct as well as comprehensive (*aśeṣaviśeṣadarśanam*). It is other than inference or testimony, because it apprehends the unique or particular nature of a thing and does not stop with the knowledge of its general nature alone like inference or testimony. It is an intimate awareness, a 'knowledge by acquaintance', in the words of Russel. It is the supreme perception (*paraṁ pratyakṣam*)[16] and is the source of testimony and inference, because they issue out of it.[17]

This *prajñā* is, thus, the true perception of the mind as distinguished from the false perception of the senses. We generally take the *pratyakṣa* or the sense-perception as the basis of all other *pramāṇas* but, in fact, it is this *prajñā* or inner perception which is at the root of all *pramāṇas,* as the Yoga system points out. Again, this *prajñā* is not something which is opposed to the intellect, but, is the very culmination or perfection of it. It is only after the highest development of the intellectual faculty and its exploration to the full have been achieved that the intuition suddenly flashes forth from the deeps. When the mind becomes utterly limpid, clear like a crystal, being freed from the memories or associations of words and images, then the object is revealed in its true nature, the subject having ceased to contribute anything to the act of cognition.[18] This intuition has also infinite ranges, beginning from the grossest right upto the subtlest. The highest form of intuition is called *tāraka* i.e. which springs of itself without any external cause or occasion. It covers all things of all times in a single moment.[19] The intellect knows only through a process of succession but here a supcrcession of the process takes place. The object is seized through a single act of intuition, the whole is revealed in an instanteneity of moment.

Thus intuition gets us in touch with the flow of life or the actual movement of the world. It brings an all-comprehensive knowledge of the entire universe and of the principle that is active in all existence or manifestation, which the Upaniṣads call Prāṇa. But the knowledge of the Ātman is still to be gained. We have pointed out, in the previous chapter, that the Ātman or Brahman is not opposed to the movement or dynamis, and hence, is not a static *being* contrary to the dynamic *becoming*. It is something unique transcending all these oppositions. This is supported once again by the method of approach to the Ātman delineated in the Upaniṣads. The Upaniṣads never try to grasp the Reality or Ātman through the intellect; and this proves that the Reality they envisage is not a mere staticity of being, for, as Bergson remarks about the method of the intellect, 'it always starts from immobility, as if this were the ultimate reality'.[20]

Inadequacy of Intuition

Again, the Upaniṣads do not seek the Ātman through, what Bergson calls, 'Intuition' or what the Yoga system calls *samādhiprajñā*. The *prajñā* or intuition, though it brings a direct knowledge of things, is still a process, and even in the highest state of *nirodha* when all processes are apparently at an end, there still remains a touch of process, which is traced or detected by the divergences in the periods of time involved in *nirodha*. In other words, *nirodba* sometimes continues for a shorter period than another *nirodha*, and again, sometimes endures for a shorter period. And this is inevitable, since intuition or *samādhi or nirodha*, after all, involves the mind and they are only deeper movements of it, and wherevcr there is mind, there must be a process. The process may be sometimes explicit, and sometimes all too implicit to be grasped at all, but still it is there all the time so long as the mind exists. Hence intuition comes and goes, it does not become an abiding vision. It, no doubt, gets to the centre but is again thrown out of it. Consequently, *vyutthāna* or return to the surface consciousness always haunts *samādhi* or the absorbed consciousness like a shadow, and is the external counterpart of the latter. So a constant war goes on for mutual overpowering between the *saṃskāras* or potencies of *vyutthāna* and *nirodha* or *samādhi*.[21] There remains, therefore, always an effort to keep the mind fixed in the level of *samādhi* or intuition. But even when the intuition becomes almost spontaneous, or the *samādhi* or the *nirodha* almost a natural state, due to an overwhelming predominance of the inward movement towards the centre, there still remains an unconscious effort to retain or rather maintain that state or level of consciousness. *Samādhi or* intuition never becomes utterly spontaneous; there is always a trace of artificiality in it, because it is produced by the efforts of the subject or the mind.

Again, the object is not truly revealed in intuition in its utter purity. Though the mind is made absolutely clear as a crystal[22] in *samādhi,* yet the object is known only as *reflected* in that clear mind and not as it is *in itself.* We still know only the image, though the image may, in this case, be very faithful, but it is not the original as yet. It is still a view of things through a medium, though the medium is seemingly nonexistent due to its utter transparency and finest nature. Still there is a film though the film may be the finest. Hence, even in this deep union brought about by *samādhi* or intuition, the subject and the object are not totally identified. There is union no doubt but not unity as yet. It is only when this last and the finest film is pierced or lifted that we reach the utter unity, the absolute transcendence. The Upaniṣadic knowledge signifies the removal of this last veil that still separates the subject and the object, the finite and the infinite.

Hence the Upaniṣads discard the intuition of the mind or the *prajñā* of *samādhi* and seek a knowledge that is neither gained through a process nor lost after a time through *vyutthāna* or return to ordinary consciousness but which is spontaneous in its nature, depending not on the effort of the subject, but aroused or generated by the object alone; to be strictly precise, which is *vastutantra* and not *kartṛtantra.* This knowledge, "by reason of the immediate character of its operation, may be called 'intuitive' but only on the strict condition that it is not regarded as having anything in common with the faculty which certain contemporary philosophers call intuition, a purely instinctive and vital faculty that is really beneath reason and not above it."[23] We may call it the intuition of the soul in order to distinguish it from the intuition of the mind, if we are keen to retain the term 'intuition'. "This faculty can also be called the pure intellect, following the practice of Aristotle and his Scholiastic successors, for to them the intellect was in fact that faculty which possessed a direct knowledge of principles. Aristotle expressly declares that the intellect is truer than science which amounts to saying that it is more true than the reason which constructs that science; he also says that 'nothing is more true than the intellect', for it is necessarily infallible from the fact that its operation is immediate, and because, not being really distinct from its object, it is identified with the truth itself."[24] Spinoza also hints at such a kind of knowledge or perception when he says, at the end of his classification of perception, that "lastly there is the perception arising when a thing is perceived only through its essence."[25] He also points out later that, "if the thing be self-existent, or as is commonly said, the cause of itself, it must be understood through its essence only".[26] The Ātman or Brahman of the Upaniṣads is essentially such a self-existent thing and hence must be apprehended only through its essence and not by any other means. In the words of Eddington it may be called 'the intimate knowledge', which 'will not submit to codification and analysis'.[27]

But the one term which truly expresses the nature of this knowledge is what the Upaniṣads use about it, viz., *sākṣāt aparokṣāt.* It is not called *pratyakṣa,* because *pratyakṣa* or perception always involves, as we have seen, the duality of the knower and the known, whereas in this knowledge there is an absolute identity of both. But any knowledge, other than *pratyakṣa* is described as *parokṣa* or indirect. The only source of direct knowledge is *pratyakṣa,* and all other modes of cognition like inference, testimony etc. are indirect. Hence, to indicate that though this knowledge is distinct from *pratyakṣa* yet it is not necessarily indirect, it is called not-indirect (*na-parokṣa*) *i.e. aparokṣa.* But this negative way of saying it merely as 'non-indirect' does not satisfy the Upaniṣads, and so they add the other word *sākṣāt* or immediate. Its immediacy surpasses even that of *pratyakṣa* or perception, for in perception the mediacy of the senses cannot be dispensed with and hence its immediacy is spurious. But here the soul perceives the soul without anything to intervene between the two. It surpasses even intellectual intuition in this that here the distinction between the subject and the object stands absolutely obliteratcd and hence the immediacy is complete. It is no doubt true that "intellectual intuition is even more immediate than sensory intuition for it is beyond the distinction between subject and object, which the lattcr allows to subsist; it is at once the means of knowledge and the knowledge itself and in it subject and object are identified. Indeed no knowledge is really worthy of the name except in so far as it has the effect of bringing about such an identification...... The only genuinely effective knowledge is that which permits us to penetrate into the very nature of things and if such a penetration may be effected upto a certain point in the inferior degrees of knowledge it is only in metaphysical knowledge that it is fully and totally realizable".[28] And here lies the superiority of this metaphysical or transcendental knowledge that intellectual intuitions and all other modes of knowledge find their final consummation in it, nay are verily rooted in it. It is the *avasāna,* the end or limit of all knowledge.

The Vedāntic view of Knowledge

The Vedāntic view of *pramāṇas* is, therefore, absolutely distinct from all other views. According to the Vedānta, the root of all *pramāṇas* is the self-revealing mode of knowledge of the Ātman (*svataḥpramāṇa*). All other modes of cognition are derived from this fundamental *pramāṇa* and are wholly dependent on it. Everywhere it is the one *Cit* that is revealed through the different modes of knowledge or *pramāṇas.* No cognition would have ben possible had there not been the selfshining *Cit* or Brahman at the background of both the subject and the object. What happens in every cognition is that the self in the perceiving subject unites itself with the self in the object perceived. In the degree that the knower has entered into the self or spirit of the thing perceived, he is said to have known that thing. Hence, 'Perception is Brahman itself, the immediate identity of knower and known'.[29] "All determinate knowledge is a self-abnegation, involving as it does a stratification of the pure consciousness or *caitanya* into three forms: *pramātṛcaitanya* or determinate self-consciousness, *vṛtticaitanya* or modes of consciousness, and *viṣayacaitanya* or empirical object."[30] So in all perception there is the coincidence of *vṛtticaitanya* and *viṣayacaitanya*[31] and it is only the unity of the apparently divided consciousness that leads to knowledge in every case.

The Vedānta recognizes as many as six *pramāṇas* or modes of knowledge, because according to it, it is the same single consciousness that is apprehended through infinite ways of approach, and so there is no need to restrict the modes of knowledge or curtail their number, once the fundamental characteristic of all of them is recognized. In every cognition the *Cit* or the Ātman is a necessary and invariable element. In fact, the whole store of knowledge lies imbedded in us and only that which is within us is revealed through the contact with outer objects. 'All knowing is but remembrance' is a truth rightly pointed out by Plato. Hence all perception is really acquired perception. What the *vṛtti* or the mode of mind does is simply the removing or lifting of the veil that covers the object (*āvaraṇābhibhava*) and immediately with the removal of the veil the object flashes forth in perception to our empirical consciousness. The covering of nescience and its occasional lifting through *vṛttis* or mental modes makes it appear that the knowledge is being generated at every moment anew, but in fact, the knowledge is eternal and uncreated. "The self is aware of all objects at all times; some being known positively and others negatively. That the self knows objects directly presented to it is of course obvious. But even in the cases of objects which arc not positively so presented, the self can be said to know them, though not as present but as absent. On being aware of an object for the first time the self remembers that it was not aware of it before. This memory clearly implies that even before the presentation of the object there was a consciousness of its absence or that it was known even then, though as absent. Thus the self may be said to be always aware of all objects, some as present and others as absent. Hence the Vedāntic dictum—"Everything is lighted up by the self, either as known or as unknown" (*Sarvaṁ jñātatayā ajñātatayā ca sākṣi-bhāsyam*)."[32]

This presentation or non-prcsentation, *jñātatā* or *ajñātatā* is the function of the intellect and hcnce we sometimes know and sometimes do not know. Our knowledge has a rising and setting, a coming and going, but to the eternal consciousness of the *Sākṣin* or the Seer it is all one awareness, without any break or interruption, regardless of the fact of presentation or non-presentation. It lights up equally both the presence and the absence of things or objects. In other words, nothing can be hid from the *Sākṣin* or the Ātman at any place or time. It even knows the absence of knowing. This proves its fundamental self-shining character. "It is in virtue of this fundamental quality that an object appears and the subject knows. Appearance and knowledge are but the two differentiated sides of the same neutral fact of immediacy. In other words, the appearance of *caitanya* as object to *caitanya* as subject or the knowledge on the part of *caitanya* as subject of *caitanya* as object, has to be credited to the fundamental self-manifesting characteristic of *caitanya*."[33] Thus perception does not bring knowledge merely from the contact of the sense with the object but 'the fact of the self knowing the object is somehow brought into connexion with the witnessing or self-shining *caitanya,* of which the self is really constituted'.[34] Everywhere the knowledge is produced through the contact of the Self or the Ātman.

Similar is the case with inference. Here, too, merely the steps of syllogism or the modes of syllogistic reasoning do not supply the knowledge, but an inner faculty of inference makes the knowledge possible. He who does not possess it can never be made to infer, even when presented with the full form of a syllogism. The jump from the known to the unknown involves something else than the mere process of syllogistic reasoning; in fact, the steps of syllogism merely serve as an occasion for the revelation of the inner flash of inferential faculty and do not produce the knowledge as such. As in perception the *vṛtti* merely lifts the veil of nescience and effects a conjunction between the two *caitanyas,* so here, too, concomitance (*vyāpti*) and the particular sign or instance (*hetu*) merely serve to connect the particular with the universal, but it is only the self-luminous *caitanya* that gives rise to the knowledge spontaneously This happens to be the fact in all forms of *pramāṇas.* In analogy, too, merely the similarity does not lead to the knowledge of one from the other ; but the joining of the two things i.e. the knowledge of the akinness is produced by an inner intuitive faculty. So with implication (*arthāpatti*) and other *pramāṇas.* It is the one consciousness that is apprehended differently at different levels of awareness and the different *pramāṇas* are nothing but the different methods devised for contacting the same *caitanya* in diverse ways as the occasion demands. The root of all knowledge, through whatever channel we may have it, is ultimately the Ātman. Hence the Upaniṣads call it *pratibodbaviditam,* cognized in every act of knowledge. It is a basic fact from which there is no escape. It is a postulate of all knowledge. It is the root of all experience and it alone makes experience possible.

The Self as the source of all Knowledge

Thus the Ātman or Brahman of the Upaniṣads is not unknowable, beyond all knowledge, but rather the very ground of all knowledge. All *pramāṇas* depend on this self-luminous light of consciousness and act only through it. As in our discussion on the problem of Reality, we found that nothing can *exist* apart from the Ātman, so from the analysis of knowledge too, it is revealed that nothing can be *known* except in and through the Ātman. That all cognition and means of knowledge or illumination depend on it is beautifully depicted in the famous discourse of Yājñavalkya and King Janaka.[35] The King asked Yājñavalkya: 'Of what light is this Puruṣa'? In other words, what is the source of illumination that makes it possible for man to work in the world? What is his guiding light ? Yājñavalkya first replies that it is the light of the Sun (Aditya) through which a man stays, moves and acts. The King then questions: 'With the setting of the Sun of what light is the Puruṣa'? The Āditya or the Sun cannot be the guiding light for all time, for it has its rising and setting but the Purusa has still to be guided, and he still needs a light and what then comes to his aid when the sun sets? Yājñavalkya replies that it is then the light of the moon which helps him to carry on his work. Again the King questions: 'With the setting of the Sun and with the setting of the moon of what light is the man'? Yājñavalkya replies that it is of the light of the fire. The King persists in his questioning and wants to know what happens after all these sources of light viz. the sun, the moon and the fire have set, and Yājñavalkya replies that then it is the light of *vāc* or word that guides. But, asks the King finally: "What is the source of light when *vāc*, too, is at rest"? Yājñavalkya then declares that it is the light of the Ātman. This points out that the final source of all lights or illuminations is the Ātman. While all other lights have their setting, this light of the Ātman knows no rising or setting. It is the Eternal Uncreated Self-luminous Light of lights.

Signifying this supreme source of light, another famous verse of the Upaniṣads declares: 'There the Sun does not shine. nor the moon nor the stars, nothing to say of this fire. Following that shining (light) all others shine, by its light all these are lighted'.[38] This, unequivocally, points out that all other sources of light or knowledge are dependent on this light of the Ātman and act only through it. The only light or knowledge which is absolutely independent and self-shining is the light of the Ātman. All other lights being borrowed lights fail to reveal the Ātman which is the very source of them all. Hence in the attempt to reveal the Ātman they can do nothing but set i.e. merge in that original light and allow it to reveal itself by its own light. In all other cognitions, the mental mode encircles the object and the light of consciousness reflected in the mode reveals or illumines the object. But in this case when the mind wants to comprehend the Ātman, what happens is that the reflected light becomes merged in the original light, which is here sought to be made the object of knowledge. In other cases, the object revealed is inconscient and material, and hence it is lighted by the reflected light of the mental mode, but here what is sought as the object is the original light itself and so instead of lighting it up, the reflected light simply merges itself in the original. Hence it is said that the *act* of mental mode applies to Ātman or Brahman, but the *effect* does not follow from it. In the technical terms of Vedānta, there is *vṛttivyāpti* in this case, but no *phalavyāpti.* The mind moves towards the Ātman, becomes modified in, or takes the form of the Ātman as in the case of cognitions of other objects, but the result that follows in other cases, viz. the revelation of the object in the light of consciousness does not follow here, because what is grasped by the *vṛtti* here is the revealing light itself. Hence the knowledge of the Ātman is not an effect or product of a process but signifies the termination of all processes.

From this point of view it is said that the mind never knows the Ātman[37] i.e. it can never make the Ātman an object of its knowledge, like other finite objects of the world. But, again, from the other point of view, it is only the mind that comprehends the Ātman,[38] for the mental mode about Brahman or Ātman must be generated, the mind must be suffused wholly by it and only then will the original light take up the reflected light within itself. The reflected light can never reveal, it is true, the original light, but it can certainly help a great deal in its revelation by putting itself face to face with the original, tallying with it point to point and thereby ceasing to exist separately. The mind or intellect in thus 'committing suicide', in the words of Bradley, does not make the knowledge of the Ātman an impossibility, but by this very act, by moving, as it were, out of the way allows the Ātman to reveal itself. The self-manifest (*svayaṁprakāśa*) Ātman then shines in its own light. "Self-manifestness of knowledge means that knowledge can behave as being immediate without being an object of knowledge. This would be an exact rendering of the explanation of the term *svaprakāśatva* (self-manifestness) as given by the Advaitins :— *avedyatve sati aparokṣa-vyavahāra-yogyatvaṁ svaprakāśatvam.*"[39].

Realization of the Self-manifest

It may still be objected that, granted that the Ātman is self-manifest, yet how is that self-manifestness to be realized? If the Ātman is self-shining, no amount of effort on the part of the mind or the intellect can ever make the Ātman known. Only if it is revealed of itself, then and then alone can it be known. But this self-revelation of the pure light of *Cit* or Consciousness can hardly be realized so long as the other false lights arc shining. The false lights must be put out one by one so that the true light may shine. We must warn that by 'putting out' we do not mean or suggest a deliberate suppression of the ordinary means of knowledge, for that is never the Upaniṣadic method, but simply indicate the transcendence of the lower method or means by the higher. The development from sensation to perception and thence to conception is all an inner unfoldment of consciousness, and as the higher keys of consciousness become operative the lower ones automatically cease to play and become included in the higher.

In order to reach the supreme state of the transcendental knowledge, our consciousness must be raised higher and higher by degrees. This is also indicated in the famous discourse of Yājñavalkya, we have just quoted.[40] There the sun, the moon, the fire and the word all stand for different methods or levels of awareness or consciousness. The light of the sun evidently stands for the sense-knowlege, for the sun is generally connected with the eye, and it is the lowest form of knowledge with which all men generally carry on their work in the world. But higher than this light is the light of the moon, which shines even when the former has set. This is the light of the intellect or the mind, for the moon is definitely connected with the mind (cf. *candramā manaso jātaḥ*). From sense-perception we thus rise to the intellect. But even higher than this faculty of intellect is the light of the fire, which evidently here symbolizes the power of intuition. It penetrates even deeper and sheds its light in a sphere where the intellect fails to enter. But even this intuitive faculty has its limit and the light of the fire, too, has its end.

The last light which comes nearest to the supreme light of the Ātman is the light of *Vāc* or Word. In a section on Oṅkāra, we shall have occasion to deal with the conception of *Vāc* fully, but here we may only point out that this *Vāc* signifies the supreme faculty of reason, which is at work behind all manifestations. Just below the Ātman is the place of *Vāc*, and hence it is nearest to the Ātman. Hence in lifting the consciousness towards the pure self-shining awareness of the Ātman, one has finally to wait here, in the plane of *Vāc*, before entering the domain of the Ātman. It is *Vāc* which gives the clue to the Ātman, being nearest to it and after serving as a pointer, it, too, vanishes or goes to rest. Hence the Vedāntins lay the supreme stress on *vākya* and assert that the knowledge of the Ātman or Brahman can only be gained with the help of the *vākyas* or words of revelation contained in the *Śruti* and never by any other means. "The consciousness of eternal freedom comes from the Word and not from anything else"[41] is the emphatic assertion of the Vedāntins.

It is therefore that the Upaniṣad, after enjoining that the Ātman is to be seen, further enjoins that it is to be heard (*śrotavyaḥ*), for it is this hearing that leads here to the seeing. We have pointed out that the nature of the Ātman is self-shining (*svayaṁprakāśa*) and it is the pre-supposition of all forms of knowledge. Hence the knowing or seeing of the Ātman simply means the recognition or realization of the fact that it is the very ground of the knowledge that seeks to apprehend it. In other words, it means simply the removal of the illusion which makes the Ātman or Brahman appear as an 'other', as an object which is to be realized or apprehended. The identity of the knower and the known which is the aim of all knowledge is here sought to be realized in its completeness. "Every form of knowledge is different from every other in the degree of identification of the object in itself with the object for consciousness, and the only resting place for knowledge is where the agreement becomes absolute. Now, if knowledge deals solely with the self which knows, it is entirely self-constituted, sclf-determined, self-contained. To be completely self-sufficient, however, is precisely what is meant by being Absolute. Absolute knowledge is the presence to consciousness of its own Self-Thought".[42]

We have seen that the Vedāntins view all modes of knowledge or *pramāṇas* as nothing but the means of the contact of the self with the self. The subject and the object arc really not two separate entities-they are one, and though the different modes of knowledge effect an union between the two and seek to bridge the gulf now and then, yet the identification is never complete. The identification is only with a part and that, too, is partial. Complete identity is not gained because all cognitions involve a process and a process necessarily presupposes a relation of separation. The Vedānta, therefore, seeks a method of processless cognition and it is only through the medium of word or *vākya* that such a cognition is found to be possible. The suggestive word, at the very instant of its utterance, brings about the knowlege in a flash by removing the ignorance that was preventing the apprehension of the fact that was already there, as in the case of *'daśamas tvam asi*'. Instanteneity is its marked characteristic. At the very moment of its birth it removes the ignorancc all at once (*sakṛtpravṛttyā*)[43], as light dispels darkness the moment it is kindled or brought. It does not require to be generated again and again nor an effort is needed to retain it, for it is not concerned with the production of what 'should be' but with the acknowledgement of that which 'is'. Its essential mark is givenness, and it does not depend on the subject. It is always the outcome of the objective factor and is the self-disclosing of the givenness. Hence the Upaniṣads symbolize this instantaneous revelation by the image of the lightning in many places.[44] In the Veda, too, we find a passage which refers to it: "By plural consciousness she brought down the mortal but by becoming lightning she has torn off the veil." And Dr. Maryla Falk rightly points out that "this is the earliest instance of the image of 'lightning' as applied to the event of instantaneous enlightenment produced by the union with the transcendent principle of universal wisdom."[45]

Hence, the removal of the illusion of separation needs nothing but the pointing out of the identity through a single suggestive word or phrase, like *'tat tvam asi'*. Consequent on the hearing of the word, if the removal of the illusion takes place, it takes place all at once and does not need to be repeated through a process. This direct and immedtate way of realization is, what is called in the Tantras, *anupāya,* or literally 'methodless' way of approach. The Ātman or Śiva, as it is called in the Tantras, being essentially self-luminous, it is felt that all methods to reveal this self-revealing reality are superfluous and futile and the self-luminous reality is hence sought to be grasped all at once by a single effort of consciousness aroused by the word of the spiritual guide (*guru*). As Abhinavagupta puts it: "The network of means cannot reveal the Śiva. Does the thousand-rayed Sun shine by the (help of the) jar? Having realized thus, the man with a wide vision attains the self-luminous Śiva in an instant."[46] Again it is said : "The Śiva is not revealed by the methods, rather they are revealed through its favour. I am that self-luminous (entity) appearing as the world. Having thus heard the words of the teacher only once, some, being convinced without any further cogitation, are found to shine full of knowledge''.[47]

But it must be remembered that the Upaniṣads always point out that this revealing word must be heard from an experienced teacher, and it Is only then that the word acts as the supreme means to an instantaneous enlightenment and not otherwise. Only one who has broken through the illusion and has realized his idcntity with the selfluminous reality can generate in another soul the same knowledge through the suggestive words. His words become charged with a significance which will be entirely missing when uttered by an inexperienced soul. That is why the *Kaṭha Upaniṣad* points out that "it can not be understood properly when taught by an inferior type of teacher, even if thought about in many ways''.[48] It must be 'taught by an able teacher' (*kuśalānuśiṣṭaḥ*).[49] For the attainment of this transcendental knowledge, the Upaniṣads, therefore, nowhere ask the seeker to go on meditating or contemplating over the nature of the Ātman. They simply ask him to arise, awake and on attaining the great ones or enlightened souls understand it'.[50] Here the injunction (*vidhi*) is not 'to contemplate' (*upāsīta*) but 'to know' (*nivodhata*). This knowing is a single act, like the opening of the eyes and the beholding of a thing in that very instant. Hence there is no process involved in it. The very hearing of the Supreme Word (*Mahāvākya*) brings back the lost consciousness and gets one established in the highest status of self-luminosity. There is no effort on the part of the recipient of this supreme knowledge, but it dawns of itself, spontaneously, and of its own accord, from the inmost depth of the soul. The short and suggestive words of the teacher work a magic in him by revealing the true nature, which was his and yet not his all this time while he was steeped in ignorance. His innate purity, which remains unsullied all through and even when he thinks that he is in the iron grips of ignorance or *saṁsāra,* is gained back. It is only an arousing or awakening of the latent consciousness that takes place in this case, merely from the living contact with the teacher and his word.

Eddington gives the striking illustration of 'humour' in connexion with what he calls 'intimate knowledge'. He points out that "humour can be analyzed to some extent and the essential ingredients of the different kinds of wit classified".[51] But all this would not make us laugh because "the classification concerns a symbolic knowledge of humour which preserves all the characteristics of a joke except its laughableness. The real appreciation must come *spontaneously, not introspectively*''.[52] And this spontaneous outburst of humour can only come 'through contact with merry-minded companions',[53] for 'probably in the recesses of his solemn mind there exists inhibited the seed of humour, *awaiting an awakening* by such an impulse'.[54] Exactly similar is the method prescribed and adopted by the Upaniṣads concerning the spontaneous generation of the knowledge of the Ātman or Brahman. Because of its spontaneous nature, this knowledge is not gained by any process of inhibition or suppression of the mind or the desires. The path of Yoga is *samādhi* or *nirodha,* while the method of Vedānta is *bodha.* The ignorance or nescience is removed only by knowledge (*bodha*) and never by any other method or process. And if this knowledge of identity between the individual self and the Brahman, generated even for once, does not remove the ignorance residing in the self then it is no knowledge at all.[55]

From this it must be clear that the knowledge, which needs to be supplemented after its birth by other processes like control of the mind or extinction of desires (*manonāśa vāsanākṣaya*), is not the true Vedāntic knowledge of which the Upaniṣads speak. It is not really *tattvajñāna* but is called so merely by courtesy. The true Upaniṣadic knowledge is self-sufficient and, as Śaṅkara points out, there is not even a trace of any process or action in it.[56] Once this knowledge dawns nothing else remains to be done and herein lies its glory and uniqueness.[57]

Relation between Jñāna & Karman

The true nature of this transcendental knowledge has been grasped by very few, and even among the followers of Saṅkara, there has been a divergence of opinion about its real character. The main dispute arises on the question of the relation between *jñāna* and *karman.* We have just seen that Śaṅkara denies all trace of *karman* or *kriyā* in this knowledge, because *karman* stands for process, while this knowledge is beyond all process. *Karman* again signifies or presupposes a relation of separation, while this knowledge aims at an absolute identification or complete unity. Hence the two can hardly be compatible and are fundamentally opposed to each other like light and darkness. 'Far apart, contradictory and leading to different ends are this pair, *avidyā* and what is known as *Vidyā* or Knowledge', declares the Upaniṣad."

This leads to two extremes: there are some who take *karman* as the sole end or aim, like the Mīmāṁsakas and reject *jñāna* altogether; while there are some who strictly adhere to pure *jñāna* to the utter exclusion of *karman.* There are, again, some who stand in the middle, trying to effect a compromise between the two. This attempt for compromise or synthesis (*samuccaya*) also takes various forms. It may first be classified broadly into two: *samasamuccaya* and *viṣamasamuccaya. Samasamuccaya* means an 'even' compromise, which gives equal scope to both, without assigning any superior status to any one of them. *Viṣamasamuccaya* means an 'uneven' compromise and it takes two forms: there are some who make *jnāna* the principal element and *karman* its auxiliary part or limb, while others make *karman* supreme and *jñāna* subordinate to it. Thus there are altogether five possible attitudes with regard to the relation between *jñāna* and *karman,* viz., two extreme attitudes, which exclude one or the other, and three compromising attitudes, of which one gives an equal degree of emphasis on both, and the other two vary in their emphasis on one or the other of the terms, though keeping the two together all the same. The Upaniṣads give equal scope to all these attitudes or viewpoints, appreciating fully the value of each at its own level, and yet at the same time not jumbling them up all together.

We have seen that the supreme knowledge is said to spring of itself and spontaneously, but the question remains: why then does it not manifest itself in every instance and at all times? The answer must be found in the presence of obstacles which prevent its manifestation. And here in the removal of obstacles the value of *karman* and its utility must be recognized. *Karman* never manifests the knowledge, for it is eternally self-manifest, but it only helps in making the conditions suitable for the revelation of that self-manifested nature of knowledge. In the level of the mind or the intellect the synthesis of *jñāna* and *karman* is indispensably necessary. Here theory and practice must join hands. We have to make the knowledge effective and enduring by acting it out; otherwise, it remains all too impotent. That is why the Upaniṣads condemn mere pursuit of knowledge as an entering into deeper darkness and enjoin a combination of both action and knowledge (*ubhayaṁ saha*).[59] The path of contemplation, which we shall discuss later, is essentially composed of these two elements, and *upāsanā* is a joint product of *jñāna* and *karman*. But as there is a level of togetherness of both (*ubhayam saha*), so there is a level of complete disparity and utter apartness between the two (*dūram ete viparīte viṣūcī*).[60] This apartness is not due to a forced separation between the two, which always leads to a darkness, because of its artificiality, but due to a natural overtopping or transcendence of the lower by the higher term.

Here the self-luminous knowledge is so potent that it does not stand in need of *karman* to make it effective. It dawns only when *karman* utterly exhausts itself and leaves the *jñāna* to shine by itself. In the level of utter ignorance, man is purely a creature of action, driven blindly by its impulses. With the first glimmer of knowledge, action assumes a new significance. It is the second level, where *karman* still predominates, but *jñāna,* too, accompanies it, though in a lesser degree. In the third level, with a further growth in knowledge, the proportion of the two becomes equal and there is a parity between the two (*samasamuccaya*). In the fourth level, the proportion of *jñāna* still increases, throwing off the balance of equality once more and this time in favour of *jñāna. Karman* is still there but only as secondary. In the last level, *jñāna* completely rids itself of all trace of *karman* and shines in its own majesty.

Our whole history of thought is the history of this gradual growth of knowledge through the overpowering of the opposite force of *karman* or ignorance. The process that we see is a creation of *karman* and the knowledge is not a product of this process. The process is concerned merely with the removal of the coverings of *karman.* As the veils of ignorance are removed the knowledge *seems* to be growing brighter and brighter, though in fact it is self-shining and complete all through, and this is realized only when we reach this final level of transcendental awareness.

As in the discussion of the problem of Reality we found the difficulty in the true comprehension of transcendence, which leads to its misrepresentation as a mere blank or utter abstraction, so here, too, the transcendental nature of Knowledge is hardly grasped. Pure *jñāna* is represented as dry intellectualism, while, in fact, it springs from the very core of being, which is the source of all knowing, feeling and willing. Again, being unaccustomed to a processless cognition we reject the conception of pure *jñāna* and drag it down to the level of the knowledge gained through a process. This is also evident from the history of Vedāntic thought itself. Even before Śaṅkara there were many Vedāntins like Bhartṛprapañca, who, though agreeing that *jñāna* is indispensable for self-realization, held the opinion that it should be combined with *karman,* or in other words, they were in favour of a *samuccaya.*

The *Naiṣkarmyasiddhi* refers to some of these views. There were some, like Brahmadatta, who held that the knowledge which is generated by the *vedānta-vākya* does not remove the ignorance all at once, but it is only after long meditation, day after day, that the ignorance is dispelled through the accumulation of thought about Brahman[61]. The central teaching of the Upaniṣads is, accordingly, to be found in injunctive statements like *'ātme' ty evo 'pāsīta'*, to which assertive propositions like *Tat Tvam Asi* are subsidiary, for they only furnish the subject-matter for the *upāsanā* enjoined therein. It is thus not the knowledge, which the latter statements convey, that directly brings about final release but rather its unremitting practice (*abhyāsa* or *prasaṁkhyāna*).

There was again another view, held by Maṇḍana, of a similar nature. 'He also understands *kriyā* i.e., *upāsanā* here as the final import of the Upaniṣads and construes the assertive propositions as depending upon it for their eventual significance. Maṇḍana also, like Brahmadatta, thinks that after knowing the nature of Brahman as taught in the Upaniṣads, one should meditate upon it; but he differs from the latter in that he makes not this meditation itself the means to liberation but a different type of *jñāna*, distilled, so to speak, out of this meditation. That is why the Upaniṣad says that one should attain the intuition after knowing' (*vijñāya prajñāṁ kurvīta*)[62].

The great Bhartṛprapañca, whom we have already referred to, also holds a similar view. Bhartṛprapañca's conception of Ultimate Reality is that of a unity-in-diversity and hence, according to him, the approach to that Reality must also be of the nature of *samuccaya*. A mere adherence to *karman* means the recognition of diversity alone and not also of the unity that underlies it. For realizing the latter, *jñāna* is essential; so the Reality is attained only by a combination of both. Hence *karman* is not to be discarded but should be performed with a realization of its full significance, i.e., with the enlightenment of *jñāna*, and not blindly. The ignorant takes a limited vision of *karman* (*paricchinnakarmātmadarśinaḥ*), while the enlightened takes a broad view of it (*aparicchinnakarmātmadarśinaḥ*),[63] and that is what distinguishes the two.

All these views draw their inspiration from the Upaniṣads and hence cannot be rejected as false or wrong. There is a kind of knowledge, the knowledge of the intellect or the mind, which always needs to be supplemented by *karman* and which never becomes potent or fruitful except through a long process of meditation. And pertaining to such a kind of knowledge of the intellectual level, the Upaniṣad enjoins meditation after the gaining of the initial knowledge, in order to make it permanent or abiding, or rather to transform the knowledge into a vision, through such statements as *vijñāya prajñāṁ kurvīta* or *ātme 'ty evo 'pāsīta.* In our discussion on *upāsanā* or contemplation we shall have occasion to refer to this kind of knowledge. But it would be wrong to make a sweeping generalization from this that all knowledge is of this nature. There is another unique kind of knowledge, which we may call the knowledge of the soul and hence processless and direct and immediate, that is quite distinct from the previous one. The true Vedāntic wisdom, therefore, recognizes this *samuccaya* in its proper sphere, while at the same time pointing to another level of knowledge where it shines in its own majesty. Sureśvara, therefore rightly says: "We do not reject *samuccaya* everywhere" , because no power on earth can refuse to recognize it in its proper sphere.[64]

The need for meditation is, therefore, admitted practically by all Vedāntins, including the followers of Saṅkara, and even among the latter a difference of opinion is found to prevail on the question, whether it precedes *jñāna* or succeeds it. In order to 'see' or realize the Ātman, so does Vācaspati opine, one must first hear about it from a teacher and get an initial knowledge about it thereby and thereafter strengthen it by reasoning and finally meditate over it. So, according to him, it is *nididhyāsana* or meditation which leads to realization, preceded, of course, by *jñāna* or knowledge gained through *śravaṇa.* But the author of *Pañcapādikā* holds the opposite view. According to him, meditation or *nididhyāsana* is only a contributory aid to the right apprehension of the meaning of the *mahāvākya.* The *pramāṇa* itself needs no direct assistance whatsoever in revealing the *prameya,* which it does, the moment conditions become favourable. Meditation or *nididhyāsana* is thus an indirect aid and precedes *ātmajñāna* instead of succeeding it.[65] It is clear, therefore, that while thinkers like Vācaspati, Maṇḍana and Brahmadatta hold, in one form or another, that the Upaniṣads by themselves cannot introduce us to the true nature of Brahman or Ātman but merely furnish a tentative conception of it and persuade us to discover its actual nature for ourselves, there are others like the authors of *Vivaraṇa* and *Vārttika* who take the *Āgama* or the Upaniṣads as the only means for the direct apprehension of the true nature of the Ātman. In any case, the Vedāntic conception of knowledge, if it is to maintain its uniqueness, must not be conceived as the product of any process, just as the Vedāntic Reality should not be conceived as the final term of a series. If this knowledge becomes a product of meditation, there is nothing at all to distinguish it from the *prajñā* that is gained through *samādhi.* That is why Sureśvara rightly points out, and Anandagiri in his commentary thereon makes explicitly clear, that even *nididhyāsana* which is prescribed by the Upaniṣads, is not a process like meditation (*dhyāna*) and lest there should be a confusion with *dhyāna,* which is very likely, the term *vijñānena* is added. It is an independent knowledge, which only results in utter liberation that is called *nididhyāsana.*[66] This is the final step of *sākṣāt aparokṣāt* as indicated by the Upaniṣads.

Western theories of Truth

Human thought is still in search of a knowledge that will be independent and self-sufficient, absolutely certain and uncontradicted for all times. The different theories of truth in the West, like those of correspondence and coherence, ultimately fail to account for the real criterion of truth. 'The correspondence theory asserts that a judgment is true, if it corresponds with fact. Now the fact is either known or not known. If it is not known, we cannot know that the judgment corresponds with it. If it is known, it is to say the least of it, unnecessary to make a judgment about it.' In other words, 'Either I know directly the fact with which my true judgment is to correspond or I do not. If I know it directly, what need is there for me to pass a true judgment about it, in order that the judgment may correspond with it? If I do not know it directly, how am I to know that my judgment does correspond with it?[67]' Thus an inherent contradiction falsifies the theory of correspondence.

The coherence theory no doubt goes ahead of correspondence in this that it tries to view the truth from a wider perspective with reference to different relations with the whole body of experience, and not merely as an isolated fact. According to this theory, 'conceivability is the essential nature of truth',[68] and 'to be conceivable' means to be a 'significant whole' or a 'whole possessed of meaning for thought'. A 'significant whole' is such that all its constituent elements reciprocally involve one another.'[69] Thus, according to this theory, 'until we know reality as a whole, we can never completely know the truth of any particular judgment,' but this applies inevitably to the coherence theory of truth itself. On its own premises then we can never know that the coherence theory of truth is true. Joachim, therefore, feels that 'a theory of truth as coherence, if it is to be adequate, must be an intelligible account of the ultimate coherence in which the one significant whole is self-revealed'[70], but, at the same time, he frankly admits that every metaphysical theory, as the outcome of experience which is partial and so far finite, is at best a partial manifestation of the truth and not the whole truth *self-revealed'*.[71] In other words, we always know only a part of truth and never the whole of it, and if we do not know the whole of it, the coherence theory can hardly stand. 'The coherence notion of truth may thus be said to suffer shipwreck at the very entrance of the harbour', and 'the voyage ends in disaster, and a disaster which is inevitable'.[72]

Joachim, therefore, ends his illuminating book, 'The Nature of Truth,' with a complete note of scepticism, and with the frank acknowledgment "that no theory of truth as coherence can be completely true; for as a system of judgments, as a piece of discursive knowledge, it must be 'other' than the truth 'about' which it is and thus it must fail of that concrete coherence which is complete truth. And again, as the knowledge of mind at a determinate level of appercipient character, it must fall short of *the complete self-revelation which is absolute truth manifest to itself*[73] (italics mine).

Human knowledge thus essentially suffers from the limitation of incompleteness and hence always remains dubious and uncertain. The note of unknowability, which Kant sounded, still remains the basic note, and rings through all our knowledge. We feel that the complete knowledge of the whole always escapes us. We are knowing more and more of the whole by bits, but cannot seize it all at one stroke. Our knowledge, therefore, always remains uncertain; though a present knowledge is working alright today it may be nullified tomorrow through the discovery of its incoherence within a still greater whole. Jeans makes a profound statement full of the deepest significance in his illuminating book, "Physics and Philosophy". He says: "Now these waves of knowledge exhibit complete determinism; as they roll on, they show us knowledge growing out of knowledge and uncertainty following uncertainty according to a strict causal law. But this tells us nothing we do not already know. *If we had found new knowledge appearing, not out of previous knowledge but spontaneously and of its own accord, we should have come upon something very startling and of profound philosophical significance"* (italics mine).[74] Modern science even after having such a complete and thorough knowledge of the workings of Nature finds that its knowledge is full of uncertainty and to its surprise, it also finds that what it has learnt so far is nothing new or unique. Hence all are looking forward to a new type of knowledge, which must be spontaneous in its nature, as well as self-revealed and appearing of its own accord. That only such a kind of knowledge can lift human thought from the sphere of relativity and uncertainty is felt both by Joachim and Jeans, and that is why the former uses the term 'self-revealed' again and again, (which we have italicised in the quotations from him) and speaks of 'absolute truth manifest to itself' Otherwise, there is no escape from a total scepticism or a complete denial of an absolute truth as is done by pragmatists.

The Upaniṣadic View of Knowledge

It is just here that the Upaniṣads come to our aid to lift us out of this hopeless position into which all our theories of knowledge or truth ultimately land us. The Upaniṣadic or Vedāntic view of knowledge, we have pointed out, is rooted in *svataḥpramāṇa* or *svayaṁprakāśa,* i.e. self-revelation or self-luminosity. The 'self-revealed' knowledge, which Joachim vaguely apprehends as the only possible solution of the baffling problem, is recognized as the very fundamental fact of all experience in Vedānta. The very definition of *pramā* shows that, according to the Vedānta, the truth of knowledge consists in its non-contradictedness and novelty (*abādhitatva* and *anadhigatatva*),[75] and not in mere correspondence or coherence. A knowledge works as true only in so far as it is not contradicted. In the sphere of our relative knowledge there is no guarantee that the truth of a knowledge will not be contradicted in any place or time. Hence what we ordinarily call *pramā* or true knowledge is only *pramā* by courtesy. The really non-contradicted knowledge or *pramā* is the knowledge of the Absolute or the Ātman or Brahman. All other knowledge that goes by the name of *pramā* is so, in so far as it reveals this non-contradictedness of the self-manifest knowledge, or rather partakes of its nature. All else is true by virtue of this absolute truth, as all else is real by virtue of the supremely real. It is the same self-manifest truth, the *svayaṁprakāśa,* that is revealed at the level of the senses as correspondence between the knower and the known, *pramātṛ* and *prameya* and again at the level of the mind as coherence or harmony of experience or *saṁvāda.* But it shines in its completeness as absolute non-contradictedness only at the level of the spirit or the level of the *sākṣāt aparokṣāt.* The knowledge of the complete system of experience or the entire whole, which alone can make the theory of coherence plausible, can come only when one transcends the system. In order to know the whole one must pass beyond the whole. The whole cannot be known by a mere aggregation of the parts, for that only leads to an approximation, and never attains finality. Hence the Upaniṣads point to a unique processless type of knowledge which takes the cognizer at one bound beyond the sphere of the whole and gets him established in the transcendental sphere. It is only on reaching this sphere that one becomes assured of absolute non-contradictedness. Hence *tattvajñāna* or 'metaphysical knowledge essentially implies permanent and changeless certitude'.[76]

Thus a bold leap is necessary in order to get the transcendental apprehension of Reality, and the supreme value of the Upaniṣads lies in this that they alone make this leap possible. The jump is taken only from the springboard of the *mahāvākyas* of the Upaniṣads. No other *pramāṇa* is of any help here except the Word or *Śabda* because, as we have already pointed out in our exposition of Yājñavalkya's description of the different lights or sources of illumination, the light of *Vāc* or the Word comes nearest to the light of the Ātman. The function of the Word or *śabda* is to point to this final light and then to go out, or retire. This pointing or suggesting is the peculiar virtue of the *śabda* or word and it is by this power of suggestion that the word transcends itself and carries one beyond its own bounds. But this suggestiveness of a word does not occur to all or is rather not caught by all, but is grasped only by one who has a keen mind, a refined intellect and who has dwelt over the problem long enough. The fall of an apple is a common event observed by all, but it was only to the mind of Newton that this all too common a fact of experience revealed the whole law of gravitation, and that was because his mind had been working all the time ceaselessly over the problem and the event just became an occasion for the final flash of revelation. Similarly the *mahāvākyas* of the Upaniṣads bring the revelation only to a mind that is seized wholly by this one passion for the supreme knowledge.

In this sense, therefore, *nididhyāsana* must precede the true revelation or knowledge, and should not succeed it. But if one, without the adequate passion for knowledge and refinement of intellect, happens to hear the *mahāvākya,* then he will certainly miss the true revelation and will be furnished merely with a tentative conception or knowledge of Reality, and in that case, *nididhyāsana* must follow *jñāna.* Thus the conceptions of the *jñāna* are different in the two cases, viz. in one case it is true revelation and in the other a mere tentative cognition, and the precedence or succession of meditation depends on the particular conception which one happens to hold about *jñāna.* In any case, the *mahāvākya* is indispensably necessary for the supreme revelation, whether it dawns all at once from the mere hearing or after a long meditation. The *manana* or *nididhyāsana* which is done independently of *śravaṇa* (i.e., without a basis of the *mahāvākyas*) is of no use whatsoever in the realization of the Ātman.

This is no dogmatism or a supercession of reason by authority to state that the words of the *Sruti* must be taken as the basis for all reasoning and meditation; a deeper reason lies behind the acceptance of *Śruti* as the starting-point of enquiry. As Prof Bhattacharya beautifully puts it: "Some provisional belief (*śraddhā*) is required to start the enquiry. A mere thought, even though necessary, can never induce belief, can never be mistaken for knowledge; for in knowledge there is an unmistakeable intuitive or 'given' character. This provisional belief can only be induced by authoritative statement (*śabda* or *āgama*) which may, for aught we know, be disproved afterwards. But the statement gains in reliability if on acting on it or after contemplation of it we attain a progressive *satisfaction* or *realization.* That is the only justification which we may expect to have of the truth of what is claimed to be revelation, from below, i.e., before we have finally realized its truth".[77] That is why Śaṅkara states that in the enquiry about Brahman, the *Śrutis* alone are not the *pramāṇa* as in *dharmajijñāsā,* but here *Śrutis* as well as the experiences or realizations are the *pramāṇa,* because the knowledge of Brahman ends in realization and pertains to a real object.[78] Thus the culmination (*avasāna*) of all *pramāṇas* or means of knowledge is in experience (*anubhava*) and hence the *Śrutis* are not accepted blindly but verified by experience.

Solution of the problem

Thus experience being the very basis of *brahmajñāna,* the question of the unknowability of Brahman does not arise at all. But this experience is not an ordinary experience of the sense or the mind, it is the supreme and unique experience of the soul. As in the discussion of the problem of Reality we pointed out that the Upaniṣadic conception of transcendence does not signify an exclusion or aloofness but only an *uniqueness* (*vilakṣaṇatā*), so here the conception of transcendental knowledge similarly signifies an *unique* type of knowledge, which flashes 'spontaneously and of its own accord' and is not exclusively an intellectual process, as is generally supposed. As the Reality or the *prameya,* so the means of knowledge or the *pramāṇa.* The transcendental or unique Reality needs a transcendental or unique mode of apprehension, and once this mode of apprehension is present, the object, that is Brahman, is automatically revealed, just as with the opening of the eyes the physical objects arc bound to be perceived, and here also lies its spontaneity. Similarly in order to seize the immanent Reality that is Prāṇa, which is by its very nature an unity-in-difference (*'mithuna'*) a method of apprehension is needed which also must be of a similar nature i.e., a combination of *jñāna* and *karman.* Lastly, when the Reality is viewed as utterly separate and distinct, as absolutely an 'other', then the method too becomes distinctly separative, like our ordinary perception. The Upaniṣads, therefore, in offering their solution to the problem of knowledge, do not exclude all the other modes of knowledge but recognize each at its own level, the *āditya, the candra,* the *agni* and the *vāc* and finally transcend them all through the conception of the self-luminous light of the Ātman, by which all others are lighted.

References

1. tam evai 'kaṁ jānatha anyā vāco vimuñcatha. MU, 2.2.5.
2. amṛtasyai 'ṣa setuḥ. Ibid.
3. tam eva viditvā 'timṛtyum eti nā 'nyaḥ panthā vidyate ayanāya. ŚU, 3.8.
4. tam akratuḥ paśyati. KTU, 1.2.20.
5. dṛśyate tv agrayā buddhyā, KTU, 1.3.12.
6. ātmā vā 're draṣṭavyaḥ. BU, 2,4.5.
7. āvṛttacakṣuh. KTU, 2.1.1.
8. na cakṣuṣā paśyati kaścanai 'nam. KTU, 2.3.9.
9. BU, 2.4.14.
10. avijñātaṁ vijāṇatāṁ vijñātam avijānatām. KU. 11.
11. pratibodhaviditaṁ matam amṛtatvaṁ hi vindate, KU, 12.
12. CE, p. 186.
13. Ibid.
14. Ibid.
15. kramānanurodhi sputaḥ prajñālokaḥ. VB, on YS, 1.47.
16. VB, on YS, 1.43.

17. Ibid.
18. YS, 1.43.
19. sarvavişayaṁ sarvathāvişayam akramam. Ibid. 3.54.
20. nirodhasthitikālakramānubhavena. VB, on YS, 1.51.
21. vyutthānanirodhasaṁskārayor abhibhavaprādurbhāvau. YS, 3.9.
22. abhijātasye 'va maṇeḥ, YS, 1.41.
23. IHD, pp. 116-7.
24. Ibid. p. 117.
25. TDI, p. 8.
26. Ibid. p. 34.
27. NPW, p. 322.
28. IHD, p. 168.
29. SIV, p. 53.
30. Ibid.
31. Tattadindriyayogyavartamānavişayāvacchinnacaitanyābhinnatvaṁ tattadākāravṛttyavacchinnajñānasya tattadaṁśe pratyakṣatvam. VP, p. 34.
32. SWK, pp. 77-8.
33. Ibid. p, 86.
34. Ibid. pp. 86-7.
35. BU, 4.3.
36. KTU, 2.2.15.
37. yan manasā na manute, KU, 5.
38. manasai 've dam āptavyam. KTU, 2.1.11.
39. SWK, p. 137.
40. BU, 4.3.
41. nityamuktatvavijñānaṁ vākyād bhavati nā 'nyataḥ. NS, 4.31.
42. STV, p. 59.
43. Sakṛtpravṛttyā mṛdnāti kriyākārakarūpabhṛd ajñānam āgamajñānam. NS, 1.67.
44. BU, 2.36, 5.4.7; CU, 1.4.2. KU, 29.30. KTU, 6.2. ŚU, 4.4. etc.
45. NRDR, pp. 10-11.
46. upāyajālaṁ na śivaṁ prakāśayed ghaṭena kiṁ bhāti sahasradīdhitiḥ/vivecayann ittham udāradarśanas svayaṁprakāśaṁ śivam āviśet kṣaṇāt. //TS, p. 9.
47. upāyair na śivo bhāti bhānti te tatprasādatas
sa evā 'haṁ svaprakāśo bhāse viśvasvarūpakaḥ/
ity ākarṇya guror vākyaṁ sakṛt kecana niścitā
vinā bhūyo'nusandhānaṁ bhānti saṁvinmayās sthitāḥ.
TL, p. 3.
48. KTU, 1.2.8.
49. Ibid. 1.2.7.
50. uttiṣṭhata jāgrata prāpya varān nivodhata. KTU, 1.3.14.
51. NPW, p. 322.
52. NPW, p. 322.
53. Ibid. p. 336.
54. Ibid. p. 337.
55. brahmātmaikatvavijñānam avidyām ātmani sthitām./
sakṛjjātaṁ na ced dhanti jñānam eva na tad bhavet.// VS,
56. kriyāyā gandhamātrasyā 'nupraveśa iha no'papadyate. ŚB, on VS, 1.1.4.
57. alaṅkāro hy ayam asmākaṁ yad brahmātmāvagatau satyāṁ sarvakartavyatāhāniḥ kṛtakṛtyatā ce'ti. ŚB, Ibid.
58. dūram ete viparīte viṣūcī avidyā yā ca vidye 'ti jñeyā, KTU, 1.2.4.

59. IU, II.
60. KTU, 1.2.4.
61. kecit sampradāyabalāvaṣṭambhād āhuryad etad vedāntavākyād ahaṁ brahme'ti vijñānaṁ samutpadyate, tan nai 'va svotpattimātreṇā 'jñānaṁ nirasyati. kiṁ tarhi? ahany ahani drāghīyasā kāleno'pāsīnasya sato bhāvanopacayān niśśeṣam apagaccati. NS, 1.67.
62. NS. 1.67.
63. ŚB on BU, 1.4.15.
64. na ca vayaṁ jñānakarmaṇoṣ sarvatrai 'va samuccayaṁ pratyācakṣmahe. yatra prayojyaprayojakabhāvo jñānakarmaṇos tatra nā' smatpitrā 'pi śakyate nivārayitum. NS, 1.58.
65. manananididhyāsanayor na brahmāvagatyuttarakālīnatā kiṅtu śravaṇavad avagatyupāyatayā pūrvakālatai 'va. PP. p. 99.
66. dhyānāśaṅkānivṛttyarthaṁ vijñāneṇe 'ti bhaṇyate. Vār, 2.4. 234. yan muktimātraphalaṁ svatantraṁ jñānaṁ tad eva nidihyāsanaṁ smṛtam. Ānandagiri on Ibid.
67. Joad : GP, p. 67.
68. Joachim : NT< p. 66.
69. Ibid.
70. Ibid. p. 170.
71. Ibid. p. 171.
72. Ibid.
73. Ibid. p. 178.
74. PHP, p. 195.
75. pramātvam anadhigatābādhitārthaviṣaya-jñānatvam. VP, p. 5.
76. IHD, p. 114.
77. SIV, p. 51.
78. na dharmajijñāsāyām iva śrutyādaya eva pramāṇaṁ brahmajijñāsāyām. kintu śrutyādayo 'nubhavādayaś ca yathāsambhavam iha pramāṇam anubhavāvasānatvād bhūtavastuviṣayatvāc ca brahmajñānasya. ŚB on VS, 1.1.2.

PART II
The Way

CHAPTER III

THE PREPARATION

We have found in our discussion of the problem of Knowledge that a transcendental mode of apprehension alone can seize the transcendental Reality. This mode is the mode of direct and immediate revelation, which is indicated by the famous dictum of the Upaniṣads: *ātmā vā 're draṣṭavyaḥ, śrotavyo mantavyo nididhyāsitavyaḥ*[1]. This is the way of *nivodhata* as distinguished from the way of *upāsīta* or *dhyāyatha*, as already pointed out. But about this way, the Upaniṣad warns that it is sharp as a razor's edge, hard to cross and difficult to tread'.[2] In other words, the straight and direct approach to the Supreme is full of great risk and open only to the exceptionally proficient seekers. 'Though there is in truth a door which leads from every house, even from the most ephemeral tenement, straight into It, yet it is a door which few can see and fewer open'.[3] Hence the Upaniṣads, being fully aware of the difficulties involved in this straight way of soaring flight or 'the Way of the Eagle', go on to propound a less hazardous circular way or 'the Way of the Ant', where one can move slowly but steadily upwards through gradual stages. This circular or spiral way is symbolized by the great *Oṅkāra*, which is furnished as the supreme support or *ālambana,* by holding on to which one may mount slowly higher and higher. Hence Vidyāranya rightly says that if that supreme consciousness does not become fixed or abiding, one must contemplate through the *praṇava or Oṅkāra.*[4] The Upaniṣads, therefore, after pointing to the hazardous way, *durgaṁ pathaḥ* show the other subtle way, *aṇuḥ pantbāḥ,*[5] but even this subtle way cannot be treaded by all. Only he can move along this way, who has already journeyed through the preliminary path of good actions, *panthās sukṛtasya.*[6] We must, therefore, begin with the *sukṛtasya panthāḥ* before taking the subtle road, *aṇuḥ panthāḥ.* In the former path or way we have a transformation of conduct and character, while in the latter, that of consciousness. We have called, for our convenience, the former path or the preliminary path as 'Preparation', and the latter as 'Contemplation'.

The Need of a Teacher

The first necessity to get on the way is to have a guide, who can lead and direct.[7] So the Upaniṣad instructs the seeker to go to the *Guru* for the special knowledge, first of all,[8] for only he can take him to the other shore beyond all darkness.[9] 'Only he who has an *Ācārya* can have the knowledge,[10] 'Only the knowledge derived from the *Ācārya* leads to the supreme goal',[11] 'Only the *Ācārya* can instruct you about the way,[12] 'Only he can know who has been taught or enlightened by a proficient teacher.[13]—thus the Upaniṣads speak again and again. The enlightenment can be had from one who is himself really enlightened and no knowledge is possible about this supreme wonder of wonders if one is instructed by somebody else, who is an inexperienced babbler.[14]

The seeker, on getting the true type of teacher, wants to have all his problems solved by him, because he does not want to let go this supreme opportunity of his life as he sits face to face with a profoundly illuminating teacher. Thus we find in the *Kaṭhopaniṣad* that Naciketas, who represents the true type of seeker, rejects all the tempting offers made to him by Yama to prevent him from making the supreme enquiry and adheres to his original enquiry about the ultimate nature of things, because he knows that he would not have such a teacher to reveal the supreme mystery.[15] The teacher is conceived as one part (*purvarūpam*) to whom the other part or counterpart (*uttararūpam*) is the disciple and their union (*sandhi*) leads to the production of *Vidyā.*[16] So in the very *śāntipāṭha* of the *Kathopaniṣad,* we find the prayer for the joint protection, and enjoyment of the teacher and the taught, whereby they may both endeavour conjointly (*saha vīryaṁ karavāvahai*) which will make their study really luminous or powerful (*tejasvin*). To generate this *tejas,* light or power, one had to betake oneself to the teacher, and in this matter the Upaniṣads do not enjoin a mcrc casual visit to him for an occasional enlightenment but asks the seeker to confine himself to the society of the teachers, rather to live in the very family of the teacher absolutely for a long time.[17] The student or seeker also prays : 'Kindly get me to the family of the teachers'.[18] It is only by living in close touch with the teacher for a long time, by becoming an *antevāsin,* a co-inhabitant that the knowledge can be expected to dawn. The teacher also instructs only that seeker, who has taken refuge in him in the proper way.[19]

About the method of approaching the teacher there is one essential feature which one finds depicted again and again in the Upaniṣads. It is the time-old custom of becoming *samitpāṇi*[20] or taking the fuel in the hand while visiting a teacher for knowledge and enlightenment. It is a very suggestive symbol, which reminds the seeker that he has come to the teacher to really kindle the flame that burns all ignorance and dispels all darkness. The aim should not be mere book-learning or *jñāna* but a deep and comprehensive knowledge of the Supreme Reality (*tadvijñānārtham*). This symbol of *samitpāṇi* also enjoins upon the seeker the duty of collecting fuel or wood daily for the teacher. It means that while he confines himself absolutely to the home or family of the teacher, his sole occupation is the gathering or collection of materials for lighting the fire. This period of collection is the first stage in the Upaniṣadic way to Supreme, which we have termed as the stage of preparation.

The period of training or Bràhmacarya

The general name for this period of collection in the Upaniṣadic terminology is *brahmacarya.* This collection means a conservation or gathering of forces which alone makes possible the supreme recollection, which leads ultimately to revelation. 'This Ātman can never be realized by one who is devoid of strength', warns the Upaniṣad.[21] To gain strength one must conserve, and that is why the term *brahmacarya* has come to signify specifically continence or preservation of the sex-energy. And so another Upaniṣad while delineating the means of getting the realization of the Ātman mentions *'dhātuprasāda'* or equilibrium of the humors as an essential requirement.[22] Wherever we look into the Upaniṣads we never miss this term when we find the seers speaking about the means of realization: 'Seeking that, one takes recourse to *brahmacarya.*'[23], 'The Ātman is to be sought by *tapas, brahmacarya* etc.'[24], 'This Ātman is attainable by eternal *brahmacarya*'[25] and so on. In all the anecdotes in the Upaniṣads we find that whenever a seeker comes for enlightenment he is enjoined to go through a period of *brahmacarya* first before he hopes to get further instructions. Thus Upakosala, we hear, carried on *brahmacarya*[26] before he obtained the knowledge, Śvetaketu was asked to go on with *brahmacarya,*[27] Indra and Virocana spent thirty-two years in *brahmacarya*[28] before they were initiated. And even the seers who were *brahmaparā brahmaniṣṭhāḥ,* absolutely devoted to the supreme quest, *paraṁ brahma anveṣamāṇāḥ,*[29] had to wait for a whole year observing *brahmacarya* before they were instructed by the great sage Pippalāda.

This method was followed by the Upaniṣadic sages because they knew that without proper conservation of energy, no retention of the imparted knowledge is possible. To hold the supreme essence, the vehicle must be made fit. Thus in the *Taittirīya Upaniṣad,* in the very opening of the *Śikṣāvallī* we find the prayer : 'May my body be immaculate. May I be fit to hold the immortal essence'.[30] Indra, the master of rhythms, is invoked to sprinkle or shower *medhā* or diligence on the seeker.[31] In the opening (*Śāntipāṭha*) of the *Kena Upaniṣad*, before the actual study begins, a prayer is uttered to refresh and fill all the different senses with divine strength.[32] In the *Praśna Upaniṣad, Prāṇa* is asked to give *śrī* and *prajñā* to the seeker.[33] Only after one is filled with supreme strength then alone the instruction begins, for otherwise if the seeker lacks the capacity to hold the truth, he will miss the entire teaching. The main thing which will lead to the final release is a constant remembrance of the Supreme. This is what is called *dhruvā smṛti* by the Upaniṣad.[34] To constantly remember, to maintain a continuous flow of the same consciousness is the very basic meaning of *Upāsanā.* When one gets this continuity or straight and unhampered flow of an identical consciousness then all the knots are untied,[35] for the continuous flow itself shows that the clogging factors which give rise to the knots (*granthi*) have been removed.

The arresting of the continuous flow comes through dirt or impurity. So the Upaniṣad prescribes *'sattva-śuddhi'* for getting *dhruvā smṛti.*[36] This *sattva-śuddhi* means the purity of the whole being and so all the parts which make up our personality must be rendered pure. The purity or impurity of our psycho-physical make-up depends on the nature of things we take in and assimilate. The quality of the food we take determines the healthy or unhealthy nature of our body. So to keep the body healthy we must consume the food that is pure. Similarly to get the purity and health of our inner being, we must first take note of the nature of food or nourishment that we are giving to it. This is what is meant by *āhāra-śuddhi*[37] in the Upaniṣad and which is shown to be the only primary step that leads to the later state of *sattva-śuddhi.* The term *āhāra* here has a wider connotation than mere eating and signifies *āhāraṇa* or gathering, i.e. intake of things.[38] So the first duty of a seeker is to make his *āhāra* pure i.e. he must first discriminate between what is good and bad and then take a vow or resolve to take the good things alone and refuse the bad ones that corrupt his system. This intake of things or *āhāra* is done not by the mouth alone but by all the different senses. It is through the door of the senses that the things of the world enter into us. So all the senses are to be cleansed and thereby prepared to welcome or take in the beneficial things alone, which will be conducive to our spiritual health and well-being, and. refuse to enjoy any other thing that leads to a deterioration of the system or structure and is detrimental to it. In the prefatory prayer in the *Praśnopaniṣad* we find this clearly stated: 'Let us hear by our ears only the good or the beneficial (word), and by our eyes behold the good alone. Thus with an equilibrium of all our limbs or parts we shall be enjoying a divine life while pleasing the gods with prayer'.[39] By training our eyes, ears etc. to attend to the good things alone, we get a calm disposition of our being. An equilibrium in all the part is established thereby and this equilibrium of the senses is termed as *yoga* in the Upaniṣad,[40] while the training which leads to this equilibrium is called *brahmacarya* or *yajña.* 'What is called *yajña* is nothing but *brahmacarya*'[41] runs the Upaniṣad. In another Upaniṣad, man himself is identified with *yajña,*[42] and the different periods of a man's life are conceived as the different oblations which are offered in the morning, the mid-day and the evening.

Significance of Yajña

Yajña thus symbolizes the period of purification. The *Chāndogya Upaniṣad* clearly states this significance of *yajña* in the following line : 'Because it purifies all this, therefore this alone is *yajña.*'[43] So *yajña* cleanses or purifies the doors of our perception and thereby brings an order and harmony in an otherwise aimless and disordered life. It draws a boundary line in a hitherto unbounded field of life, instils a purpose or aim in all our actions, to the fulfilment of which we must strive and strain. It is *yajña* which distinguishes man from the animal, for the animal is guided by blind impulses alone, while for man *yajña* ushers in the enlightened reign of reason, which he may utilise for his benefit or walk his own reckless way if he so chooses. Man has this choice before him which the animal does not have. This is the unique privilege of man.

Śreyas and Preyas

Here lies his freedom: in the choice between impulse and reason, passion and prudence, *preyas* and *śreyas.* 'One is *śreyas* (the good), the other is *preyas* (the pleasant); they both try to bind man with different purposes. But of them, he who chooses the *śreyas* is wise and he who courts *preyas* loses his purpose'.[44] The criterion of a true seeker is that he never falls a prey to the allurements of *preyas* or the pleasant. Most people sink in this stream of the pleasantry. Thus with the choice of the *śreyas* begins the life of the spirit and that is why Yama opens his spiritual discourse with this topic of *śreyas and preyas* and extols Naciketas as the true type of seeker because he has refused to be tempted by the offers of *preyas* and has instead exihibited his steadfast attention to the *śreyas* alone. As one should resolve to tread on the right path of *śreyas,* so must he promise to quit the evil way of *preyas,* for one cannot walk on both ways together. The old track must be quitted first before the new road can be taken. In similar and almost identical terms the great mystic Plotinus utters a warning: 'He, I say, will not behold this light, who attempts to ascend to the vision of the Supreme while he is drawn downwards by those things which are an impediment to the vision.'[46] Hence as the Upaniṣads ask the seeker to observe *brahmacarya,* follow the truth, perform *tapas* and so on in a positive manner, they similarly point out in a negative way the things to be desisted from or avoided. 'None can attain this (Ātman) unless he has ceased to rcvcl in the evil ways of life, unless he is calm and concentrated and his mind tranquil'.[47] 'He who does not carry on a vow should not (be allowed to) read this (*brahmavidyā*).'[48] 'One who is devoid of reason, (*avijñānavān*) of uncontrolled mind and ever impure (*amanaskas sadā aśuciḥ*) can never attain this status (*padam*) but only goes down in *saṁsāra*'[49].

Kratu or Resolution

Thus this period of preparation consists of two elements: the acquirement or acceptance of the good and the rejection of the evil ways and things. This must be taken as a vow or resolve. That is why the term '*kratu*' has an important bearing in the Upaniṣads. '*Kratu*' primarily means firm resolve and secondarily sacrifice or *yajña.* 'A man is made of *kratu'* says the Upaniṣad[50], i.e. as his resolution so is his evolution. A right resolve makes a right man. To insert the right resolve, to instil the holy desire in the heart, the Upaniṣads use the strongest imperatives, as we shall presently find while discussing the premilinary virtues to be acquired. 'Therefore he must do *kratu*'[51], asks the Upaniṣad. Another Upaniṣad asks the resolving faculty of man, at the time of his last breath, to remember and take into account of what he had done or accomplished (*kṛtam smara*)[52], because only the thing he had passionately desired and sought with his whole being in life will determine his post-mortem state of existence, and future embodiment.

Thus we find that *brahmacarya* has been identified with *yajña* and *yajna,* or *kratu* is esssentially composed, of a right vow or resolve. This vow has been called the *śirovrata* in one Upaniṣad[53]. It means the carrying of the fire on the head. The fire symbolizes reason or wisdom; and therefore to constantly carry the fire on the head means to be constantly guided by reason alone. So it becomes clear now that the approach to the teacher, with which the *brahmavidyā* begins, signifies the assent of the seeker to be guidcd by the superior reason embodied in the teacher, and the preparatory period of *brahmacarya* begins with a vow to abide by the instructions of the teacher who represents the voice of reason and thereby reject the evil promptings of impulse. In this way, by strictly following the guidance of reason, one gathers strength, *vīrya* or *bala,* without which the Ātman cannot be realized. The impulses bring distraction and from distraction comes diffusion of energy which gradually results in waste, draining away of all strength. So conservation is the first essential condition to stop this waste, and with conservation comes recollection. Patañjali in his system of Yoga rightly shows the gradual steps when he speaks of *smṛti* or recollection following from *virya* or conservation of energy or strength. The ultimate aim is *prajñā* or right knowledge. But right knowledge can never dawn without *samādhi* or absorption, and *samādhi* can hardly come without *smṛti* or constant recollection. For this *smṛti, vīrya* or conservation is essential.[54] This conservation must be absolute and total. The waste has to be stopped all around. So one must know in detail the virtues one has to cultivate in order to gather strength. Let us try to find out what the Upaniṣads enjoin in this respect, i.e. the necessary observances for the preparatory period.

Satyam or Truth

In the *Śiksāvalli* of the *Taittirīya Upaniṣad* we find some instructions peremptorily given to the students or seekers. The very first instruction is: 'Speak the truth'.[55] Truth is the very basis or foundation of the Upaniṣads and the *Kena Upaniṣad* expressly declares it.[56] By first becoming truthful in speech, we can gradually hope to be truthful in spirit. The initiation in the life of the spirit begins with the cultivation of truth. 'On what is initiation based? On truth,' answers the Upaniṣad.[57] 'Therefore is the initiated asked to speak the truth because in truth is the initiation based. On what is truth based? On the heart, it was replied. By the heart is truth known, therefore in the heart alone is truth based.'[58] This passage is significant as it makes clear the source or basis of truth. *Hṛdaya* and *buddhi* have been identified in many places in the Upaniṣads, as we shall find in our discussion about the *dahara-vidyā;* so, by saying that truth is based on the heart, the seer is hinting that the *buddhi* or reason is the true home or abode of truth. By adhering to truth in speech we gradually get established in reason and consequently there remains nothing irrational or impulsive in our nature. It is truth which is at the root of creation and the world of unreality or falsehood is really sustained by truth alone. 'In the beginning were the waters; they created truth, truth created Brahman, Brahman the Prajāpati, Prajāpati the Devas or Gods; those gods worship Truth alone-these three letters—'sa', 'ti' and 'yam.' The first and the last letters are truth, in the middle is the falsehood. Therefore this unreality or falsehood is sustained on both sides by truth.'[59]

The supreme value that is attached to truth is also made clear through the famous story of Satyakāma Jābāla. Satyakāma was uncertain about his *gotra* or lineage and when he resolved to go in for a period of *brahmacarya* he wanted to ascertain it correctly from his mother Jabālā. She replied that she herself was ignorant about his *gotra* because in her youth she was much too busy in serving many people and as such had no opportunity to ascertain his *gotra.* 'I do not know what family or *gotra* you belong to. My name is Jabālā and your name is Satyakāma. Therefore call yourself only as Satyakāma Jābāla.' He went to Hāridrumata Gautama and said, 'I shall observe *brahmacarya* under you and so have approached you.' Gautama asked, 'What is your family, O gentle one?' He replied, 'I do not know it, I asked my mother about it but she replied that she had got me while serving many men and hence she knew not what was my *gotra* or family. I am simply Satyakāma Jābāla.' Then the Ṛṣi said, 'Not a non-Brāhmin can speak like this (i.e. such fearless expression of truth is possible only for a Brāhmin). Bring wood, I shall initiate you as you did not flinch from truth.'[60] This clearly depicts that truth and truth alone was counted as the supreme qualification for discipleship.

Again we find a reference to a novel method of finding out a real culprit by giving in his hand a heated axe. If he is a liar and tries to conceal his guilt he will be burnt by it and later killed for his crime. But if he has not perpetrated the act and is truthful (*satyābhisandhaḥ*) then even if he takes hold of the heated axe he will not be burnt and then will be released.[61] Thus whether in determining the fitness of a disciple or in detecting the real culprit, the standard of judgment always was fidelity to truth in the Upaniṣadic age. 'One is dried from the very roots if he tells a lie' is the express opinion of the seer in the Upaniṣad.[62] So concealment and deception were things unknown to seers of old. While instructing others, they never kept anything concealed, and taught only that much about whose truth there was not a shadow of doubt in them. They never taught or talked about a thing beyond their range of experience. Their whole conduct is truth (*ṛṣīṇāṁ caritam satyam*),[63] because they knew that in order to reach the supreme status of truth (*satyasya paramaṁ nidhānam*) one must tread the celestial way (*devayāna*) and that way is made wide by truth (*satyena panthā vitato*).[64] The *Praśna Upaniṣad* declares: 'They alone attain this *brahmaloka* who have performed *tapas* and *brahmacarya,* in whom is the truth established'; 'Theirs is that pure *brahmaloka* in whom there is no crookedness, falsehood or deception.'[65] Thus truth is a standard of judgment, a rule of conduct and a means for the attainment of the highest world.

Dharma or the true Law of Life

Along with the cultivation of truth in speech, one must also tread the path of *dharma.*[66] As *satya* is a quality of *vacana* or speech ,(*vada*), so *dharma* is a matter for *ācaraṇa* or conduct (*cara*). Dharma is thus the actualization of truth. The *Bṛhadāraṇyaka Upaniṣad* says: 'What is *dharma* is verily truth; therefore when one speaks the truth he is said to be speaking *dharma* (i.e. rightly) or when one tells *dharma* he is said to be telling the truth'.[67] Thus these two are inter-changeable terms. In the Vedic terminology it is *ṛta* or the right law or norm of conduct. What the supreme vision reveals as *satya* is sought to be expressed in action as *ṛta or dharma.* As one knows, so must he act. If one knows the truth, he must act in the right manner. If he acts wrongly, his knowledge of truth is merely a pretension. Action and thought must be brought to a harmony, and then *dharma* will be established.

Dharma is not religion or virtue as it is generally understood or translated. *Dharma* is the basic or inherent nature of a thing which sustains it. To transgress *dharma* is to forfeit one's own existence. According to our scriptures, *dharma* is comprised of two things: *abhyudaya* and *niśśreyasa.* To grow and prosper and then to have complete freedom or release from the fetters of life is the goal of *dharma.* So the essential meaning of *dharma,* i.e. its definition is *'codanā'* i.e. the incentive or inspiration to all actions. The inspiration must come always from the highest centre. One must be spurred to action by the command from above and not by the promptings of the lower nature, which leads one to *adharma.* Every action should thus be inspired by a noble purpose, and this is the significance of the command to act according to dharma (*dharmaṁ cara*).[68]

Tapas or Force of Concentration

After discussing the general nature of *dharma,* let us try to find out, if possible, some specific acts of *dharma* enjoined by the Upaniṣads. The *Chāndogya Upanīṣad* explicitly mentions three constituent elements of *dharma,* viz, *yajña, adhyayana* and *dāna.*[69] *Yajna* generally means sacrifice or the offering of the self. It is a very wide term which generally applies to the whole stage of preparation or purification. We have already seen from a passage in the Upaniṣad that *yajña* has been identified with *brahmacarya.*[70] Here it is said: 'The first (i.e. *yajna*) is nothing but *tapas.'* This term *'tapas'* is met with very frequently in the whole Upaniṣadic literature. *Tapas* primarily means heat, that is why *tapas* plays an important part in the process of creation, We hear that the Supreme, when He desired to create (*akāmayata*), found Himself tired and then performed *tapas* (*tapo atapyata*), and from Him, tired and then heated through *tapas* (*taptasya*), glory and energy sprang out.[71] In the Vedic description of creation, too, we find a similar reference to *tapas.* 'From enkindled *tapas, ṛta* and *satya* were born'.[72] Thus *tapas* means the supreme force or energy, the primal heat which produces the universe, or is rather at the root of creation.

So in going back to the source of creation one has again to take recourse to *tapas.* 'Enquire about Brahman through *tapas. Tapas* is verily Brahman.'[73] The intenser the *tapas* grows, the brighter comes the revelation. Thus Bhṛgu, by higher and higher *tapas,* came to know by stages the different forms of Brahman, beginning from *anna* or matter right upto *Ānanda* or Bliss. *Tapas* with its primary meaning of force, thereafter came to mean forcible endurance of afflictions, i.e. penance. Such austerities or self-inflicted mortifications generate a heat or force, which ultimately purifies the soul. By denying to the self all forms of sense enjoyment, one gathers the force which is generally frittered away in trivial enjoyments. This force or heat helps to slacken or soften the otherwise hardened encrustations lying heavily on the soul. Heat causes things to expand and so the heat of *tapas* expands the soul by releasing it from its small and narrow existence. Patanjali, too, while delineating *kriyāyoga,* which is the primary requisite of *samādhi* yoga, mentions *tapas* first, and Vyāsa, in opening his commentary thereon, says that success in yoga cannot come to one who has no *tapas.*[74] Only by cleansing the cloth first, one should think of dyeing it. To dye an unclean cloth is to disfigure it and make it uglier still. This primary work of cleaning is done through *tapas* and that is called *yajña* here, which forms an integral part of *dharma.*

Sri Aurobindo makes the conception of *tapas* clear in a remarkable note on that particular term, which we reproduce here: "Tapas means literally heat, afterwards any kind of energism, askesis, austerity of conscious-force acting upon itself or its object. The world was created by *tapas* in the form, says the ancient image, of an egg, which being broken, again by *tapas,* heat of incubation of conscious force, the Purusha emerged, soul in Nature, like a bird from the egg. It may be observed that the usual translation of the *word 'tapasyā'* in English books, 'penance', is quite misleading—the idea of penance entered rarely into the austerities practised by Indian ascetics. Nor was mortification of the body the essence even of the most severe and self-afflicting austerities; the aim was rather an overpassing of the hold of the bodily nature on the consciousness or else a supernormal energising of the consciousness and will to gain some spiritual or other object."[75]

Svādhyāya or Study

The next constituent of *dharma* is *adhyayana* or study. We have seen that the preparatory stage begins with the approach to the *Guru* or *Ācārya.* The approach is made in order to have knowledge, and to have knowledge, study must be prosecuted unremittingly. 'Do not be unmindful to your studies' warns the Upaniṣad.[76] Along with the cultivation of other virtues, *svādhyāya* and *pravacana,* study and teaching must go on without any interruption, because study is the sole occupation or pursuit of the student. So the *Taittirīya Upanisad* mentions all the different virtues, *ṛta, satya, tapas, etc.* separately and attaches to each of them the term *svādhyāyapravacane ca,* thereby showing that this is the common and indispensable factor in the list of virtues.[77] If one acquires other virtues to the neglect of studies, then all those virtues will be of no avail to him, because mere acquirement of virtues is not the goal but real illumination is the aim of all these preparations. This illumination can never be had without absolutely devoting oneself to studies to the exclusion of everything else. Therefore it cannot be dispensed with in any case, even when one is acquiring other virtues.

But mere study by oneself, or *svādhyāya* does not make the knowledge sure or secure. So *pravacana* also must be undertaken, *adhyāpana* must also be practised and not *adhyayana* alone. By *pravacana* or teaching, one not only enhances his own knowledge but by thus handing it down to another, he helps in keeping the chain of tradition unbroken (*jñānatantusaṁrakṣaṇa*), which also happens to be a supreme duty for him. Without distributing what he has acquired, one is not freed from the debt that he owes to his preceptor.

In the *Mahābhāṣya* of Patañjali there is a memorable line which points out the conditions which make knowledge or *vidyā* really fruitful. There are four steps through which a *vidyā* becomes useful. First by the coming of it from the teacher, secondly by the studying of it, thirdly by the teaching of the same, lastly by its application.[78] When these four things combine, real knowledge dawns, and that is why the Upaniṣads lay so much stress on *svādhyāya-pravacana.* It must be noted in this connexion that the *svādhāya* or study must be confined to the Vedas alone. It is not the study of secular literature, all and sundry, that is enjoined here but the reading of the *Śruti* which is the very embodiment of *Śabda-Brahman.* Thus by *svādhyāya-pravacana* one tries io maintain a constant contact with the supreme Logos or *Śabda-Brabman.*

Dāna or Dedication

The third and last of the components of *dharma* is *dāna* or dedication. The Upaniṣad itself explains this last element thus: 'The third is to confine oneself absolutely to the family of the teachers.'[79] This means that one who wholly gives himself up to this quest and with that end in view resolves to spend his whole life in the home of his teacher, is really the man who has made a gift (*dāna*) of himself. In explaining the second factor of *adhyayana* the Upaniṣad had said: 'The second is the *brahmacārin* residing in the family of the *ācarya*'.[80] But here residence is absolute (*atyantam*) and not confined to the period of *brahmacarya* alone. Hence it is a total dedication, a complete consecration of one's life that the term *dāna* here signifies.[81]

Its secondary meaning of charity naturally follows from this primary sense of dedication. Through the cultivation of charity we are released from our isolated existences or private universes and get connected with the wider universe that lies around us. We feel indissolubly bound by a tie of relation with our fellow beings and then cndeavour to our best capacities to fulfil all these relations.

Dāna thus connects us with the human world and this is made clear in the *Bṛhadāraṇyaka Upaniṣad,* where we hear that the gods, demons and men all had gone for enlightenment to their common father Prajāpati, and he cryptically instructed them with only a single syllable, *'da'*. The gods understood it as *dama* or self-control, the demons as *dayā* or compassion, and men as *dāna* or charity.[82] Thus *dāna* is essentially a human virtue, because man being a social being must think of others around him and come to their aid by curtailing his own enjoyment. Hence man transgresses his own *dbarma* or rather, goes against the inherent law of his nature if he hoards everything for his own enjoyment and is not charitable in his disposition. Not wealth alone but whatever treasure one happens to possess must be distributed among and shared with his fellow beings.

That this ideal was always kept in view by the Upaniṣadic sages is clear from the numerous illustrations of ungrudging exposition of the nature of Reality to a true seeker. Nothing was kept as a closely guarded secret or as one's own private experience. They tried to disseminate the truths they had experienced as much as possible. In a remarkable passage in the *Taittirīya,* we find the sage inviting the *brahmacārins* to come to him from all quarters : 'As do the waters flow downward, or the months move towards the year, similarly O Lord, let the *brahmacārins* flock to me from all quarters'.[83] He is sending a call all around and is praying and hoping that he will have response to it from all quarters. This shows his anxiety to share his experiences with others.

As in the case of spiritual treasure, so in the matter of earthly treasures, too, there are ample illustrations of gift or *dāna* in the Upaniṣads. The case of Janaka, who made a lavish gift to his preceptor Yājñavalkya at the end of his teaching, shines out in a singular blaze of glory. The *Kaṭhopaniṣad* verily begins with this theme of *dāna.* There it has been shown that the gift of bad and useless things takes the donor to cheerless states of existence (*anandā lokāḥ*)[84], and to prevent the same thing happening to his father, Naciketas offers himself as a gift and presses his father again and again to give him to somebody, which ultimately so much enrages the father that he gives over his son to Death or Yama. But from this supreme gift of the son, though made in anger, there comes the great enlightenment to Naciketas. Thereby the Upaniṣad teaches that no gift should be made of useless things in a careless manncr and the gift of a supremely valuable thing, like a son, though heedlessly made brings its fruit. So the *Taittirīya Upaniṣad* points out in detail the right manner of making a gift. 'One should give with reverence. Nothing should be given with contempt. The gift must be made lavishly. With humility should it be given and also with fear and right knowledge'.[85]

Thus by the three components of *dharma* a connexion is established with the three spheres of existence. By *yajña* or sacrifice one is linked with the world of gods, through study or *adhyayana* one is joined with the supreme sphere of *Śabda-Brahman,* the world of the seers or ṛṣis and lastly through *dāna,* self-giving or gift of things one gets connected with the human world. Dharma thus covers all the spheres of life and is not an isolated state of thing, as is clear from the Upaniṣadic conception of it.

Importance of Śraddhā or Faith

All these virtues are to be cultivated with adequate faith or *śraddhā.* It is *śraddhā* which protects the seeker like a mother[86]. It is nothing but the utter transparency of the mind (*cetasas samprasādaḥ*), as Vyāsa defines it in his commentary on Patañjali's *Yoga-Sūtra*[87]. Only a transparent mind can hold or retain the truth. The truth gets stamped indelibly upon such a mind and thus the conviction becomes unshakeable. That is why Āruṇi while imparting the supreme instruction to Śvetaketu asks him to have faith in his sayings (*śraddhatsva somya*)[88]. Śaṅkara in his commentary thereon says : 'Though a thing established through reasoning and testimony is known exactly to be so, yet the most subtle things are hardly apprehended without a deep faith by one who is attached to outward objects and follows his own nature. Therefore it is said : 'Do have faith'. With faith the mind becomes attentive to the thing desired to be known and from that follows its knowledge'[89]. Elsewhere in the Upaniṣad it has been pointed out that one begins to think or contemplate over a thing only when he has faith in it and thus at the root of *manana* or reasoning lies faith.[90]

In the *Bṛhadāraṇyaka Upaniṣad* it is stated that *yajña* or sacrifice rests on *dakṣiṇā* or dedication and that *dakṣiṇā* is again based on *śraddhā.* 'When one is full of faith then only he makes the gift'. The Upaniṣad goes on to show the root of faith too. On what is faith based? On the heart, it was replied. By the heart is the faith recognized. Therefore in the heart alone is faith established or founded'.[91] Thus to have faith means to set one's heart upon the thing, according to the Upaniṣads. Unless one takes a thing to heart he cannot make it the sole pursuit of his life, and without this singleness of purpose the supreme knowledge of Brahman cannot be gained. So at the very root of the supreme enquiry lies faith. It is *śraddhā* which got hold of Naciketas (*śraddhā āviveśa*)[92] and prompted him to think seriously about the acts of his father. So in his case too reflection ensued (*so amanyata*)[93] only after *śraddhā* had entered into him (*āviveśa*). He also makes a demand on Yama to tell him about the Supreme Secret because he is full of faith.[94]

Śraddhā is thus the essential pre-requisite of this supreme search because it makes one fit for holding the truth. Hence in this preparatory stage we find *śraddhā* mentioned along with the other virtues already discussed : 'By *tapas, brahmacarya* and *śraddhā*',[95] '*śraddhā, satya, brahmacarya* and *vidhi'*,[96] 'offerings made with *śraddhā*',[97]. 'Those who cultivate *tapas* and *śraddhā* in the forest'[98] and so on. The *Taittirīya Upaniṣad* while enjoining charity warns the student that the gift must be made with faith and never should anything be given without faith.[99] Thus each and every act enjoined herein must be done with absolute faith, without which even a pious act becomes useless and even perverse (*asat*), as the Gītā points out.[100] The *Taittirīya,* while delineating the different forms of the Ātman beginning from the *annamaya,* makes it explicitly clear in the exposition of the *Vijñānamaya*

Ātman that *śraddhā* is verily the source of *vijñāna* or knowledge. 'Its head is *śraddhā* alone', it declares.[101] Echoing the Upaniṣads, Patañjali in his *Yoga-Sūtras* places *śraddhā* at the very beginning of the evolution of the intellect which culminates in *prajña.*[102] In the Vedāntic scheme, too, of the acquirement of knowledge, it is *śraddhā* again which leads to *samādhāna.* 'The man with faith gets knowledge', declares the Gītā.[104]

Thus everywhere it is made unmistakeably clear that to have Knowledge, *prajñā, vijñana* or *samādhāna* or *jñāna, śraddhā* is the indispensable pre-requisite. 'It is a living responding of the soul to God' as Radhakrishnan puts it.[105] Sri Krishna Prem in his illuminating book on the *Kaṭhopaniṣad* says that 'the *śraddhā* which entered Naciketas is the true faith, the Fair Faith as Hermes calls it, which is a form of Knowledge that has been realized at deeper levels of being. In technical terms it is the reflection in the personal mind of the Knowledge that results from the union of the higher *manas* with the *buddhi.* For the personal mind it is not quite knowledge, because that personal or lower mind is not yet properly united to its higher self and therefore the latter's knowledge can only appear as the reflection which we term faith'.[106] Thus with the dawning of faith comes a glimpse of the light that lies beyond, which initiates the quest or search as well as sustains the seeker to the very last limit of his journey.

Sri Aurobindo analyzes the nature of faith in the following words: 'First of all, faith does not depend upon experience; it is something that is there before experience....... All men of action, discoverers, , inventors, creators of knowledge proceed by faith and until the proof is made or the thing done, they go on inspite of disappointment, failure, disproof, denial, because of something in them that tells them that this is the truth, the thing that must be followed and done.......Faith is the soul's witness to something not yet manifested or not yet realized but which yet the Knower within us, even in the absence of all indications, feels to be true or supremely worth following or achieving'.[107]

Reverence for Parents

Another important teaching inculcated in *Taittirīya Upaniṣad* is the attribution of divinity to the parents and the guest as well.[108] They arc to be looked upon as emblems of divinity, for they are the visible gods on earth who represent the Invisible Supreme. We have already seen the supremely important place occupied by the *ācārya* in the scheme of *Brahmavidyā.* The position of the parents, too, is no less important. Not only do we owe our physical existence to them but our whole spiritual make-up too. So the father is not only our *pitā* but the *pitṛdeva,* the divine in the form of the father and the mother is the *mātṛdeva,* the divine incarnated as the mother. The whole aim of *Brahmavidyā* is to find the divine in every form and nowhere else it is more easily grasped and apprehended than in the living and concrete form of the parents. Hence the Upaniṣad enjoins the student to look upon the parents with supreme reverence.

The primary virtues are first imbibed from the parents. Thus Satyakāma Jābāla who earned the Supreme Knowledge because of his unswerving adherence to truth acquired this spirit of truthfulness from his mother, Jabālā. He was absolutely in the dark about his origin or caste, and had the mother chosen to deceive him by attributing a false origin, Satyakāma would have had no means to correct it or even to know that it was false. But the mother gave out the truth to her son in utter frankness and sincerity of spirit and the son, too, repeated the same thing in an exactly similar and simple way to his teacher when the latter questioned about his origin.[109] On the contrary, the flouting of the authority or disregard for the superiority of the parents debars one from getting the illumination that he seeks, however much he may presume to know and pretend to succeed. Thus we find in the *Kaṭha Upaniṣad* that the very first boon that Naciketas sought from Yama was about the pacifying of the angry and ruffled spirit of his father. The prayer was that the father may be *śāntasaṅkalpa, sumanāḥ* and *vītamanyuḥ,* of a calm disposition, happy mind and devoid of anger[110]. Naciketas, being the ideal type of a seeker, knew that without the propitiation of the father—though in his case the father was in the wrong, yet even then—no knowledge can be gained, because the wrath of the parents blocks the whole road to progress and makes further advancement impossible. By mutual cooperation the son and the father should proceed on the journey and so by adoration and surrender the son must propitiate the father and identify himself with the spirit of his progenitor. The son does not only inherit the material properties and earthly belongings of his father after he passes away, but the whole spiritual inheritance accrues to him. He must enrich the inheritance, so he has to take the torch entrusted and handed over to him further in regions left unexplored by his predecessor and continue the march from the place where his father fell, who charges him to complete the journey which he could not finish.

We find in the Upaniṣad the remarkable picture of this supreme relation between the father and the son depicted in what is called *Sampratti*[111] i.e. *sampradāna* or entrusting. The dying father calls the son to his bedside and gives him a report of the progress he had made, of the summits he had gained in life. But still higher summits remain to be scaled or conquered to make the journey complete. So he entrusts his son with this work after leaving to him the whole wealth of his experience gained during the journey. This is described as his entering into the son, as it were, i.e. he identifies himself in spirit with him[112] at the time of his departure from this world[113]. Thus the duty of the son, which is obtained from the very basic meaning of the term *'Putra'*, is to liberate the father by completing the work left unfinished by him[114]. This function of *sampradāna* is worked out in detail in the *Chāndogya Upaniṣad* too.[115] Similarly in the *Chāndogya Upaniṣad,*[116] we find the sage Kauṣītaki asking his son to enrich the experience of his father by multiplying the rays i.e. by knowing the reality in all its various aspects or numerous phases, of which he had only a general and non-detailed knowledge. The father had only a partial knowledge of truth and so he asks his son to have a comprehensive knowledge of the same and thereby complete his experience.

Such is the glorious and ideal relationship between the father and the son which was envisaged by the seers of the Upaniṣads and that is why in the very beginning of the spiritual discipline, the student is trained to look upon his parents as gods. The tradition of the Brahmavidyā was also generally handed down from the father to the son, as we find from numerous instances in the Upaniṣads.

Respect for the Guest

Lastly, the *atithi* or the guest too, is to be looked upon as a god and worshipped as such[117]. The act of hospitality should not be a formal one but must be carried out in a spirit of worship, for when the guest comes at our door, he should not be looked upon as a stranger or an outsider but as the very emblem of the Supreme Spirit. In the Vedic imagery, Agni and Soma, too, are termed as *atithi,* because they are like guests come from heaven to adorn the sacrifice. So in *Kathopaniṣad*[118] it is expressly stated that when a Brāhmin guest enters the house one must take it as an entry of the Agni itself (*vaiśvānaraḥ praviśati*). Even the all-powerful Yama is very much apprehensive of a calamity befalling him because of his failure to attend to the guest who is *namasya* or adorable, due to his absence from home; and so on his return, he immediately goes to propitiate Naciketas by offering him the grant of three boons for the three nights he had been left uncared for and unattended. This shows what a great reverence was accorded to a guest during the age of the Upaniṣads.

This ideal of service to the guest has permeated the whole fabric of Indian life. Whether one reads the ancient Upaniṣads or the later epics like *Rāmāyaṇa* and *Mahābhārata* or the works of Kālidāsa like the drama of *Śakuntalā,* everywhere is found this supreme importance of *atithisevā* stressed again and again. It is the *nṛyajña,* by performing which we fulfil our obligation to the whole human race and feel that none is a stranger to us in this world and the same divine spirit inhabits all forms. The *Muṇḍakopaniṣad,* while enumerating the flaws that spoil the *agnihotra* sacrifice, mentions the absence of worship of the *atithi* (*atithivarjitam*) as one of the main defects.[119]

We may note, in passing, that this scrupulous fulfilment of all duties demanded here shows that the Upaniṣadic seers looked upon the tree of life as an organic whole and hence tried to fulfil all the relations scrupulously, not only of man to man but to all created things. The vision of supreme unity is the final aim and the seeker is trained from the initial stage to imbibe this spirit of unity in all spheres of life.

After enjoining these duties the seer again warns the student not to falter or fail in scrupulously carrying out each of the above injunctions and so repeats them all over again with the warning '*na pramaditavyam*'[120] attached separately to each of them. This shows how in this period of preparation one has to be constantly on vigil and ever alert lest a slip should occur and spoil the whole work. It also makes clear how exacting the sages were in this respect, viz. in the scrupulous conformity to the moral law or *dharma,* though their ultimate aim was to transcend the sphere of morality, pass beyond all *dharmas* whatsoever.

No stress on Ahiṁsā or Īśvara Praṇidhāna

Of all the virtues enumerated so far, non-violence or *ahiṁsā* seems to occupy no privileged position in the Upaniṣads, which is a thing to be noted. It is mentioned just only once along with other virtues, in the *Chāndogya Upaniṣad:* 'Now *tapas, dāna,* simplicity, *ahiṁsā* and truth in speech, these are his *dakṣiṇās* or fees.'[121] It seems that the stress on *ahiṁsā* came with the later Buddhist tradition and so Patañjali, in his enumeration of *yama,* mentions *ahiṁsā* first of all.[122] The stress varied between truth and nonviolence in later schools. Some thought that *satya* or truth is the primary thing without which no *ahiṁsā* is possible. A really truthful man alone will never injure another. The opposite view is that one could hardly be established in truth without first cultivating the spirit of *ahiṁsā.* How can one flinch from truth whose vow is non-injury to others? The debate is interesting, though the ultimate issue is not so much a matter of dispute, as the final outcome is practically the same whichever way the stress is laid.

Another thing to be noted is that, though the Upaniṣads lay stress on *tapas* and *svādhyāya*, yet they nowhere mention in the preparatory stage any form of *Iśvara-praṇidhāna,* as we find it in the *kriyāyoga* of Patañjali's system, which has been defined by Vyāsa in his commentary as 'the offering of the fruits of all actions to the Great Lord', (*sarvakarmaphalānāṁ paramagurau arpaṇam*),[123] This teaching of *'phalārpaṇa' was* made more popular by the Gītā as a preparatory purification. There is a theistic element involved in it, while the Upaniṣadic scheme of preparatory virtues has a more humanistic basis, as they are to be acquired and adhered to unflinchingly by man himself without bringing in a god at whose feet he may lay bare the burden of his soul. Here he must stand on his own strength (*uddharet ātmanā 'tmānam*) and should not lean or depend upon any external agency or factor—this seems to be the pointer.

Instruction through the syllable 'Da'

In the *Bṛhadāraṇyaka Upaniṣad*[124] there is a peculiar cryptic formula of *'da'*, by which syllable three virtues arc taught to the three different species of beings, viz. the gods, the demons and the human beings, all the offsprings of Prajāpati. All the three approached their father for instruction and after having observed *brahmacarya* prayed for the knowledge. To all the three he imparted the instruction through the same single syllable *'da'*, and each understood its meaning according to his own peculiar disposition and character. The gods took it as *dama* or self-control because they needed it more than anything else as a check or corrective to their excess of power. Without *dama* they were liable to misuse the divine energy at their disposal. The human beings understood it as *dāna* or offering because being essentially social beings their foremost virtue lay in this gift or offering of each to the other, which keeps the human society going. The demons thought it to be *dayā* or kindness, for their fierce and cruel nature needed to be softened by the benign influence of kindness all around. Thus, at three levels, three forms of virtue arc prescribed here: the divine needs self-control, the human needs self-giving and the demoniac needs kindness.

Condemnation of Immoral acts

The Upaniṣads also condemn many immoral acts and warn that the perpetrators of such heinous crimes go down as well as those who are the abetters. 'By stealing gold, drinking wine, polluting the bed of the teacher and killing a Brahmin—these four go down as well as the fifth who acts with them'.[125]

The Upaniṣads also discourage too much of learning as it amounts to mere verbiage. 'One should not absorb oneself in many words, for that only tires the speech'.[126] Mere scholarship is not prized but the simplicity of a child is adored and prescribed. 'After fully exploring knowledge one should desire to remain as a child'.[127] The Upaniṣadic seers were aware that too much of learning only leads to arrogance and to distraction and entanglement in a net of words. Instead of straightening and simplifying the issue it only leads to an increasing complication and confusion of the same. Only in a heart free from all bias and prejudices, the truth is revealed. That is why the innocence and simplicity of a child is sought to the exclusion of all outward scholarship or learning. After a thorough search through the intellectual mazes one must let everything go and wait for the revelation through a simple intuition.

Summary of the teachings and their significance

The period of preparation which we have surveyed so far is essentially a period of purification or purgation. It begins as we have seen with the surrender of the charge of life to the teacher, who henceforward sits at the helm, guiding the course of life of the disciple. Under his exacting discipline the gathering of forces or the conservation of energy begins, which is called *brahmacarya.* This entails the rejection of many sweet and comfortable things which are described as *preya,* and the deliberate endurance of many hardships and rigours and restraints. Thus one goes in for *tapas,* which 'only means the development of soul-force, the freeing of the soul from slavery to body, severe thinking or energising of mind'.[128] For this development of soul-force adherence to truth at all costs is the most essential need. The seeker must know that 'it is truth alone which is (ultimately) victorious and not falsehood'.[129] Without this basic belief or faith in the ultimate success of truth, it is not possible to move forward in this hazardous path. That is why *śraddhā* or faith has been found to be an indispensable requirement for the seeker. If one follows with faith the way of truth, one's power is sure to grow imperceptibly and only the man with power can get hold of the Ātman, because it can never be realized by one devoid of strength or power as the Upaniṣad declares.[130] The purpose of the gathering of strength is to kindle the fire, which alone can burn all impurities whatsoever, free the soul from the crooked ties of sin and lead one along the path of goodness (*supathā*) towards plenitude (*rāye*) and fulfilment.[131] With the kindling of fire life turns into a *yajña* or sacrifice, and the seeker signifies his earnestness for kindling the fire and turning his life into a *yajña* by carrying the *'samidh'* or load of wood in his hand while approaching the teacher. The seeker confines himself to the home of the teacher and devotes himself absolutely to the study of the scriptures. In order to test his assimilation of the subject taught, he goes on to make an exposition of the subject to others which makes his knowledge secure and sound.

Thus *svādhyāya,* or study and *pravacana* or exposition are the two main occupations in the prepatory period. The sage Nāka Maudgalya calls this *svādhyāya and pravacana* as the only form of meditation or *tapas*[132]. That this happens to be the primary and essential thing in this period is also clear from the *Taittirīya Upaniṣad,* where the other virtues like *ṛta, satya* etc. are all separately enumerated with the clause *'svādhyāya pravacane ca'* attached to each of them[133]. This signifies that the other virtues should be cultivated along with the study and exposition of scriptures and not to the exclusion of the latter in any case. This period of studentship is thus solely meant for the acquirement or gathering of knowledge along with the conservation of energy or force which, as we have seen, is termed *brahmacarya.* These two things viz. knowledge and strength or force should be collected to the full and it is only the fullness of knowledge as well as of strength that brings liberation. A complete development of all the parts from the physical upto the intellectual is, therefore, demanded.

This shows that the Upaniṣadic *sādbanā* or approach to Reality is not a mere intellectual gymnastic; it is a growth, a development. It is a growth from animality to humanity, from humanity to divinity, and from divinity to infinity. Diffusion or dissipation of energy or wastage of force must be checked at all costs and that is why so many vows are to be taken and strictly adhered to. The injunctions about right conduct can hardly be driven home with more emphasis or strength than as here in the Upaniṣads. With the strongest imperatives are they imparted to bring home to the novitiate the supreme importance of them. Scrupulous conformity to them is demanded by a repetition of the warning again and again : *'mā pramada',* 'do not fail or falter'.

We draw the attention of those scholars who find a complete disregard for morality in the Upaniṣadic teaching to this emphasis on right conduct repeated over and over again in the Upaniṣads. It is an astounding charge which Western scholars like Hume, Deussen, Gough and Keith have levelled again and again against the Upaniṣadic tradition. Dr Hume observes: "There is a wide difference between the Upaniṣadic theory and the theory of the Greek sages, that the man who has knowledge should thereby become virtuous in character or that the result of teaching should be a virtuous life. Here the possession of some metaphysical knowledge actually cancels all past sins and even permits the knower unblushingly to continue in 'what seems to be much evil' with perfect impunity, although such acts are heinous crimes and are disastrous in their effect for others who lack that kind of knowledge"[134]. Evidently Dr Hume has completely misunderstood the nature of the 'metaphysical knowledge' to which he refers here. Does not the Upaniṣad declare unequivocally 'None can attain this Ātman unless he has ceased to revel in the evil way of life'?[135] To let the animal in us have its full play and yet to pretend to grow divine is a colossal self-deception of which the Upaniṣadic seers were very well aware. So the seeker is warned again and again to be on his guard against the attacks of the enemy, the *asura*, who is the very incarnation of sin (*pāpmā*). One must bid good-bye to the animal in him before he can hope to welcome and usher in the divine.

Not one Upaniṣad here and there mentions the necessity of moral discipline but all the Upaniṣads uniformly and unfailingly stress this point. Thus the *Kena Upaniṣad,* which devotes itself exclusively to the exposition of the nature of Brahman, does not forget to remind its readcrs while concluding its discourse that *tapas, dama* and *karman* are the foundations of this supreme knowledge and *satya* or truth is the very basis of it[136]. Again, in the *Kaṭha,* while expounding the nature of the Ātman, Yama gives the warning that one who is devoid of reason (*avijñānavān*), of uncontrolled mind and ever impure (*amanaskas sadā'śuciḥ*) can never hope to attain this status (*padam*) but only goes down in *saṁsāra.*[137] If one wants to reach the end of the way, Yama adds, one must have reason as his charioteer and a composed mind as the bridle to check the senses, which are like wild horses.[138] Next, the *Praśna Upaniṣad* also sings to the same strain, when it says that the stainless sphere of Brahman can be attained only by those who have practised *tapas* and *brahmacarya,* who are established in truth and free from all crookedness, falsehood and deception.[139] The *Muṇḍaka* is emphatic on this point that the Ātman can be realized only through *tapas, brahmacarya*, *satya* and right knowledge (*samyag jñānena*).[140] The *Taittirīya* begins with the *Śikṣāvallī* and devotes a whole section to this essential basic training in moral virtues before it goes on to expound the nature of Brahman in later chapters. The *Chāndogya,* in the very beginning, brings in the topic of the classic struggle between the *devas* and *asuras* and thereby reminds us that the way is not so smooth as we think, because we must first free ourselves from the clutches of *asura* or *pāpmā* who holds us in its iron grips.[141] Lastly, the *Bṛhadāraṇyaka,* though solely engaged in the exploration of the Ātman, opens with the description of the *Aśvamedha,* the highest sacrifice, which literally means the purification of the animal or the *aśva.*[142] Thus we find the same note ringing through all the Upaniṣads about the supreme necessity of having a virtuous life in order to qualify for the supreme knowledge of the Ātman or Brahman.

Everywhere in the Upaniṣads we find that the supreme knowledge is not imparted all at once but the seeker is asked again and again to perform further *tapas* and thereby purify himself before he can hope for the ultimate enlightenment. Moreover, when one aspires to attain higher and higher levels of perfection he has to pass through more rigorous and stricter moral discipline as he rises in the scale of spiritual advancement.

But it should be remembered that all this purification is not an end in itself and the Upaniṣads are not mere codes of virtues or morals. We have seen that purification or *āhāraśuddhi,* rather the cleansing of the doors of perception is meant for *sattvaśuddhi* or purity of the essence or being, which leads to a constant and uninterruptcd remembrance of the supreme spiritual principle. With this continuous flow of fixed remembrance, the knots of the heart are all unloosened and then comes the utter freedom. This freedom, by its very nature, implies a transcendence of all laws and regulations. The liberated soul is neither bound to abide by any rule nor can he be forced to flout any sacred law. There is no binding on him in either way, for any form of limitation will frustrate the very freedom by keeping him imprisoned in a particular realm of law. That is why the *Bṛhadāraṇyaka Upaniṣad,* in a celebrated passage, describing the nature of the liberated soul says: 'He is not tormented by doing or non-doing.'[143] Neither is there any feeling of depression in him on account of brooding over past sins nor is there any elation in him at the thought of virtuous acts previously performed. The 'ought' no longer applies to him and so the thought of any unfinished duty does not torment him.

The moral plane is the sphere of stress and torment, for it is a battle-ground of two opposing and hostile forces, the *devas* and the *asuras,* the forces of light and darkness. So here the injunction is to hold steadfastly to the forces of light, to abide strictly by the dictates of reason. Every time one fails to be faithful to the promptings of reason he is seized with a torment. There is no escape from it. But with the birth of the spiritual element the story becomes different. The strife ends, the struggle ceases, the torment disappears. With the birth of the spirit comes a taste of freedom due to a transcending of the sphere of conflict. Consequently he acts 'unblushingly', as Humc calls it, in every way. 'Blushing' signifies a sense of guilt or sīn, and one who has passed beyond the realm of sin can never have any 'blushing' for any act whatsoever. But when Hume says that the knower is allowed unblushingly to continue 'in what seems to be much evil', he grossly misrepresents the thing. There can be no question of the knower continuing in the ways of evil, because, as we have seen, the Upaniṣad expressly declares that none can be a knower of the Ātman if he does not desist from the evil ways of life. So one must part company with 'what seems to be much evil', but ultimately he must also part company with what seems to be much good. Good and evil alike are transcended here because good also presupposes the existence of evil, the notion of virtue calls up the opposite notion of vice. To have real freedom one must pass beyond both of them.

Signifying this supreme state of liberation the Upaniṣad says: 'In that highest state a thief is not a thief, a murderer not a murderer. He is not followed by good nor followed by evil, for he then overcomes all the sorrows of the heart'.[144] Echoing this the Gītā says: 'Killing all these people he does not kill nor is himself killed.'[145] All these extreme statements are made just to show that the realized soul rises above the sphere of moral good and evil, and they are not meant to indicate a deliberate continuance in the ways of evil or the wilful perpetration of 'heinous crimes' as suggested by Hume. Neither is there any suggestion that once 'the knowledge of the Ātman has been gained, every action and therefore every moral action also has been deprived of meaning,' as Deussen thinks.[146] With the dawning of the knowledge all actions assume a supreme meaning, to say nothing of moral actions alone. The meaning attached to moral actions is imposed from without and is hencc contingent and artificial but here in the state of knowledge the meaning springs from the soul of being and spontaneously accompanies all actions whatsoever. Here 'law is fulfilled in love.'

References

1. BU, 4.5.6.
2. KTU, 1.3.14.
3. YK, p. 79.
4. sā dhīś cen na tarhi praṇavena vicintayet. AP, 6.58.
5. BU, 4.4.8.
6. MU., 1.2.1.
7. KTU, 1.3.14.
8. MU, 1.2.12.
9. CU, 7.16.2.
10. CU, 6.14.211.
11. CU., 4.9.1.
12. CU., 4.14.1.
13. KTU, 1.2.7.
14. ananyaprokte gatir atra nā 'sti Ibid, 1.2.8.
15. Ibid, 1.1.22.
16. TU, 1.3.2.
17. atyantam ācāryakule avasādayan. CU, 2.23.2.
18. prāpaya na ācāryakulam. CU, 4.5.1.
19. upasannāya samyak. MU, 1.2.13.
20. MU, 1.2.12, PRU, 1.2.
21. MU, 3.2.4.
22. KTU, 1.2.20.
23. Ibid., 1.2.15.
24. PRU, 1.10.
25. MU, 3.1.5.
26. CU, 4.10.
27. Ibid., 6.1.

28. Ibid., 8.7.3.
29. PRU, 1.1.
30. TU, 1.4.
31. Ibid.
32. āpyāyantu mamā 'ṅgāni, etc.
33. PRU, 2.13.
34. CU, 7.26,2.
35. sarvagranthīnāṁ vipramokṣaḥ. Ibid.
36. Ibid.
37. āhāraśuddhau sattvaśuddhiḥ. CU, 7.26.2.
38. āhriyata ityā 'hāraḥ. ŚB, on Ibid.
39. bhadraṁ karṇebhiś śṛṇuyāma etc.
40. tāṁ yogam iti manyante sthirām indriyadhāraṇām. KTU, 2.6.11.
41. CU, 2.23.1.
42. puruṣo vāva yajñaḥ. Ibid., 3.16.1.
43. CU, 4.16.1.
44. KTU, 1.2.1.
45. majjanti bahavo manuṣyāḥ. KTU, 1.2.3.
46. EN, VI. 9. IV, Taylor's trans.
47. KTU, 1.2.23.
48. MU, 4.2.11.
49. KTU, 1.3.7.
50. CU, 3.14.1.
51. Ibid.
52. ĪU, 17.
53. MU, 3.2.10.
54. YS, 1.20.
55. TU, 1.11.1.
56. KU, 4.33.
57. BU, 3.9.23.
58. Ibid.
59. BU, 5.5.1.
60. CU, 4.4.
61. Ibid., 6.16.2.
62. PRU, 6.1.
63. Ibid., 2.8.
64. MU, 3.1.6.
65. PRU, 1.15.
66. TU, 1.11.1.
67. BU.1.4.14.
68. TU, 1.11.1.
69. CU, 2.23.1.
70. Ibid., 8.5
71. BU, 1.2.6.
72. RV, 10.190.1.
73. TU, 3.2.
74. nātapasvino yogas sidhyati. VB, on YS, 2.1.
75. LD, p. 420.
76. svādhyāyān mā pramada. TU, 1.11.1.
77. TU, 1.9.
78. caturbhiś ca prakārair vidyo 'payuktā bhavaty āgamakālena svādhyayakālena pravacanakālena vyavahārakālene'ti. PMB, p. 6, Keilhorn's ed.
79. CU, 2.23.1.
80. Ibid.
81. In the interpretation of this text from *Chandogya* 2.23.1, viz. *trayo dharmaskandhāḥ* etc., I have followed an independent line which differs widely from the interpretation put to it by Śaṅkara. The difference arises from the divergence in the method of splitting the actual text. I have put a stop after *'dānam iti'*, but Śaṅkara stops after '*prathamaḥ*' and so he has put all the three viz. *yajña, adhyayana* and *dāna* together

as the first of the three components of *dharma*. Śaṅkara means to connect the *dharmaskandhas* with the three *āśramas,* viz. *brahmacarya, gārhasthya* and *vānaprastha* and interprets the text accordingly, keeping the fourth *āśrama* of *sannyāsa* rightly beyond all dharmas, and hence not included in the *dharmaskandhas.* But I beg to differ from Śaṅkara here and think that after enumerating the three component elements of *dharma* as *yajña, adhyayana* and *dana,* the Upaniṣad itself puts a stop with the term 'iti' and then goes to explain them one by one. Śaṅkara has also been forced to twist the meaning of the term '*prathamaḥ*' into '*ekaḥ*' i.e. one, while in my interpretation its natural import i.e. 'first' is preserved. The difference in the method of splitting is very interesting, though it must be borne in mind that Śaṅkara's interpretation is equally cogent and acceptable and the two interpretations do not clash with each other nor are they in fundamental opposition. It is mentioned here only to point out the absolute flexibility of the Upaniṣadic texts.

82. BU, 5.2.
83. TU, 1.4.3.
84. KTU, 1.1.3.
85. TU, 1.11.3.
86. VB, on YS, 1.20.
87. YS, 1.20.
88. CU, 6.12.3.
89. Ibid. ŚB.
90. CU, 7.19.1.
91. BU, 3.9.21.
92. KTU, 1.1.
93. Ibid.
94. prabrūhi taṁ śraddadhānāya mahyam. KTU, 1.13.
95. KTU, 1.13.
96. PRU, 1.2.1.10.5.3.
97. MU, 2.1.7.
98. Ibid, 1.2.2.
99. Ibid, 1.2.11.
100. TU, 1.11.3.
101. Gitā, 17.21.
102. TU, 2.4.1.
103. YS, 1.20.
104. Gitā, 4.40.
105. ERWT, p. 337.
106. YK, p. 17.
107. AG, pp. 257-59.
108. TU, 1.11.2.
109. CU, 4.4.1-4.
110. KTU, 1.1.10.
111. BU, 1.5.17.
112. ebhir eva prāṇais saha putram āviśati. BU, 1.5.17.
113. asmāt lokāt praitī. Ibid.
114. sa yady anena kiñcid akṣṇayā' kṛtaṁ bhavati tasmād enaṁ sarvasmāt putro muñcati, tasmāt putro nāma. BU, 1.5.17.
115. Kauṣī, 2.15.
116. CU, 1.5.2.
117. TU, 1.11.2.
118. KTU, 1.7.
119. MU, 1.2.3.

120. TU, 1.11.1.
121. CU, 3.17.4.
122. YS, 2.30.
123. Ibid., 2.1.
124. BU, 5.2.
125. CU, 5.10.
126. BU, 4.4.21.
127. BU, 3.5.1.
128. RPU, p. 91.
129. MU, 3.1.6.
130. Ibid, 3.2.4.
131. IU, 18.
132. TU, 1.9.
133. Ibid.
134. TPU, p. 60.
135. KTU, 1.2.23.
136. KU, 4.33.
137. KTU, 1.3.7.
138. Ibid, 1.3.6.
139. PRU, 1.15.
140. MU, 3.15.
141. CU, 1.2.
142. BU, 1.1.
143. BU, 4.4.22.
144. BU, 4.3.22.
145. Gītā, 18.17.
146. PU, p. 362.

CHAPTER IV

CONTEMPLATION

We now move to the second stage in the Upaniṣadic approach to Reality. In the first stage of preparation we have found that, through a rigid discipline and strenuous endeavour, the attainment of purity of being (*sattvaśuddhi*)[1] has been aimed at. This purity is not an end in itself but is sought to be achieved in order to qualify for the *Brahmavidyā* proper, which is *upāsanā* or contemplation. Thus the Upaniṣad says: 'To such a soul, who is free from the taint of impurity (*mṛditakaṣāyāya*)[2] the teacher shows the way to the other shore beyond darkness (*tamasas pāraṁ darśayati*).[3]

Devas & Asuras

In the famous prayer in the Upaniṣad:

'Lead me from the Unreal to the Real,
Lead me from Darkness to Light,
Lead me from Death to Immortality,'[4]

the first line seeks deliverance from unreality, i.e., emancipation from the false self, and thereby makes an affirmation of the true self. There is a ring of falsehood in all our actions while we remain mere creatures of impulse. With the guidance of reason there begins an assertion of truth and with this assertion ensues a struggle between the two forces, eternally hostile to each other, of truth and falsehood. This is the classic struggle between the *devas* and the *asuras,* with which open the *Chāndogya Upaniṣad,*[5] the repository of most of the *vidyās* or methods of contemplation, and thereon Śankara rightly comments: 'this struggle for mutual overpowering and predominance is the struggle between the *devas* and the *asuras,* which is going on from all eternity among all creatures and in each body.'[6] The term *devas,* derived from the verb '*div,*' signifying illumination, stands for the functions of the senses illuminated by reason, while the term *asuras* signifies the exactly opposite thing, viz., the natural and impulsive actions of the senses, which are prompted by a desire revelling in the objects of vital pleasure (*asu*).[7] In the stage of preparation the whole energy is devoted to the purification of the functions of the senses by a process which has been called *āhāraśuddhi*. *Āhāraśuddhi* means the knowledge of the objects (*viṣayavijñānam*) freed from the taint of attachment and repulsion.[8]

But this attempt to free each of the senses separately from the taint of attachment or sin (*pāpman*)[9] hardly becomes wholly successful. This is clearly brought out in the Upaniṣadic parable of the fight between the *devas* and the *asuras* and in the description of the methods adopted by the former in overcoming the latter. The *devas* tried first to overpower the *asuras* by enhancing or extending the powers of the different organs of sense, but every time they failed because the *asuras* intruded and struck them down by smiting them all, each of the particular faculties, with an attachment or liking. Attachment is sin (*pāpman*), for it causes a limitation, a narrowness, brings a fixed gaze on the particularities of a thing and thereby deprives one of the wide vision of the universal. Thus one gets absorbed in a world of particulars with their inherent duality of good and bad. Hence the nasal breath takes both the bad and the good smell, the organ of speech tells a lie as well as the truth, the eye beholds a beneficent form as also an ugly and reprehensible object, the ear hears good and beneficial words as well as lends itself to the reception of such talks as are not fit for hearing at all.[10] In a word, all the senses are thus inherently stamped with this duality of good and evil.

Therefore we find in an opening beneficial prayer (*śāntipāṭha*) of one of the Upaniṣads: 'May we hear by our ears only the beneficial (words or speech), may we behold through our eyes only the beneficial (form)[11]. To ensure the victory of good over evil, of *sat* over *asat* is the aim of the preparatory level. That is why we find the categorical imperative in force there. The seeker is asked to tread the way of *dharma* and forsake the way of *adharma,* to speak the truth, and avoid the telling of a lie and so on. Definite instructions are thus given to choose the right and reject the wrong, and thereby the right will is sought to be infused, the right resolution instilled.

Inadequacy of the first step

In this way through the preparation, though one finds himself lifted from *asat* to *sat*, from the sphere of falsehood to that of truth, yet darkness envelopes him. The fear of the *asuras* is not dispelled as yet, as the *devas* do not feel completely immune from their attack. The *Chāndogya,* while introducing the contemplation on *Oṁkāra* as *Udgītha,* makes this point crystal clear by bringing in again the topic of the *devas*. The *devas,* afraid of death, entered into the three *vidyās'* i e., the three Vedas or scriptures. In other words, they first tried to flee from death by making their actions conform strictly to the standards of truth and law as embodied in the scriptures. 'They covered themselves with the rhythms (*chandas*); because they covered themselves thereby (*ācchādayan*), therefore are the *chandas* termed as such'. But there Death found them out as are fishes detected in the waters. Knowing this (that they have again been spotted out by Death) they lifted themselves above the *ṛk, yajus* and *sāman* and entered into the *Svara* or the Sound.[12] Thus the covering by the rhythm of reason proved inadequate, as Death pursued and haunted them even there. It did not prove to be a shield thick enough to make them invisible to Death, i.e., it did not lift them altogether from the sphere of Death, did not free them absolutely from its clutches. The aim was to transcend the sphere of Death but that has not been achieved as yet. Fear persists, darkness is not yet dispelled, death is yet to be transcended. Hence the second and third line of the prayer run: 'Lift me from Darkness to Light, from Death to Immortality'.

But it should be noted here that the first step of preparation did not prove to be absolutely useless, only because it failed to free the gods from Death. That they were still being pursued by Death and were not yet free from its clutches could be apprehended by them only because they were already in part purged and purified in being (*saṁskṛtāś śuddhātmānaḥ*)[13] by their pious deeds or their fight with the powers of Darkness, This consciousness would not have dawned on them but for this primary purification or struggle they had gone through. The value of the first step is not minimised by proving it to be inadequate but rather enhanced by this very fact. The enquiry about the next step cannot come to one who has not explored to the full the possibilities of the first approach. The limitations thereof are apprehended, and the inadequacy realized only when the method is given a complete trial. This is clearly brought out in this parable in the Upaniṣad where it is shown that the *devas* tried to overcome the *asuras* through the help of each of the senses, one after another and only when all of them failed to overpower them that they took recourse to the *Mukhya Prāṇa,* the central principle of life.

But why the senses, each and every one of them, failed to overcome the *asuras?* Because the attempt to intensify the powers of the senses or to magnify and stretch too far the particular functions always leads to a stress and strain which, ultimately, is bound to end in absolute failure and spell even disaster. There is no escape from it so long as one remains confined to the sphere of particulars and is not lifted towards the universal, which is the *Mukhya Prāṇa.* But there is a utility of this attempt to expand the particular powers or faculties, which cannot be denied anyhow, just as none can deny the utility of modern science, though it has brought our civilization to the very brink of total extinction. The search for the universal begins only after the complete exploration of the particular methods. And hence after exploring each of the particular means to the full and finding each of them inadequate, the *devas* thought of a different device.[14] One must try the several methods himself and find out their worth and then reject them all ultimately if they are found wanting. But to reject them on hearsay and jump for the next higher step is to frustrate the whole aim of the approach to the Supreme. Thus Yama tests Naciketas by offering him a whole world of things of temptation and enjoyment and only when he becomes sure that he is calm and unruffled (*dhīra*), and has spurned (*atyasrākṣīḥ*)[15] all his offers, he begins his discourse on the Ātman. The *Muṇḍaka* also says that the *Brahmavidyā* is imparted to one who is of a calm disposition (*praśāntacittāya*) and possesses self-control (*śamānvitāya*).[16] In order to have this calm disposition one must have a feeling of complete detachment (*nirveda*). But this detachment cannot come unless one has tried all the means in the different spheres of action (*parīkṣya lokān karmacitān*),[17] and found them wanting. 'The Brahmins wish to know (this Supreme Reality) by *yajña, dāna, tapas* and *anāśaka'*,[18] 'One sees the Self in the Self by becoming calm, self-controlled, detached, full of fortitude and concentration'.[19]

The relation of the two steps

Thus the second step, with which we now propose to deal, necessarily presupposes the first, as is evident from all the Upaniṣads.

We have stressed this point because the first step is generally skipped over on the plea of its ultimate inadequacy and consequent futility, but that only leads to an utter stagnation of the spirit because without the necessary purification, no contemplation, in the true sense of the term, is possible. Through the purification undergone in the stage of preparation, one becomes *dhīra,* calm and collected, a term very favourite with the Upaniṣads and strewn all over the Upaniṣadic literature. Nacikctas forsook everything else by his strong will (*dhṛtyā*) because he was *dhīra.*[20] 'Only the *dhīra* chooses the *śreya,* the good, in preference to the *preya* or the pleasant'.[21] 'Exceptionally only a *dhīra* with his eyes turned inwards beholds the inner Ātman desiring immortality'.[22] 'Only the *dhīras* look into the source of all creatures',[23] 'the *dhīras* attaining the all-pervading reality all around'.[24] Thus the attainment of the state of *dhīra* is an indispensable necessity according to the Upaniṣads and one can never become *dhīra* unless he is frecd from the taints of sin (*mṛditakaṣāya*). This is attempted to be achieved through the methods employed in the stage of preparation we have gone through.

Thus, through the exhaustive methods of purification prescribed in the state of preparation, one becomes partially freed from the taints of sin (*pāpman*) and thereby realizes the hidden presence of the *asura* still in his being. Aimless and impulsive actions are replaced by a rhythmic regularity of functions, which is termed here as *chandas* , through a conformity to the dictates of the scriptures or the revealed Reason. But as this, too, proved an inadequate covering, the devas took recourse to *svara* or the sound or the melody (indicating a deeper harmony). And what happened then? 'The *devas* entering it became immortal and fearless' (*amṛtā abhayā abhavan*).[25] They were taken out of the sphere of Death by the uplifting power of *svara* or *nāda* or the sound. They had drawn themselves inward through *chandas* or rhythm, now they are raised upward through sound or *svara,* far beyond the reach of the *asuras.* With this upward movement begins the second stage of the Upaniṣadic approach or way and that is why the *Chāndogya Upaniṣad* opens with this *Udgītha Upāsanā*, which literally means the contemplation through the uplifting power of music or rhythmic sound or reason.

But this uplifting sound or energy can hardly be generated by any of the organs of sense, because, being limited, there is a disturbing element present in each of them which breaks up the sound into fragments or disharmony and causes diffusion and dispersion and thus prevents it from moving upward. This disturbing element is the *pāpmān*[26] or the sin of attachment, which inevitably brings in the duality of likes and dislikes, good and bad. This causes a turning, one way or the other and thus deflects the energy from the straight path and makes the sound, too, quivering, unsteady and discordant.

That is why the *devas* failed to raise the *Udgītha* again and again through each of the particular limited sense-organs. After repeated defeats at the hands of the *asūras,* they found out, at long last, the real centre which could generate the uplifting sound. It is the *Mukhya Prāṇa,*'[27] the vital Energy or *Caitanya Śakti,* literally the life-principle residing in the mouth. As they resorted to the *Mukhya Prāṇa,* '[27] a miracle happened. Even the effort of taking an offensive against the *asuras* was not needed, it was not even required of them to strike at the enemy but as the enemy came to strike them, they themselves perished all at once like a clod of earth going to pieces on hitting a piece of stone.[28]

The Nature of the Mukhya Prāṇa

But what is the secret behind this miracle? How was it possible for the *Mukhya Prāṇa* to vanquish the *asuras* so easily without any effort whatsoever, while the sense-organs had failed even with the most strenuous endeavour? The secret is that the *Mukhya Prāṇa* is not attached to any particular organ and is thus free from self-regard and the bonds of attachment; and what transcends the sphere of selfish attachment can never be assailed by the *asuras* or death. It is thus immune from all attack by the hostile forces and is stationed in a sphere of natural freedom.

By locating it in the *mukha* or the mouth it has been indicated that it is not stationed in any of the sense-organs but is situated in a neutral place, free from the taint of likes and dislikes, and is central too. 'Neither the good scent nor the bad is known by it, it has totally extinguished or exterminated all sin (*apahatapāmpā hy 'eṣa*), and therefore whatever it eats or drinks, by that it protects or sustains all the other vital functions'.[29] It is thus clearly an universal principle which sustains all the other particular functions which absolutely depend upon it. The sense-organs are all selfish, as they keep the best thing for themselves and give only the rest to others, as the

Bṛhadāraṇyaka describes them.[30] But the *Mukhya Prāṇa,* being universal in its very nature, has nothing to keep for itself but its sole function is to sustain and nourish others and lift them all from the sphere of death, attachment or limitation.

Hence it is termed *āṅgirasa,* the sustaining essence of all the limbs (*aṅgānām hi rasaḥ*).[31] It is also called '*dūr*'[32] or the 'distant' because death keeps itself at a distance from it. Having exterminated (*apahatya*) death in the form of sin, it carried (*atyavahat*) or took each of the senses and lifted them all beyond the sphere of death (*mṛtyum aty amucyata*)[30] and thereby gave them all their divine forms which shine gloriously, having transcended death (*mṛtyum atikrānto dīpyate*).[34] Thus, through the awakening of the universal principle, all the particular centres of consciousness, too, arc released from their imprisonment of selfishness and sin, and each gains a resplendent divine form, free from death.

The drawback of the methods adopted in the preparatory stage was that they all tried to purify or divinise each particular centre or organ separately and they failed to hit upon a central principle which could sustain and nourish as well as divinise them all. So was the prayer uttered for lifting the soul from darkness and death to illumination and immortality. The Upaniṣad enjoins that those who desire to make a higher and higher ascent (*abhyāroha*)[35] should make a *japa* of this particular prayer, i.e., repeat these lines constantly, and thus become inured to the underlying idea.

Distinction of the two steps

The parable, with which we have been dealing so long, makes two things clear: firstly, the shortcoming of the previous methods and secondly, the unique importance and significance of the *Mukhya Prāṇa* for the next step to be taken. This next step we have termed contemplation, which the Upaniṣads call *upāsanā.* In the preparatory stage the methods involved more or less those connected with the body and the speech. There the main injunctions are signified by the terms '*vada*'[36] and '*cara*' which mean 'speak' and 'act'. Here the injunction is '*upāsīta*'[37] i.e., 'contemplate', or literally 'get near', which involves the mind. Several virtues had to be culled from without or the outer world in the preparatory stage, and so the seeker had to acquire them by a severe effort of the body and the will. Here the inner being is to grow from within, and so the only necessity or requirement is to let the flow of consciousness move uninterruptedly towards that one goal, which is to be achieved. This is called *dhruvā smṛti*[38] or constant remembrance by the Upaniṣad, and it is this process of constant remembrance which is termed *upāsanā.*

The Nature of Upāsanā

Śaṅkara defines *upāsanā* as the steady maintenance of one-pointed devotion of thought towards a particular object, in the way sanctioned by the scriptures, uninterrupted by any other thought apart from it.[39] *Upāsanā* thus involves three factors: (i) a subject who contemplates, the *upāsaka*; (ii) the object of contemplation, *ālambana* or the *upāsya;* and (iii) the act of contemplation, or *upāsanā.* The act of contemplation, thus, seeks to link the subject with the object and ultimately to merge the one into the other through a gradual process of identification. To make this identification possible, the subject must be utterly passive and calm, and so the Upaniṣad enjoins: '*Śānta Upāsīta*'[40]. The object, too, as Śaṅkara points out, should not be something imaginary, i.e., which is conjured up through one's sweet fancy, but it must be '*yathāśāstrasamarthitam*',[41] sanctioned by the scriptures; for, otherwise, one only moves in a world of imagination, without getting anywhere near concrete realization. In order to give a definite line to the process of thought, one must look into the scriptures and direct his thoughts accordingly. Lastly the act of contemplation, in order to be really potent, must have in it the combination of three factors : '*vidyā*' or right knowledge, '*śraddhā* or faith and '*upaniṣad*' or mystic insight.[42] These three things help to bring in more force in the act (*vīryavattaraṁ bhavati*)[43] than is usually found when an act is performed mechanically. *Upāsanā,* is not, therefore, a mechanical act but an act illumined by knowledge, sustained by faith and crowned with a mystic faculty.

Upāsanā literally means to 'come near' a thing. Here the thing to be approached is the very self of the seeker and not something external to him. 'He is to be searched, he is to be enquired about',[44] 'Seeking the Ātman through *śraddhā vidyā*' and all such lines signify that the object of approach is the Ātman or Brahman. It is inherent in us, Yet we have to get near it because we have moved far away from it by the outward-looking tendencies of mind, and have, thus, lost all touch with it. It is the purpose of *upāsanā* to get in touch with it again, to restore the lost contact. We are completely oblivious of the treasure we possess, though we are always carrying it with us. The Upaniṣad makes this clear with an apt simile. As men, ignorant about the worth of a plot of land (*akṣetrajñāḥ*), move about over it, again and again, without knowing that a mass of gold lies buried under it, so are all creatures ignorant about the supreme treasure that lies within them (*anṛtena hi pratyūḍhāḥ*).[45] There are thick layers of ignorance which are to be removed one by one to make it possible for the self to reveal itself in all its majesty. This probing through the coverings of ignorance is the purpose of *upāsanā* and consequently, there are different degrees of contemplation according to the depth of the sinking or penetration.

The Purpose of Upāsanā

The purpose of *upāsanā* is thus twofold—a lifting of the veil of ignorance and a consequent extension of vision and thereby narrowing the division between the subject and the object and finally, reaching the identification. To approach an object, to get to the very self of it and lastly to identify oneself with it is the purpose of *upāsanā*. The approach signifies a movement, and movement is life, and thus *upāsanā* is essentially a function of life or Prāna. We have seen that the upward movement, which is *upāsanā,* is possible only through the help of the *Mukhya Prāṇa.* It is not the vital air that is meant by *Prāṇa* but the Cosmic Energy which is at the root of creation. It is thus not a blind force but a power informed with consciousness. It is the joint product of *jñāna and karman,* illumination and action. There is thus a *samuccaya* or fusion between *jñāna* and *karman* in *upāsanā.* So the *Īśa Upaniṣad* rightly lays stress on this point of togetherness or fusion (*ubhayaṁ saha*)[48] between *Vidyā* and *Avidyā.* Here *jñāna* without *karman* leads to idle speculation and *karman* without *jñāna* leads to mechanical repetition. They must join hands to make the act of contemplation really fruitful and beneficial.

Distinction between Jñāna & Upāsanā

Upāsanā is thus neither pure *jñāna* nor pure *karman* but a biune process comprising both. The distinction between *jñāna* and *upāsanā* is thus an important one, which has been emphasized by the later Vedāntins.[47] In *jñāna* there is no process, nor does it admit of any degree or hierarchy. It is a revelation which is immediate and complete in itself. Neither does it depend upon the effort of the seeker, because it is not a product, brought about by the endeavours of an individual. It purely rests with the object itself, the subject has no contribution to it. If the object reveals itself then it is revealed, otherwise not even a thousand effort on the part of the subject can make it reveal itself. In *upāsanā,* on the contrary, there is a process and consequently a degree or hierarchy. It does not give birth to an immediate and complete revelation but reveals the reality through a mediate and incomplete manifestation, which gradually grows clearer and more complete. It entirely depends upon the agent who contemplates because, here, things are moulded according to thought. As he thinks so he becomes.[48] This becoming or transformation signifies the presence of the element of *karman* in *upāsanā.* As it is a becoming or a process and involves effort on the part of the subject, one has, therefore, to hold on to it steadfastly till the last breath of life. 'Until one gets identified with the reality of the thing contemplated, one should go on thinking over it and later hold on to it till death'.[49] *'Upāsanā* may be done, undone or otherwise done according to the individual and therefore he should (because it rests with him alone) maintain always a continuous flow of consciousness.'[50] It, thus, requires uninterrupted effort for the whole span of life in order to get established in the divine consciousness. The thing contemplated becomes firmly established, the smooth flow (*praśāntavāhitā*)[51] becomes ensured. as Patañjali says, only with long and continuous practice carried on with supreme care.[52] The smooth flow of consciousness is interrupted primarily by the entry of a whole brood of aimless thoughts or *rajas* and secondly, by the onset of inconscience or *tamas.* Our consciousness, thus, has been broken up in different compartments, the waking (*jāgrat*), the dream (*svapna*) and the sleep (*suṣupti*) states. We pass from one state to another without being able to maintain a link with the previous state. Thus the waking consciousness is cancelled first and only then ensues the other state of dream. We cannot enter into the other state unless the former is abandoned. This causes a split or division in consciousness and the aim *of upāsanā* is to remove this division. By constant thinking, the thing contemplated sinks into the subconscious and continues to be revealed even in the dream state (*svapnādāv api*).[53]

Element of devotion in Upāsanā

But the subconscious or the dream state reveals only those things which we desire most, and hold dearest to our heart. Hence the object of contemplation must be a thing of supreme adoration. Without devotion or sincere attachment, no contemplation is possible. One must be passionately fond of the thing he contemplates upon, for otherwise his interest will slide back and take his mind off from the object of contemplation. With deep attachment the thing intrudes on the mind of itself, even when one is engaged in other distracting activities. As a woman, intensely seeking the company of her lover, thinks of him alone even while engaged in her household work, so does a contemplative soul meditate on his object of contemplation even while engaged otherwise.[54] Thus the element of feeling plays an important part in the act of contemplation, and that is why the leading exponents of the Bhakti school of thought, like Rāmānuja, lay their whole emphasis on this *dhruvā smṛti* or *anudhyāna,* constant remembrance as the supreme means of *sādhanā*.

The identification of *dhruvā smṛti* with *upāsanā* is very old and not a new theory propounded by Rāmānuja, for one of the oldest Vedāntins, Brahma-Nandin is credited with a statement, quoted by Rāmānuja in his *Śrī Bhāṣya*, in which he says definitely that *Upāsanā* is nothing but constant remembrance.[55] Vedāntadeśika also quotes a verse which very clearly shows the different steps through which *upāsanā* leads to *bhakti* or absolute devotion for the object of contemplation. It says: 'Knowledge ends in meditation, meditation culminates in constant remembrance, that leads to a seeing or realization i.e. an insight into Reality, and this insight begets devotion'.[56] Rāmānuja clearly points this out while showing the way to realization. 'The means of the realization of Brahman is only supreme devotion (*parābhaktir eva*), which is of the nature of constant remembrance (*anudhyānarūpā*), generated by the extreme loveability of the thing and which is preceded by a knowledge of the Reality acquired from the scriptures and brought into being by the pursuance of the path of devotion, helped by his own actions or *karman.*'[57] He also quotes Yāmunācārya thus: 'The Supreme can be realized by the sole and absolute devotion of a man whose mind has been purified by both (*jñānayoga* and *Karmayoga*)'.[58] In this connexion he quotes the famous saying of the *Īśa Upaniṣad* on *Vidyā* and *Avidyā* and explains *Vidyā* as contemplation which is of the nature of devotion (*bhaktirūpāpannaṁ dhyānam ucyate*).[59] He also refers to the famous utterance in *Kaṭha* that the Ātman cannot he realized by teaching, nor by knowledge nor by hearing profusely, but only he attains it who adores it most of all and to him it reveals its own form; and he comments thereon that the Supreme Purusa is realized by the seeker only when an extreme attachment to that constant remembrance is generated in him.[69] This devotion or attachment, too, is not a mere blind feeling, but Rāmānuja calls it a form of *jñāna* or knowledge (*jñānaviśeṣa eva*), in which the Supreme is realized to be the most adorable thing to the exclusion of all other things and which also gives rise to an utter dislike for everything else.[61] The *Nārada-Bhakti-Sutra* says that *bhakti* requires absolute devotion to the object of contemplation as well as an indifference to all other things opposed to it.[62]

Integral nature of Upāsanā

Thus the Upaniṣadic *Upāsanā* is neither purely emotional nor merely intellectual by nature but is an illumined act of the mind suffused with adoration or love. This has been clearly indicated by the three terms: *vidyayā, śraddhayā* and *upaniṣadā*.[63] Other statements in the Upaniṣads, such as, 'This Ātman is perceived by those of subtle perception through the refined and one-pointed intellect',[64] 'Pierce that goal, by drawing (the bow) with the mind suffused by that feeling (*tadbhāvagatena cetasā*),[65] 'Those become immortal who know it revealed through the heart, the clear intellect and the mind',[66] 'Those become immortal who know it residing in the heart through the heart and the mind',[67] and so on, all equally point out that each of the elements, which constitute our psychic being, has its share in the act of *upāsanā*. It is not an one-sided approach either through the heart or through the intellect but an integral seeking of the whole being. The Upaniṣad shows that by realization of the Ātman, not only is our knowledge completed because by knowing it we know all, but our love, too, is fulfilled because it happens to be 'dearer than the son, dearer than the wealth, dearer than everything else, because this self is the inmost thing'.[68] Hence love, knowledge and action, feeling, knowing and willing, affection, cognition and conation, too, are all involved in this act of *upāsanā*.

In *upāsanā* we have first to get an *ālambana*, literally a 'support' i.e., an object for contemplation and then hold on to it firmly through an unflinching act of the will or concentration and thereafter direct the thought-process along a definite channel; and this becomes smooth and spontaneous with the growth of an insight into and consequent attachment to the object. One must make it the central passion of his life and steadily pursue that definite end, with his whole being. By making the *Mukhya Prāṇa* the main instrument of *upāsanā,* the Upaniṣads have sought to impress upon the seeker that the whole man, the totality of all parts that constitute him, should be engaged or harnessed in this act of contemplation.

Integral nature of Upāsanā

Thus the Upaniṣadic *Upāsanā* is neither purely emotional nor merely intellectual by nature but is an illumined act of the mind suffused with adoration or love. This has been clearly indicated by the three terms: *vidyayā, śraddhayā* and *upaniṣadā.*[63] Other statements in the Upaniṣads, such as, 'This Ātman is perceived by those of subtle perception through the refined and one-pointed intellect',[64] 'Pierce that goal, by drawing (the bow), with the mind suffused by that feeling (*tadbhāvagatena cetasā*),[65] 'Those become immortal who know it revealed through the heart, the clear intellect and the mind',[66] 'Those become immortal who know it residing in the heart through the heart and the mind',[67] and so on, all equally point out that each of the elements, which constitute our psychic being, has its share in the act of *upāsanā.* It is not an one-sided approach either through the heart or through the intellect but an integral seeking of the whole being. The Upaniṣad shows that by realization of the Ātman, not only is our knowledge completed because by knowing it we know all, but our love, too, is fulfilled because it happens to be -dearer than the son, dearer than the wealth, dearer than everything, else, because this self is the inmost thing'.[68] Hence love, knowledge and action, feeling, knowing and willing, affection, cognition and conation, too, are all involved in this act of *upāsanā.*

In *upāsanā* we have first to get an *ālambana,* literally a 'support' i.e., an object for contemplation and then hold on to it firmly through an unflinching act of the will or concentration and thereafter direct the thought-process along a definite channel; and this becomes smooth and spontaneous with the growth of an insight into and consequent attachment to the object. One must make it the central passion of his life and steadily pursue that definite end, with his whole being. By making the *Mukhya Prāṇa* the main instrument of *upāsanā,* the Upaniṣads have sought to impress upon the seeker that the whole man, the totality of all the parts that constitute him, should be engaged or harnessed in this act of contemplation.

Characteristics of Upaniṣadic Contemplation

Having glanced through the general nature of the Upaniṣadic *upāsanā,* let us now look into the characteristics of the methods by means of which the *upāsanā* is carried on. *Upāsanā* being essentially a movement, we find that, everywhere in the Upaniṣads, the movement starts from the outer extremities and gradually penetrates into the inmost recesses of the soul. This is a marked characteristic of all the *vidyās* in the Upaniṣads, which we shall try to trace out clearly later on. A second feature of the *upāsanās* or *vidyās* in the Upaniṣads is that the whole investigation is conducted in two spheres, in the subject as well as in the object, in the individual as well as in the world, in the *'aham'* as also in the *'idam',* in the *'adhyātma'* and also in the *'adhidaiva'* spheres. This method is repeated everywhere. A third trait of the *upāsanās* is that the contemplation is carried on in two ways: synthetically as well as analytically, through *'āpti'* as well as *'samṛddhi',* which the Gitā calls *yoga* and *vibhūti.* The *vidyās* do not rest content in knowing the reality simply as a whole but proceed further to comprehend it in all its infinite details too. That is why the Sagc Kauṣītaki asks his son to recount the rays of the Sun, all around,[69] to sing repeatedly the Prāṇas in a profuse manner[70] and thereby to attain richer fruits of experience than he. He had comprehended the reality in a common non-detailed way, or got a general view of it and now requests his son to know it in all its aspects and thus complete his partial realization. The *Chāndogya Upaniṣad* opens with the *Udgitha Upāsanā,* which is a part of *Sāma Upāsanā* and thereafter in the second chapter goes on to expound the synthetic nature of *Sāma Upāsanā* (*samastasya khalu sāmna upāsanam*).[71] Thus the *upāsanā* is carried from the parts to the whole, from the analytic to the synthetic aspect and vice versa. There is also a graduated hierarchy in some of the *upāsanās,* as we find in the *Parovarīyān Udgītha* and *Parovarīyaḥ Sāma Upāsanā*[72], in which higher and higher gradcs are gradually unfolded and grasped. This is also found in the famous *Nārada-Sanatkumāra-saṁvāda,*[73] where the next is shown to be *bhūyān* i.e., higher than the former in the exposition of the nature of the Ātman. But it should be rcmcmbered that the higher includes the lower and adds something more to it and never rejects it. The lower has its fulfilmcnt in the higher and finds its consummation there but never faces extinction.

The *vidyās* in the Upaniṣads also abound in so-called symbolism; and some symbol is adopted in some form or other in all the spheres of enquiry. But it must be remembered that the symbols of the Upaniṣads are not so many fanciful constructions of the mind which are provided as a support for contemplation. They all represent a deep truth of spiritual experience and hencc are not products of mere wishful thinking. The truths of the symbols become revealed only after one gets an insight into them. We shall try, while discussing the *vidyās,* to account for the various symbols adopted in them, i.e., to find out why those very symbols like the heart-lotus, the cavity of the heart etc, are adopted and why the imagery cannot be altered as we choose. We note this in order to guard against the common and popular view of symbolism, which misses its true significance.

The divisions of Upāsanā

The grades of *upāsanā* are necessitated by the difference in the levels of the intellect. Contemplation, being essentially a function of the intellect. differs in nature according to the composition or quality of the mind which contemplates. Our mind always functions in the realm of relations, the most fundamental of the relations being that subsisting between the subject and the object. The aim of *upāsanā* we have seen, is an identification of the two, by removing the gap that separates the one from the other. It must be incidentally noted here that the subject and the object are, in fact, two aspects of the same one Reality and unless the division is healcd, truth cannot be attained. This healing of the gap is effectcd in two ways: sometimes, by making the subject predominant and sometimes, by giving predominance to the object. This has led to the traditional classification of *upāsanā* in two groups: the *pratīka* or the symbolic, and the *āhaṁgraha* or the subjective. The first is, again, divided into four classes and the second in two, thereby making the total number of classification or varieties of *upāsanā,* six. The subdivisions of the first are: *sampat, āropa. saṁvarga* and *adbyāsa. Sampat,* literally meaning 'wealth', signifies that form of symbolic meditation in which a wealth of qualities is attributed to an otherwise small or insignificant thing.[74] As for example, the mind has been called the infinite and the seeker is asked to contemplate over it as such, though it is well-known that the mind is a finite thing which engages itself with only one thing at a time. The second, *āropa,* literally meaning 'attribution', signifies that form of *upāsanā* in which the relation of the whole with a particular thing is attributed to the parts as well.[75] This is illustrated in the *Udgītha Upāsanā,* where the *Udgītha* happens to be a part of *Sāman* and because *Sāman* happens to be connected with *Oṅkāra,* the *Udgītha,* too, is looked upon as closely related thereto, and contemplated as such. In the third form, viz., *saṁvarga,* a particular action or function is taken as an analogy and attributed as such to the object of contemplation.[76] The destructive wind called *saṁvarga,* literally meaning 'all-engrossing', has the power of enveloping and thereby destroying or controlling all creatures at the time of destruction of the universe (*pralaya*). This great function of universal control is attributed to the vital breath, *prāṅa,* which is supposed to bring under control all the inner and outer senses and hence it is worshipped as such. The last, called *adhyāsa,* is nothing but the attribution of a particular virtue to a particular thing, only because it has been ordained by the scriptures, in spite of the fact that such an attribution is manifestly absurd and contradicts our normal experience.[77] For example, in the *Pañcāgnividyā,* the woman is conceived as fire and contemplated as such, though it is well-known that a creature of dust can hardly be taken as fire itself. To sum up, in *sampat* a quality is attributed, in *āropa a* relation, in *samvarga* an action, and in *adhyāsa* anything found in the scriptures. In all these, the object predominates and is made to assume an importance through the attribution of some quality or activity which distinguishes it from everything else and this special feature grips the mind and makes it absorbed therein. Hence all these forms of *upāsanās* are called outer (*vāhya*) because it is the outer object which is predominant here.

The *ahaṁgraha upāsanā,* however, is termed inner (*āntara*) contemplation because, here, one turns inward towards his own self and contemplates, accordingly, with a feeling of identification of the object contemplated with the subject himself. This *upāsanā* is divided in two classes: *saguṇa* and *nirguṇa.* When some qualities are attached to the self and the contemplation goes on in that manner then it is termed *saguṇa,* and when all qualities are stripped of the self and the contemplation seeks an identification with the very essence of being it is then termed *nirguṇa.* The *upāsaṇā* of *Oṅkāra* has this double aspect, both *saguṇa* and *nirguṇa,* as the *Praśna Upaniṣad* makes it clear that the *Oṅkāra* signifies both the *Para* and *Apara* Brahman i.e., the *Saguṇa* as well as the *Nirguṅa,* and the knower attains any one of the two phases by this contemplation on *Oṅkāra.*[78] Similarly the

Bṛhadāraṇyaka enjoins the *upāsaṇā* of the Self alone.[79] When one concentrates on the Self in the *nirguṇa* form it is only then that one seeks an identification with the basic reality which is indicated both in a positive and a negative manner in the Upaniṣads. 'Brahman is Bliss',[80] 'Brahman is the Supreme Consciousness and Bliss',[81] 'Brahman is Truth, Consciousness and Infinite',[82] point to the reality in a positive way, and there are other expressions like 'It is neither gross, nor subtle, neither short, nor long etc.'[83], 'That which is invisible, intangible, without sound, touch, form, immutable',[84] and so on, which indicate the reality in a negative manner. So in the contemplation of the Self one should gather or collect together all the different descriptions, both positive and negative, made about the Self or Brahman in different contexts and contemplate accordingly. The *nirguṇa* form of contemplation being essentially of one type—because the basic reality cannot be of two kinds—it is enjoined that all the attributes or adjectives should be collected together, as they all signify the same essential reality and the contemplation must proceed with this convergence of everything upon the Self. This gathering together of attributes is technically termed *'guṇopasaṁhāra'*. In two different *sūtras,* Vyāsa has enjoined the unity of these positive and negative characteristics attributed to Brahman.[85] In a word, the Ātman is sought to be realized as a unity and hence the different characteristics are not meant for showing the plurality of the Ātman but for pointing to the one and the same thing from various aspects.

Grades of Contemplation

Thus from this traditional classification it is clear that the *upāsanās* are graded according as they approach nearer and nearer the reality. As it becomes difficult for the mind to contemplate without an object, a concession is made to it by providing it with suitable symbols. But as the contemplation grows deeper and deeper, it is felt that 'the object is nothing but a part of the subject and finally comes an identification which takes the form of the feeling, 'That is I', *So'ham asmi.*[86] This identification with the Self is first made through the medium of qualities or attributes, which is called *saguṇa-upāsanā* and finally comes the identification with the very core of being or reality through *nirguṇa-upāsanā.* The superior quality of an *upāsanā* is thus recognized according to its proximity to the supreme realization of identity. Hence the *nirguṇa-upāsanā* is taken to be the best form of contemplation because it gradually leads to the highest knowledge.[87] The *Pañcadaśī* shows the grade thus: 'Better than the acts of the devil is the performance of good acts, better than that is the *saguṇa* contemplation and better than it is the *nirguṇa* one'.[88]

We have already lifted ourselves from the sphere of the devil through the performance of the good and virtuous acts prescribed in the state of preparation.

We shall next engage ourselves with the *saguna* form of contemplation through the different *vidyās* and then go in for the *nirguna-upāsanā* mainly through the help of the analytic methods and finally find a synthesis of the two methods in *Oṅkāra.* All the forms of contemplation have only one aim : to lead to the Supreme Knowledge or *Jyoti,* and hence they are termed *vidyas* and through *vidya,* the Upaniṣad declares, one attains immortality, (*amṛtam aśnute*[89]), nay, rather *vidyā* itself is *amṛta, amṛtam tu vidyā.*[90]

Varieties of approach

Before specifically dealing with the different *vidyās* we propose to examine the characteristics which pertain to the Upaniṣadic approach to Reality. We have already noticed some common features subsisting among the different forms of approach and we must now turn to the special features stamped on them. In other words, we must now ascertain the varieties of approach as we have traced the unity of it. The seeds of all the divergent approaches of later schools of philosophy can be easily traced to the Upaniṣads.

The Upaniṣad uses in many places the expression *dhyāyatha*[91], *dhyāyan apramattaḥ,*[92] *dhyānayogānugatāḥ,*[93] which shows that the method of *dhyāna* or *Yoga,* too, is implied in the *upāsanā* of the Upaniṣads. In fact, the term *Yoga,* too, is found defined in the *Kaṭha* as the calm holding of the senses,[94] which reminds one of the calmness of the limbs generated by *āsana,* with which the Yoga properly begins. Again, in another place, one is asked to separate the Ātman from one's own body very patiently (*pravṛhet svāt śarīrāt*)[95]. This is clearly a method of *viveka* or discrimination, which is elaborated in the Sāṅkhya system. The famous instruction to surrender the speech to the mind, the mind to the *Jñānātmā* or Conscious Self, the Conscious Self to the *Mahān Ātmā,* the Vast Self and that Vast Self finally to the Calm Self,[96] is clearly a method of absorption (*laya* or *nyāsa*).

Japa, too, which happens to hold a very important place in the Tantra system is prescribed in some places, notably in connexion with the famous prayer, *'Asato mā sad gamaya'*.[97] Sometimes absorption through feeling, (*bhāvagatena cetasā,*[98] *tanmayo bhavet*),[99] is asked for, which clearly gives scope to *bhakti. Jānatha*[100] or *Vijijñāsasva,*[100] 'know' or 'enquire', is very frequently enjoined all over the Upaniṣads, which clearly has given birth to the famous *brahmajijñāsā* of the Vedāntins. Thus we find a rich variety in the methods of approach, all of which, of course, press towards the same goal.

Mystic practices

There are traces of mystic practices which later came to occupy a prominent place in the scheme of *sādhanā,* especially in the Tāntric system. We have already seen that the *Udgītha-vidyā* is mainly pursued by the help of the uplifting sound to be generated through the *Mukhya Prāṇa*. This function of sound or *nāda* as the connecting link between the human and the divine is emphasized again and again in the Tantras. In fact only with the generation of *nāda,* the upward flow or current is known to be active. The *Chāndogya,* while showing the means of realizing the presence or existence of the supreme luminosity of the self in the body (*antaḥ puruṣe jyotiḥ*), refers to the hearing of the sound, similar to that generated by the movement of the chariot (*ninadam iva*), or like that of the bellowing of the bull (*nadathur iva*) or resembling the sound of the burning fire, by closing or stopping the ears.[102] The *Bṛhadāraṇyaka* also refers to this hearing of the sound (*ghoṣa*) by stopping the ears and thereby establishes the existence of the great fire *Vaiśvānara* within the human body.[103] This certainly came to be developed as an independent line of *sādhanā* later on, as we find many mystic schools of later times taking to this practice of hearing the internal sound, which is called *nādānusandhāna* and thereby stilling the mind to reach the supreme goal.

Another important yogic practice, that of *prāṇāyāma,* though not explicitly mentioned in the earlier Upaniṣads, is certainly hinted at in a mystic way in many places. In the description of the *UdgīthaUpāsanā* there is a mention of *vyāna,* which is said to be the junction or meeting-point of the two breaths, *prāna* and *apāna.* It must be remembered that by the term *prāṇa* is signified the exhalation and by *apāna,* the inhalation, and *vyāna* signifies the cessation of both. The term *vyāna,* in the Upaniṣads, carries a special sense and does not signify that function of the vital air which pervades all through the body or the skin, as described in the Sāṅkhya and other later philosophical systems. Hence, by signifying that the *vyāna* is the junction of *prāṇa* and *apāna, recaka* and *pūraka,* the Upaniṣad is clearly hinting at *kumbhaka,* where both the outgoing and the ingoing movements cease and meet. This is made all the more clear by the mention of the various acts of valour (*vīryavanti karmāṇi*) which are generally done by stopping the breath-movement, i.e., through *vyāna,* such as the churning of the fire, the running of a race, the drawing of a stiff bow.[104] Thus all acts, which require supreme concentration and energy, are done through *vyāna* and hence in contemplation, which needs extreme attentiveness and alertness, *vyāna* is indispensable and hence, in the *Udgītha,* it comes to play such an important part. The *Kaṭha Upaniṣad,* too, refers to it in a more cryptic way, where it is said that the *prāṇa* is moved up and the *apāna* is thrown down and all the gods worship that little (literally 'dwarf') one, resting in the middle.[105] 'This resting in the middle' is the same as the *'sandhi'* or meeting point, which is *vyāna.* It is called *'vāmana',* the 'dwarf' or 'little' one, because it is of so little a duration that it almost escapes one's notice. In the *Bṛhadāraṇyaka,* this *'vāmana'* of the *Kaṭha* is referred to as *'śiśu'* or the child and there it is explicitly stated that this *śiśu'* is nothing but the middle *prāṇa.*[106] Hence it is without doubt the middle state of equipoise, which in the Tāntric terminology is called the *suṣumnā,* and which lies in the middle of the two opposite currents of *iḍā* and *piṅgalā;* and the whole aim of *sādhanā* is to get hold of this synthetic point and through it move upward.

The two opposite currents, one moving inward, the other coming outward, always keep the mind moving and distracted. In the middle comes the rest, a lull, a stop and in this moment of equipoise, the doors of heaven are ajar and one catches a glimpse, gets a flash, however fleeting, of the luminosity that lies beyond. But it does not abide, because the coming and going movement ensues once more immediately afterwards. But it leaves an indelible impress on the mind, though its duration is so short. Hence the supreme importance of *sandhi* in the Hindu view of contemplation. The *Taittirīya* devotes a whole section to trace out the two opposite forces as well as its *sandhi* in various spheres.[107]

As we find hints about *nāda* and *prāṇa* as instruments of contemplation, so *jyoti*, too, comes to play an important part, as is evident from the Upaniṣads. The colours are given different ranks, and the experience is tested and ranked according to the visualization of the particular colour. Thus the white lustre *śuklam bhāḥ*)[108] of the Sun is referred to, and deeper than that is the intense blue and dark hue (*Yan nīlam paraḥ kṛṣam*).[109] And Śaṅkara comments that this dark hue is visible only to him, whose vision is intensely concentrated (*atyantasamāhitādṛṣṭer dṛśyate*).[110] One who pierces through this dark hue beholds inside it the Golden Puruṣa, who is wholly golden in hue from the hairs down to the nails.[111] The *Madhu-vidyā* places the scheme of colours thus : first comes the red colour (*rohitam rupam*)[112] of the Sun; secondly, the white (*śuklam rupam*);[113] thirdly, the intensely dark hue (*param kṛṣnam rupam*)';[114] lastly comes the liquid lustre, which is found moving in the centre of the Sun (*madhye kṣobhata iva*).[115] Another verse runs thus: 'They see the lustre of the eternal cause all around like the day (light) and this supreme lustre shines in the luminous (Brahman).[116] Śaṅkara comments : 'Those who have realized Brahman, whose eyes are turned inwards, and hearts purified by the practice of *brahmacarya* etc. behold all around the effulgence' (*a samantato jyotiḥ paśyanti*).[117] Another famous verse refers to moving towards the variegated from the dark and again from the variegated to the dark, (*śyāmāc chavalam śavalāc chyāmam prapadye*).[118] Colours are attributed even to the arteries or *nāḍīs* of the heart and their correspondence is shown to the different colours in the Sun. All these arteries of the heart are existing through a subtle essence of a pink colour, as well as white, blue, yellow and red. This Sun, too, is pink, white, blue, yellow and red.[119] Lastly, in the famous *Janaka-Yājñavalkya-saṁvāda*, one is led ultimately to the supreme *Jyoti* or lustre, through the different *jyotis* of *Āditya, Candramā, Agni,* and *Vāk*.[120] Thus *jyoti* or light and colour come to play a significant part in the Upaniṣadic approach to Reality.

In later Upaniṣads, like the *Śvetāśvatara*, there are clear references to the Yogic practices of *āsana, prāṇāyāma, dhāraṇā* etc. as well as to the vision of various lights as indicative of the revelation or experience of Brahman.[121] What are stated explicitly in the later Upaniṣads, are expressed cryptically and in a very concealed manner in the earlier ones. The *Bṛhadāraṇyaka* and the *Aitareya* repeat an identical statement which says that the gods are fond of indirectness (*parokṣapriyāḥ*) and hatc the direct or open method.[122] This seems to apply truly to the method of the earliest Upaniṣads, where they mostly speak as in parables, whose mystery it is difficult to unravel.

Two broad features

From the survey of the characteristics found in the different approaches to Reality in the Upaniṣads, two broad features come out very prominently. The first is an approach through the methods of *yoga,* more or less mystical and the second, through the methods of *viveka* or *vicāra,* more or less the method of Sāṅkhya or *jñāna.* The one proceeds in a synthetic way, seeking out correspondences or harmonies between the outer and the inner self, and the other proceeds through an analytic way searching after the supreme cause, penetrating deeper and deeper by casting off, one by one, the outer wrappages that hide that one reality. Of course, the two methods arc found side by side in many of the Upaniṣads, yet the stress varies. Thus the *Chāndogya* begins with the *Udgītha-upāsanā* which, evidently, comes under the synthetic approach, while the *Bṛhadāraṇyaka's* keynote is to be found in *Ātma ity eva upāsīta'*,[123] in the contemplation of the Ātman itself, which belongs to the second way. Thus, in these two great Upaniṣads, though many things are found to be common and even repeated in both places and though both the methods find place in each of them, yet there is a predominance of the first method in the *Chāndogya* and that of the second in the *Bṛhadāraṇyaka.* That is why the Vedantins find their supreme sustenance from the *Bṛhadāraṇyaka,* while followers of the *Bhakti* school get invaluable guidance from the *Chāndogya.* Similarly, the *Īśa* definitely favours the synthetic approach (*ubhayam saha*), while the *Kena* leans towards the method of discrimination (*ne' dam yad idam*).[125] The *Kaṭha* steers a middle course and tries to do justice to both the ways. The *Praśna* is mostly synthetic, though there is a touch of the other approach towards the end. The *Muṇḍaka* closely follows the *Kaṭha* in giving equal scope to both. The *Māṇḍukya* gives scope to the method of synthesis (*pāda mātrā mātrāś ca pādā*)[126] while finally giving predominance to the other way of analysis (*nā''ntaḥprajñam* etc.)[127] The *Taittirīya* in different sections allots definite places to both the methods. The *Aitareya,* tracing out the source of creation, ultimately finds *prajñā* at the root and its correspondence with all the functions of the mind, nay with everything (*sarvam prajñāne pratiṣṭhitam*).[128]

References

1. CU, 7.26.2.
2. Ibid.
3. Ibid.
4. BU, 1.3.28.
5. CU, 1.2.1.
6. anyonyābhibhavodbhava-rūpas saṁgrāma iva sarvaprāñiṣu pratidehaṁ devāsurasaṁgrāmo anādi-kālapravṛtta ity abhiprāyaḥ, ŚB, on CU, 1.2.1.
7. devā divyater dyotanār-thasya śāstrodbhāsitā indriyavṛttayaḥ. asurās tadviparitās sveṣv evā'suṣu viśvagviṣayāsu prāṇana-kriyāsu ramaṇāt svābhāvikyas tama-ātmikā indriyavṛttaya eva. ŚB on CU, 1.2.1.
8. ŚB on CU, 7.26.2.
9. CU, 1.2.1.
10. CU, 1.4.2.
11. Ibid.
12. CU, 1.4.3.
13. ŚB on CU, 1.4.3.
14. CU, 1.2.
15. KTU, 1.2.3.
16. MU, 1.2.13.
17. KTU, 2.11.
18. BU, 4.4.22.
19. BU, 4.4.23.
20. KTU, 2.11.
21. Ibid, 2.2.
22. Ibid, 4.1.
23. MU, 1.1.6.
24. MU, 3.2.5.
25. CU, 1.4.4.
26. CU, 1.2.2.
27. CU, 1.2.7.
28. CU, 1.2.7.
29. CU, 1.2.9-10.
30. BU, 1.3.9.
31. BU, 1.3.9.
32. Ibid.
33. BU, 1.3.12.
34. Ibid.
35. BU, 1.3.28.
36. TU, 1.11.1.
37. CU, 1.1.1.
38. CU, 7.26.2.
39. ŚB on CU, 1.1.1.
40. CU, 3.14.1.
41. ŚB, Ibid.
42. CU, 1.1.10.
43. Ibid.
44. CU, 8.7.1.
45. CU, 8.3.2.
46. IU, 11.
47. PD, 9.74.
48. taṁ yathā yathā upāsate tad eva bhavati. ŚBR, 10.5.2.20.
49. tathai' vā' mṛti dhārayet. PD, 9.7.8.
50. Ibid. 9.80.
51. YS, 1.13.
52. Ibid. 1.14
53. PD, 9, 82.
54. PD, 9.83-84.

55. upāsanaṁ syād dhruvānusmṛtir darśanān nirvacanāc ca. Śrī Bh. p. 34.
56. vedanaṁ dhyānaviśrāntaṁ dhyānaṁ dhruvā smṛtau/ sā ca dṛṣṭitvam abhyeti dṛṣṭir bhaktitvam ṛcchati. SD, p. 136.
57. brahmaprāptyupāyaś ca śāstrādhigatatattvajñānapūrvakasvakarmānugṛhītabhaktiniṣṭhasādhyānavadhikātiśayapriyaviśadātamapratyakṣatāpannānudhyānarūpaparabhaktir eve' ty uktam. VAS, pp. 248.
58. ubhayaparikarmitasvāntasyai' kāntikātyantikabhaktiyogalabhya iti. Ibid. p. 142.
59. VAS, p. 143.
60. Ibid p. 146.
61. Ibid p. 147.
62. NBS, 9.
63. CU, 1.1.10.
64. KTU, 1.3.12.
65. MU, 2.2.3.
66. KTU, 2.6.9.
67. SU, 4.20.
68. BU, 1.4.8.
69. raśmīṁs tvaṁ paryāvartayāt. CU, 1.5.2.
70. prāṇāns tvaṁ bhūmānam abhi gāyatāt. Ibid. 1.5.4.
71. CU, 1.9.2.
72. Ibid. 2.7.1
73. Ibid. 7.2-15.
74. SG, 12. 10.
75. Ibid. 12.11.
76. SG, 12.13.
77. Ibid. 12.12.
78. PRU, 5.2.
79. ātme'tyeva upāsīta. BU, 1.4.7.
80. TU, 3.6.1
81. BU, 3.9.28.
82. TU, 2.1.
83. BU, 3.8.8.
84. MU, 1.1.6.
85. VS, 3.3.11. & 3.3.33.
86. ĪU. 16.
87. yāvad vijñāasāmīpyam tāvat śraiṣṭhyaṁ vivardhate/ brahmajñānāyate sākṣāt nirguṇopāsanaṁ śanaiḥ. PD, 9.12.2.
88. Ibid. 9.12.1.
89. ĪU, 11.
90. SU, 5.1.
91. MU, 2.2.6.
92. CU, 2.22.2.
93. SU, 1.3.
94. KTU, 2,6,11.
95. Ibid 2.6.17.
96. Ibid, 1.3.13.
97. BU, 1.3.28.
98. MU, 2.2.3.
99. CU, 2.2.4.
100. MU, 2.2.5.
101. TU, 3.1.
102. CU, 3.13.8.
103. BU, 5.9.
104. CU, 1.3.4-5.

105. KTU, 2.5.3.
106. ayaṁ vāva śiśur yo' yaṁ madhyamaḥ prāṇaḥ. BU, 2.2.1.
107. TU, 1.3.
108. CU, 1.6.5.
109. CU, 1.6.6.
110. ŚB on Ibid.
111. Ibid.
112. CU, 3.1.4.
113. Ibid. 3.2.5.
114. CU, 3.3.3.
115. Ibid, 3.5.3.
116. Ibid. 3.17.7.
117. SB, on Ibid.
118. CU, 8.13.1
119. Ibid. 8.6.1
120. BU, 4.3.2-6.
121. ŚU, 2.8.11.
122. AU, 1.3.14
123. BU, 1.4.7.
124. IU, 11.
125. KU, 1.4.8.
126. Mā, 8.
127. Mā, 7.
128. AU, 3.3.

CHAPTER V

THE SYNTHETIC WAY

The way of synthesis essentially seeks a centre, a meeting-point where all the divergent lines converge and coalesce. Thereby the separation of the inner and outer spheres is sought to be removed, the sundered life is sought to be integrated. There are three principal centres where this synthesis is easily realized. These three points of synthesis are : the Heart (Hṛdaya), the Life (Prāṇa) and the Sun (Āditya). Even outwardly viewed, it is too well-known a fact that the heart is the central thing in the physical organism. The Prāṇa, too, is the most vital and central thing, rather the pivot round which moves the whole system of corporeal existence. This has been made clear, again and again, in the Upaniṣads through numerous parables and specific statements. The Sun, similarly, comes to occupy the same position in the solar system, and so what is inwardly Prāṇa or Prajñā is outwardly Āditya or the Sun. 'Āditya is verily the outer Prāṇa' declares the Upaniṣad.[1] We shall try to get in touch with these three centres through the help of three principal *vidyās* in the Upaniṣad, viz., the *Dahara-vidyā,* the *Udgītha-vidyā,* and the *Madhu-vidyā.* The *Dahara-vidya* tries to plumb the depths of the heart, the *Udgītha-vidya* seeks to generate the reconciling rhythm of Prāṇa, and the *Madhu-vidya* wants to explore the path of the immortal essence through the rays of the Sun.

(i) *The Dahara Vidyā*

The *vidyās* in the Upaniṣads form the rungs of the ladder of divine ascent, of which the *Dahara-vidyā* is the highest, and so we begin with it, first of all.

The text of the Upaniṣad runs:, 'Of all the *vidyās* the heart is the sole shelter' (*ekāyanam*).[2] In other words, all the *vidyās* are rooted in the heart. The supreme virtues like *śraddhā,* (faith) *satya,* (truth) ete., with which we dealt in the preparatory stage, are all ultimately referred to the heart. In what is faith rooted? In the heart, because through the heart is the faith known'.[3] In what is truth found? In the heart; through the heart is the truth recognized, therefore in the heart is the truth established.'[4] Yājñavalkya teaches King Janaka about the heart in the following manner: 'What is stability? The heart is the stability. The heart is the shelter of all creatures, the heart is the root or the ground of all creatures, in the heart are all creatures sheltered. The heart is the Supreme Brahman'[5]. Thus the heart is here identified with the Supreme Brahman itself and it now becomes clear how everything in the universe—all the virtues, all the *vidyās,* all the creatures, all the meanings and values—is rooted there. Brahman being the supreme source of the universe, all things are naturally rooted in it and the heart being identified therewith gives shelter to everything. Unless one enters into the heart, there is no stability (*sthitatā*) for him. He is in the grip of instability, a ceaseless flux or movement, so long as he does not get an entry into the heart. No contemplation (*upāsanā*) can really begin until the self enters into the heart, because he must first get a stable tranquil position and only then can he think of moving upwards and approaching the Supreme, which is contemplation. The constant whirl of the outer movement allows no fixity to the self and keeps it constantly on the move. To counteract the outer movement the inward movement is initiated and when it becomes complete it reaches the end, which is the heart. The self now gets a secure station or anchorage, rather gets his own self back, and now can begin his journey upwards.

The secret, behind the fact of the heart being the station of all, lies in this that inside the heart is the *ākāśa,* the supreme space, which is beyond the touch or taint of other gross matters because of its extremely subtle nature. It is the utter emptiness or void, the cavity (*suṣiram*), where the distracting noises never penetrate and hence its eternal and utter stability. Therefore the heart is identified as the seat of the self in numerous statements: 'in the heart is the Ātman'[6]. 'This my Ātman is inside the heart, subtler than a grain and this my Ātman is inside the heart, bigger than the earth, the heaven and all the worlds.'[7] 'The inner self, who is the Puruṣa of the size of a thumb, is ever ensconced in the heart of all men.'[8] Echoing the Upaniṣads the Gītā says: 'The Lord resides in the region of the heart of all creatures'.[9]

The very etymological meaning of the word *hṛdaya* signifies, as the Upaniṣads show, that it is here that the Ātman resides. 'This Ātman is in the heart; therefore this is its etymology: 'In the heart is this (*hṛdi ayam*), therefore (is it called) *hṛdayam* or the heart'.[10]

Thus everything testifies to the importance of the *hṛdaya* as the place where the Ātman is to be found. Hence, the *Dahara-vidyā* opens thus: Now in this city of Brahman is the subtle abode of lotus and inside it is the very subtle *ākāśa* or space. That which is inside it that is to be searched after, that is to be enquired about.'[11] Here first comes the imagery of the city of Brahman, *brahmapura.* As the city of a king contains his subjects and attendants who carry out his behests, similarly this body is the city of Brahman containing the several senses, the mind and the intellect, all serving the purpose of the master.[12] The *Kaṭha,* similarly, refers to the city of eleven gates of the Unborn Self.[13] The *Śvetāśvatara* also speaks of the nine-gated city of the bodily self (*navadvāre pure dehī*).[14] The *Chāndogya,* in another context, refers to the five luminous apertures of the heart (*pañca devasuṣayaḥ*) which are the five vital breaths.[15] They are like the gate-keepers of the city of heaven (*svargasya lokasya dvārapāḥ*).[16] Śaṅkara comments: 'By these, viz., the eye, the ear, the tongue, the mind and the vital air or life, outwardly engaged, are the doors of the realization of Brahman, residing in the heart, closed. It is an experienced fact that the mind does not dwell on the Brahman in the heart, being covered by ignorance due to the attachment to outer objects because of the senses remaining uncontrolled.'[17] Thus it is clear that the outer senses, whether enumerated sometimes as eleven or sometimes as nine or five, are the doors of perception through which the self makes contact with the outer world, But to enter into the inner sanctuary of the self, these must be closed. This is sought to be conveyed by the imagery of the city of Brahman.

The inner abode of the self is the subtle lotus of the heart. 'Inside one's body, above the navel, within a region of twelve fingers, of the shape of a lotus-bud with its face downwards and slightly blooming, covered all around by a network of nerves, is the abode of the Universal Self. Within that lotus is a subtle aperture which is the *ākāśa* or supreme ether. In that *ākāśa* resides the Supreme Brahman unmoved.'[18] The imagery of the lotus (*puṇḍarīska*) evidently signifies that the heart is the centre of the *buddhi,* for the lotus is the symbol of the intellect which blossoms forth, petal by petal, as it gets in touch with the light of the Sun of the Spirit. That the heart signifies the deepest centre of *buddhi* is clear from the use of the term *'guhā'*, again and again, in the Upaniṣads, where the Ātman, we are told, remains concealed: 'Of this creature, the Ātman is concealed in the cave'[19], 'Having entered the cave in the supreme ether'[20], 'Know this as hidden in the cave',[20] 'He who knows it hidden in the cave'[22] and so on. The *Taittirītya,* after enunciating the nature of Brahman, says: 'Who knows it as hidden in the cave, founded in the supreme ether'[23]. The *guhā* or the cave and the heart are identical, as is evident from the use of such terms as *guhāgranthi*[24] and *hṛdayagranthi*[25] in the same sense. The knots that bind the soul are all in the *buddhi,* for it is through the *buddhi* that the soul gets connected or entangled with the outer world in infinite ways. This is also physiologically signified by the description of the innumerable nerves which create a sort of network inside the heart (*antarhṛdaye jālakam iva*).[26] We also hear of the hundred and one *nāḍīs* of the heart, of which only one leads upward and the others move in multifarious directions.[27] Thus what is physiologically shown as the heart, from which proceed the numerous channels of conscious movement, i.e. the whole network of *nāḍīs,* is psychologically depicted as the *buddhi* or the intellect, which is the centre from which radiates the innumerable rays of impressions and experiences. That the *hṛdaya* is identical with the *buddhi* is further made clear by such statements as the desires are all deposited in the heart',[28] or 'one crosses beyond all the sorrows of the heart',[29] where the term *'hṛdayam'* evidently signifies the *'buddhi',* which is the store of all desires and sorrows and other allied feelings. The *Aitareya Upaniṣad* makes it explicitly clear that the heart (*hṛdayam*), the mind (*manas*) and all different functions of the intellect. as *saṁjñāna, ājñāna, vijñāna, prajñana* etc. are only different names of *prajñāna* or the *buddhi.*[30]

Thus it is clear beyond doubt that the *'hṛdaya', the 'guhā',* the *'hṛtpuṇḍarika'* all signify the *buddhi,* which is the subtle abode of Brahman (*daharaṃ veśma*).[31] Inside this is the subtle *ākāśa* or other[32]. The abode being subtle, the *ākāśa* is subtler still. This *ākāśa* is not physical space but is only a name of Brahman and signifies that alone, as Śaṅkara makes it clear. Brahman is called *ākāśa* because of the common features of bodilessness, subtleness, and all-pervasiveness.[33] The very root meaning of the term *ākāśa* points to the all-pervasive luminosity which is Brahman (*ā samantāt kāśate prakāśate iti*). Thus by penetrating through the heart one must get hold of this extremely subtle *ākāśa* and again piercing through it search for that which lies inside it. From the outer ranges of the *brahmapura* or the city of Brahman one first enters into the inner abode of the heart, from the inner abode of the heart one proceeds further inside into the supremely subtle *ākāśa* and finally dives into the bottomless depths to get at the core of being, the foundation of all foundations. The Upaniṣadic way everywhere leads the seeker thus from the outer to the inner and then to the inmost realm step by step. All this points to the fact that the *ākāśa* is the outer symbol of Brahman, *buddhi* the inner and the Ātman which surpasses even these in subtleness is the real Brahman.

Now, the doubt naturally arises that when word *'dahara'*, which signifies extreme smallness or subtleness, has been used as an adjective for both the lotus-abode (*puṇḍarīkaṁ veśma*) and the *ākāśa* or space therein, then the thing inside it, which is to be searched after, must be smaller still. Then what is the use of such a search after the smallest thing ? Is it not an almost entirely fruitless exertion that leads to nothing? The subtleness goes on to be finer and finer as one penetrates farther and farther, till it almost seems to be reaching the vanishing point. Hence a doubt naturally crops up that makes one feel the utter uselessness of this search, because it seems to be leading to a zero or a void. So the Upaniṣad itself voices the doubt by raising the question thus : "Now if he (the teacher) is asked: 'In the city of Brahman, the subtle lotus-abode and inside it in the subtle space, what does exist, what is to be enquired about"?[34] Then he should reply: 'The *ākāśa* inside the heart is as much as this *ākāśa.* Both the heaven and the earth is truly existent herein, both the fire and the wind, the sun and the moon, the lightning and the stars or planets. Whatever is of it here and whatever not, all are truly stored in it".[35] The reply, thus, effectively removes the misconception about the smallness of the space inside the heart and the consequent nothingness attributed to the thing inside it, by showing that the *ākāśa* inside the heart is of an identical magnitude with the physical sky or space. Not only that; it is of an unlimited magnitude, as is made clear by the reference of everything existing or non-existing to it. As Sankara rightly points out, the analogy of the physical space is taken,[36] simply because there is no other appropriate analogy to signify the infinitude of the inner realm of the heart, and so it is not to be misunderstood that the inner space is of an identical size or magnitude as the physical space.

Here the Upaniṣad also clearly points to the absolute correspondence between the microcosm and the macrocosm. By stating that the earth and the heaven, all elements, gods and planets, nay everything that is and is not, are to be found herein within the heart, the Upaniṣad wants to emphasise the great fact that there is really no distinction or opposition between the outer and the inner universe. Our body is verily the universe and hence it is termed here as *brahmapura,* or the city of Brahman. As nothing can exist apart from Brahman and as this Brahman itself verily inhabits the body, therefore all things whatsoever exist in it, and can be found here within the body itself, only if one can wake up in the deepest level of consciousness which is the heart, the central point of integration. From the heart, which is the true centre, one can get in touch with all the different centres of harmony or synthesis which can be found symmetrically set and arranged all through the body.

'Whatever is here that is there, and whatever is there that is here'[37] is the great truth which is sought to be imparted through the different *vidyās* in the Upaniṣads. There is nothing in the outside universe which is not inside the body. Only one has to be awake in those centres, i.e. make those centres active, and immediately the particular is joined to the universal and the two are found to be identical. Hence, once this consciousness of highest integration is gained, the mind becomes creative, and whatever is desired springs forth, of itself, immediately with the thought of it. So the Upaniṣad describes that whatever *'loka'* or sphere is desired to be attained by such a realized soul, that particular *'loka'* comes to him only from his *'saṅkalpa'* or desire.[38] Śaṅkara rightly comments that like Īśvara, he too being full of the purest essence (*viśuddha sattva*), his desires always become true and fruitful and are never falsfied,[39] i.e. never remain unrealized. The Ātman is said to be *'satyakāma'* and *'satyasaṅkalpa'*, and the seeker now being identified with the Ātman, all his desires and resolutions become unhindered and unhampered, or in other words, here all oppositions vanish. The desires of wordly creatures are baulkcd at every step and often remain unrealized but the case is totally different with Īśvara[40] or the Self who realizes his identity with Him. He, being the Lord of Nature, makes her yield whatever He wants, while the worldly creatures, being her slaves, remain at her mercy.

Thus it has been made clear that within the apparently small space in the heart lies embedded the whole universe. But yet a difficulty remains. Through the imagery of the city of Brahman the body was referred to and thence, a reference was made to the heart-lotus and the subtle space therein, and it was finally shown that all things rest there. But is not the body, though called by the magnified name of 'the city of Brahman', a perishable thing? And, then, with its perishing, all the things, which were said to rest within it, must also necessarily perish. Then what remains? Ultimately does it not all come to nothing? The Upaniṣad replies : 'By its decay, it (the *ākāśa*) does not decay, by its death, it is not killed, this is the immovable or true *brahmapura,* all the desires rest herein. This Ātman is free from all, sin as well as from old age, death, grief, desire for eating or drinking, and is of true resolutions and true desires, As here the subjects carry out the injunctions (of a king), so whatever he desires, whichever place or land, those very things are brought into being'[41]. This is the secret cave of the heart which is the repository of the highest *prajñā,* in which shines the Supreme Self in his full effulgence. In fact, it is the byss beyond which is the Abyss.

Thus it is taught that the *ākāśa* is imperishable, and with the decay or the perishing of the the body, that suffers no decay or death. If the *ākāśa* itself is imperishable like that, then what to speak of the Ātman or Brahman which is even subtler than it?[42] Hence the term *'brahmapura'* does not signify the perishable body but Brahman itself,[43] who is the supreme abode (*pura*) of all beings and where all desires are stored. By referring all desires to the *brahmapura,* the Upaniṣad asks the seeker to turn inwards for the fulfilment of his desires instead of looking outwards and running after the worldly objects to get his desires fulfilled. Thus the turning inwards is not meant for a suppression of desires or for killing them out, but only to seek their complete fulfilment and actualisation or sublimation.

Finally, the nature of the Ātman is described in detail because that is the supremely imperishable thing. To find that utter imperishability one had entered into the cavity of the heart. The abode was found, and now the inhabitant thereof is discovered, who is free from all taint and even beyond the *ākāśa* (*virajaḥ para ākāśāt*)[44]. It is in this imperishable being that the *ākāśa* is contained.[45] 'It is this which resides in the *ākāśa,* which is subtler than it, and whom the *ākāśa* doee not know, whose body is the *ākāśā,* who inwardly controls it'.[46]

Thus the *Dahara-vidyā* essentially concentrates on the centre of the *buddhi* and through it seeks to realize the Ātman that dwells therein.

The centre is conceived as a lotus because it blooms only in the rays of the Sun of the Spirit and springs from the waters of life. Buddhi is the joint product of life and spirit and hence its unique position as a centre of synthesis. Here this centre is utilised effectively for the realization of the Ātman in a unique way.

(ii) Udgītha Vidyā

The *Udgītha* is a part of *Sāman* and its unique importance lies in the fact that it occupies the mid-position or the point of conjunction among the different constituent parts of the *Sāma Upāsana*. The parts of the *Sāman* are sometimes taken as five[47] and sometimes as seven.[48] The five parts are: (i) *Hinkāra,* (ii) *Prastāva,* (iii) *Udgītha,* (iv) *Pratihāra,* and (v) *Nidhana*. The seven parts are enumerated as follows : (i) *Hinkāra,* (iii) *Prastāva,* (iii) *Ādi,* (iv) *Udgītha,* (v) *Pratihāra,* (vi) *Upadrava,* (vii) *Nidhana*. Thus it is clear that the *Udgītha* occupies the third place in the scheme of five, and the fourth place in the scheme of seven and thus happens to be at the mid-point of both forms of *Sāma Upāsana*. It is the pivot round which moves the whole *upāsanā* through *Sāman*.

The secret of all *upāsanā* lies in this *sandhi* or mid-point. *Upāsanā* being essentially a function of the *buddhi* or *prāṇa,* its success depends on rightly grasping the central point from which radiate the infinite streams of consciousness. *Prāṇa* or *buddhi* elaborates itself into grades and levels and as such, is a complex whole made of parts and is not a simple unity like the Self. Hence also the importance of the central point in the ladder of consciousness or the scale of being. Only from the centre an integration or harmonisation is possible and so the *Udgītha* serves the purpose admirably and hence its importance.

The *Chāndogya Upaniṣad* opens with this *Udgītha-upāsanā* and tries to show its importance from various aspects. First, it is identified with the mystic syllable Om,[49] because the *Udgītha* or the singing of the hymn begins with Om[50]. Next it is shown, by tracing the different sources of things step by step, that the *Udgītha* is the supreme essence of all things. 'The earth is the essence of the creatures; of the earth, the waters are the essence, of the waters, the herbs or plants are the essence, of the herbs, the *puruṣa* or man is the essence, of man, *vāk* or speech is the essence and of *vāk,* the *ṛk* or the verse is the essence, of *ṛk*, the *sāman* or the song is the essence, and of *sāman,* the *Udgītha* is the essence'.[51] Hence the *Udgītha* is the ultimate essence of all essences.[52] It is composed of *ṛk* and *sāman,* which are again identified with *vāk* and *prāṇa* respectively.[53] *Vāk* signifies reason, and *prāṇa* signifies action or movement. Thus the *Udgītha* is a combined product of reason and action, *jñāna* and *karman,* illumination and vibration. With the fusion (*mithuna*)[54] of these two complementary parts comes fulfilment and deployment, fruition as well as creativity and prosperity thereof (*samṛddhi*)[55]. Thus it is clear that the *Udgītha* is not mechanical music or vibration but the song of reason or the song celestial. It is an intelligently generated rhythm of music and this touch of thought or reason in the song adds to its strength or force (*viryavattaraṁ bhavati*)[56].

The Upaniṣad, here, clearly gives a hint, by the way, about making contemplation really forceful and successful. It says that there is a lot of difference between a thing done with knowledge and a thing done ignorantly. Whatever is done with knowledge as well as faith, combined with the secret science (*upaniṣadā*), that verily becomes more forceful.[57] By adding the word 'more' (*taram*) it has been sought to be conveyed that mere mechanical action, devoid of reason, is not absolutely without use or power. But it is not potent enough to lift one out of the sphere of darkness and death. So it is essential to add reason to action and thus make it more forceful, as here in the *Udgītha.*

But the song of *Udgītha* can hardly be produced with success by any of the particular organs. They all fail to generate the right rhythm or vibration because these organs are all particularized or localized in their functions and hence cannot be the fit instrument to generate the universal music of *Udgītha.* This particularization causes the narrowness of attachment which is termed sin (*pāpman*), with which all the particular sense-organs are said to be smitten (*pāpmanā hy eṣa viddhaḥ*).[58] The universal music thus needs a universal centre, from which it can be rightly expressed, faultlessly generated and ideally represented. The gods, after failing to produce the *Udgītha* through the sense-organs, finally hit upon the *Mukhya Prāṇa* as the right centre for it and thereby lifted themselves from the sphere of death, as well as made themselves immune from the attacks of the *asuras.*[59] The *Mukhya Prāṇa*, we must remind, is not the vital breath but the highest principle of Conscious Energy, *Cit-Śakti* which sustains the whole creation as well as the individual beings. The *elan vital* of Bergson approximates to some extent this *Mukhya Prāṇa* of the Upaniṣads, especially in its characteristic of an universal principle. But the *Mukhya Prāṇa* is not a blind force like the *elan vital,* which moves and moves onward without any definite end or aim. It is a combined product of *jñāna* and *karman* and as such, the ideal instrument for *sādhanā.*

What is inwardly Prāna is outwardly the Āditya, for with the rise of the Sun is removed the dread of darkness, the Sun comes singing and showering plenitude on the creatures.[60] As the *Udgātā* sings his *udgītha* for the fulfilment of all wants, so also the Sun rises singing and bringing fulfilment thereby, for without its rise no production is possible on earth and thus all production and consequent fulfilment of wants depend on the Sun. With the rise of the Sun all darkness disappears of itself. No particular effort is needed for the removal of the gloom, but one feels lifted automatically from the region of darkness with its rise. This power of 'lifting up' makes it identified with the *Udgītha,* for the very basic meaning of the term *'Udgītha'* signifies this 'uplifting' or 'moving up,' as we shall see presently.

Āditya is everywhere identified with Prāna in the Upaniṣads. The *Praśna Upaniṣad* expressly says: 'Āditya is verily Prāna,'[61] 'Āditya is the outer Prāṇa',[62] 'This is the *Vaiśvānara,* the Universal Form, Prāṇa, Agni that is rising as the Sun.'[63] Here the identification is depicted all the more clearly by a reference to the similarity of their action, quality as well as the effect they produce. 'This and that is equal',[64] because this is warm and that too.[65] The quality of warmth is found to be common between Prāna and Āditya. Secondly, Prāṇa is called *'svara'* i.e. coming or moving, and Āditya, too, is called *'svara'* as well as *'pratyāsvara'* i.e. coming and returning i.e. rising and setting.[66] Thus their names, which signify their action, are also similar. Prāṇa dedicates itself to others and sustains all the parts, being the universal principle; similarly, Āditya rises for the benefit of the whole world and sustains the entire creation. Prāna removes all sin, Āditya, too. removes all darkness and fear.[67]

Thus Prāṇa and Āditya are only two aspects of the one supreme principle and there is absolutely no difference between the inner and the outer manifestations. The seeker has first to get hold of it within himself through the Prāṇa and then proceed to know it even outside himself through the Āditya. Thus he comes to realize the one universal principle running through all, within him and without him, inside him and outside him, in his heart as well as in the heaven.

After thus identifying Prāṇa and Āditya, the Upaniṣad again turns inward and shows a point of synthesis even among the different vital breaths or functions. We have pointed out in the very beginning that the *Udgītha-upāsanā* is essentially engaged in finding out a mid-point of harmony all around. Here also we find that the *vyāna*[65] is taken as an instrument of the *Udgītha,* simply because it happens to be the point of conjunction (*sandhi*) between *prāṇa* and *apāna*, the inner and the outer breath. In the centre of conjunction lies concealed the store of energy, and the *vyāna* being such a centre, all acts of valour like the churning of the fire, the running of a race, the drawing of a bow etc. are done by means of the *vyāna* i.e., by suspending the breath-movement totally.[69] The breath-movement causes a dissipation of force and by stopping it, one gathers strength or energy. By thus conserving the energy at the *vyāna,* one rekindles the flame or sharpens his hunger for the spirit (*dīptāgnir bhavati*).[70] Hence the *Udgītha,* to be made forceful and effective, has to be sung through the *vyāna,* i.e., with a total suspension of inhalation and exhalation. For this reason the *vyāna* is to be worshipped as the *Udgītha,* says the Upaniṣad (*etasya hetor vyānam eva udgītham upāsīta*).[71]

The *Udgītha-upāsanā* is, thus, first conducted through Prāṇa, then through Āditya and next, with a combination of both the inner and the outer symbol. To make the *Udgītha* really forceful, the central point of the vital function, viz., *vyāna* is referred to as the right centre for producing it. The Upaniṣad, then, goes on to show that even the very name *'Udgītha'* carries a hidden significance, and by meditating on it, one can attain the fruits of contemplation. As Śaṅkara says: "Even by the contemplation on the letters of the name, the named itself is contemplated" (*nāmākṣaropāsane' pi nāmavata eva upāsanaṁ kṛtaṁ bhavet*).[72] Thus even the letters of a word become a symbol for reality inasmuch as they are all impregnated with the power of the Spirit, filled with a deep significance.

To kindle the Spirit is everywhere the aim of Brahmavidyā and the technique is made so perfect that even a name carries within it the power to generate in the mind the thoughts of the Spirit, Here the meditation is not enjoined on the mere letters or the *word 'udgitha'* separately, but on the letters of the *name 'udgītha',* as is evident from the attaching of the word '*iti*' after *udgītha.*[73] Thus it is the contemplation of the meaningful word or concept, because a name signifies something which is beyond the letters. The term *'Udgītha'* is hence a significant word, because it carries a hidden meaning or idea behind it, and that is to be explored now.

The name '*Udgītha*' is composed of three letters or syllables, '*ut*' '*gī*' and '*tha*'. The letter '*ut*' stands for Prāṇa because '*ut*' signifies an 'uplifting' or rising up.[74] Only that which is full of life is found to rise and prosper and a thing devoid of life stands inert and motionless. Prāna is thus the lever to raise the soul and hence its significant name '*ut*'. Then '*gī*' stands for '*vāk*' or speech because '*gīh*' or '*girah*' is a common name for speech used by all.[75] Then, lastly, '*tham*' stands for '*anna*' or food, because '*tha*' signifies '*sthiti*' or resting and everything ultimately rests on food.[76] Thus we get three things from the name '*Udgītha*': Prāṇa, *vāk*, and *anna*. We have already pointed out that the *Udgītha* is the joint product (*mithuna*) of Prāṇa and Vāk and the very letters, too, that compose the word, point to the same thing.

The first need is to feel the uplifting surge of life, the full flood of rise and growth. It is only by invoking the Prāṇa that this can be effectcd. Next, after raising the key of life to a higher pitch one must take recourse to '*gī*' or '*vāk*' for the supreme enlightenment or knowledge. In the Vedic symbol she is Sarasvatī, the repository of all knowledge. She makes the milk flow from her breasts and causes the divine nectar to drip for the sake of the seeker, who becomes immortalized with that divine ambrosia. 'For him Vāk milks the milk, the milked product of Vāk'.[77] In other words, Vāk draws from herself her own inner essence for the sake of the seeker[78] and hands over the same to him. But this supreme essence even when received is not of any use unless it can be held and retained. This is signified by the '*tha*' or *sthiti* or fixity. It must become the permanent food or *anna* for nourishing the soul. Not only should the seeker raise himself up occasionally and enjoy the flow of reason or wisdom but he must also have his permanent station there, a fixed abode for himself. Thus the term '*Udgītha*' peculiarly signifies all the essential steps in contemplation, viz., the rising, the drawing and the retaining. One must rise through Prāṇa, draw through Vāk and finally retain it as the permanent fruit of coatemplation, which sustains him like food.

The Upaniṣad then proceeds to show that this principle of three pervades everywhere, whether in the '*lokas*' or in the '*devas*' or in the 'Vedas'. Of the three '*lokas*', the '*dyuloka*' or the heaven is the '*ut*', because it stands high above all the spheres, the *'antarīkṣa'* or the sky is the '*gī*', because it envelopes all (*giraṇat lokānām*)[79] and the earth is the *'tham'*. Similarly of the gods, the Āditya or the Sun is the *'ut'* as it occupies a high position, the Vāyu is the '*gī*' as it envelopes Agni and others, and Agni is the '*tham*' because all sacrifices rest in it. Lastly, of the Vedas, the Sāman is '*ut*' as it is praised as celestial, the Yajus is '*gī*' because the gods consume the offering given through it and Ṛk is the *'tham*' as it happens to be the ultimate basis of all.[80]

Having indicated the all-pervasive nature of the three components of the *Udgītha,* the Upaniṣad goes to declare the effect of such contemplation: 'One becomes full of food and its eater or enjoyer, who worships these letters of the *Udgītha'*.[81] In other words, he becomes full of plenitude and enjoyment, because he comes to know the secret of creation and thereby can easily manipulate the sources from which flow all the things required or sought.

The Upaniṣadic *upāsanā* is based on thoroughly scientific methods and its results too are, therefore, always sure and certain. To ensure prosperity or fulfilment of desires (*āśīḥ samṛddiḥ*)[82] the Upaniṣad indicates the methods of directing the thought during the contemplation. The thought most be concentrated on the particular hymn, as well as on the seer who has composed it and finally on the deity who is to be praised.[83] Not only that, the particular rhythm of the hymn and even the direction through which the approach is being made, is to be reflected upon.[84] The thoughts must be kept consistently moving (*upadhāvet*) along these lines. Lastly, the thought must be directed on oneself (*ātmānam antataḥ upāsṛtya*),[85] and the concentration on the desired thing must be unflinching, and pursued with extreme care (*apramattaḥ dhyāyan*)[86]. Śaṅkara comments on *'apramattaḥ'* thus: without making any mistake in the vowels, labials or consonants. i.e. by becoming very careful about pronunciation of the particular hymn.

We have already seen the significance and value that is attached to the letters of a word and hence the Upaniṣad is very particular about the right pronunciation of each letter, whether it is a vowel or a consonant or a labial. According to the Upaniṣad, each letter or syllable of a word is charged with divine power, and is, rather, the very self or embodiment of a particular divinity. 'All the vowels are the selves of Indra, all the labials the selves of Prajāpati, all the consonants the selves of Mṛtyu'.[88] Hence the Upaniṣad asks the devotee to take refuge (*śaranaṁ prapannaḥ*)[89] in those particular divinities, if he is charged with any mistake in their pronunciations. It also enjoins the right method of pronouncing them. The vowels must be pronounced resoundingly and forcefully (*ghoṣavanto balavanto vaktavyāḥ*), the labials should be pronounced in the centre of the mouth without casting them out (*anirastāḥ*), and the consonants must be pronounced each separately without the least inter-twining (*leśena anabhinihitāḥ*).[90]

From this it is clear, how particular and careful the Upaniṣads are in making every part of contemplation faultless, however basic it may be. Without the basic things being made right, the higher notes can hardly break forth. Only right vibrations produce right thoughts and feelings. Thoughts and feelings are not within one's grasp or control, but the vibrations are. They can be produced at will, rightly or wrongly, and that is why so much stress is laid on making them faultless. The force of a hymn (*mantra*) depends, thus, on the right pronunciation of the letters composing it and the right vibrations thereof. The right vibrations set the body in tune, fill it with a superabundance of strength (*balam dadānī'ti*).[91] and release it from the grip of the stupor of death (*mṛtyor ātmānaṁ pariharāṇī'ti*).[92] With this accession of strength it becomes possible for the mind to maintain itself on the higher levels, alert and attentive, which leads to a deeper contemplation till finally the revelation dawns. Thus the term *'apramattaḥ'* carries a deep significance for contemplation.

Having thus indicated the nature and method of the *Udgītha-upāsanā,* the Upaniṣad again repeats the injunction about doing the *Udgītha-upāsanā* with Om,[93] and shows how the gods were lifted from the sphere of death through Om. The return to Om is made to show that the *Udgītha,* the *Praṇava* and the Āditya are really identical,[94] and the seeker is asked to know the reality in its various aspects and not from one side alone, as Kauṣītaki says to his son.[95] A deeper approach is now made through the *Udgītha.* The way to prosperity through the *Udgītha* was indicated before, but the Supreme Person or Reality is yet to be found and seen. So, through the Āditya, a deeper and deeper penetration is made. One begins with the white lustre (*śuklaṁ bhāḥ*)[96] of the Sun, then finds the deep dark blue (*yan nīlaṁ paraḥ kṛṣnam*)[97] within it, which is visible only to one with concentrated vision, as Śaṅkara points out.[96] Finally, one views the Supreme Self within the Sun, who is magnificently lustrous all over, of golden hue from the hairs down to the nails.[99] As in the Sun, so in the eye, too, this Supreme Self may be viewed by going deeper and deeper inside.[100] With this vision comes utter fulfilment. He attains this world as well as all the other worlds beyond it; divine enjoyments come to him, Not only that. He can bring fulfilment of any desire asked for,by anybody, as it were, through a mere song. Such becomes his power of the song of *Sāman* or *Udgītha.* In fact, as Inge aptly says: "If our ears were attuned to the Divine Voices, we should, in the words of the great living poet-prophet of India 'hear the music of the great 'I AM' pealing from the grand organ of creation through its countless reeds, in endless harmony.''[101]

As in the *Dahara-vidyā* the end was to find the Ātman within the heart or in the self or subject, so here, too, the ultimate end is the vision of the Purusa within the Sun or in the eye of the subject. There also we found the fulfilment of all desires following from the vision, here also the same result accrues to the seeker when he gets the enlightenment..

(iii) The Madhu Vidyā

The Madhu-vidyā occupies a unique place in the Upaniṣadic scheme of *upāsanā,* due to its supremely hidden significance and peculiarly mystic presentation. It has got two different versions, one in the *Chāndogya*[102] and another in the *Bṛhadāraṇyaka.*[103] The *Chāndogya* version takes up the Āditya or the Sun as the main symbol and works out the *vidyā* thereon, while the *Bṛhadāraṇyaka* depicts a long series of cause and effect, showing their mutual interdependence and finally leads to the Ātman which is shown to be the supreme source of everything else. The two versions do not differ in their ultimate end or outcome, though the approaches seem to be different.

'Madhu' literally means 'honey'; secondarily, it signifies sweetness or delight. What brings delight or sweetness of satisfaction in us? Evidently the fruition of a work, its successful outcome or result. So Śaṅkara takes *'madhu'* to mean 'effect' (*madhu kāryam*),[104] and he also accepts the primary sense of delight (*modanān madhu iva madhu*).[105] The effect of an action is enjoyed by everybody and with this enjoyment comes delight. Āditya is the sum-total of the results of the actions of all creatures (*sarvaprāṇikarmaphalabhūtaḥ*) and as such it nourishes and sustains everything in the universe. Āditya also intoxicates

the gods with delight, because, of all sacrifices performed for the sake of the gods, the ultimate fruition is the Āditya. Thus the term *'madhu'* in the sense of ultimate effect or essence as well as the source of delight rightly applies to the Sun.

The imagery of the honey is then worked out in detail. The heaven is taken as the slanting pole on which hangs the sky which is imaged as the bee-hive, and the rays of the Sun are taken as the whole brood of bees.[106] The rays of the Sun cause things to grow and mature and, as such, are like channels for the production of the ultimate effect, which is the *'madhu'*. Hence they are taken as bees and as the bees cling to the bee-hive, so the rays, too, inhere in the sky, which here stands for the bee-hive. But the ultimate support for this whole honey-making process is provided by the *dyaus* or the heaven. The sphere of action has always its basis in the domain of light, which is *dyaus,* depicted here as the pole which supports the bee-hive in the form of the sky. The rays are all engaged in producing through this bee-hive the celestial or divine honey (*devamadhu*),[107] which is the Āditya.

The Upaniṣad, then, goes on to show how Āditya is the store of all effects, the essence of all things and thoughts, the repository of all wisdom from which come forth, from different directions, the four great Vedas. The rays coming from the east are taken as the eastern channels of honey (*prācyo madhu-nāḍyaḥ*).[108] In those channels are engaged the *ṛks* or the hymns as bees producing the honey. They draw the honey from the Ṛgveda, which is like the flower storing the honey. Śaṅkara explains that, here, by the term 'Ṛgveda' is signified the actions ordained in the Ṛgveda,[109] for only from the actions can there be a flow of the juice of honey i.e. the result or the effect and the enjoyment thereof, but from mere collection of words the flow of enjoyable effects is not possible (*karmaphalabhūtamadhurasanisrāvāsambhavāt*).[110] Therefore from the actions enjoined in the Ṛgveda, the *ṛks,* which are like the bees, collect the essence and make the honey. The essence is here called the immortal waters because the effects of actions arc really indestructible and hence immortal.

These hymns, drawing the immortal essences, heat up, as it were, the Ṛgveda and this heating (*abhitāpa*) causes the honey to flow, which otherwise lies concealed within the flower.[111] We have seen that the real meaning of *'tapasyā'* is 'heat' and *tapasyā is* at the root of creation. Here also the Upaniṣad hints at the same thing by using the word *'abhitāpa'*. No drawing of the honey, no production of an effect, no realization of an end is possible without this heating. All actions prove ineffective, all efforts turn out to be barren, unless they are rightly warmed up or heated. The technique of tapping the right sources and getting thereby the flow of desired effects without any hindrance is here taught in the *Madhu-vidyā* through the use of the word *'abhitāpa'*.

From the heating of the Ṛgveda flowed the following effects: fame, lustre, perfect sense-organs, strength, as well as food and all eatables.[112] In other words, the organs and powers of enjoyment as well as the objects of enjoyment are all found in their fullness through this heating. The Upaniṣads nowhere ask the seeker to choose the ideal of a beggar, who has nothing to possess. On the other hand, they prompt the seeker to gain the whole wealth of the divine kingdom, attain the highest development, grow to the fullest stature. All the *vidyās* teach this technique of growth through the gathering of the honey.

The effects that flow are not mere imaginary things but are actualities that become visualised. So the Upaniṣad goes on to say that these effects ultimately take shelter in the Sun, which fact is attested by the red form of the Sun.[113] In other words, the red form of the Sun is the embodiment of the fruits of action that follow from the Ṛgveda. Every effect takes shape in a particular form or colour, which signifies its concretisation and completion. The honey that was being drawn through the heating now comes out completely extracted and stands shining in front as the dazzling red form of the Āditya.

Similarly the southern rays are connected with the Yajurveda and through a similar process of heating the honey is drawn, which here takes, the white form (*śuklaṁ rūpam*)[114] of the Āditya. Next, the western rays become the channels for drawing the honey that is in the Sāmaveda and its ultimate form is found to be dark (*kṛṣṇam rūpam*)[115]. Again, the northern rays are taken to be connected with the Atharvaveda, from which the honey, when drawn, takes the deep dark hue, (*paraṁ kṛṣṇaṁ*)[116]. Thus, from the four quarters, are drawn the essences of the four Vedas and the deeper the essence drawn, the deeper becomes its colour or representation, signified by the red, white, dark and deep dark hues.

Then the Upaniṣad proceeds to unravel the supreme secret. The drawing of the honey is still not complete, for the Vedas do not exhaust the whole of reality. The Vedas, no doubt, cover all existence, but there is something beyond existence too and the supreme essence lies there alone. The search was so long being conducted in a downward direction along the four quarters and now that being completed, one turns upward to get hold of the higher channels of honey. The upward moving rays are the higher channels of honey here, the secret teachings or commandments are the bees, and the flower from which the honey is to be sipped or culled here is Brahman itself.[117] By means of the secret methods of disciplines prescribed—like the prayer first to unlatch, then to leave the doors ajar and lastly to throw them wide open, for a look into reality,[118]—this Brahman, who is here *Praṇava,* the Śabda Brahman, is to be heated, which, will then pour out the supreme essence. Here the essence or the honey has no particular form or colour, because it happens to be beyond all manifestation. Still it is the highest source of all manifestation and hence in its bosom there is a heaving. So the honey here is recognised not by any form or colour but only by the heaving at the centre of the Sun (*madhye kṣobhata iva*).[119] Śaṅkara reminds again that only one whose vision is calm and collected can behold this heaving (*samāhitadṛṣṭer dṛśyate*).[120]

Thus the *Madhu-vidyā* is essentially a science for extracting the honey or the supreme essence. The honey is first to be drawn from all quarters by extracting the Vedas, the repository of all wisdom. What was signified by the milking of *vāk* (*vāgdoham*) in the *Udgītha* is here indicated by the heating (*abhitāpa*) of the Vedas, the concrete representations of *vāk*. The Upaniṣadic contemplation is mainly based on this milking and heating, the sole purpose of which is the dynamisation of the whole being, through the flowing current of divine energy, essence or honey. The essence must not only be drawn but made to flow especially (*vyakṣarat*),[121] and finally take concrete shapes in the effulgent forms of Āditya. These effulgent forms are the essence of all essences (*rasānāṁ rasaḥ*).[122] the nectar of nectars (*amṛtānām amṛtāni*).[123] The Vedas are taken as the essence of all the worlds and hence are immortal or eternal and these, being the essence of the Vedas, are naturally the supreme essence, the highest immoratality.

The Upaniṣad, after drawing the immortal essence, says that the gods neither eat nor drink it but become satisfied only by looking at the effulgent form.[124] In other words, the vision itself brings complete fulfilment and satisfaction and hence, no necessity is felt for taking in the thing through any outer means. But do they merely look on? No, they plunge into this form (*etad eva rūpam abhisaṁviśanti*)[125] and again rise from this form (*etasmād rūpād udyanti*).[126] By plunging in that sea of luminosity, they come out with their whole being recast, shining and resplendent.

The aim of the Upaniṣadic contemplation is not a loss of being or personality but its highest development through the divine transmutation. We found how the *Mukhya Prāna,* after vanquishing death, carried each of the senses beyond death (*mrtyum atyavahat*)[127] and they all became shining and resplendent, being freed from the clutches of death (*mṛtyum atikrānto dīpyate*).[128] The keynote of *upāsanā,* as we have indicated, is this freedom from darkness and death, sometimes sought through the heart as in the *Dahara-vidyā,* sometimes through Prāṇa as in the *Udgīthavidyā* and sometimes through Āditya as here in the *Madhu-vidyā.* The heart (*hṛdaya*), the Prāṇa and the Āditya are only three forms of the same thing and hence are identical.

But the darkness is not entirely dispelled for all times so long as one remains in the sphere of the relative, even though the shining forms of Āditya are visualised. The light of the Sun has been gained, it shines resplendent, yet it has a setting, and with the setting of the Sun there is again an onset of darkness. Thus there is a limit to the freedom and lordship (*svārājyam*)[129] gained. It endures for the period beginning from the rise of the Sun in the east till its setting in the west (*yāvad ādityaḥ purastād udetā paścād astametā*).[130] But when the upward moving rays are got hold of, the story becomes different. 'Then, thereafter, rising above, it neither rises nor sets but stays alone in the middle'.[131] 'There surely is neither a coming down or setting nor any rising at any time whatsoever'.[132] As Śaṅkara comments: 'this is the Brahmaloka which is devoid of rising and setting' (*udayāstamayavarjito brabmaloka iti*).[133] The Upaniṣad concludes by saying that, to him, who gains this knowledge, there dawns the eternal day (*sakṛddivā*)[134] which knows no rising or setting. Thus one ultimately reaches the sphere of eternal light, where it is only day and no night at all. This is the sphere of self-luminosity, according to Śaṅkara (*svayamjyotiṣtvāt*),[135] where the knower becomes the Eternal Uncreated Brahman, free from the limitations of time.

The *Bṛhadāraṇyaka* version also leads to the same end by working out in detail the different essences, all of which ultimately rest in the supreme essence of the Ātman. The search for the essence begins with the *pṛthivī* or the earth, which is found to be the essence of all *bhūtas*[135] or creatures, because it happens to be the ultimate effect produced through the efforts of all creatures. Śaṅkara comments: 'As a bee-hive is produced by the joint effort of numerous bees, so this earth is produced by all the creatures'.[137] Again, the creatures are also the effects of the earth and hence, in turn, its essence. Thus they mutually produce each other and hence are identical. This mutual production of one from the other becomes possible because of the presence of an identical principle in both. This principle is here shown to be the effulgent immortal Purusa which equally inhabits both the earth and the corporeal frame.[138] 'This is the Ātman, this is the Immortal, this is Brahman, this is all'.[139] Thus, this same principle is found inhering in the whole series of causes and effects. As in the earth so in the waters, fire, wind, sun, quarters, moon, lightning, cloud, or the sky— in a word, it all the elements and principles active in the universe, the same correspondence of cause and effect and the final identity of the spiritual principle is traced and found.[140] Not only in the physical components or elements but even in the moral principles like *dharma* and *satya*, the same chain of mutual cause and effect is found, indissolubly binding the one to the other.[141] All these physical and moral or psychical principles ultimately make up the species man (*mānuṣam*),[142] who in turn produces those principles, for it is only for him that they all exist. Beyond the species is the composite self (*kāryakāraṇasaṁghātaḥ*)[143] of body, mind etc., which is the product of all that has gone before and again, in turn, the producer of all this.

But still we have not reached the Supreme Self which is neither the product nor the producer of anything. This comes last of all, and this Ātman is described as the Lord, the King of all *bhūtas* and is thus not a product of them.[144] By the term'*adhipati*' or Lord, it is signified that it is independent of all the *bhūtas* (*sarvabhūtānāṁ svatantraḥ*)[145] and the use of the two terms, '*adhipati*' as well as '*rājā*', signifies that its kingship is not conditional but absolute and independent. As the spokes of a wheel rest in the axle of the chariot, so all these created things, all of them rest in the Ātman. Thus the whole world is finally found to rest in the Ātman. Hence the Ātman is termed *puruṣa* because it rests in all the *puras* or bodies by entering into them.[147] There is nothing which is not covered by it, there is nothing which is not permeated by it.[148] Whether inside or outside, it is the same principle everywhere as *nāma* or *rūpa*, evolving as cause and effect.[149]

In each form it has expressed itself, it has taken up all these forms only to manifest itself.[150] The Supreme Lord assumes all these forms through his *māyā*[151] i.e. the supreme principle of intelligence or *prajñā,* as Śaṅkara comments.[151] Thus finally one finds the Supreme Brahman, which has neither before nor after, neither in nor out, which experiences all.'[153] And this Brahman is the Ātman (*ayam ātmā Brahma*), the very self of the seeker. Thus, step by step, the Upaniṣad leads to the complete identification of the self with the highest object that is Brahman and with the dawning of this consciousness one reaches the sphere of eternal day, as envisaged in the *Chāndogya.* Then everything, beginning from the self down to the very earth, is found to exist and inhere only in and through the Ātman or Brahman. Nothing exists apart from it and hence everything is of the nature of everything (*sarvaṁ sarvātmakam*). This is the consummation of the search for the essence or *'madhu'*. Here is the ultimate fulfilment, the completest enlightenment which is not clouded any more in any part of time. We started with *dahara, ākāśa* or *vyoman,* then came down to *vāyu* or *prāṇa* and ended with *āditya, sūrya.* From the vacuum to the vibration and finally to the illumination.

References

1. āditya ha vai vāhyaḥ prāñaḥ. PRU, 3.8.
2. BU, 2.4.11.
3. BU, 3.9.21.
4. BU, 3.9.23.
5. BU, 4.1.7.
6. PRU, 3.6.
7. CU, 3.14.3.
8. KTU, 2.6.17.
9. Gītā, 18.61.
10. CU, 8.3.3.
11. CU, 8.1.1.
12. ŚB, Ibid.
13. KTU, 2.5.1.
14. ŚU, 3.18.
15. CU, 3.13.1.
16. ŚB, Ibid.
17. ŚB, CU, 3.13.1.
18. DVP, p. 8.
19. KTU, 1.2.20.
20. ŚU. 3.20.
21. KTU, 1.1.14.
22. MU, 2.1.10.
23. TU, 2.1.1.
24. MU, 3.2.9.
25. MU, 2.2.8.
26. BU, 4.2.3.
27. KTU, 2.6.16. CU, 8.6.6.
28. kāmā ye 'sya hṛdi śṛtāḥ. BU, 4.4.7.
29. BU, 4.3.22.
30. AU, 3.2.
31. CU, 8.1.1.
32. Ibid.
33. ŚB, on Ibid.
34. CU, 8.1.2.

35. Ibid, 8.1.3.
36. ŚB, on Ibid.
37. KTU, 2.4.10.
38. CU, 8.2.
39. ŚB on CU, 8.2.1.
40. ŚB on CU, 8.1.5.
41. CU, 8.1.5.
42. ŚB on CU, 8.1.5.
43. brahmai'va puram. Ibid.
44. BU, 4.4.20.
45. BU, 3.7.12.
46. BU, 3.8.11.
47. CU, 2.2.
48. CU, 2.8.
49. CU, 1.1.1.
50. Ibid.
51. CU, 1.1.2.
52. CU, 1.1.3.
53. CU, 1.1.5.
54. CU, 1.1.6.
55. CU, 1.1.8.
56. CU, 1.1.10.
57. CU, 1.1.10.
58. CU, 1.2.2.
59. CU, 1.2.7.
60. CU, 1.3.1.
61. PRU, 1.5.
62. Ibid. 3.8.
63. Ibid. 1.7.
64. CU, 1.3.2.
64. Ibid.
66. Ibid.
67. CU, 1.3.1.
68. CU, 1.3.3.
69. CU, 1.3.5.
70. ŚB on CU, 1.3.7.
71. Ibid.
72. ŚB on CU, 1.3.6.
73. ŚB on CU, 1.3.6.
74. prāṇena hi uttiṣṭhati. CU, 1.3.6.
75. CU, 1.3.6.
76. Ibid.
77. CU, 1.3.7.
78. ŚB, Ibid.
79. ŚB, on CU, 1.3.7.
80. Ibid.
81. CU, 1.3.7.
82. CU, 1.3.8.
83. CU, 1.3.9.
84. CU, 1.3.12.
85. CU, 1.3.12.
86. Ibid.
87. ŚB, Ibid.
88. CU, 2.22.3.
89. Ibid.
90. CU., 2.22.5.
91. CU, 2.22.5.
92. Ibid.
93. CU, 1.4.1.
94. CU, 1.5.1.
95. CU, 1.5.2.
96. CU, 1.6.5.
97. Ibid.
98. ŚB. Ibid.
99. CU, 1.5.9.
100. CU, 1.7.1.4.
101. PP, p. 23.
102. CU, 3.1.11.
103. BU, 2.5.
104. ŚB on. BU, 2.5.1.
105. ŚB, on CU, 3.1.1.
106. CU, 3.1.1.
107. Ibid.
108. CU, 3.1.2.
109. ŚB on Ibid.
110. Ibid.
111. CU, 3.1.3.
112. CU, 3.1.3.

113. CU, 3.1.4.
114. CU, 3.2.
115. CU, 3.3.
116. CU, 3.4.
117. CU, 3.5.1.
118. apajahi parigham. CU, 2.24.6. lokadvāram apāvṛṇu paśyema tvā vayam. CU, 2.24.4.
119. CU, 3.5.3.
120. ŚB. on Ibid.
121. CU, 3.1.4.
122. CU, 3.5.4.
123. Ibid.
124. CU, 3.6.1.
125. CU, 3.6.2.
126. Ibid.
127. BU, 1.3.11-14.
128. Ibid.
129. CU, 3.6.4.
130. Ibid.
131. CU, 3.11.1.
132. CU, 3.11.2.
133. ŚB on Ibid.
134. CU, 3.11.3.
135. ŚB on CU, 3.11.3.
136. BU, 2.5.1.
137. ŚB on Ibid.
138. BU, 2.5.1.
139. Ibid.
140. BU., 2.5.2-10.
141. BU, 2.5.11.-12.
142. BU, 2.5.13.
143. ŚB on BU, 2.5.14.
144. BU, 2.5.15.
145. ŚB, on Ibid.
146. Ibid.
147. BU, 2.5.18.
148. BU, 2.5.18.
149. evam sa eva nāmarūpātmanā' ntarvahirbhāvena kārya-kāraṇarūpeṇa vyavasthitaḥ. ŚB on BU, 2.5.18.
150. rūpaṃ rūpam pratirūpo babhūva. BU, 2.5.19.
151. Ibid.
152. māyābhiḥ prajñābhiḥ. ŚB on Ibid.
153. tad etad brahmā 'pūrvam anaparam avāhyam. BU, 2.5.19.

CHAPTER VI

THE ANALYTIC WAY

(*1*) *The Sleeping Man*

As the synthetic method tries to realize the Ātman through a particular centre specially suited to hold in harmony the discordant notes of experience, so the analytic way tries to grasp the Ātman more directly by dispensing with all such centres and instead concentrating itself on a searching analysis of the very states of the Self. The analytic method discards all outer symbols through which the Ātman reveals itself, because the very symbol or the medium, through which the Ātman is viewed, proves to be a bar to a naked view of it; and because the numerous variety of symbols makes the Ātman, too, appear different and varied, though, in reality, it is one and the same in all circumstances. The approach through a symbol has the fatal defect that it views the reality from one aspect alone and is thus deprived of a comprehensive knowledge of it. It is like viewing the reality in different fragments and not in its unity, which is the very soul of it. Again, being accustomed to view the reality through a symbol, one is apt to get lost and bewildered when the symbol is withdrawn and there is a consequent failure to apprehend the reality any further. Hence the analytic method proceeds the other way to get hold of the reality directly, shorn of all outer vestures or trappings and thus ensure the true knowledge of the Ātman, whereby one is enabled to view the Ātman under all circumstances, behind all vestures or symbols, as the same single unity. The superiority of the analytic way of search and the drawback of the symbolic approach are clearly shown in the famous Gārgya—Ajātaśatru episode in the *Bṛhadāraṇyaka Upaniṣad*,[1] which we propose to study now.

Gārgya-Ajātaśatru episode

Gārgya, pretending to have a complete knowledge of Brahman and therefore haughty and proud (*dṛpta*) approaches King Ajātaśatru with the intention of teaching him about the true nature of Brahman. He begins with the symbol of the Sun and declares that he worships the Self in the Sun as Brahman and prescribes the same method to Ajātaśatru.[2] Ajātaśatru immediately stops him from elaborating this symbol any further, as he happened to know it in full already. In his commentaty, Śaṅkara makes Ajātaśatru's reply clear in the following manner: "Do not narrate more about this Brahman. If you know anything else, tell me about that Brahman and not of one that I know already. If you think that I know Brahman alone (in a general way) and not the results of its particular contemplations, then that, too, is not correct, because I happen to know all that you are saying."[33] In order to prove this, the king immediately narrates himself the special effect of such a particular contemplation of Āditya Puruṣa as Brahman.[4] The king then allows Gārgya to proceed further and further to elaborate his experience of Brahman. Gārgya takes up one symbol after another but each time the king stops him from elaborating his point by declaring the effects of such contemplations himself, and thereby showing that he is already fully aware of all such approaches to Brahman.[5] Gārgya thus exhausts all the particular symbols by means of which he had apprehended Brahman and finally concludes with the universal symbol of the Ātman or the Self.

Gārgya's knowledge extends only upto this collective apprehension of Brahman as the Purusa in the Self or Ātman. This is the state of Prajāpati, as Śaṅkara rightly points out while explaining the meaning of the term '*ātmanvī*'[7]. That Śaṅkara is right may be proved by a reference to the Upaniṣad itself where it explains the term '*ātmanvī*, which is also used here to explain the result of such contemplation. Thus run the opening lines of the second section of the first chapter in the *Bṛhadāraṇyaka*: "In the beginning there was nothing here; it was covered by Death or Hunger. Hunger is Death. So He created the mind, (thinking that) I shall become self-conscious (*ātmanvī*)"[8]. Thus the state of *Ātmanvī* is the first state of self-consciousness, the state of Prajāpati , when from the state of absolute inconscience emerges the cosmic mind, out of which is manifested the whole creation. So while tracing back the creation in search of the Self the last point that is reached here is the state of the primeval selfconsciousness. This is the highest limit of the intellect beyond which it cannot go. So Gārgya comes to a stop and remains mute. He has exhausted the whole range of his experience and fails to proceed any further.

But Brahman is not truly known as yet. That the knowledge so far gained is inadequate is categorically stated by the Upaniṣad itself here: 'By this much it is not known' (*nai'tāvatā viditaṁ bhavati*).[9] This signifies that the search has to be pursued still further in order to have the truest and most fundamental knowledge of Brahman. But it should be remembered that the knowledge so far gained is not utterly useless and so the previous realizations are not to be despised or looked down upon. Śaṅkara, in course of his elucidation of this passage in the Upaniṣad, raises the question: 'Is this knowledge, gained so far no knowledge at all?' and answers that the knowledge is very real because it carries concrete results behind it.[10] It should not be thought that the results of such knowledge, which have been set forth, are mere empty praises (*arthavāda*), and are not meant to be taken as true. On the contrary, they prove the practical usefulness of the knowledge gained and hence are set forth in details separately along with every special kind of knowledge or realization. Hence the Upaniṣad does not mean to dispense with such knowledge, for then the king would have stated "you know nothing" but instead he merely says "by *this much* it is not known", thereby signifying that something more is to be known or added in order to make the knowledge complete. In other words, the king, representing the true voice of the Upaniṣads, does not annul the previous knowledge or experience gained by Gārgya but only wants to supplement it by further exploration into the nature of the Supreme and thereby make it true and complete. Śaṅkara says: 'As this much knowledge is the door to the knowledge of the Supreme Brahman, it has, therefore, been rightly said, "by this much it is not known"'.[11]

Thus the previous knowledge, though inadequate, is indispensably necessary for the gaining of the true and adequate knowledge, for the very inadequacy of the former can hardly be realized by one who has not travelled the whole way himself so far. To pretend to know its inadequacy, without having the experience of it, is to indulge in a colosal self-deception. The true knower of Brahman, here represented by the king, does not confine his knowledge to one aspect alone, dogmatically clinging to it as the best and the highest but possesses a comprehensive and minute knowledge of Brahman in all its different phases and aspects and hence can faultlessly judge the inadequacy of other's knowledge and can help him to make it complete and adequate. By stopping Gārgya again and again and recounting himself the various effects of the different approaches to Brahman, the king shows the richness of his experience and then proceeds even further than Gārgya in order to set forth the true and complete nature of Brahman.

Thus two lessons emerge from this historic statement of the king, 'by this much it is not known': firstly, the inadequacy of the knowledge gained through the symbolic approach, and secondly, its absolute indispensability and value for the achievement of the supreme knowledge, because we are accustomed to a spirit of rejection of that which seems inadequate. But the Upaniṣadic spirit is never of rejection but of completion and fulfilment of the lower by the higher. This is here signified by the statement, 'not by this much' which suggests that something more is to be added to the 'this much' knowledge already gained and the 'this much' knowledge is not to be thrown away as utterly useless. Thus it is evident beyond doubt that the synthetic approach is supplemented and completed by the analytic and there is no spirit of opposition between the two methods of approach, as is commonly assumed.

The unprejudiced spirit of the Upaniṣads never allows the seeker to remain contented and confined to his own way of thinking but always prompts him to get his own view extended and broadened through the help of a more enlightened spirit. Even the proud (*dṛpta*) Gārgya who was so long pretending to teach the king, submits himself immediately for further enlightenment to that very king, having realized the incompleteness of his own vision. He did not indulge in a contest for establishing the superiority of his own realization nor did he challenge the king to establish the inadequacy of his knowledge, but instead, humbly approached the king as a submissive disciple, for getting more light in the matter.[12] Such was the free spirit of the Upaniṣadic age.

Gārgya having approached the king now for further knowledge, the latter feels embarrassed in accepting the position of a teacher to a Brāhmin, being a Kṣattriya himself, for it was contrary to the usual practice, (*pratilomaṁ cai'tat*).[13] This signifies that usually, as a rule, the Brahmins happened to be the instructor in Brahmavidyā, for they possessed the supreme knowledge and it was a case of rare exception when a Kṣattriya instructed a Brāhmin. The king, however, promised to make the reality truly known to Gārgya and took recourse to a novel method. He took Gārgya by the hand and they both rose and went up to a sleeping man. Then he called that sleeping man by different names like *Bṛhat, Pāṇḍaravāsāḥ, Soma, Rājan,* which are particular appellations of Prāṇa but yet he did not wake up. Then he gave him jerks by the hand and this finally awakened him.[14]

What is signified by this strange method of instruction adopted by the king? Evidently the king wanted to give the fundamental knowledge about Brahman and in order to have it, one must go down to the deepest level of being, where the naked reality may be found in its utter purity and freedom, detached from everything else. But this is not possible so long as one remains in the surface consciousness, wide awake to the plurality of impressions coming and going. The state of sleep brings, in a natural way, an absolute quiescence and makes the soul withdraw to his own station by temporarily giving up his identification with the body. Gārgya had a complete knowledge of the Self in its different states of identification with different *upādhis* or symbols but he did not know how it could exist even apart from all identifications whatsoever, in absolute detachment and freedom. That is why the king takes recourse to this sleeping state in order to demonstrate the true nature of the Self.

He also proves to Gārgya the incompleteness of his knowledge through this novelty of the method of teaching. Gārgya had taken the state of Prāṇa as the true status of being or reality for, all the different gods beginning from Āditya down to Prajāpati, with all of whom he had identified Brahman, are nothing but different aspects of Prāṇa, as has been unmistakeably made clear by Yājñavalkya elsewhere.[15] Now this Prāṇa functions as usual, rather with more noise and force, during the state of sleep, but yet it does not respond to the calls made through its different names. This fact of unresponsiveness of the manifestly existing Prāṇa during sleep proves beyond doubt that the principle of consciousness does not inhere in the Praṇa alone but lies imbedded far deeper in the soul. That inherent consciousness came back, as it were, from somewhere else manifesting itself like a flame (*jvalanniva*) through the act of jerking.

Now the question naturally arises: Where was the conscious Self lying so long and wherefrom did it come, as it were, again in the body? This very question was put by the king to Gārgya but the latter did not understand it at all, as he had no knowledge of the Self as distinct from all associations.[16] Then the king himself proceeded to enlighten him on this point. The two questions complete one another, for to know the Ātman or Brahman truly, both these things must be known adequately viz., where did it lie, away from the surface consciousness, so long and also whence did it come back hither again. It may be thought that the second question is superfluous, for by knowing where it was, it is also known whence did it come. But that is not so, for here the Upaniṣad aims to give a complete knowledge about Brahman and in order to have it, one must not only know how it rests apart from all associations in its own station but also the details of the process of its identification with the body or the psycho-physical apparatus. The two movements, namely the going in and the coming out, must both be comprehended correctly in order to make the knowledge complete, and this is the significance of the two questions put together. The second question is as important as the first and is not a mere repetition of the latter.

To make known the status of the Self as withdrawn from all outer association, the king recounts in detail the two states of dream and deep slumber, for it is through these states that the dissociating process gradually moves. When the Self enters the state of deep sleep it takes into itself the whole consciousness of the life and the senses and rests inside the space of the heart. This space is no physical space but the very ground of the Self and hence, by the statement that it rests in the space of the heart, it is meant to be conveyed that it rests in its own true nature, in the deepest core of its own being. We have already dealt with the significance of the heart in our discussion about the *Dahara-vidyā* and we need not repeat the same here. That the Self becomes identified with its own true essence, i. e. rests in itself during deep slumber, is attested to by the Upaniṣad itself through numerous statements. 'Then he becomes one with Reality, O gentle one'[17] teaches Uddālaka to his son Śvetaketu, while explaining the state of deep sleep. Nay, the very name, *'svapiti'* carries within it the import of the attainment of one's true nature, as the Upaniṣad points out: 'Then he attains himself, and he is, therefore, called asleep'[18]. Through this state, one is everyday carried to the Supreme Brahman, though unconsciously[19]. Then be becomes covered all over with the light of the soul and everything being overpowered with that light (*tejasā' bhibhūtaḥ*)[20] even the dream states, which bring up different pictures of desire, cease altogether. It is like a state of undifferentiated mass, all enveloped in that excess of light. As to their home, the tree, fly the birds, so everything takes refuge in that Supreme Self'[21]. All the scattered faculties of consciousness are collectcd together in the Self, as do the rays of the setting Sun gather themselves and become unified in the disc of light[22]. Thus, in the state of sleep, the Ātman rests in itself, the diffused emanations of consciousness being retracted and absorbed into itself.

The dream state stands in the borderland between waking and deep sleep. It is a state of expanded consciousness, for then the Self moves unfettered as it likes (*yathākāmam*)[23]. Thus here the desires find free play. The particular functions of the senses, too, cease here and yet all the acts of seeing, hearing etc. are accomplished by the mind alone. In this state, then, the Self withdraws its identification with the senses but still remains in unison with the mind. With the help of the mind, it goes on creating shapes and forms, situations and circumstances to fulfil its unrealized desires of the waking state. The fetters of material sphere do not cling to the Self in this state and hence the knot of identification, though not removed here, is yet definitely loosened. It is thus an intermediate state between the state of close identification with the gross level and the state of total detachment from all identifications whatsoever.

But when this identification with the subtle states of the mind is also removed, the consciousness of particularities completely ceases. The innumerable channels of thought, which are pictured as the arteries called *hitā,* cover up the whole body[24]. Through the spreading of this network of nerves or channels of thought, the Self carries on its work during the waking state; and during sleep it hauls up the net, as it were, and rests in itself. With the casting of the net, distractions become inevitable and consequently there is distress and and sorrow, but with its withdrawal, utter peace is gained and there follows an all-exceeding delight, which removes all sorrow absolutely (*atighnīm ānandasya*)[25]. This feeling of delight is a clear and unmistakable evidence about the Self attaining its own true status during deep sleep, for nothing but the attainment of one's own self can generate this supreme delight transcending all sorrow. It is the seeking of the outer objects that causes distraction and distress, but with the vanishing of the outer world and even the mental world of imagined objects, there is nothing to draw out the Self. Then poised in itself, it feels and enjoys perfect bliss.

Thus, through the instructions of the king, it has been made abundantly clear that the self resides in itself during sleep and not in something else apart from itself, and thereby the first part of the question, 'whence it was' has been answered. Now the second part of the question 'where did it come' is also to be answered. Here also the answer will show that it comes from itself and not from something separate from itself. The term 'where' carries the significance of a locus and the term 'whence' also points to a limit of separation and these two are generally conceived as, and also happen to be, separate from the thing located or separated. But, here, by the answer given in the Upaniṣad about the 'where' and 'whence' of the Ātman during and after sleep, it has been sought to be conveyed that no separate thing exists apart from the Self to which it may fly or from which it may come. It goes to itself and comes again from itself. It is that one principle which is working through all these mutually exclusive states, sometimes going back and resting in itself and sometimes coming down from its own station identifying itself with the different states of consciousness. This contraction and expansion give rise to the two states of sleep and waking, but as we pass from the one state to the other in utter inconscience, we cannot follow how the Self withdraws gradually to its own station and then comes back to the outer sphere. These two movements of coming and going must be watched and followed consciously in order to know the Self, and this is the supreme significance of the instruction imparted here through the illustration of the sleeping man.

Thus it is shown that nothing exists apart from the Ātman, that everything follows from it, and that it is the supreme source of all existence. "As the spider spreads out the net from its own self or as from the fire shoot forth the small sparks all over, so from the Ātman follow all life, all the spheres, all the gods, and all creatures"[26]. It is the prius of the whole creation which is sustained by it. The vesture of apparent truth that the world wears is borrowed from that supreme source, the truth of all truths[27]. That highest truth is the final goal of the Upaniṣadic quest, and it must be known directly, shorn of all outer wrappings. Here by the analysis of the sleep and dream states, an attempt has been made to delve down to the deeps and get in touch with this final source of everything. But it Is not a mere negative approach, through denial and dissociation but a very positive approach which makes one see not only the true nature of the Ātman but also how the whole universe follows from and is sustained by it. We have seen how Gārgya had identified the Self with the different manifestations of Prāṇa and could not go beyond them and so it became necessary for the king to instruct him further. Here he concludes by saying that the Prāṇa is a truth no doubt but it is not the ultimate truth. Beyond it lies the highest truth.[28] the association with which turns all else true and real.

Finally, it must always be borne in mind that the analogy of the state of sleep is not taken to signify the utter blankness of the nature of the Ātman but simply to show that it exists in its own right and is not annihilated even when all the states of consciousness cease to exist. The Ātman is not a mere aggregate of conscious states as is sometimes assumed by the Buddhists and other allied schools of thought, and this can only be proved by a reference to the state of sleep, when through a natural process the incessant flow of thought is brought to a stop and yet the light of consciousness is not extinguished or put out. And once this is proved, one must try to realize it consciously and with its conscious realization the necessity for leaving one state of consciousness and entering into another undifferentiated state of apparent unconsciousness ceases altogether. Then one feels the independence of the Ātman even while awake to the numerous states of thought or consciousness. There is no further necessity of contracting the thoughts once this absolute freedom of the Ātman is gained or realized, for the Ātman neither contracts nor expands. It is only the mind that possesses this twin aspect of contraction and expansion, and the Ātman, being in close identification with it, appears to be contracting and expanding. Hence it seems, at one time, withdrawing itself and again coming out and spreading itself all around, as the mind goes to rest and again becomes active. There is no withdrawal on the part of the Ātman, for it is everywhere and all the time the same identical reality, without any contraction or expansion whatsoever in itself.

Hence it must be carefully remembered that only because, in the waking state, it becomes impossible to have any idea of the Ātman in its purity, free from its identification with the states of consciousness, one is taken to the state of sleep, where through a natural process the states of consciousness cease and it becomes easy to get hold of the Ātman as it is *per se.* The analogy of *susupti* or deep sleep is thus taken, not to prove the inconscient nature of the Ātman but to demonstrate the existence of the supreme consciousness even in the state of inconsciencc. As one must pass beyond the state of waking, so also must one move beyond the state of sleep, for both are equally states of the mind, and the Ātman is not a state but an unchanging entity which remains the same in all states and conditions.

(*ii*) *The Five Sheaths*

As the states of consciousness are brought under severe analysis, similarly the constituent parts of the embodied self are also critically analyzed and examined in order to find out the ultimate ground of the Self. These several parts have been termed *kośas* or sheaths, because inside them lies concealed the Supreme Self. These are like so many covering vestures that the Ātman wears while revealing itself in the world, and so again the veils are to be lifted one after another in order to apprehend the true nature of reality. The whole purpose of creation lies in this covering and revealing of reality the total concealment of the spirit under the cloak of the thickest and grossest matter, and again, its complete emergence from all wrappages as the pure naked spirit.

It must be remembered that throughout this apparent concealment, the purity of the spirit remains unsullied and hence when the freedom is gained, there is no stain left of the vestures that are cast off. With the dawning of the supreme illumination the sheaths vanish like the morning mist before the Sun, because they are all creations of ignorance. These sheaths are like so many bodies which are taken up by the Self in order to function at the different levels or spheres of consciousness. As the material sphere needs a material form, so the other higher spheres demand similar forms, constituted of subtler stuffs, which make it possible for the Self to function freely and normally at those levels. Every level has its appropriate body i.e. the instrument for making contacts with that particular sphere. This is stressed, again and again, here by a repeated reference to the likeness of the different sheaths to the human form (*tasya puruṣavidhatām*)[29] and also by enumerating their different limbs, head, sides etc.[30]

The final aim is no doubt the realization of the Reality that is beyond all forms in its utter nakedness and purity. But before it can be apprehended as such, one has to make the film that covers it finer and finer And thereby feel a growing awareness, an increasing illumination of it. In a word, one must become awake in the higher levels of his being, take a new birth and embodiment in those spheres. The personality must be preserved and developed to the highest degree before one hopes to attain the Impersonal.

It must also be remembered that the Impersonal does not negate or annul personality as we generally suppose, but transcends it in a way far beyond our conception. To lose personality before attaining the Supreme Reality is to lose all consciousness. It leads to a state of blankness and utter inconscience, like that of the *prakṛtilayas* of the Sāṅkhya. To guard against this danger, the Upaniṣad, again and again, refers to the *'puruṣavidhatām'* or the features of personality persisting in all the higher levels of being.[31] The exposition of the five sheaths (*pañcakośas*) is thus taken up by the Upaniṣad to trace the gradual evolution of personality, the increasing development of the human soul and its final emergence from all coverings. The Upaniṣad recounts how from the imprisonment in the thickest shell of matter, the embodied self bursts out into the freedom of delight and finally attains the utter freedom of the Self. Thus for the true apprehension of the Self, the knowledge of the five levels of personality is indispensably necessary and a close analysis of them essential.

The *Brahmavallī* of the *Taittirīya* opens with the assertion that the knower of Brahman attains the Supreme[32]. It then goes on to expound the nature of Brahman by defining it as Truth, Consciousness and Infinite.[33] It lies hidden in the cave, established in the supreme ether.[34] Thus it cannot be gained easily, all at once, because it does not lie on the surface but remains concealed in the depths of the cave, which, we have seen, means the heart or the buddhi. One must penetrate through the deepest layer of consciousness in order to have direct contact with the reality lying underneath. But it is not possible to go down to the deepest layer by a sudden and single effort; there lie numerous thick hard layers in between, which have to be penetrated through first of all. The personality, of which we are ordinarily conscious and in possession now, is purely material (*puruṣo annarasamayaḥ*).[35] It is the last outcome of the spirit's downward movement, which begins with the ether (*ākāśa*) and ends with the earth (*pṛthivī*). From this earth spring the crops, which produce the food, which ultimately gives birth to the corporeal frame of man. Thus the imprisonment of the spirit is complete here, and so the movement for release, too, must begin from this level first of all.

As matter imprisons the spirit, so the spirit again releases matter. 'By creating it all He entered into it' *says* the Upaniṣad.[36] Hence, matter, being infused with spirit, forsakes its mere materiality, gives up its dead inertia. It feels an urge to expand, to outstrip itself, an impelling drive to grow and, evolve. The touch of spirit thus works a magic in matter. This is the secret behind the "emergent evolution" of which Alexander and Lloyd Morgan speak so much. They have noted the phenomenon but have given no satisfactory explanation of this urge or nisus for growth and evolution. Here the Upaniṣad throws a flood of light when it says that the spirit has entered into matter and hence matter, too, can no longer rest in its materiality but must move from its narrow and small boundary towards the vast and the illimitable.

Matter is not to be despised or neglected, for whatever rests in the earth (*pṛthivīṁ śritāḥ*)[37] depends on it, rather owes its very existence to it. It is the material food that sustains the material body, and hence it is the foremost of all created things (*bhūtānāṁ jyeṣṭham*)[38]. Hence also it is called the supreme medicine for all (*sarvauṣadham*),[39] which alone relieves the agony of hunger. The Upaniṣad, thus, never neglects the material basis of spiritual life but wants to make a firm footing in this level before moving further. Absolute material prosperity is promised to one who worships matter as Brahman. All food flows to him who achieves this realization (*sarvaṁ vai te annam āpnuvanti*).[40] 'Grow more food' (*annaṁ bahu kurvīta*),[41] is an ageold command uttered by the Upaniṣad long ago, for the seers knew that want in the material plane handicaps the soul in its upward ascent. Hence, only after ensuring plenitude in the material plane, they moved forward to explore further in the field.

But it must be remembered that the knowledge of mere matter or the mere hoarding of food is not the goal but the realization of the Self that is encased in matter (*annamaya ātmā*). Only then can it be realized how mere dead inert matter in the form of food becomes transformed into the very constituent elements of a living organism, when consumed by a man i.e. how it goes to contribute to the formation of living cells and tissues, bones and muscles etc. If there were no common principle between the consumer and the consumed (*anna* and *annāda*). this assimilation and absorption of one by the other would not have been possible. Underlying matter is life and by the latter it is filled, (*tenai'ṣa pūrṇaḥ*)[124], and that is the secret of its contribution to the growth of life. As the vital being (*prāṇamaya*) is the informing spirit which fills matter all over so the *prāṇamaya,* too, has its footing in matter (*pṛthivī paccham pratiṣṭhā*)[43]. Matter is instilled with life and life is sustained by matter, rather rooted in it.

Thus the frontiers of matter and life are not rigidly marked out and absolutely closed to each other but the one runs into the other and there is an easy and spontaneous passage from one to the other. Here is the secret behind the custom among the Hindus to offer food, first of all, to the different forms of Prāṇa viz., *Prāṇa, apāna, vyāna, udāna* and *samāna.* The *prāṇamaya* or the vital self is the consumer. (*bhoktā*) and that is why we hear in most of the *Prāṇavidyās* that one who has this realization becomes full of consumable goods as well as a great consumer himself (*annavān annādo bhavati*)[44]. The food (*anna*) changes into the immortal essence (*amṛta*) to one who realizes this state of *prāṇamaya ātmā.* This becomes possible because the vital self acts as a link between matter and spirit. It has its station in the earth but its self is the ether (*ākāśa ātmā*)[45], and hence it connects the earth with the heaven. With its foot on earth it stretches itself towards the heaven and the upward ascent thus begins here. The immobility of matter gives way to the fluidity of life and there ensues an irresistible movement towards growth and expansion.

As the attainment of the material self leads to the cure of all ills or problems of the material plane because *anna* happens to be the all-curing drug (*sarvauṣadha*), so the realization of the vital self ensures a full span of life (*sarvam eva ta āyur Yanti*)[46] i.e. the movement for growth becomes unimpeded and is not cut short in the middle by any accident or calamity. Hence the significant name of *prāṇa* is *sarvāyuṣam*[47]. The span of existence on the material plane depends absolutely on the inherence of life (*prāṇa*) in the body. Thus the material self is wholly dependent on the vital self and exists solely through it. Therefore the *prāṇamaya* is called inner than the *annamaya ātmā* (*anyo antara ātmā prāṇamayaḥ*)[48] because it happens to be subtler than the material as well as the sustainer of it.

But inner than the *prāṇamaya* or the vital self is the *manomaya* or the mental self. By the latter is the former filled or sustained. We have seen that the *prāṇa* is the consumer or the enjoyer, but the enjoyment presupposes desires, for the fulfilmcnt of which one indulges in the enjoyment, moves forward for their satisfaction. Thus the movement of the *prāṇamaya* is guided by the desires, which are stored in the *manomaya.* The mental self is constituted of desires, *saṅkalpa* and *vikalpa* and hence it is sometimes called the desire-body (*liṅgaśarīra*). Unless and until this desire-body is dissolved, embodiment in the material plane is inevitable, for it is this which impels life to move forward towards an embodiment in the material plane in order to gather the material objects and consume them to fulfil or satisfy the desires. Wherever desire subsists, a seeking of objects must necessarily follow. This seeking or urge is signified by the *prāṇamaya* but at the root of the seeking is the *manomaya,* who gives the incentive or the directive to go forward. Thus life is not a blind movement but instilled with a consciousness or purpose. It is filled by the *manomaya* (*tenai'sa pūrṇaḥ*)[49]*,* the principle of consciousness, whose whole body is composed of the different Vedas, the *yajus* being its head, the *ṛk* and *sāman* its two sides and the *atharvan* its hinder part[50]. This signifies that it is wholly constituted of a principle of knowledge or consciousness.

Our ordinary sphere of existence is constituted of these three principles matter, life and mind. We live in a world of desires, vital urges and material satisfactions. Freud's thesis about the primacy of the subconscious over all the functions of the human life holds true upto a certain point. Anticipating him, as it were, our scriptures have said long ago: 'Whatever a creature does is nothing but the movement of desire[51]. All these signify that the mental self holds a predominant position in our ordinary state of consciousness and directs all the actions of each and every creature. It is the prompting of desire that goads a man to action and thus the cycle of *avidyā, kāma* and *karma* goes on moving, thereby perpetuating the creation (*saṁsāra*). But we generally cannot get in touch with the sub-conscious, which is the fountain-head of all our inspirations and actions. We remain scattered on the surface and cannot sink to the deeper levels of our being.

One who can be awake in the subconscious, rather can consciously identify himself with this *manomaya ātman,* attains a relative freedom from all fear because he gets a glimpse of the fullness of delight that remains concealed within his very self.

The mental self thus signifies a state of expanded consciousness, where one gets hold of all the desires at once, it being the seed or repository of all of them. Ignorance about the course of evolution or the future shape of things to come, causes fear. So long as one is in the dark about the working of the inner springs of action, he is liable to feel apprehensive and nervous. But once the original source of action is seen, once the sub-conscious comes into view, then all fears and apprehensions vanish. The whole cycle of evolution, the whole journey through time is then beheld in a single vision within this mental self and that is why fear vanishes for all time to come.

But the knowledge of the whole cycle of creation or evolution or the journey through time, comes only when one reaches the source from which streams out the flow of life or creation. One has thus to move beyond the mental self in order to know the mental mechanism of creation. The mind, no doubt, makes an earnest effort to unravel the mystery of creation even by an attempt to overreach itself, but is forced to return baffled (*nivartante aprāpya*)[52], without attaining a vision of the source of creation. The return (*nivartante*) signifies that there was a movement on the part of the mind and the senses towards the source but the attempt proved abortive, for the mystery of creation lies beyond the reach of the mental self in the secret depths of the *vijñānamaya* or the Knowledge-Self. This *vijñānamaya* possesses the whole knowledge of creation, for it is this *vijñāna* that initiates all actions, all movements, nay, the very 'sacrifice' of creation.

All the gods worship it as the eldest Brahman (*brahma jyeṣṭham upāsate*).[54] This clearly signifies that this *vijñāna* is the first evolute, hence *jyeṣṭha,* the eldest offspring of the Supreme Reality. Hence it is the Prajāpati, the lord of creation, the Prāṇa, which is the twin principle of knowledge and action. That the *vijñāna* signifies the state of Prāṇa is proved conclusively by the use of the term *jyeṣṭha* which is an appellation of Prāṇa, as is clear from the *Bṛhadāranyaka.*[55] This is further proved by the statement here that the soul of this *vijñānamaya* is *yoga* or union (*yoga ātmā*)[56]. This *yoga* evidently points to the biune nature of the *vijñāna,* which is called in the *Chāndogya* as *mithuna* or a state of fusion, the state of one-in-two, of unity-in-difference. Prāṇa or Vijñāna cannot exist if the two parts that constitute it are severed or kept asunder. Its very existence depends on the fusion of the two, the joining of the division. Hence this *yoga* or fusion has rightly been called the very soul of the *vijñānamaya.*

With the realization of this *vijñānamaya* there follows inevitably the fulfilment of all desires and freedom from all sin, even while in the body.[57] The *Chāndogya,* too, in identical terms describes the effect of the realization of the state of *mitbuna."* That the freedom from all sin is the very nature of Prāṇa is recounted again and again through all the Upaniṣads.[59] Thus it is clear beyond doubt that the state of *vijñānamaya* is identical with the state of Prajāpati or Prañā or Prajñā, all of which mean the same thing in the Upaniṣadic terminology.

We have seen that *yoga* is the very soul of *vijñānamaya.* Hence it is the link-principle that connects the Absolute and the relative, the Uncreated and the created, the Infinite and the finite. It stands in the middle, joining the two hemispheres, the upper and the lower. So its footing or station has been indicated as the vast or *mahas* (*mahaḥ pucchaṁ pratiṣṭhā*)[60]. The sphere of *mahas* stands in the middle of the seven spheres that embrace the whole creation. Below it are the three, *bhūḥ, bhuvaḥ,* and *svaḥ* and above it the other three, *jana, tapas* and *satya.* The point of junction is the *mahas.* When the upward movement begins from the level of *bhūḥ* and the three lower spheres are gradually transcended, then one first feels the taste of freedom and delight here in the sphere of *mahas* or *vijñāna* and thence proceeds further onwards. Similarly when the lower Movement is initiated, when the urge for creation moves forward, then again it is from this sphere of *mahas* that the plunge into the darkness of ignorance is taken. Below is the sphere of utter darkness, above is the sphere of eternal light, and in the middle lies this region of twilight.

Hence those who seek a synthesis of the two contradictory principles, a compromise between the two opposing forces of light and darkness lay their whole emphasis on this plane of *vijñāna.* That is why Sri Aurobindo, being essentially imbued with a spirit of synthesis, makes his philosophy move on this central principle of *vijnāna*, which he has chosen to call 'supermind', in his own terminology. He believes that with the descent of this higher faculty of supermind, a total transformation and regeneration of the ordinary man is inevitable. Through the agency of the supermind the higher light will illuminate the lower spheres of matter, life and mind. Hence to get in touch with the sphere of light that lies beyond and then to bring it down to the earth-consciousness, one must rend this veil of supermind or *vijñāna.*[61] This will unravel the mystery of creation, solve the riddle of the universe.

Alexander, too, dreams about the emergence of a still higher faculty than the mind, for he believes that the evolution does not stop with the birth of the mind but holds within it the possibility of the emergence of a still higher principle than it. The emergence of this higher faculty is inevitable because the creative urge of evolution is charged with this aim. God is 'in the making', according to Alexander; he is not a finished product as such. Hence the entire creation, limited by space and time, moves towards the making of the deity,[62] according to Alexander.

We have mentioned these modern views in passing in order to show how remarkably the Upaniṣadic conception of this *vijñānamaya* self tallies with these conceptions. We have seen that the *vijñāna* signifies the state of Prāṇa or Prajāpati, which Alexander chooses to call the 'deity'. At the apex of creation it stands, and its realization seems to be the crowning achievement of the whole evolution, for which it strives. That sphere, whence speech and mind return baffled, now seems to be within one's reach through the achievement of this new faculty of *vijñāna.* One is now in touch with the realm of delight that lies beyond.

Thus in our analysis of the sheaths of the Self, we have been brought to a junction-point. The thick shells of matter, life and mind have been penetrated through and the luminous sheath of *vijñāna* or knowledge first brings definite intimations of the hidden reality that lies beyond. *Vijñāna,* no doubt, brings a complete knowledge of the process of creation, because, as we have seen, it is the source from which the whole creation proceeds or extends (*tanute*).[63] But the reality that lies beyond is still not revealed in its utter purity and nakedness, the *vijñāna* itself being a sheath which covers that reality. That is why the Upaniṣad proceeds still further and reaches the final sheath of *ānanda* or bliss, which lies beyond *vijñāna.*

This *ānandamaya* or bliss-self is composed all over with bliss from its head to foot, as the Upaniṣad here describes its different limbs in terms of different varieties of bliss, like *priya, moda, pramoda, ānanda* etc.[64] This signifies that it is brimming with the fullness of delight or bliss. This delight is the delight of self-projection or self-extension. It is from the overflowing of this ocean of delight that the creation begins and it is also sustained by it and finally returns to it. Thus the initial movement for creation begins here in the *ānandamaya kośa,* and the *vijñānamaya* only extends it (*tanute*), i.e. carries it far and wide, down to the *annamaya* or physical self. The signal to start or to go forth is given here and the *vijñānamaya* then executes the plan, works out the details, actualizes the project. Hence the *vijñānamaya* is said to be filled with this *ānandamaya*[65] or is rather the very first offspring (*jyeṣṭham*) of the latter. As we found the *vijñānamaya* to be identical with the first-born Prajāpati or Hiraṇyagarbha or Prāṇa, so this *ānandamaya* naturally occupies the status of Īśvara, who is the progenitor of the world.

Now, what particular characteristic is sought to be conveyed through this term *'ānandamaya'* and how does it excel the *vijñānamaya*, which, we found, contains within it the whole solution of the riddle of creation? What is the necessity of positing still another sheath beyond the *vijñānamaya?* The *vijñānamaya* is no doubt stationed in the vast (*mahas*) but yet it is not infinite in its own nature. Its greatness or universality is essentially a product of conjunction (*yoga*), which is its very self (*ātmā*), and hence a created thing and not inherent in itself. *Ānanda* signifies a fullness or spontaneity; hence it is free from all mixture, an absolutely unalloyed joy which wells up from the very being of the Self. So the *ānandamaya* is described as rooted in Brahman itself (*brahma puccham pratiṣṭhā*),[66] from whose being flows out this exuberance of joy. This joy is not a product of an union of two principles but the very fundamental nature of reality that lies behind all creation. Hence the process of creation is as effortless and unconscious an act as breathing. 'Whose breathing are the Vedas' says Sāyaṇa in the benedictory verse of his commentary on the Vedas.[67] The Veda or the supreme *vijñāna,* the repository of all knowledge which brings into existence the whole of creation, comes out of it with as much ease and spontaneity as the act of breathing. The overflowing fulness or the utter spontaneity of this level of *ānandamaya* sharply distinguishes it from the *vijñānamaya.* What becomes a conscious act on the part of *vijñānamaya* is only an unconscious projection for the *ānandamaya.*

The Upaniṣad is well aware of the difficulty in the comprehension of this supernal delight on the part of a human being and so draws a gradual hierarchy of delight beginning from the human and ending with that of Brahman.[68] A human being considers himself perfectly happy if he is full of health, wealth and youth. But in the scale of delight drawn by the Upaniṣad it occupies the lowest rung of the ladder. The delight goes on increasing in the higher sphere of the gods and lastly in that of the Prajāpati, the delight is the highest of all the gods. But his delight, too, becomes insignificant before this delight of Brahman, which far exceeds all of them. In connection with this exhaustive scale of delight drawn here, one thing is to be particularly noticed. It is the refrain *'śrotriyasya cā 'kāmahatasya'*[69] attached to all the different grades of delight. This signifies that no delight is inaccessible to one, who has freed himself from the fetters of desire and devoted himself to the Vedas alone i.e. who is guided solely by the Supreme Reason in all spheres of life. Even the highest and the most supreme delight of Brahman is not difficult of achievemcnt for him, because it is only the desires that deprive one of the delight that is inherent in him, and so the Upaniṣad declares : "When all the desires, pertaining to the heart, are removed, immediately the mortal becomes immortal and here achieves Brahman".[70] There is no interval of time between the cessation of desires and the revelation of delight. As the one goes, the other which is the very basic nature of the self reveals itself immediately. The term *'akāmahatasya'* also makes it clear that this delight is not the short and ephemeral happiness that follows from the gratification of desires.

Finally, the distinction from the level of *vijñānamaya* is made absolutely clear by the Upaniṣad itself while it recounts the effect of realization, as distinguished from the former. We found that after the emergence from the sheath of the mind and with the entering upon the level of *vijñāna,* there resulted a taste of delight which in its turn freed the seeker from fear for all time to come (*na vibheti kadācana*). Here also the same result is repeated in identical terms but with only one slight change. There it was *'kadācana',* 'never', in no moment of time and here it is *kutaścana,* 'from none' whatsoever. The *vijñānamaya,* having within its vision the whole cycle of time or evolution, has nothing to fear so far as time is concerned. But as it is a product of two, *'yoga'* or fusion being its very soul, it fails to banish all fear from a second. The seed of division is in its very self and so it is not possible for it to transcend all fear from an 'other', which practically means for it a transcending of its own nature, which is impossible.

But the *ānandamaya,* springing from the very depth of the one indivisible Reality, has nothing to fear from anything whatsoever. because all things happen to be of the very stuff of delight and hence is not separate from it or alien to it. Here again, only at this level, does one transcend the sphere of dualities. For such a liberated soul the distinction between right and wrong ceases altogether. 'Only him such thoughts do not torment: what virtuous deeds have I not done, what sins have I committed'[71]. Doing or non-doing do not bind him at all. This is the sphere of utter freedom, of absolute fearlessness.

Now this final sheath of *ānandamaya* has given rise to a sharp difference of opinion between Śaṅkara and Rāmānuja.[72] We need not discuss it here in details but must try to judge impartially the truth of things by a direct reference to the texts of the Upaniṣads and then decide the issue as far as practicable. The point at issue is: does the *ānandamaya* signify the ultimate reality, in whose quest the analysis of the sheaths was undertaken or is it still one of the sheaths, though the last and the finest, and has to be cast off or transcended in order to reach the ultimate goal? The difficulty has arisen because the Upaniṣad stops with the description of *ānandamaya* and does not specifically denote whether the journey's end has been reached or not. But if one looks closely into the passages of the text that follow, then it will not be difficult to arrive at a definite conclusion. Reference to other Upaniṣadic texts will also help us to clear up the confusion.

In opening this discussion about the sheaths we found that the goal was first of all set as the Supreme Brahman, who is described as *Satyam, Jñānam* and *Anantam.* Thereafter the process of creation beginning from *ākāśa* down to the *puruṣa* was sketched and thence began the unfoldment of the different *purusas* or selves lying inner and inner, the one inside the other. This has finally brought us to the *ānandamaya* self and there can be no doubt that there is no higher self than this *ānandamaya.* If the aim of our search is the highest *puruṣa* or *ātmān* i.e. the *Paramātman,* then undoubtedly the consummation is reached here, as is rightly concluded by Rāmānuja. But as the Upaniṣad, in the very opening, reminds the seeker that the true goal is Brahman, the Infinite, the Supreme Truth and Consciousness, so in the end, too, it does not fail to bring into view that at the background of this highest *ātman or* puruṣa stands the eternal Brahman as the very foundation of it (*brahma puccham̐ pratiṣṭhā*). And the Upaniṣad immediately adds a warning lest one should ignore this ultimate foundation, which upholds and sustains all these different manifestations. If the final ground or foundation of all existence is denied then it inevitably leads to nihilism. The very existence of the seeker is thereby imperilled: 'by apprehending the Brahman as non-existent, he himself becomes non-existent' i. e. faces extinetion' and 'by knowing it as existing, he, thereafter, knows himself too as existent'.[73] In other words, it is through the existence of this foundation that all derive their existence or reality and hence to deny the foundation is to deny the existence of the whole structure. This warning seems quite out of place in the context of the *ānandamaya,* but it fits admirably if one takes it along with the statement *'brahma puccham pratiṣṭhā'*.

That the Upaniṣad is following a definite logical order is amply made clear by the passages that follow. As in the opening immediately after the enunciation of the goal as the Supreme Brahman, the process of creation is exhibited, so here, too, the same procedure is adopted after the conclusion is reached. In the opening, the process of creation was brought in with a view to point out the existence of *puruṣa* and here, in the end, the topic is revived again to show that all these different sheaths are the cloaks through which the same one reality reveals itself at different levels, for, after creating it all, he has verily entered into it.[74] This gives the whole rationale of the movement beginning from the *annamaya* and ending with the *ānandamaya.*

But how does the Supreme Reality sustain this whole creation by entering into it? "He is the Essence or Bliss; on attaining this Essence does this (being) become delighted. Who would have breathed and who would have lived had not this ether been full of bliss ?"[75] Echoing this the *Bṛhadāraṇyaka* says : "Of this Supreme Bliss all the other creatures taste a fraction and live thereby"[76] Here the Upaniṣad makes clear the actual function and utility of the *ānandamaya.* It is only in relation to the creation that it stands supreme and indispensable. The whole creation will cease to exist even for a moment if *ānanda* does not sustain it. Hence *ānanda* is the ultimate refuge of the world. But is there anything beyond this *ānanda?* The Upaniṣad continues: "When he verily attains station in this invisible, incorporeal, inexpressible, unfathomable one, then does he attain freedom from fear"[77]. Thus, again, the seeker is finally reminded of the ultimate ground, the ineffable reality with which the enquiry started. The same sequence is maintained throughout and there is no ambiguity whatsoever in the Upaniṣadic text.

Thus it is clear from the actual text of the Upaniṣad that both Śaṅkara and Rāmānuja are equally right in their respective points of view. Rāmānuja's goal is the Īśvara who stands at the root of creation, sustaining it by His own being. And this sustaining principle is the *ānanda* and hence Rāmānuja has no need to posit another reality behind the *ānandamaya.* But Śaṅkara is in search of the transcendent Braliman, the immutable, unfathomable Reality and he can, therefore, hardly finish with the *ānandamaya.* He cannot rest content until he has reached the *turīya,* which is described in the *Māṇḍukya,* solely by means of negative terms. The *Māṅḍukya* also throws a flood of light on this *ānandamaya* as it expressly identifies it with the *prājña* state.[78] And this *prājña* is the Īśvara, as is unequivocally stated there[79]. But beyond this is the fourth, the supreme, the non-dual eternal reality.

Thus a close scrutiny of the Upaniṣadic texts makes all the dispute about the *ānandamaya* utterly useless, for nowhere do the Upaniṣads leave any ambiguity whatsoever about its true status or position. Hence, to our view, both Śaṅkara and Rāmānuja, are right according to their own respective standpoints. Rāmāṇuja, with his leaning towards a personal god, *parama, uttama puruṣa* rightly stops with the *ānandamaya,* because, that is truly the state of Īśvara, according to the Upaniṣads. Śaṅkara with his look fixed on the Supreme Absolute, and ultimate foundation, *brahma puccham pratisṭḥā* leaves the *ānandamaya* behind and moves forward. But we must remind once again that to reach this supreme background, the ineffable reality, one must pass through the *ānandamaya,* and that is the whole purpose behind the presentation and elaboration of this topic of five sheaths.

To lead to the absolute transcendence through complete immanence is everywhere the sole method of the Upaniṣads, which we are trying, to depict all through by a direct reference to the Upaniṣadic texts alone and a close scrutiny of them. As we found in the topic of the sleeping man that the king did not reject the relative truth of Gārgya's realization but only completed it by leading him further, so here, too, in the gradual awakening and growth of consciousness from one sheath to another, the consciousness of the lower sheath is not rejected but fulfilled and transcended in the next higher one. This is signified, again and again, by the repetition of the phrase *'tenai 'ṣa pūrṅaḥ'* which seeks to remind that the lower is included in the higher and is never rejected as a mere nothing.

Thus the analytic method is not, in any way, a path of exclusion and does not stand in a relation of opposition to the synthetic one, but they go hand in hand, the one completing the movement initiated by the other. It is the same one movement in which the technique is changed to complete the knowledge. It is one circular movement in which the two arcs are the analytic and the synthetic methods. This complete circle, this integral whole is symbolized by the great *Oṅkāra.*

Finally, one more point in connection with the five sheaths is to be noted. As the Self is found to contain within itself inner and inner forms, so the outer world, too, contains exactly similar levels of being. As the macrocosm so the microcosm, and there is a complete correspondence between the two. And that is why in the next *bhṛguvallī* the same topic is raised again by a direct question about the creation, sustenance and dissolution of the world.[80] As in the individual is discovered the inner and inner *ātman,* so in the heart of the world is gradually found the deeper and deeper forms of Brahman. Here, too, it is finally found that *ānanda* is the ultimate cause from which all beings spring, by which they are sustained, and to which they finally return.[81] Thus the world and the individual spring from the same source and hence the last word of the Upaniṣads: Brahman is the Ātman, the Ātman is Brahman.

References

1. BU., 2.1.
2. BU, 2.1.2.
3. ŚB on Ibid.
4. Ibid.
5. BU, 2.1.2-13.
6. BU, 2.1.13.
7. ātmani prajāpatau. ŚB, Ibid.
8. BU, 1.2.1.
9. BU, 2.1.14.
10. ŚB, Ibid.
11. etāvadvijñānadvāratvāc ca parabrahmavijñānasya yuktam eva vaktuṁ nai 'tāvatā viditaṁ bhavati 'ti. ŚB, on BU, 2.1.14.
12. BU, 2.1.14.
13. BU, 2.1.15.
14. BU, 2.1.15.
15. katama eko deva iti praṇā iti ca. BU, 3.9.9.
16. kvai'ṣa tadā'bhūt kuta etad āgād iti. BU, 2.1.16.
17. CU, 6.8.1.
18. svam apito bhavati tasmād enaṁ svapiti' ty ācakṣate. Ibid.
19. ahar ahar brahma gamayati. PRU, 4.4.
20. PRU, 4.6.
21. PRU, 4.7.
22. Ibid, 4.2.
23. BU, 2.1.18.
24. Ibid, 2.1.19.
25. BU, 2.19.
26. BU, 2.1.20.
27. satyasya satyam. BU, Ibid.

28. Ibid.
29. TU, 2.2.
30. Ibid.
31. TU, 2.2, 2.3., 2.4, 2.5.
32. TU, 2.1.
33. satyaṁ jñānaṁ anantaṁ brahma. TU, 1.1.
34. Ibid.
35. Ibid.
36. TU, 2.6.
37. TU, 2.2.
38. Ibid.
39. Ibid.
40. Ibid.
41. TU, 3.9.
42. TU, 2.2.
43. Ibid.
44. CU, 1.3.7, 1.13.4, 2.8.3. TU, 3.6., 3.7., 3.8., 3.9.
45. TU, 2.2.
46. TU., 2.3.
47. TU, 2.3.
48. TU, 2.2.
49. 2.3.
50. Ibid.
51. yad yad dhi kurute jantus tat tat kāmasya ceṣṭitam.
52. TU, 2.4.
53. vijñānaṁ yajñaṁ tanute karmāṇi tanute'pi ca. TU, 2.5.
54. Ibid.
55. prāṇo vāva jyeṣṭhaś ca śreṣṭhaś ca. BU, 5.1.1.
56. TU, 2.4.
57. śārire pāpmano hitvā sarvān kāmān samaśnute. TU, 2.5.
58. āpayitā ha vai kāmānāṁ bhavati. CU, 1.2.9.
59. apahatapāpmā hy eṣah. CU, 1.2.9.
60. TU, 2.4.
61. Cf. LD.
62. Cf. STD, last chap.
63. TU, 2.5.
64. Ibid.
65. tenai'ṣa pūrṇaḥ. Ibid.
66. TU, 2.5.
67. yasya niḥśvasitam vedāḥ.
68. TU, 2.8.
69. TU, 2.8.
70. KTU, 2.3.14.
71. TU, 2.9.
72. Cf. their *bhāṣyas* on *Brahma Sūtra.*
73. TU, 2.6.
74. TU, 2.6.
75. TU, 2.7.
76. BU, 4.3.32.
77. TU, 2.7.
78. prajñānaghana evā 'nandamayo. Mā, 5.
79. eṣa sarveśvara eṣa sarvajña eṣo antaryāmy eṣa yoniḥ sarvasya prabhavāpyau hi bhūtānām. Mā, 6.
80. TU, 3.2-6.
81. TU, 3.6.

CHAPTER VII

THE OṄKĀRA

The Nature of Om

The synthetic as well as the analytic way we have surveyed so far meet and converge in Oṅkāra, which is the great symbol of integration and synthesis in the Upaniṣads. We now propose to make a detailed study of the Oṅkāra to find out why it has been adored so much in the spiritual life and why it is looked upon as the most concrete expression of the most abstract principle or reality viz. Brahman.

OM means 'yes' and it is the supreme principle of affirmation or assent and hence negation or rejection is foreign to its very spirit. As Bhartṛhari points out in his *Vākyapadīya,* in the world there are numerous schools of thought, monistic, dualistic etc.,[1] but Pranava or Oṅkāra is unopposed to all doctrines or points of view, i.e. has no conflict with any of them. It is 'sarvavādāvirodhinī',[2] reconciles all views of diverse character. Puṅyarāja points out in his commentary thereon that all the systems of philosophy rise from and set in this vast womb of Oṅkāra,[3] and it gives its assent to all forms of description about Brahman as well as rejects them all.[4] It accepts all views because they all contain some truth and yet rejects them, because they do not contain the whole truth. It contains them all as well as exceeds them, fulfilling and completing the partial truths they contain. This simultaneous acceptance and rejection is the great paradox which baffles them who are bound by partial dogmas and prejudices. Only when one is freed from all bias of a partial vision, then and then alone can he appreciate the values of all viewpoints as well as complete the knowledge by exceeding them all. The reconciliation comes only through transcendence, by going beyond all viewpoints to the very heart of Reality, and Oṅkāra, being the Supreme Reality itself, naturally harmonises all by exceeding all. This will be borne out by a close examination of the nature of Oṅkara.

Correspondence of Pāda & Mātrā

The two broad approaches to Reality, namely the analytic and the synthetic, proceed by an analysis of the states of consciousness or self and a synthesis through the rhythms of harmony or integration respectively. In the Oṅkara, the states of consciousness and the measures or degrees of harmony coincide as is evident from an explicit statement in the Māṇḍukya[5] and a consequent exposition in detail of this harmony between the three states of the self, viz. *jāgrat, svapna,* and *suṣupti* and the three components of Oṅkāra, viz. a, u and m. The transcendent nature of the self, again, corresponds with the supreme state of Oṅkāra which is beyond all mātrās or measures. Thus there is an absolute correspondence between the two, and hence, rhythm and reason or as the English idiom goes, 'rhyme and reason' are identical. The expression of reason is always accompanied by a revelation of rhythm and vice versa. As the rhythm so the reason, and that is why we hear that the Brahmin is generated through the supreme rhythm of *Gāyatrī* and the Kṣatriyas and the Vaisyas are born out of other rhythms. The rhythmless is the Śūdra and hence he gets no entry into the realm of reason or Vidyā. Oṅkāra being the supreme rhythm, and the one source of all rhythms, is attainable only by one who has reached the final stage of development, the last order of life, viz. *sannyāsa*. Only then can he wield this great weapon furnished by the Upaniṣads (*aupaniṣadam mahāstram*). The entire edifice of Upaniṣadic wisdom is based on and sustained by this one little syllable OM. The different vidyās and methods of contemplation are only partial refractions of this one great luminary of OM and they all ultimately lead towards it and find their fulfilment in it. In fact we may say that the other mantras are only a drawing out and a rendering more comprehensible of the meanings contained in the OM. As such, when the pupil has advanced a certain distance, he is allowed to drop them and retain only the Om which is thus the essence of all the Vedas.'[6]

Significance of the component syllables

That the OM comprehends within it all the systems of thought, all the rhythms and sounds, nay the whole world, is also palpable from an analysis of the very component syllables in it. It epitomises the entire gamut of vocal sounds, for it commences with the 'A' sound produced at the back of the throat and finishes with closed lips for the 'M'.[7] Thus it covers the entire region of the mouth beginning from the inmost region and ending with the outermost extremity. It begins with a complete opening of the mouth and ends with a total close of it. With its opening through 'a' is generated the complex world of waking experience (*jāgaritasthāna*) and with its closing in 'm' is withdrawn the entire universe into the ultimate cause and there ensues the sleep of inconscience (*suṣuptisthāna*).[8] Thus the analysis of the sound-elements itself reveals a world of meaning and points to the unique significance of Oṅkāra. And, again, its very visual image also suggests how it covers the whole existence by the encircling coils and again transcends it through the moon-digit and the dot.

Oṅkāra has been called the bow to which must be affixed the shaft of the soul sharpened by means of contemplation.[9] Contemplation refines the soul, cleanses it of its impurities and attunes it to the object of contemplation. But to pierce the supreme goal, this contemplative self must identify itself with OM. The supreme goal is the Imperishable (*Akṣara*), the Para Brahman and who can attain it unless he first identifies himself with the Śabda Brahman? OM is at once the Para Brahman and the Apara Brahman or Sabda Brahman, as expressly stated in the Upaniṣad.[10] Hence it is at once the end as well as the means. In its aspect of Śabda Brahman it casts out or projects an arm and he who can grasp it is lifted from the sphere of finitude and finds his shelter in the Infinite. That is why it has been called the 'bridge of immortality' (*amṛtasya eṣa setuḥ .*).[11] There is an yawning chasm between the finite and the infinite, an unbridgeable gulf between the relative and the absolute, an irreconcilable opposition between time and eternity. Here Oṅkāra comes in to link up the two by including within its circuit both of the opposing aspects. It is, as it were, the stalk which holds and supports this great lotus of the world with its innumerable petals, and, in tracing the source from which this lotus springs, one must go along the line of the stalk to find out whence it arises. To miss the stalk is to miss the link and then it would seem that the lotus floats without a stem. So to those who have missed it the world has appeared as a fortuitous creation, a meaningless flux, a chance appearance. That is why we find in a system like the Sāṅkhya that the duality between matter and spirit, *prakṛti* and *purusa* has not been resolved in spite of the very best efforts and so the final aim has been only to keep the two sundered from each other. The healing of the wound comes only through the instrument of this great sound of OM and where its music of harmony is absent, separation is inevitable. The distracting notes of the universe must first be brought within the harmony of universal sound and thence one must pass to the supreme silence, which again, we must remind, does not signify an absence of all sounds but a transcendence of them all in its ineffable status. The uniqueness of the Upaniṣadic teaching will be entirely missed unless one penetrates into the mystery of this OM.

Śabda Brahman

Thus Sabda Brahman represents the main aspects of Oṅkara, though Para Brahman, too, is not excluded from it but stands at the background as the ultimate support. The *Māṇḍukya* makes this clear when it says that 'the past, present and future are all only Oṅkāra, and that other, which is beyond the three divisions of time, also is Oṅkāra alone.'[12] Thus the timeless and the temporal are both signified by Oṅkāra. The timeless as such is beyond our reach and comprehension and so the aspect which is in time interests us more because it is intimately bound up with creation.

Let us now look more closely into this concept of Śabda Brahman. 'It corresponds to what the Graeco-Egyptian mystics referred to as the Logos, the formative divine utterance which gives pattern to the cosmos.'[13] The Bible also refers to it as the Word and it says that in the very beginning of creation was this Word and that the Word was with God, nay the Word was God. Thus the conception of the Śabda or the Word as the first principle of creation is universal and as old as creation itself. We ordinarily fail to comprehend how it can be possible for a mere word to create a concrete world of matter. But a deeper reflection will convince us that a word or sound not only creates but also destroys form. When a sound becomes condensed, it is bound to reveal itself through a form. We need not go into the mystic details of this secret of the creative word or sound, but modern science, through its newly-found branch of supersonics, is also lending support to this conception of the supreme potency of sound, which can hardly be challenged. The Śabda Brahman is thus in other words, the first vibration in the calm ether of being, the first reflection of the supreme consciousness. The Śabda Brahman is also identified with the principle of 'Reason' 'because the faculty known to us by that name is essentially the ordering and pattern-making faculty in our world.'[14] It is also identified with the Sun or 'Ravi', the very etymological meaning of the term signifying its identity therewith (*rauti śabdam karotī'ti raviḥ*). As the Sun produces the whole world and sustains it, and happens to be the central principle of creation, so, too, the Sabda Brahman. 'This Word, then, or Logos, is the one central Principle round which revolves all the rich symbolism of the Vedas as unerringly as the starry heavens revolve round the Pole-star.'[15]

The Components of OM

The Śabda Brahman being the supreme sound or vibration has its grade or scale of notes. The main notes that go to compose it are generally enumerated as three : 'a', 'u' and 'm'. The Tantras add two more, viz. *bindu* and *nāda* and make it five.[16] There is also a five-fold classification of the measures in which OM is pronounced, viz. *hrasva, dīrgha, pluta, sūkṣma* and *atisūkṣma*.[17] The Tantras make this principle of five pervasive in five spheres, i.e. they make five groups of five,[18] each corresponding with the other according to the different stages. We have already enumerated two of the five-fold classifications, viz. *a, u, m, bindu* and *nāda* as well as the *hrasva, dīrgha, pluta, sūkṣma* and *atisūkṣma*. The other three are : (i) the five-fold gods signified by the different measures, viz. *Brahmā, Viṣṇu, Rudra, Īśa* and *Sadāśiva;* (ii) the five-fold principles (*tattvas*) residing in them, viz. *Dharā, Prakṛti, Māya, Īśvara* and *Sadāśiva*; and (iii) the five-fold states of the pronouncer, viz. *Jāgrat, Svapna, Suṣupti, Turīya* and *Turīyātīta*.[19] 'More elaborate analysis including a seven-fold one, are also known' but the classification into three or four (if the *amātra* is included) is 'the most usual and convenient'. The *Māṇḍukya* makes an elaborate analysis of the three *mātrās* as well as of the fourth beyond all *mātrās* and traces their correspondence with the states of the self as follows :

The first mora is '*a*' and it is identified with the state of waking because, as all letters and words are permeated by the syllable '*a*', so the whole world of experience is held or covered by the state of waking. Thus *'āpti'* or '*vyāpti*', i.e. all-pervasiveness is common between the two.[20] The Upaniṣad speaks of another common feature, *ādimatva*[21] viz. both stand first in their respective spheres. The '*a*' is the very first of all letters and so is the state of waking which precedes the other two states of dream and sleep.[22] Similarly, the second syllable '*u*' stands on a par with the state of dream because both have this thing in common that they excel the previous state or syllable (*utkarṣāt*) and also stand in the middle (*ubhayatvāt*), i.e. the syllable '*u*' stands in the middle of the other two '*a*' and '*m*' ; and similarly the state of dream between those of waking and sleep.[23] Finally, the state of sleep is identified with the last mora '*m*', because of two common features, viz. both measure, or delimit, as it were, the other two as well as unify them within itself (*miter apīter vā*).[24] The two moras '*a*' and '*u*' come out of and enter again into '*m*', and similarly, the two states of waking and dream have their source in sleep from which they issue forth and to which they return again. The distinctive features of waking and dream are all merged and unified in the state of sleep, and similarly the two moras, '*a*' and '*u*' become merged in the final mora '*m*'. As Anandagiri points out that if one continuously goes on uttering Om, he will realise that *a* and *u* enter into *m* and again come out of it.[25] Thus there is a rising and falling of Om. As the sound rises it begins with *a* and gradually through *u* enters finally into *m*, but when the sound first comes down from the supreme level the order becomes reversed. The very first sound then is *m*, which gradually comes down to *a* through *u*.

Our consciousness, too, has its ascent and descent in an exactly similar pattern. The Absolute first draws a curtain over itself and becomes the *Prājña,*[26] who like a seed holds within itself the whole world yet unmanifest. This potentiality of creation gives it the name of *'Prajñānaghana'*,[27] in whom consciousness has been condensed, as it were, into a dot or seed. The all-pervasive light of the Absolute concentrates itself in this state into a point, which later bursts into the diversity of the waking world through the intermediate state of the world of idea, that is dream. This concentration verily implies a limitation, because it gives a boundary to a hitherto unbounded sphere of consciousness. This limitation or boundary or measurement is signified in the system of Vedānta by the term '*māyā*'. The very basic meaning of the term '*māyā*' is the principle which measures, limits or marks off a thing (*mīyate anayā iti*). Here the term '*mātrā*' also signifies the same thing. *Mātrā* is the measure and beyond is the *amātra,* the immeasureable. *Mātrā* always signifies *mṛtyu*, the death, due to limitation, as expressly declared by the Upaniṣad (*tisro mātrā mṛtyumatyaḥ*),[28] and the *amātra* is the *amrta*, the truly immortal. Hence with the very first appearance of *mātrā* in '*m*' there ensues a limitation and though this state is called *prājña* yet it is the *suṣuptasthāna,*[29] the sphere of sleep because the seed of self-forgetfulness is laid here.

It may be asked here that if it is a state of inconscience like sleep, why is it called *prājña*? The answer is, it is so called because it knows the whole creation in all the aspects of time, past, present and future; in a word, because it holds within it the entire universe. Hence the complete knowledge of all manifestation is here alone, and hence it is rightly called *'prājña',* as Śaṅkara points out (*bhūtābhaviṣyajjñātṛtvam sarvaviṣayajñātṛtvam asyai've'ti prājñah*).[30] The Upaniṣad even goes further and exalts this state in more glorious terms : This is the Lord of all, this is the All-knower, this is the Indwelling Spirit, this is the source or womb of the creation and destruction of all creatures (*eṣa sarveśvara eṣa sarvajña eṣo' antaryāmy'eṣa yoniḥ sarvasya prabhavāpyayau hi bhūtānām*).[31] Thus it is clearly the state of Īśvara, which is signified by this *prājña* or by the mora 'm', or by the state of sleep. In the case of individuals (*jivas*), *suṣupti* only signifies a total absence of all consciousness, they being creatures of ignorance, but in the state of Īśvara it gives rise to the entire knowledge of creation, He being free from the domination of ignorance. But still it is a state of ignorance even for Him, though the ignorance is wilful and not imposed from without. He is full of complete knowledge about creation or manifestation but is ignorant of or rather has wilfully turned His eyes from the supreme status of the Absolute. The world is here held together in an undifferentiated unity, and in the next state of dream the differentiations begin to manifest themselves, and finally they take concrete forms and become actualities in the state of waking. In the return-movement, too, one must proceed along the same steps through which he has come down. The waking world of differentiation must first be resolved into the ideal state, where the fetters of finitude are slackened because the world that was appearing quite external and independent of the subject is here included and taken in completely within the mind of the knower. Hence this state is called superior (*utkarṣāt*)[32] to the former state of *jāgrat,* and it also stands intermediate (*ubhayatvāt*)[33] between the two extreme states of absolutely inward and completely outward consciousness. Through this state one must pass to the next state of *susupti* and enjoy the lordship, attain the super-consciousness and only thence pass to the supreme status from which he originally fell.

The Amātra or the Turīya

This supreme status is called *Amātra* or the Immeasurable, the *Turīya* or the Fourth. By the term *Amātra* one should not misapprehend that there is an entire absence of all *mātrās* in it or that it is without any *mātrā* whatsoever. On the other hand, it signifies its infinitude of *mātrās* and hence its immeasurability. That is why Gauḍapāda in explaining this term uses both terms together; *'amātro' nantamstraśca',*[34] and Saṅkara rightly comments thereon that it cannot be measured as this much (*nai' tāvatvam asya parichhettum śakyata ity'arthaḥ*).[35] It is also sometimes called the *Ardha-Mātrā* or 'echoing half-beat' and as the *Durgāsaptaśatī* describes it, 'it is the eternal half-beat which is especially unutterable'.[36] The other measures or beats come within the sphere of utterance but this remains beyond all utterance. Signifying this highest state, the Upaniṣad has elsewhere said that words or speech return baffled thence,[37] because it is the speechless depth of being. This unutterable (*anuccārya*) nature makes it also '*avyavahārya*'[38] beyond all actual use. But if it cannot be brought to any use, then it is reduced almost to a mere nothing. So the Upaniṣad immediately states that it is '*prapañcopaśama*',[39] i.e. it is the ultimate substratum in which the world rests at its withdrawal or destruction.

Distinction between the Turīya and the Prājña

But one must be very careful in drawing the distinction between the withdrawal of the whole existence in the state of *turīya* and that in the state of *prājña.* In both there is a withdrawal of the manifest world, but the *prājña* holds it within him as a seed, just as a cause holds the effect within it, whereas in the *turiya* there is no relation of cause and effect and hence the '*upaśama*' is absolute, as no seed is left from which it may spring forth again as in the state of *prājña*. The whole existence is here transcended and not withdrawn or retracted or taken back into itself as in the *prājña*. Hence there is no *'prabhava* and *apyaya*', coming out or going back here but all is '*śānta*', absolute peace, *'śiva',* absolute good, because it is '*advaita*',[40] without a second, no seed of duality being left in it. But we must warn again that this state should not be imagined to be a featureless blank or an inert staticity of being. The only thing that is sought to be conveyed by the Upaniṣads, again and again, is the miracle of the Absolute who creates not in the manner of the usual cause and effect series or relation but by transcending this relation, by remaining relationless and yet causing all relations. This is the superb magic or '*māyā*' of the Absolute.

OM as the supreme 'support' for meditation

The examination of the mātrās has taken us deep into metaphysics but this was inevitable because as we observed, the states of the Self are intimately bound up with the different rnoras of OM. This metaphysical discussion was also necessitated by the fact that OM is at once the end as well as the means. But here we are mainly concerned with the method of approach to Reality and as such must devote ourselves now to consider why the OM is counted as the best means for realisation. 'This is the best means (of attainment); This is the highest support', declares the Upaniṣad. Sri Krishna Prem rightly translates the word '*ālambanam*' in two ways, as the means, as well as the support, because it signifies both. He adds : "*ālambanam* means a support, that from which anything hangs and also by a special application of this idea, a 'support' for meditation, a springboard, as it were, from which to plunge into the waters that are beyond the mind. Such 'support' may be of many kinds, a visual form, a sound or an idea. Here the OM is stated to be the best of all such."[41] He continues : 'In the first place it affords a convenient combination of all the three types of mental support previously mentioned. It is at once a visual form, ॐ, a sound and an idea or rather combination of ideas."[42] Oṅkāra, thus becomes an ideal *ālambana* or 'support' for meditation from all points of view. OM is thus a name as well as an image of the Brahman. As Śaṅkara points out : 'It is known in the whole of Vedanta to be the best means of meditation of the Supreme Self as a name as well as a symbol.'[43] This letter OM is the nearest appellation of the Supreme Self or Paramātman. On this name being applied He becomes pleased like a man when he is called by his favourite name.[44] OM thus becomes the closest signifier of the Supreme, as Patañjali also indicates in his *Yoga Sūtras*.[45] Vyāsa, in his commentary thereon, makes clear that this denotation or signifying is not done through mere convention or *saṅketa* nor does it establish a new relation with the thing or object signified. But it only reveals what was already there, as a lamp reveals the objects already existing in darkness (*pradīpaprakāśavat*) or as the statement 'This is his father, this is his son' merely reveals the relation between the father and the son which was already existing.[46] Thus Oṅkāra, as in a flash, reveals the Supreme by dispelling all darkness, it being the closest name or signifier. But even shorn of all meaning or signification, the bare letter itself (*śabdasvarūpamātram*)[47] stands as an image or symbol of the Supreme like an idol or picture. This is denoted in the *Chāndogya* by the attachment of the particle '*iti*' after OM.[48] The '*iti*' denotes that only the letter itself should be meditated upon, even apart from its signifying characteristics. Thus Oṅkāra suffuses the mind with the idea of the Supreme, grips the eye with its visual image as well as fills the ear with its ineffable music or harmony. Hence OM has no equal so far as symbols are concerned. It is the veritable image of the Supreme Brahman and hence by the utterance or singing of OM, the divine is attracted and made to occupy the heart of the seeker. So the Upaniṣad asks the seeker to meditate upon the Self as OM and thereby pass to the other shore beyond all darkness (*Om ity 'evam dhyāyatha ātmānam*).[49] The *Praṇavakalpa* rightly says : 'Delight or roam in this celestial *praṇava* and never in any other mantra mistakenly because it is covered all over by that form of Brahman. What more is to be said ? There is nothing comparable to *pranava*. All the Vedas sing about it, all the sages meditate on it.'[50]

OM as the best means of attainment

Another meaning of the term '*ālambana*' is the 'means'. We have seen that it provides an ideal 'support' for meditation; what more is signified by the second meaning, viz. 'means'? It signifies that OM not only offers a support or something to hold on to for the mind but also carries it forward to the ultimate end. It is extremely difficult to raise the consciousness from its ordinary sphere to the supreme status without some aid to lift it. And this aid is provided by the moras of OM, because it is comparatively easy to generate the vibrations, which are in the level of action and hence within one's control, whereas the mind or consciousness is intangible and not within one's easy grasp. The right vibration being roused, the consciousness, too, is automatically raised to the corresponding level. That is why, as we have seen already, the Upaniṣad asks the seeker to attach himself like a shaft to the bow that is Oṅkāra.[51] Only when it is attached to the bow, the shaft gets the momentum or the force to move forward towards its goal. Here the very symbol of the bow throws a flood of light. The bow when it is rightly drawn gives out a sharp twang or sound, and this sound (*nāda*) is the essential movement that carries the soul forward.

Flow or movement is the essential nature of *nāda*. In the process of creation, nāda occupies the primary place. The first movement towards creation is signified by *nāda* and that is why the *Śāradātilaka* places it only next to *Śakti*, in the order of evolution from *Saccidānanda*[52]. It also stands everywhere in the middle to connect two principles, as in the order, *śakti-nāda-bindu* and also in *bindu-nāda-bīja.*[53] Thus it is the link-principle that always connects two spheres or entities. It connects, because it moves or flows, and thus flow or movement constitutes the very nature of *nāda*. Oṅkāra, as we have seen, has been called the *'setu'*[54] or bridge and hence *nāda* constitutes an essential characteristic of OM, because the function of bridging or linking essentially belongs to *nāda*. The aspirant who feels himself cut off from his original source and tries desperately to link up with it again gets an invaluable aid in this *nāda* of OM.

He finds that his consciousness is cut off in three different and distinct segments of *jāgrat, svapna* and *suṣupti,* all mutually exclusive states. An impenetrable barrier separates each state from the other and only by cancelling one state, the other state is ushered in. By obliterating the *jāgrat*, the *svapna* commences and vice-versa, and by effacing them both ensues the inconscient state of *suṣupti.* Thus his consciousness is cut in fragments and he fails to maintain a continuity between the mutually cancelling states. Here the '*setu*' of *nāda* comes to his aid, which makes him feel that there is a continuous flow which pervades all through and is not interrupted anywhere. By attaching himself to this sound or *nāda*, he is automatically carried to the goal. There is no effort needed on the part of the seeker any more. The sound has its inherent motion and being attached thereto, the self also moves spontaneously along with it. The *mātrās* carry him to the higher and higher *pādas* or states and finally in the *amātra*, he attains the highest state of *turīya.* Thus as the means, 'the *praṇava*, Om is indeed the leader, *praṇetṛ* : while three-fold, he is the cosmic tree turned upside down and thus the fountainhead of the manifold elementary manifestation constituted by its branches, but by steady meditative concentration (upa-as) upon OM the intimate leader (*praṇetāram ... jñeyam nihitam guhāyām*) can be rendered "one" again and thereby become the awakener, the producer of *bodhi : eko'sya sambodhayitā'*.[55]

OM as the end

It is now clear to us why OM is regarded as the best *ālambana,* because it not only offers a shelter or 'support' for meditation but also leads the meditator forward towards the goal through its own inherent force, lifts him upward through its supernal vibrations. But OM is not only the means but also the end, as we have stated earlier. The Upaniṣad declares: 'This Word is indeed the Brahman. This Word is indeed the Supreme[56]. OM is Brahman'.[57] The Oṅkara is the Para and Apara Brahman'.[68] Thus 'not only is it a symbol of the dual Brahman, the manifested Brahman which is this universe and the unmanifested Brahman beyond: it is also an expression or manifestation of it, for all true and living symbols are manifestations of that which they symbolize. This is what differentiates them, in fact, from the artificialities of mere allegory. Hence, says the teacher, it can itself be spoken of as the Brahman and is not only the best support for meditation but is also itself that which is the support of all.'[59] While discussing the *mātrās* we tried to probe into the nature of OM, let us now try to plunge deep into its mystery to realize its true significance as the ultimate end or goal.

Its three aspects

The Chāndogya Upaniṣad while enjoining the contemplation of OM as the *Udgītha* tries to reveal its true nature by positing three aspects of it. The first is its *rasatama* aspect, where it is viewed as the fundamental essence of all essences, i.e. the ultimate principle, the final ground in which all rests. Hence it is called the Supreme, deserving an equal status with *Paramātmā* (*Paramātmā-sthānārhah*),[60] and also the eighth or the Trascendent. It does not come within the series of seven but overtops it and hence the supreme aspect of transcendence is suggested here by the term '*aṣṭamaḥ*'. But immediately after describing its transcendental nature as *rasatama*, the Upaniṣad goes to unfold another aspect of OM which is termed as '*mithuna*' or a 'coalescence'. What was viewed as a pure unity in the state of *rasatama* is here represented as composed of two things, a mixed product, a one-in-two or biune reality. The two things that go to constitute its nature are *vāk* and *prāṇa*, or *ṛk* and *sāman*.[62] Thus this mixture attaches to the letter OM, says the Upaniṣad"' and the fruit of this coalescence or union is complete fulfilment. Hence OM is famous for its quality of fulfilling all desires (*sarvakā-māvāptiguṇavattvam*).[64] Division gives rise to desire and that being healed here by a fusion of the two complementary parts, there ensues an utter fulfilment and complete fruition of all desires. What becomes sundered later on into the fragments of innumerable effects is here held together as in a point; the diffusing rays of light are held together, as it were, within a disc or orb. This reminds one of the state *prajñanaghana, sarveśvara* or *sarvajña* as described in the *Māṇḍukya.* And the turiya there corresponds with the *rasatama* here, which lies beyond this seed-state or mixed nature in its unalloyed purity.

The Nature of Vāk

But what are the principles that are involved in this coalescence or *mithuna*? The Upaniṣad answers that the two things which are coalesced here are *vāk* and *prāṇa.* In the description of the process of creation in the Upaniṣads we find reference to this '*mīthuna*' again and again. In the opening of the *Bṛhadāraṇyaka* we find that the Supreme Purusa desired a second, and then made a '*mithuna*' between mind and speech.[65] Again, a little later one finds the description that the Purusa was not at ease when alone and so had the desire for a second. Then He split himself up into two, the male and the female, and one become the husband, the other the wife.[66] Thus this 'mithuna', it is clear, is composed of two opposite principles, viz. the male and the female, and only from the union of them the creation proceeds and also the fulfilment of desire is achieved. *Vāk* has everywhere been identified with the female principle involved in this '*mithuna*'; The Upaniṣad specifically states that *vāk* is the wife (*vāg jāyā*)[67] and the *Śatapatha Brāhmana* expressly states : '*prāṇa* is the male, the mate of *vāk'*. Thus *vāk* is the *prakṛti* or *śakti,* the matrix of all creation, which is described in the *Gītā* as the Mahat Brahman, which is the *'yoniḥ'* or source in whose womb the Purusa lays the seed of creation.[69] Hence *vāk* is sometimes identified in the Upaniṣads with the *virāṭ* or the vast whose body is this universe (*yā vāg virāṭ*).[70] Thus the infinite variety of manifestations becomes possible only through the agency of *vāk.* The richness of the Infinite would have remained a sealed book to all had not *vāk* revealed it. That is why Bhartrhari states that the Supreme Consciousness or *Prakāśa* would never have been revealed but for the eternal form of *vāk,* which is the instrument for the act of revealing (*prakāśanakriyāsādhanam ity arthaḥ*).[71] Thus the whole universe is the evolution of *śabda* or *vāk* and Puṇyarāja,[72] in his commentary, quotes a verse from the *Ṛgveda* which clearly states this : 'It is only *vāk* which became this whole universe, all is *vāk*, that which is immortal as well as that which is mortal.'[73] This Ṛgvedic verse points to two aspects of *vāk*—one, the immortal, the other the mortal.

Four-fold division of Vāk

Another verse of the *Ṛgveda*, quoted in the *Nirukta*, indicates a fourfold division of Vāk, of which only the fourth is spoken by human beings.[74] What the Veda meant by the four-fold classification is not very clear from the Veda itself but it must have been of the nature of the later four-fold classification of *vāk* into *parā, paśyantī, madhyamā* and *vaikharī*. The *vaikharī* is the fourth which is the spoken speech of human beings, as indicated by the Ṛgvedic verse. It is generated by the vital breath, assumes definite forms of letters through the contact of the vital breath with the different places in the mouth, and is also audible through the ear, as well as carries a definite meaning.[75] The third or *madhyamā* transcends the function of the vital breath, i.e. is not generated by it like the *vaikhari* nor is it perceived by the ear, but it is of the nature of an inner muttering or vibration (*antaḥsaṁjalparūpā*) in an exact sequel of letters corresponding to the *vaikhari* and is purely conceptual.[76] In other words, the *madhyamā* is a sort of inner replica of the outer *vaikharī*, corresponding to it exactly in every respect, but distinguished only by its ideal or mental nature as opposed to the actual of the *vaikharī*. Rising still higher, one gets in touch with another level of *Vāk*, called *paśyantī*. Here the series of letters or their sequences are all lost in a non-differentiated unity. It is like the indistinguishable creative egg-fluid of the peahen (*māyūrāṇḍarasopama*), in which the infinite richness of colour of the peacock remains concealed, as it were, under one mass or fluid. But this *paśyantī* is self-revealed (*svayamprakāśa*) which is a distinctive feature of it.[77] It is the self-luminous seed which breaks out into an innumerable sequence of letters, and hence its significant name, '*paśyantī*' or 'seeing', i.e. self-revealing. Beyond this, too, is the supreme state of *vāk*, the *Parā* or *sūkṣmā vāk,* the imperishable or eternal sound, which knows no rising or setting, modification or running down.[78] This is the primary vibration or *nāda* which is generated by the ruffle or perturbation in the supreme *bindu*. This is what is termed the Śabda Brahman, which, as we have found, forms an essential aspect of Oṅkāra. That is why the very term Brahman is found primarily to signify vāk alone, 'the female power of the personal All-God Puruṣa.'[79]

Oṅkāra and Gāyatrī

Thus *Vāk* forms an essential part of OM, and it is also clear that the *mātrās* of Om are a direct outcome of the inherence of *vāk* in OM. The four stages of *vāk*, which we have just noted briefly, show that vāk being essentially of the character of vibration has a hierarchy of mātrās, which is reflected in OM too. Hence OM contains within it all the different forms and levels of *vāk*, nay, it is the very essence of all *vāk*. This has been made amply clear by the Upaniṣad while it describes how Oṅkāra was generated in the beginning of creation.[80] Prajāpati first heated up the worlds in order to extract the supreme essence out of them (*sārajighṛkṣayā*). This heating up or *'abhitāpa'* is a peculiar and characteristic technique which is resorted to in the matter of drawing an essence, as is found in the *Madhuvidyā*. By this heating, there flowed out of the worlds the three *vidyās* or the Vedas. From the latter, too, again, being heated, came out the three letters, *'bhūḥ'*, *'bhuvaḥ'* and *'svaḥ'*. These three, again, were heated and finally flowed out the Oṅkāra. Thus Oṅkāra is the quintessence of all the lokas or worlds, and Vedas and finally of the *vyāhṛtis*. The *vyāhṛtis, 'bhūr-bhuvaḥ-svah'*, immediately remind one of *Gāyatrī*. She represents in herself the whole of the Veda and that is why the Upaniṣad here shows that the extract drawn out of the three Vedas was the three letters, *'bhūr-bhuvaḥ-svah'*. *'Gāyatrī* is all the creatures and everything that is here,' declares the Upaniṣad.[81] It further states: 'Gāyatri is verily *vāk* and *vāk* is all these created things.'[82] This specific statement leaves no shadow of doubt about the true nature of Gāyatri and also throws a flood of light on the close connection between Oṅkāra and *Gāyatrī*.

Gāyatrī is also represented as *'catuṣpadā'* or 'four-footed' and our discussion of the four states of *vāk* makes this term easily comprehensible to us. It is also stated that only one of its feet is all these creatures, the rest three being in the immortal heaven,[83] which also tallies exactly with the Ṛgvedic verse about *vāk* which we have already quoted. There also it was stated that of the four-feet of vāk (*catvāri vāk parimitā padāni*) only the fourth (*turīyām vācam*) is spoken by men and the rest three are hidden in the cave (*guhā triṇi nihitā*) and are only known by the enlightened Brahmins (*brāhmaṇā ye manīṣiṇaḥ*). *Gāyatrī,* thus being *vāk* herself is only an elaboration of Oṅkāra and the latter, in its turn, the essence of *Gāyatrī*.

The contemplation of *Gāyatrī* is essentially a contemplation of

Savitṛ, the *Ravi* who is identified in the Tantras with the Śabda Brahman.[84] This is the golden lid which covers the face of Truth and so the prayer goes out to the Sun, the Sustainer, the Sole Seer, the Ordainer to remove the veil so that the true vision may dawn, which will reveal Reality in its utter purity and nakedness.[85] In the Vedic imagery, this *Savitṛ* or *Gāyatrī* is represented variously as *Iḍā, Bhāratī, Sarasvatī,* all signifying the state of *Vāk*. She is the *Kāma* (*kāmākhyo raviḥ*), representing the original desire for creation, from whose womb comes out this infinite multiplicity of existence. It is she who gives the incentive to all actions (*pracodayāt*), guiding all movements in the heavens as well as in the hearts of creatures. Her domain extends over all the three spheres of *bhūr, bhuvaḥ* and *svaḥ,* and the three states of the self : *jāgrat*, *svapna, suṣupti*. These three spheres correspond, again, to the three letters of OM, '*a*', '*u*' and '*m*', as Manu states it : 'Prajāpati milked or extracted out of the three Vedas, *akāra, ukāra* and *makāra* as well as *bhūr, bhuvah* and *svaḥ*.'[87] Thus the close correspondence of the *vyāhṛtis* with the three letters of OM as well as the intimate connection between OM and *Vāk* or *Gāyatrī* is now clear beyond doubt. And that is why the Upaniṣad concludes with the statement: 'As all leaves are permeated or penetrated through and through by the stem, so all *Vāk* is penetrated all over by Oṅkāra and Oṅkāra is all this.'[88]

Oṅkāra and the Vedas

This account of the creation of Oṅkāra by Prajāpati also brings into relief the close connection between Oṅkāra and the Vedas. Oṅkāra has been shown to be the essence of the three *vyāhṛtis* and the *vyāhṛtis,* in their turn, are the essence of the Vedas. The Vedas, again, form the essence of the *lokas* or worlds. This makes clear the statement of Sāyaṇa that the Supreme Lord created the whole universe through the Vedas.[89] But the Vedas are the representations of the different aspects or *vyāhṛtis* of Vāk and hence the Vedas are regarded to be the concrete image of Śabda Brahman, holding within them the whole store of knowledge, because all knowledge is nothing but a production of Vāk. 'There is no knowledge in the world which is not accompanied by Śabda (or Vāk)', declares Bhartrhari.[90] Thus behind the wisdom of the Vedas stands Vāk and behind Vāk is Oṅkāra and hence Oṅkāra is the very foundation of the Vedas, their supreme essence. 'The Brahmins call Oṅkāra itself as the Veda. It is regarded as the Veda because through it is known the knowable Brahman.'[91] Therefore through its use, the whole Veda with all its collections is taken as used. Hence know the Veda as Oṅkāra. This also incidentally throws a flood of light on the conception of '*apauruṣeyatva*' of the Vedas. The Oṅkāra which represents the whole Veda is not a produced thing or a product of an individual being or purusa but is at the root of all production. It is itself not a created thing but the eternal presupposition of all creation, the Uncreated Word or Logos which makes the world evolve, the Imperishable or the *Akṣara*, the *Śabdatattva,* the supreme principle of Word, the Brahman which is without beginning or end.[93] Hence its *'apauruṣeyatva'* or uncreated nature.

The Nature of Prāṇa

Let us return, however, to our original analysis of the nature of OM as *mithuna*. One component of the twin principle is Vāk, the nature of which we have surveyed so far. The other principle involved in the *mithuna* is *prāṇa*. Now what is *Prāṇa*? The Upaniṣad expressly states '*Prāṇa* is *prajñā* or the principle of knowledge.'[94] As *Vāk* signifies *śabda* or *pada* or word, so *prāṇa* signifies *artha* or meaning and only the combination of the two gives rise to the *'padārtha'* or the object. We have also seen a passage from the *Śatapatha Brāhmaṇa* which represents *prāṇa* as the male, the mate of Vāk. This reminds one of Aristotle's rēpresentation of matter as the female principle and of form as the male. It is through the medium of matter or *Vāk* that the form or *prāṇa* gives concrete shape to itself. *Prāṇa* is, thus, the formative principle, while *Vāk* the executive, and it is only through their union that the actualization of an effect is possible. Hence *Vāk* and *Artha* are in eternal coalescence and the great poet Kālidasa rightly pictures Hara and Pārvati to be in a similar indissoluble union, while offering his obeisance to them.[95]

The progenitors of the universe (*jagataḥ pitarau*) are always of the nature of one-in-two or *ardhanārīśvara*. Oṅkāra is essentially constituted of these two principles of *Vāk* and *Prāṇa*, because it is permeated by *Vāk* as well as generated by *Prāṇa* (*vāṅgmayatvam omkārasya prāṇaniṣpādyatvācca mithunena samsrṣṭatvam*).[96] But it must be remembered that this coalescence (*mithuna*) that is effected in OM is not of two mutually exclusive principles but they are of the very stuff of the self of Oṅkāra. It is the one indivisible unity of *Rasatama* that apparently splits into two, and again comes into coalescence. So Śaṅkara rightly reminds that this *mithuna* is '*svātmānupraviṣṭa*,'[97] enters into the very self of OM and is not the product of something external to itself. The fulfilment that follows from the coalescence also proves it, for it would never have been experienced if the two halves had not been originally parts of an integral whole.

From this coalescence (*mithuna*) follows the third aspect, *samṛddhi*,[98] the exuberance, the infinite richness of creation, the unending series of desire. The command seems to have been received, the assent seems to have been given, to 'be fruitful and multiply' and so the thousand-fold stream of desires flows thence in its ever-swelling dimensions. Hence OM is called the letter of command or assent (*anujñākṣaram*),[99] for without the initiative coming from OM, no movement for creation is possible. Utter disintegration and complete chaos would follow if OM is not there to sustain and direct the flow of creation. That is why Manu observes that the Brahmin must always put OM at the beginning as well as at the end, for everything disintegrates and later breaks into fragments if it is not sustained by or attached with OM.[100] Thus from the analysis of the nature of OM we find that the flow of creation is OM, the root or seed of creation is OM, and that which is beyond creation is also OM.

Oṅkāra as the last thought

As we have found the intimate connexion between OM and creation, from the analysis of OM given in the *Chāndogya*, so in the matter of dissolution or death, too, Oṅkāra plays a very important part, because it alone determines the postmortem movement and state of existence. This topic is dealt with in the *Praśna Upaniṣad.*[101] The contemplation of OM must be pursued till the time of the final departure (*prāyaṇāntam*),[102] for the last thought must be fixed on and suffused by Oṅkāra, because only then the morae of OM will lift the departing soul to higher spheres. It is the last thought of a man that determines and shapes his future state of existence, and hence if this last thought concerns itself with something of the world then it is impossible to get a way out for an upward movement. He is doomed to revolve round and round the unending cycle of *saṁsāra.* So discarding all worldly thoughts one must get wholly attached to Oṅkāra during the last moment of his earthly existence.

But Oṅkāra lifts the soul according to the mora (*mātrā*) he contemplates upon. If he contemplates only on the first mora, i.e. the lowest measure of it, then he is carried to the human world by the *ṛks* and quickly attains celebrity there, being endowed with *tapas, brahmacarya* and *śraddhā,* i.e. all the best human virtues.[103] But if his mind becomes fixed on the two morae of OM, then the *yajus* carries him to the *Somaloka* or the sphere of the moon, the intermediate region (*antarikṣa*). He is lifted above the human world in this case, but he has to return again after enjoying eminence there for a limited period.[104] The highest movement, however, is initiated if one contemplates on the supreme Purusa through the three morae of the letter OM alone. Then he attains the sphere of the Sun, and as the snake casts off its slough, so does he totally shake off the shackles of sin. The *sāman* lifts him to the highest *Brahmaloka* and there he attains the vision of the supremest Purusa, who resides in all bodies.[105] Thus it is made clear that as the morae of OM so the movement or upliftment to higher and higher spheres. The Vedas, too, are represented here as carrying to a definite sphere, each of them separately. Thus the *Ṛk* leads to this world of human beings, the *Yajus* to the *antarikṣa* or intermediate world and the *Sāman* to the supreme sphere of *Brahmaloka.* But all these spheres as well as the Calm, Imperishable, Immortal and Fearless Supreme can be attained by the enlightened soul only through the medium of OM.[106] Hence the great importance of the contemplation of OM at the dying moment. Echoing this the Gita says. 'He who departs, casting off his body, uttering OM, the one-lettered Brahman, and meditating on me, attains the highest status.'[107]

Correct utterance of OM

This, incidentally, brings in the question of the proper utterance ot OM. OM, as we have seen, comprises within it the two aspects of *vāk* and *artha* and so, in the proper application of OM, too, both these aspects come into play. As *vāk* it needs '*vyāharaṇa*' utterance, and as *artha* it requires '*anusmaraṇa*' or constant remembrance or contemplation. These two things go hand in hand and so Patañjali after indicating the OM as the symbol of God prescribes both its *japa*, utterance as well as *arthabhāvana* i.e. contemplation on its meaning or significance.[108] From the analysis of the four states of *Vāk*, we have come to learn that the actually pronounced word is called the *vaikharī* and hence the pronunciation of OM, too, begins with the *vaikharī*, then it moves to the level of *madhyamā,* where it is only inwardly pronounced without any connexion with the outer organs of speech, then it is lifted to the sphere of *paśyantī* or 'seeing' *vāk*, where the flash of illumination comes, and finally reaches the state of *Parā* or the highest sphere of *Vāk,* the pure primal vibration (*nāda*), the all-encompassing sound or harmony. Thus, beginning from the gross level of *Vaikharī*, the utterance becomes subtler and subtler till it finally reaches the stage of *Parā*. The scale of *'artha'* or meaning, too, rises in an exactly similar correspondence with the levels of utterance. That is why it has been declared in the Upaniṣad that 'he, who with knowledge can utter the OM, can certainly, as the verse says, gain whatever he desires (*yad icchati tasya tat*), for in it is the whole power of the creative Logos.'[109]

Sri Krishna Prem rightly points out 'that by correct utterance is not meant any mere pronunciation that can be learnt by studying the throat and lip movements of another man. Not by mere instruction, as a later verse tells us, is the utterance to be learnt nor will any known science of phonetics avail to write it down. The word must be uttered not with lips alone but with the whole four-fold being of the psyche if it is to manifest the creative power which we have described above. It is in the heart that we must utter it or rather must unite with its eternal utterance, for no man can pronounce it but only 'God' himself.'[110] Thus the pronunciation must not be confined to the level of *vaikharī* but must be taken to the level of *paśyantī* or uttered 'in the heart' and finally reach the state of *Parā* where it will 'unite with its eternal utterance'. Then one comes in touch with the eternal *Nāda* or Sound which, the *Bhāgavata,* while tracing the origin of Oṅkāra, says, was generated from the ether of the heart of the Supreme Brahman and which, it adds, can be heard or realized only with the cessation of all modifications of the mind and the senses (*vṛttirodhāt*).[111] In the words of Sri Krishna Prem 'Then in the very centre it wells up, a throbbing fountain of Sound which rolls echoing around the deep caverns, impressing itself on their walls in ten thousand hieroglyphic forms which contain, for him who can read them, all knowledge, human and divine.'[112]

The meaning of 'Praṇava'

We have exhaustively surveyed the nature of OM so far, but we have not mentioned another synonym for Oṅkāra which is very commonly used in the Upaniṣads. It is the term 'Praṇava' and this term is not the product of a later age, but is as old as the *Chāndogya Upaniṣad* which in a statement, expressly identifies it with OM (*eṣa praṇava om iti*).[113] It is difficult to determine the true significance of this term but it is interesting to study the different interpretations put upon it. The *Śabdakalpadruma* derives the term from the root '*ava*' which means 'to protect' and then the term would signify that which properly protects. *Śabdakalpadruma* also makes it mean the '*avyayam*' or the imperishable. A later Upaniṣad suggests two meanings : it makes the whole vital being go to dissolution, or makes all parts of our being bent upon or inclined towards the Supreme and hence it is called *Praṇava*.[114] Another later Upaniṣad draws a delightful sequence from OM to the Supreme with a long chain of terms and incidentally explains both the terms, OM as well as *Praṇava.* It runs thus : 'Now that which is Oṅkāra is Pranava, that which is Pranava is all-pervading, that which is all-pervading is infinite, that which is infinite is redemptive, that which is redemptive is bright, that which is bright is of the nature of lightning and that which is of the nature of lightning is the Supreme Self.'[115]

Then it goes on to explain each term of the long series, but of which we shall only take the first two here : 'Now why is it called OM? Because by its very utterance it lifts the whole being (literally, all the life-principles) upwards, therefore it is called Oṅkāra. Now why is it called Praṇava? Because by its very utterance it brings down to the Brahmins all the Vedas, *ṚK, Yajus, Sāman and Atharvan,* therefore is it called *Praṇava.*'[116] The *Śivapurāṇa* suggests some other meanings of the word *Praṇava* : '*Pra*' signifies *prakṛti,* the vast ocean of the world and '*ṇava*' signifies a boat, and thus, both together signify the boat that carries one beyond the ocean of the universe.[117] Or '*Para*' signifies the '*prapañca*' or wordly existence, '*na*' signifies absence, '*vaḥ*' denotes 'yours', i.e. *Praṇava* declares that the 'world' of division and duality does 'not' exist for 'you', i.e. the seeker. It brings this supreme message of deliverance and hence it is significantly called *'Praṇava'*.[118] Or it is called *Praṇava* because it 'leads' in the best manner to liberation.[119] Or because it makes the sage entirely 'new', i.e. creating him anew or endowed with a pure form, hence the seers know it as *Praṇava.*[120] It recasts the whole being of the man who makes 'Japa' of it by extinguishing all his action and freeing him from the taints of māyā. Thus it is clear, from all these numerous explanations of the term, that Pranava carries within it the whole significance of OM and hence it is used everywhere as a synonym of the latter.

OM as the synthesis of all approaches

Oṇkāra is, thus, the very soul of the whole *Brahmavidyā* in the Upaniṣads, and here the way or the approach to the Supreme Brahman finds its consummation. What was sought through the partial approaches of the *Vidyās* is grasped here in its integrality. We found that the symbolic approach needed a supplementing by the analytic to achieve completion, but Oṅkāra, being complete in itself and comprising within it all the approaches, the synthetic as well as the analytic, the symbolic as well as the introspective, stands in need of nothing else and hence its unique character. It may be questioned that if OM alone is the best way, integrating within it all the diverse approaches, then why should one take recourse to the other *Vidyās,* which are only partial by nature ? The Upaniṣad itself gives the answer to it when it says that one should affix the shaft of the soul to Oṅkāra only when it is *upāsāniśitam,*[191] i.e. sharpened through contemplation. The Vidyās or methods of contemplation make the soul refined and sharpened and thereby make it fit to finally get identified with OM. Our search for the way begins through the rigorous discipline of the stage of preparation, which makes the soul fit for contemplation by making it '*śānta*' or calm, and thereafter the practice of contemplation refines it still further to enable it to merge finally in OM. Thus all the steps that we have traced so far in the Upaniṣadic approach are absolutely inter-linked and one logically leads to the other. To skip over any of them is to delay the progress and miss the goal. To gather strength through *brahmacarya* in the stage of preparation is *yajña*, then to learn the technique of the art of refinement of the soul through. contemplation is *yoga* (*yogaḥ karmasu kauśalam*)[122] and only after passing through these two stages one becomes able to handle the supreme weapon of the Upaniṣads, the OM (*aupaniṣadam mahāstram*).[123] To one who is devoid of strength as well as ignorant of the techniques, the supreme weapon will bring only his self-extinction and a complete disaster if handled rashly by him. That is why to the completely mature man, who has entered the last order of life, viz. sannyāsa, the Oṅkāra is prescribed for meditation and not to all and sundry.

Before concluding we must take note of a remark by Dr. Keith that the Oṅkāra 'is recognised by the Kaṭha but its importance belongs to the later Upaniṣads, which delight in mystery regarding it'.[124] But we would beg to differ from his statement that its importance belongs to the later Upaniṣads alone. Almost each and every Upaniṣad, later as well as earlier, resounds with the song of glory to OM. The great *Chāndogya* verily opens with the topic of Oṅkāra, the *Praśna* devotes a whole section to it, the *Muṇḍaka* lays the supreme stress on it and points it out as the great Upaniṣadic weapon, the *Taittirītya* also devotes one full *anuvāka*(1.8) to it, the *Kaṭha* not only 'recognised' it, as Keith says, but the supremely secret teaching of the whole Kaṭha is based on it and finally the *Māṇḍukya* is totally concerned with OM alone. In a word, the whole Upaniṣadic wisdom is based upon and contained in that little syllable OM. It is the eternal seed of all mantras, Upaniṣads and Vedas, as the *Bhāgavata* points out.[125] By its three syllables it holds or sustains the three qualities, *sattva, rajas* and *tamas*, the three names or Vedas, the three objects or worlds, *bhūr, bhuvah, svah* and the three states of waking, dream and sleep.[125] Not only that, it is without beginning, middle, or end, the cause of delight, the Truth, the bliss, the immortal, the Supreme Brahman, the final refuge.[127] 'With OM the universe was breathed forth, with OM it is maintained in being now and with OM it will be again withdrawn at the end of the Cosmic Day. With OM the Heavenly Sphere with all its stars and planets revolves around the earth, with OM rise and fall the waves of that Leaden Sea we call the solid land, with OM the rivers flow towards the ocean and with OM that ocean beats for ever on the land. With OM, too, the hosts of men rush forth to battle, with OM they clash together and again with OM they leave their outer shells to tread an unseen path.'[128]

Thus OM is not a thing of later invention but the eternal presupposition of all things, the very foundation over which rises the supreme edifice of the Upaniṣads, the supremest goal as well as the surest and best approach, the greatest end and the finest means.

References

1. ekatvinām dvaitināñ ca pravādā bahudhā matāḥ. Vākyapadīya. 1.8.
2. satyā visuddhis tatroktā vidyai'vai'kapadāgamā/ yuktā praṇavarūpeṇa sarva-vādāvirodhinī// Ibid.
3. sarvadarśanodayapratyastama-yayonih. Punyaraja on Vākyapadīya. 1.9.

4. sarvathe'dam brahmā' bhyanujānāti sarvathā ca pratiṣedhati. Ibid.
5. 'pādā mātrā mātrāś ca pādā'
6. YK, p. 98.
7. Ibid.
8. Ma. 5.
9. praṇavo dhanuḥ. MU. 2.2.4.
10. PRU. 5.2.
11. MU. 2.2.5.
12. Ma. 1.13.
13. YK. p. 95.
14. Ibid.
15. Ibid. p. 96.
16. praṇavah pañcadhāvasthaḥ. STA. 6.22.
17. Ibid. 6.4.
18. pañcapañcakasaṁyuktaḥ. Ibid. 6.13.
19. Ibid. see comm.
20. Ma. 9.
21. Ibid.
22. Ibid. 10.
23. Ibid. 10.
24. Ma. 11.
25. Om ity omkārasya nairantaryeno'ccāraṇe saty akārokārau prathamam makāre praviśya punas tasmāt nirgachantāv' ivo' palabhyate. Ibid. Anandagiri.
26. Ibid.
27. Ibid. 5.
28. PRU. 5.6.
29. Ma. 5.
30. Ibid.
31. Ma. 6.
32. Ma. 10.
33. Ibid.
34. GPK. 1.29.
35. Ibid. SB.
36. *ardhamātrā sthitā nityā yā'nuccāryā viśeṣataḥ.*
37. TU. 2.9.
38. Ma. 12.
39. Ibid.
40. Manḍ. 12.
41. YK. pp. 97-98.
42. Ibid.
43. *nāmatvena pratīkatvena, ca paramātmopāsanasādhanam śreṣṭhatamam iti sarvavedānteṣv'avagatam.* SB, CU. 1.1.1.
44. *Om ity etad akṣaram paramātmano' bhidhānam nediṣṭham. yasmin hi prayujyamāne sa prasīdati priyanāmagrahaṇa iva lokaḥ.* Ibid.
45. YS. 1.27.
46. VB. on Ibid.
47. SB. on C.U. 1.1.1.
48. CU. 1.1.1.
49. Om ity evam dhyāyatha ātmānam svasti vaḥ parāya tamasaḥ parastāt. MU. 2.2.6.
50. Ramantām praṇave divye na tu mantrāntare bhramāt/
    idam vyāptam yatas tena brahmarūpeṇa sarvaśaḥ//
    Kimatra vahuno 'ktena praṇavena tulā na hi/
    gāyanti śrutayaḥ sarvā japanti munayaṣ tathā// P.K. p. 9 & pp. 19-20.
51. MU. 2.2.3-4.
52. ST. 1.7-8.
53. Ibid. Also see an article by M.M.G. Kaviraj on 'Nāda-Bindu and Kalā' in GRI Journal, Feby. 1945.

54. MU. 2.2.5.
55. NRDR. p. 42.
56. KTU. 1.2.16.
57. TU. 1.8.1.
58. PU. 5.2.
59. YK. p. 98.
60. SB. on CU. 1.1.3.
61. CU. 1.1.3.
62. CU. 1.1.5.
63. CU. 1.1.6.
64. Ibid. SB.
65. BU. 1.2.4.
66. BU. 1.4.3.
67. BU. 1.4.17.
68. SBR. 7.5.1.7.
69. Gita.
70. CU. 1.13.2.
71. Vāgrūpatā ced utkrāmed avabodhasya śāśvatī/ na prakāśah prakāśeta sā hi pratyavamarśinī// VPD. 1.125.
72. Śabdasya pariṇāmo' yam ity āmnāyavido viduḥ. Ibid. 1.121.
73. Vāgeva viśvā bhuvanāni jajñe/ vācā it sarvam amṛtam yac ca martyam// Puṇyarāja's comm. on Ibid.
74. Catvāri vākparimitā padāni tāni vidur brāhmaṇā ye manīṣiṇah/ guhā trīṇi nihitā ne'ñgayanti turīyām vāco manuṣyā vadanti// Nir
75. RT. pp. 30-31.
76. Ibid.
77. Ibid.
78. svarūpajyotirevāntaḥ sūkṣmā vāg anapāyinī/ nāstameti naco'deti na śrānto na vikāravān// Ibid. p. 32.
79. Cf. NRDR.
80. CU. 2.23.2-3.
81. CU. 3.12.1.
82. Ibid.
83. CU. 3.12.6.
84. Śabdabrahmātmako raviḥ. RT. p. 33.
85. IU. 15.
86. VVR. p. 71.
87. MS. 2.76.
88. CU. 2.23.3.
89. yo vedebhyo' khilam jagat nirmame.
90. Na so'sti pratyayo loke yah śabdānugamād ṛte. VPD. 1.24.
91. oṅkāro veda eve'ti brāhmaṇās'tu pracakṣate/ vedā'nena yato vedyam brahma vedas tato mataḥ// VAR. 5.1.126.
92. tasmin prayujyamane'taḥ sarvo vedaḥ sasaṅgrahaḥ/ prayuktaḥ syād ato veda oṅkāra iti gamyatām// Ibid. 5.1.13.
93. anādinidhanam brahma śabdatattvam yad akṣaram. VPD. 1.1.
94. yo vai prāṇaḥ sā prajñā yā vā prajñā sa prāṇaḥ. KSU. 3.2.
95. vāgarthā'viva sampṛktau. RVS. 1.1.
96. SB. on CU. 1.1.6.
97. Ibid.
98. CU. 1.1.8.
99. CU. 1.1.8.
100. MS. 2.74.
101. PRU. 5.
102. Ibid. 5.1.
103. Ibid. 4.3.
104. Ibid. 4.4.
105. Ibid. 4.5.

106. PU. 5.7.
107. Gita 8.14.
108. YS. 1.28.
109. YK. p. 99.
110. Ibid. pp. 99-100.
111. Samāhitātmano brahman brahmanaḥ parameṣṭhinah/
hṛdyākāśād avūn nādo vṛttirodhād vibhāvyate// BH. 12.6.37.
112. YK. p. 100.
113. CU. 1.5.1.
114. Prāṇān sarvān pralīyata iti pralaya (praṇavaḥ). prāṇān sarvān paramātmani praṇāmayatī'tyetasmāt praṇavaḥ. ASU. 1.10.
115. ya oṅkāra sə praṇavaḥ yaḥ praṇavaḥ sa sarvavyāpi yaḥ sarvavyāpi so'nantaḥ yo'nantas tat tārakam yat tārakam tac chuklam yac chlukam tad vaidyutam yad vaidyutam tat paramātme' ti. ASU. 44.
116. Ibid.
117. pro hi prakrtijātasya saṁsārasya mahodadheh/
navam nāvāntaram iti praṇavam vai vidur budhāḥ// SP. 17.4.
118. prah prapañco na nā'sti vo yuṣmākam praṇavam viduḥ. Ibid. 17.5.
119. prakarṣeṇa nayed yo'smān mokṣam vā praṇavam viduḥ. Ibid. 17.5.
120. prakarṣeṇa mahātmānam navam śuddhasvarūpakam/
nūtanam vai karotīti praṇavam tam vidur budhāh// Ibid. 17.7.8.
121. MU. 2.2.3.
122. Gita 2.50.
123. MU. 2.2.3.
124. PVU. p. 591.
125. sarvamantropaniṣadvedabījam sanātanam. BH. 12.6.41.
126. dhāryante yai' strayo bhāvā guṇānām arthavṛttayaḥ. Ibid. 12.6.42.
127. Ādimadhyāntarahitam ānandasyā' pi kāraṇam/
satyam ānandam amṛtam param brahma parāyaṇam// RS. 18.10.
128. YK. p. 99.

PART III

The Attainment

CHAPTER VIII

THE PROBLEM OF LIBERATION

Our study of the Upaniṣads has provided us, so far, with the solution of two major problems, viz., that of Reality and of Knowledge. We have been furnished with a picture of the goal or Reality, as well as with a complete map of the journey or the way. We have been told of the various methods of knowledge or *vidyā;* but *vidyā* is not an end in itself, it leads to *amṛta* or immortality, says the Upaniṣad (*vidyayā vindate amṛtam*).[1] So we have to engage ourselves finally with the problem of this immortality, *amṛta* or *ānanda.* The three problems are not separate and isolated from one another but are closely bound together. In fact, it is the same one problem viewed from three aspects or points of view. All the problems centre round the one supreme and ultimate principle, viz., Brahman, and Brahman being *Saccidānanda* or triune by nature, the problem, too, necessarily becomes threefold. We have found the answer to the problem of *Sat* or Reality as also to the problem of *Cit* or Knowledge and now the answer is to be found to the final problem of *Ānanda* or Fulfilment or Attainment.

Mokṣa as the end of all darśanas

This attainment is generally known by the term *'mokṣa',* which is counted as the last of the four-fold aims of life (*caturvarga*) as well as the supreme end of all human beings (*puruṣārtha*). Incidentally it may be pointed out that it is this conception of *mokṣa* that distinguishes the Indian systems of *darśana* from the Western systems of philosophy. All the *darśanas* are guided by this one aim, viz., the attainment of *mokṣa,* though their conceptions of it differ widely, while philosophy in the West keeps no such concrete aim in view. In India, a concrete realization, an actual enjoyment of freedom and joy has always been the only demand in the pursuit of knowledge, while the West has remained content with a mere logical apprehension of and intellectual speculation about Reality. Here knowledge is intimately bound up with life, and the dawn of knowledge automatically transforms all life. The knowledge, which does not bring a release from misery, or does not give birth to *ānanda* or bliss is totally barren, and as such, does not deserve to be called *jñāna,* or knowledge. Hence, Śaṅkara rightly points out that one, who has known the nature of Brahman, can no longer continue to be a man of the world as before, and he who remains as such has never known it.[2] That alone is *vidyā* which leads to *vimukti.* Knowledge is thus tested only by its effect. The Upaniṣads, at every step, recount the effects that follow from each particular knowledge, and it is from these effects that it becomes possible to assess the worth of the different modes of knowledge and their respective values. Brahmavidyā, being a perfect science of the soul, promises exact and definite results which are bound to follow from different experiments in the search for the Supreme.

The relation of Knowledge and Delight

The Upaniṣads, therefore, do not contain mere theories of soul or creation and the like, but they embody the saving wisdom that lifts one from the sphere of sorrow and suffering and bestows the gift of delight supernal. That is why we find in the *Bṛhadāraṇyaka* that the verses of *Gāyatrī* and *Madhumati* are used together in the *Manthavidyā.*[3] One line of the first is followed by another line of the second, which depicts that as knowledge grows through *Gāyatrī* delight flows through *Madhumatī.* Knowledge and delight move in an exact ratio, and so the steps of *Gāyatrī* are followed equally by those of *Madhumatī. 'Madhu'* thus stands for the aspect of value, which forms an integral part of the Upaniṣadic Brahmavidyā, and *'mokṣa'* signifies nothing but the realization of the highest value, the *'rasānāṁ rasatamaḥ',*[4] the *'ānandarūpam amṛtam'.*[5]

The Nature of the Problem

But the problem arises as soon as we try to comprehend the nature of this *ānanda* or *amṛta* or immortality. The Upaniṣad says: 'Only in the Vast is bliss, not in the little is there any bliss. What is the Vast that is Immortal and that which is little is mortal'.[6] Here the term *'bhūmā'* signifies the Infinite, and the opposite term *'alpam'* denotes the finite. True bliss or immortality is said to reside only in the Infinite and all that is finite is characterized by a lack of bliss or delight, and bears inevitably the stamp of mortality. The world, being essentially finite, is a realm of sorrow; then, does *mokṣa* or *amṛta* imply a getting out of the world? Again, the individual, too, is finite by his very nature, and so, if he seeks immortality should he bring about a self-extinction? As Radhakrishnan poses the question: 'Is the highest state of religious realization, the atonement with the supreme godhead, a mere vanishing into nothingness'?[7] In other words, is *amṛta* or *mokṣa* an escape from the world, an utter self-extinction? Closely related to this problem is the second problem which, practically, arises out of the first: Is the attainment of this immortality not possible while one exists in the world or as an individual? The first problem is concerning the 'what' or the true nature of *amṛta* or *mokṣa* and the second centres round the 'when and where' of it.

Various Conceptions of Liberation

The answer to the first problem has been varied and diverse. The answers differ according to the differences in the conceptions of Reality. Thus, to the Cārvākas, there being no soul apart from the body, the very extinction of the body is liberation (*dehocchedo mokṣaḥ*).[8] In fact, they do not recognize *mokṣa* at all as a desired end, for, to them, the only things that matter are *artha* and *kāma,* wealth and gratification of desires.[9] Of the Bauddhas, the Yogācāras hold that the cessation of the modes of the mind is liberation, the Sautrāntikas take it as the objectless flow of consciousness, the Vaibhāṣikas conceive of it as a flow of consciousness free from *'kleśas',* while the Mādhyamikas take it as complete void.[10] The Jainas conceive of the soul as of the size of the body and as covered by eightfold *karman* and when these ties of *karman* are slackened, one attains the four infinites, viz., knowledge, vision, strength and happiness; thereafter the soul moves, higher and higher, in the *'alokākāśa'* or boundless space.[11] One thus attains independence (*svātantrya*) or becomes free, just as an encaged bird becomes free on the breaking open of the cage. This freedom is thus liberation, according to them.[12]

Then, among the six systems of *darśana* too, the conceptions are found to be widely divergent. The Vaiśeṣikas take the Self as *'vibhu'* or all-pervasive and also as the repository of nine special qualities and it is the complete annihilation of these nine qualities that constitutes liberation, according to them.[13] The Naiyāyikas, again, take the utter extinction of twenty-one forms of misery as *mokṣa.* Another school of them views it as the total annihilation of all actions.[14] The Sāṅkhya views it as the absolute cessation of the threefold misery, viz., *ādhyātmika, ādhibhautika* and *ādhidaivika,* which follows from the discrimination (*viveka*) between Puruṣa and Prakṛti.[15] According to Patañjali, it is the absence of the union between Puruṣa and Prakṛti or the dissolution of the *guṇas* and the regaining of the true status of pure consciousness.[16] Then, of the Mīmāṁsakas, the school of Prabhākara regard it as the total rooting out of all relations with the body and the senses, caused by the extinction of *dharma* and *adharma,* while the Bhāṭṭas are often described as regarding it as the manifestation of eternal bliss caused by eternal knowledge.* Some of the latter, again, take it as merely the absence of misery.[17] Of the Vedāntins, there are some who regard *mokṣa* as nothing but the merging of the effect in the cause, others take it as the attainment of the Supreme Lord, and again, there are others who hold that it is nothing but the attainment of an unchanging state by the forsaking of the changeful state.[18] Maṇḍana, in his *Brahmasiddhi,* refers to some more views about liberation. As for instance, some conceive of it as the non-generation of future consciousness of body and senses, or another regards it as a transformation into the nature of Brahman.[19] Maṇḍana himself prefers to take it as the attainment of one's true nature by the removal of the taints of attachment.[20]

Apart from the six systems, there are other theistic schools who have their own idea about liberation. The Pāśupatas, for example, regard it as going to Paśupati or the Great Lord without further return, while the Vaiṣṇavas take it as the attainment of the domain of Viṣṇu (*Viṣṇuloka*).[21] The Hairaṇyagarbhas conceive of it as the attainment of Hiraṇyagarbha through the path of light (*arcirā*).[22] We also hear of numerous other views about liberation, such as the loss of the subtle body,[23] the attainment of immutable body in a special region, the absorption in the Supreme Self through the knowledge of identity with the Self, the imbibing of the qualities of Maheśvara after the extinction of all impure grandeur or power through the favour of Maheśvara and so on.[24] Even there is the ridiculous conception of the devils, to whom devotion to wine and to the gods constitutes liberation. In fact, every individual, not to speak of the different systems, has his own idea of final fulfilment, and the conception differs according to one's taste and mental bias.

The Upaniṣadic conception is, however, distinct from all else. The Upaniṣads conceive of it as nothing else than the attainment of the Ātman or Brahman and in this attainment lies the highest bliss. It is within this grand conception that all other conceptions of liberation find their place, and practically they are all vague articulations of this one supreme end, which the Upaniṣads clearly set forth.

The Universal demand for Liberation

Though we get innumerable conflicting viewpoints regarding the ultimate nature of the attainment or consummation, yet one thing stands out clear from all of them. It is the fact that there is a dissatisfaction with the present state of things and a consequent striving to get out of it. As the *Vārttikasāra* beautifully puts it: 'All people virtually seek liberation, in as much as they desire the attainment of supreme happiness and the end of misery'.[26] *Mokṣa* or *mukti* literally means a 'release', which necessarily pre-supposes a state of bondage. The bondage is nothing but the absence of the awareness of the true nature of the Self and the release is similarly nothing but a gaining back of the lost awareness. The Upaniṣad beautifully states the plight of the man in bondage thus : 'Just as he, who does not know the hiding place of a treasure of gold, does not find it, although he may pass over it again and again, so none of these creatures find the world of Brahman, although they daily enter into it (in deep sleep); for, they are covered by falsehood (or ignorance').[27] Thus the Upaniṣad makes clear that attainment consists in nothing but an awareness of the possession that eternally belongs to the soul.

The very consciousness of imperfection implies a transcendence of it. The idea of perfection eternally abides with us and goads us on towards it even in the midst imperfection. We carry the supreme treasure in our hearts and that is why all earthly possessions of value are cast off as useless even when one gets a glimpse of it. 'This then dearer than the son, dearer than wealth, dearer than all else is this inmost Self',[28] and it is supremely dear because it is most nigh, so close to the heart. Hence, according to the Upaniṣads, 'emancipation is not to be regarded as becoming something which previously had no existence'.[29] It 'is not properly a new beginning but only the perception of that which has existed from eternity, but has hitherto been concealed from us'.[30] 'Thus Deliverance and total and absolute Knowledge are truly but one and the same thing; if it be said that

Knowledge is the means of Deliverance, it must be added that in this case means and end are inseparable, for Knowledge, unlike action, carries its own fruit within itself; and moreover, within this sphere, a distinction such as that of means and end can amount to no more than a mere figure of speech, unavoidable no doubt when one wishes to express these things, in so far as they are expressible, in human language. If, therefore, Deliverance is looked upon as a consequence of Knowledge, it must be specified that it is a strict and immediate consequence'.[31]

The Eternal nature of Upaniṣadic Liberation

It becomes necessary to stress this point while making clear the Upaniṣadic conception of liberation, because, according to the Upaniṣads, liberation is not a product which is generated at a particular time or place or state of existence, for if it be conceived as something produced or newly brought into being, then certainly it is liable to be destroyed sometimes or other. All that is created is bound to perish, only the Uncreated is the eternal and truly immortal. All systems are unanimous on this point that the state of liberation must be eternal and unchanging, but it is only the Vedānta that points out that it becomes truly so only if it is conceived not as a product or effect of something but as a mere revelation of that which eternally is. Hence the Vedānta strongly asserts that 'deliverance is not effected by the knowledge of the Ātman, but it consists in this knowledge; it is not a consequence of the knowledge of the Ātman but this knowledge is itself already deliverance in all its fulness'[33].

Hence Śaṅkara points out that *mokṣa* is neither a thing to be generated (*utpādya*) nor something to be transformed or changed (*vikārya*), for in either case *mokṣa* will be transient in nature. Similarly, it is neither a thing to be newly had or attained (*āpya*), for Brahman is all-pervasive like the ether and hence already in possession of all; nor is it a thing to be modified or polished (*saṅskārya*), for a modification is made in two ways: either by the adding of some qualities or by the removal of some defects. Brahman, which is verily *mokṣa,* is not liable to further increase, being eternally self-complete and hence no addition of qualities is possible to it. Similarly, the question of the removal of defects does not apply to it at all because it is eternally pure by nature[34]. Hence, as in the conception of knowledge we found that the Upaniṣads point to a unique type of processless cognition, so here too, in the conception of liberation, the Upaniṣads equally signify its processless nature.

Objections to the conception answered

But it may be objected that such a conception of liberation takes away the very value and significance of it. If it is neither *utpādya, vikārya* nor *saṅskārya* nor *āpya,* then the effort to achieve it turns out to be useless and utterly futile. It will rather be wiser to give up all efforts to attain liberation and take to inaction. But this charge is made from an utter ignorance of the Upaniṣadic or the Vedāntic standpoint. The Upaniṣad, no doubt, asserts that nothing but ignorance (*ajñāna*) withholds the supreme treasure from man which is eternally in his possession, and it is only *jñāna,* the mere awareness that reveals what always was there, yet this awareness or knowledge is not gained easily. Without the removal of the obstacles that stand in the way, the *vidyā* or knowledge cannot be manifest and that is why even one who is well-versed in the Vedas and their meanings does not become free or is not liberated[35]. The obstacles or impediments are in the *buddhi* or the mind and until the mirror of mind is cleansed, the luminosity, which is always there but only covered by dust, cannot come out or make itself manifest. In this clearing up of the dust or the impediments, a sincere and total effort is needed. So the Upaniṣads do not damp the spirit by declaring that *mokṣa* is not produced by action, but rather, by this very assertion, infuse a new spirit of enthusiasm in the heart of the seeker, for it brings the assurance that liberation is not problematic or uncertain but within one's possession which can be realized simply by piercing through the veil of ignorance. One has just to resolve to shake off the impurity of sin just as a horse shakes off the dust from its body (*aśva iva romāṇi vidhūya pāpam*)[36], in order to gain back the pristine purity. The removal of ignorance means the removal of limitation, and to be utterly unlimited or free is to attain liberation. The call for liberation is, therefore, a call for growth and development through a perpetual overcoming of limitations, which constitute bondage.

It is utterly wrong to think that behind the Upaniṣadic conception of liberation is 'the underlying idea that the world of human existence is a ceaseless meaningless round, a "bondage of everlasting sorrow", from which we may escape, but over which we cannot hope to obtain any victory'[37], or to say that 'it is this longing for deliverance, rather than salvation, in the full sense of the term, which the philosophical thought of the Upaniṣads sets itself to satisfy'[38]. There is not a single passage in the Upaniṣads which states that liberation consists in getting out of 'the meaningless round,' or in an escape from 'everlasting sorrow' over which no victory is possible. The Upaniṣads are not unaware of the conception of 'victory' and the term 'conquers' or 'obtains victory' (*jayati*) has been used times without number to state the results of the different *vidyās*.

The Western critics are not ignorant of this fact that the Upaniṣadic conception of liberation includes the idea of 'victory' or supreme power, but they unfortunately misinterpret it to such an extent that it almost appears to be ridiculous. The remark of Keith is an example to the point, which is both amusing and annoying to all sincere students of the Upaniṣads. He says: "The emancipated self possesses autonomy but it is not an ethical state; it is merely a condition of unhindered power, the ideal of a despot, the state of the man who goes up and down these worlds, eating what he desires, assuming what form he desires"[39]. Evidently the word *'kāmacāra'* has misled Keith here and it is regrettable that a scholar of his eminence has failed to appreciate the true bearing of the term which signifies only utter freedom. It is neither out of a pessimistic disgust nor out of a lust for power that the Upaniṣadic conception of liberation took its rise. It rose out of the innate craving in man to return to his original nature, out of that nostalgia or homing instinct that drives man perpetually to come back to his own self.

The Purpose of Liberation

According to the Upaniṣadic conception, liberation, therefore, means nothing but the attainment of one's true nature or Self or *'svarūpa'*. The conception of the true nature of the Self, no doubt, differs with every system, but we have found that the Upaniṣadic conception of it is so comprehensive as to include within it all the varied points of view. Similarly, in the conception of liberation we find an almost identical comprehensiveness which contains all the divergent opinions that are current in the different systems about it. Before trying to find out the true Upaniṣadic conception, we must first try to find out the value and utility of liberation, or in other words, its rationale. Liberation, being the attainment of one's own nature (*svarūpa*), bondage necessarily implies a fall from the original nature, and this is known as *saṁsāra*. Now, what this fall is due to? Again, what is the guarantee that such a fall would not come to happen again after one attains liberation? The Ātman was in its own nature (*svarūpa*) before the fall, and if liberation means nothing but merely a return to that nature, then the possibility of the fall remains as before.

But, as we have pointed out, there is a deep purpose, according to the Upaniṣads, behind this fall or the plunge into ignorance, and that purpose is simply to make itself known (*tad asya rūpaṁ praticakṣaṇāya*)[40], and it is in this knowing that delight consists. The Ātman originally, while alone, felt dreary and desolate (*sa vai nai'va reme*)[41] and that is why he created a second to relieve the gloom of his isolation. He was also seized with fear (*so'avibhet*)[42], being alone and this also prompted him to seek the company of a second. This creation of a second, rather the splitting of oneself into two, (*ātmānaṁ dvedhā pātayat*)[43] was the signal for the plunge into *saṁsara*. Immediately with the birth of a second sprang forth the principle of desire, and this desire (*kāma*) is just the opposite principle of delight (*ānanda*). So long as there is a second outside oneself, there is bound to arise a desire for it and so long as desire is there, delight must be absent, for delight signifies a fullness, and desire a fragmented and sundered state of being. Hence for the attainment of delight the other part thrown out of one's being must be reabsorbed into itself, or, in other words, the second must be recognized not as an other but as identical with oneself and this is taught by the great sayings of the Upaniṣads, *Tat Tvam Asi, Aham Brahmā 'smi*. It is in this recognition that the delight consists, and this *ānanda* is the *amṛta* or immortality, the true *mukti* or freedom.

Though it is true that *mukti is* not a newly produced thing nor the effect of any action, but merely a discovery of an already existing fact, yet that does not take away the delight out of it but, on the contrary, enhances it. This discovery brings a delightful surprise and it is this element of surprise that increases the delight all the more. A thing, however pleasant, which follows in the natural sequence, fulfilling a normal expectation, does not cause so much delight as an absolutely unexpected and undreamt of event does. The plane of determinism has no delight to offer, for everything is predetermined and absolutely fixed there. It is only in the plane of freedom that there is joy, for nobody knows what surprising revelation awaits him just round the corner; and this plane of freedom is the plane of the Ātman. Hence the Upaniṣad says about this Brahmavidyā that 'wonderful is its teacher and wonderful, indeed, is he who knows it[44]. Wonder and delight are its characteristic marks.

Element of Delight in Liberation

Thus liberation, though it means nothing but the attainment of one's true nature, is not just a mere relapse into the original state of being from which one fell, but the element of delight in it points out that it is something more. If mere removal of the ignorance of one's true nature be the sole characteristic of liberation then it would turn out to be a mere negative state, but the Upaniṣads are emphatic that the positive mark of *delight* distinguishes that state. The fall, we have pointed out, is marked by two prominent characteristics, viz, fear and absence of delight, and the reattainment is similarly marked by the very opposite of these two characteristics, i.e., fearlessness and delight (*abhaya* and *ānanda*). The Upaniṣads specially speak of these two characteristics. viz, *abhaya* and *ānanda,* again and again, whenever they describe the state of liberation : 'Then he becomes free from fear', (*atha so'bhayaṁ gato bhavati*), 'He has no fear from anything having known the delight of Brahman', (*na bibheti kutaścana*)[46], 'Theirs is the eternal happiness', (*teṣāṁ sukhaṁ śāśvatam*)[47], 'He delights having attained the blissful', (*sa modate modanīyaṁ hi labdhvā*)[48], and so on. We have also seen that desire (*kāma*) signifies the opposite principle of delight (*ānanda*) and so the Upaniṣads also invariably describe the state of attainment as the absorption or fulfilment or conquering of all desires: 'He conquers those spheres and those desires' (*jayate tāṁś ca kāmān*)[49], 'Here and now all his desires utterly vanish' (*ihai'va sarve pravilīyanti kāmāḥ*)[50], 'He attains verily all desires' (*āpnoti ha vai sarvān kāmān*)[51] etc. Now this *abhaya, ānanda* and transcendence of desires, all these are due only to the cognition that the second or the 'other' is nothing but one's own self, absolutely identical with one's own being. Only the consciousness of absolute identity can make one completely free from fear and desire and sorrow. At the time of the fall, the Self was, *as it were,* unconscious of its own fulness or majesty, and that is why it felt impoverished in being, lonely and desolate, needing an 'other' to make it full and complete, and now after the return through liberation it feels its fulness, having absorbed within itself the whole wealth of diversity.

It should not, however, be wrongly assumed from this that the Self is endowed with a new quality or characteristic by the act of liberation, which was lacking in it before. There is no 'excess' (*'atiśaya'*) or a new addition from the standpoint of the Ātman, but there is certainly a world of difference from the standpoint of its cognition, between the *'svarūpa'* or reality that is known and the *'svarūpa'* that is not known. The reality which is not known is almost equal to an unreality, and hence the supreme value and importance of knowing it and it is only in this knowing or the cognition that the original fall finds its justification. Metaphysically, the Ātman has neither any fall nor any regeneration as such, neither any bondage nor any liberation, yet it *'plays* at being bound' in order to create the richness of delight. Hence the *Vārttikasāra* rightly points out that from the standpoint of the Ātman there is no 'excess' (*'atiśaya'*), but from the standpoint of the mind, the cognition (*'bodha'*) itself is a great addition no doubt[52].

The Sāṅkhya-Yoga conception of Kaivalya

Thus we have found the significance and value of liberation from the concept of *ānanda* inherent in it. Without a complete reabsorption and identification of the second or the 'other' with oneself, this delight is not possible of achievement. Hence those who hold the second as eternally and actually an 'other' or an alien principle, the very opposite of the Self, have necessarily to conceive of their liberation in merely negative terms, as a cessation of sorrow or an absence of contact with the opposite principle. This becomes very clear especially from a study of the Sāṅkhya-Yoga conception of liberation. Both Śāṅkhya and Yoga are frankly dualistic and, according to them, both Puruṣa and Prakṛti are equally real entities and also absolutely opposed to each other, the one being pure Spirit and the other pure Matter. Bondage consists, therefore, in the coalescence of these two principles, which brings in its train misery and suffering. Liberation, consequently, consists in nothing else but the severance of the connexion between the two, (*saṁyogābhāvo hānam tad dṛśeḥ kaivalyam*)[53]. Vyāsa, in his commentary, makes it clear that it means a 'non-mixed' state or in other words, a further absence of connexion with the *guṇas (puruṣasyā-'miśrībhāvaḥ punar asaṁyogo guṇair ity arthaḥ)*[51]. The very term for liberation used in Sāṅkhya-Yoga viz. *'kaivalya'* signifies that the aim of these systems is to secure an 'aloneness' by severing all connexion with the second or the other, for, according to them, the root of all miseries is in the *'saṁyoga' or* connexion between Puruṣa and Prakṛti. The Sāṅkhya-Yoga can never think of resolving one of the terms into the other, for both of them are recognized as real as well as absolutely independent and of contradictory natures. Even when the discriminating knowledge (*vivekajñāna*) causes the separation between the two, Prakṛti does not vanish into nothingness but remains intact with all her potencies. Hence the Mīmāṁsakas, who take the view that nothing but the exhaustion of all actions can lead to liberation, rightly condemn the Sāṅkhya view as of no value, since the potencies remain there still, and there is no guarantee that they will not cause further bondage. As Keith puts the Mīmāṁsā view: 'The Sāṅkhya theory of liberation by knowledge is without value, since the potencies will remain able to come again into activity. Knowledge, it must be recognised, can never give freedom from bondage, which can be attained only by the exhaustion of action, for which the Sāṅkhya metaphysics affords no adequate possibility, owing to the infinite potentiality of nature'[55].

The Nyāya Vaiśesika View

Similarly, the Nyāya-Vaiśeṣika theory, we have seen, aims at the utter extinction of all the nine special qualities which pertain to the Ātman, or the total annihilation of the twenty forms of misery, and it is patent that the Nyāya-Vaiśeṣika school conceives of the liberation in terms of exclusion and negation. There is absolutely no place for *ānanda* in either the Sāṅkhya-Yoga or the Nyāya-Vaiśeṣika conception of liberation, for it is precluded by the very metaphysics which these systems envisage. The Nyāya-Vaiśeṣika even go further than the Sāṅkhya in this that they not only deny the existence of *ānanda* in the final state of liberation, but also that of *jñāna* or consciousness, for, according to the former, *jñāna* is essentially a quality which is produced in the Ātman through the contact with the mind and is not the inherent nature of it, as the Sāṅkhya-Yoga think. Hence some have ridiculed the Nyāya-Vaiśeṣika system by saying that their final aim is merely to turn into a stone![56] If even consciousness is denied in the final state of liberation, then there remains nothing to distinguish the Ātman from pure inert matter. Thus, in their zeal to root out misery, the Nyāya-Vaiśeṣika even do not hesitate to go to the ridiculous extreme of rooting out consciousness, too, in the process. Such is always the danger behind the extreme attitude of exclusion and negation.

The Upaniṣadic View distinguished

We have especially dealt with the Sāṅkhya-Yoga and Nyāya-

Vaiśesika conceptions of liberation because the Upaniṣadic view is often represented as practically identical with or of the same nature as the *kaivalya* of Sāṅkhya-Yoga or the inert static *mokṣa* of Nyāya-Vaiśeṣika. A study now, of the Upaniṣadic texts which describe the supreme state of attainment, will reveal how utterly distinct and absolutely unique is this conception from all else, and yet how it includes all the diverse views by placing each of them in its proper place within the hierarchy of values. The Upaniṣads, undoubtedly, recognize that there is a tendency towards exclusion or escape in the movement towards liberation and that this is a necessary and very important phase of it. The Sāṅkhya rightly points out that the urge towards liberation arises only from the impact of misery[57], and similarly the Nyāya, too, very closely analyses the successive steps in liberation describing how the release from one preceding thing automatically leads to the release from the next one following it, which is, in fact, the effect of the former, and there it is shown that misery is the ultimate form which the original evil of ignorance takes finally[58].

Release from misery is, no doubt, the basic demand in man, and further when he finds that the whole of existence is full of misery, the demand takes the form of one for a release from existence as such. If birth or embodiment inevitably implies misery, as the *Nyāyasūtra* points out, then it necessarily becomes imperative to seek a release from birth or life itself. This attitude, for getting out of life is born of a spirit of disgust and frustration. The very term *'mukti'* or '*mokṣa*' which signifies 'release', is generally taken to represent this attitude.

But the Upaniṣads are always careful in this that whenever they speak of 'release', they also immediately add that there is also an 'immortality' to supplement and complete the former. We have said that the conception of liberation depends closely on the conception of Reality and is in fact inseparable from the latter. There is no escape from a conception of it as *kaivalya* if one takes the Reality as distinctly two and utterly independent. But the Upaniṣads, we have seen, do not view the two as distinct and separate, but, on the contrary, as nothing else but the splitting into two halves of the same one original principle (*ātmānaṁ dvedhā pātayat*)[59]. We have also seen that this twin principle (*'mithuna'*) or one-in-two is known as Prāṇa in the Upaniṣads. Now this Prāṇa has a double movement: one negative and another positive. The negative movement attempts to free the Prāṇa from impurities, while the positive one seeks to attain its pure and perfect form. A separation is, no doubt, needed and here the Sāṅkhya-Yoga are right. But what is separated or excluded is the imperfect form alone, and hence the Sāṅkhya-Yoga represent only one side of the movement, because to be relieved of the imperfect form is not enough. Another movement, and this of union, must lead to the attainment of the perfect form. In the words of the Upaniṣads, one must not only 'cross beyond death' but also 'attain immortality' (*mṛtyuṁ tīrtvā ... amṛtam aśnute*)[60], one must become 'freed' or 'released' and also have immortality (*mucyate ... amṛtatvaṁ ca gacchati*).[61]

Such statements make it absolutely clear that, according to the Upaniṣads, the crossing or passing beyond death is not the same thing as the attainment of immortality. Immortality is something more than a mere release from mortality, for it is not merely negative in nature but carries a positive significance. This is clearly brought out in another context in the Upaniṣad, where it is stated that after rising out of the body and on attaining the supreme light one becomes endowed with his own true form, he becomes the Supreme Purusa'[62]. The casting off or the rising out of (*samutthāya*) the body is the initial negative movement, which leads to the attainment of the pure light of consciousness. Many stop with this negative movement and on attaining this *'jyotis'* or light, become merged in it and feel that they have reached the final goal, wrongly taking this light itself as the Brahman or the Ātman. This happens to those who take *'kaivalya'* as the final attainment.

But the Upaniṣads, unfailingly, point out that there is still a higher evolution even after the attainment of this light. One rises from that vast ocean of light with a new resplendent form, which is truly his own form (*svena rūpeṇa abhiniṣpadyate*). What he had cast off before entering into the light was his false form, a mere shadow of the original, which had been projected only to carry on the work in the temporal world of illusion. But there is an eternal world of reality, which Plato conceived of as the World of Ideas, and which the Upaniṣads call the supreme sphere of Brahman or *Brahmaloka.* To function in that sphere one needs a form alike to it in nature, i.e., eternal and pure. The Upaniṣads, therefore, speak of the endowment of a new form, original and truly own, after the attainment of the light. In other words, the true personality is gained only here, after one casts off the false one and emerges out of the pure light with all his limbs bathed by it.

The Upaniṣads, therefore, do not advocate the ideal of a suppression of personality but always insist on its fullest and completest development. In the context of the *Madhu-vidyā,* it is stated again and again, as we have seen, that one enters into (*abhisamviśati*) that particular form of immortal essence (*amṛta*), but again rises out of it (*udeti*)[63]. Not a merger or dissolution of the self but an elevation or development of it is always the end that is kept in view. The attainment is, thus, not 'a sleep and a forgetting' but a waking and remembering, not a *'laya'* but an *'udaya'* or rising.

It is again not an escape through isolation but a victory through subordination of the forces of Nature. This sufficiently distinguishes the Upaniṣadic conception from the Sāṅkhya one, for there is no conception of victory in the Sāṅkhya theory of liberation nor can there be any in it because of its wrong metaphysics. But the Upaniṣads, in recounting the effects of the different *vidyās,* speak of the attainment of victory or kingship, again and again[64].

Another feature of the Upaniṣadic conception sharply distinguishes it from *kaivalya.* It is the identity of the liberated self with the whole of existence which is held up as a prominent characteristic. 'He, the all-knower, enters into all'[65], 'Those calm and self-united souls, having attained the All-pervading all around, enter into all', and such other statements[66] point out that the universe is not something separate from or alien to the Self but the very stuff of its being. Thus the absorption and inclusion of the whole existence or Prakṛti by the Self, and not its isolation or separation from it, is the mark of the final state of attainment, according to the Upaniṣads. The Upaniṣads do not rest content by merely absorbing the universe within the Self but also move further to transcend it, of which we shall speak later.

That the Upaniṣadic conception is also not akin to the inert staticity of *mokṣa,* as conceived by the Nyāya-Vaiśeṣika, becomes all too patent even from a casual scanning of the texts. 'There he moves all around, eating, playing, enjoying ' (*sa tatra paryeti jakṣan krīḍan ramamānaḥ*)[67], 'Having known thus, he has his love in the Self, play in the Self, enjoyment in the Self, delight in the Self' (*evaṁ vijānan ātmaratir atmamithuna ātmānandaḥ*)[68], 'With his play in the Self, love in the Self, full of activity is the highest of the knowers of Brahman' (*ātmakrīḍa ātmaratiḥ kriyāvān eṣa brahmavidāṁ variṣṭhaḥ*)[69], and such other texts signify that, according to the Upaniṣads, the final state is not one of staticity but of the highest activity and movement. We have pointed out that the Nyāya-Vaiśeṣika even deny the existence of consciousness in the Ātman. After the enlightenment (*tattvajñāna*), according to them, the mind, though existing as an entity (*tattva*), ceases to function, and hence consciousness, too, ceases.

But the Upaniṣads take just the opposite view, for, according to them, in the Ātman the organs of knowledge and action, the senses and the mind do not exist and yet all the particular functions go on even without the existence of the organs! 'He is without hand and feet and yet (moves) fast (or is swift), and is the knower. He sees though without eyes, he hears though without ears'[70]. Such is the paradoxical nature of the Upaniṣadic Ātman. The movement or the functions do not cease but become all the more perfect in the Ātman, because the limitations of the organs are transcended here. The Ātman can see, hear, know and feel and carry on all functions independently of all organs, because the organs themselves are dependent on the Ātman and not vice versa. This is clearly brought out through repeated statements concerning the different functions of the senses in the *Kena Upaniṣad:* 'That which does not see through the eye but through which the eyes see' and so on[71]. The infinite consciousness does not stand in the need of organs to contact the world of objects. Our finite consciousness is so limited and dependent by nature that it cannot conceive of dispensing with the organs and yet have knowledge. The Nyāya system, being merely an account of our empirical consciousness, naturally conceives that the Ātman, in its pure state, is without all functions and consciousness. But the Upaniṣads go deeper and point out the independent and creative nature of the infinite consciousness.

Other texts examined

We have sufficiently distinguished the Upaniṣadic conception of liberation from those of the Sāṅkhya-Yoga and the Nyāya-Vaiśeṣika, yet we may be accused of having deliberately suppressed other texts of the Upaniṣads which run contrary to our contention. There are texts which clearly picture the final state as an utter self-loss : 'As the flowing rivers disappear in the sea, losing their name and form, thus a wise man, freed from name and form, goes to the divine person who is beyond all'[72], or again, 'As a lump of salt which is thrown into the water dissolves and cannot be gathered up again, but wherever water is drawn, it is salty, so truly is it with this great being, the endless, the unlimited, the fullness of knowledge, from these beings it came into view and with them it vanishes. There is no consciousness after the great departure'[73].

We have stated more than once that the conception of the attainment is inseparable from the conception of Reality. So long we have been dealing with the attainment from one aspect of that Reality, viz., Prāna, and have quoted texts which point to its dual nature, negative as well as positive, especially emphasising the dynamic and creative character of the attainment. But we know, the Upaniṣads view the Reality not merely as Prāṇa but also as *prāṇasya prāṇaḥ* or *satyasya satyam.* The texts, we have just quoted above, describe the attainment of this supreme aspect of Reality, and these texts are liable to be interpreted as signifying a state where there is 'a survival without consciousness, where body is dissolved and mind extinguished, and all is lost in a boundless darkness'[74].

As in our discussion on Reality, we pointed out that it is impossible to describe the transcendent Reality, save through negative terms, so here, too, in the description of the attainment of that Reality. a negative character or colour is inevitable and unavoidable. Such terms as 'disappear' or 'dissolve', no doubt, appear 'alarming' to us, but they, are divested of such an import if we bear in mind that they are not used for suggesting an annihilation or a loss, but merely for pointing to the unique nature of the realization which baffles or exceeds all description. This exceeding nature we always confound with the excluding one, and hence that which is beyond consciousness is taken as without consciousness. The confusion is quite natural, since the state beyond consciousness and that without consciousness look so similar outwardly and their descriptions too necessarily happen to be of the same nature.

That we are not thrusting our own interpretation and trying to read the Upaniṣadic texts in our own light, ignoring or twisting their real import, will be evident, if one cares to read further the remaining portion of the Upaniṣadic text itself, quoted above. Even at the risk of repetition, we point to it once more in order to show that the Upaniṣads are not unaware of the fact that this supreme state of attainment is liable to be interpreted as a state of annihilation or a vanishing into a mere nothing, and so have guarded against it themselves, and this proves beyond doubt that the texts in question do not signify a loss or extinction but a gain which is infinite and immeasurable. On hearing from Yājñavalkya the lines quoted above, Maitreyī observes: 'This speech of thine that there is no consciousness after the great departure perplexes me'. Yājñavalkya replies : 'I tell thee nothing perplexing, it is quite comprehensible. Where there is a duality of existences, one can see the other, one can smell the other, one can speak to the other, one can hear the other, one can think of the other, one can apprehend the other. But where everything has turned into his Ātman, by whom will he be seen and whom will he see?' and so on[75].

This makes it quite clear that the description in question is meant just to convey the sense of utter unity, where all traces of difference (*bheda*) *is* absolutely obliterated. The unity is here so deep that it baffles all description. At the level of Prāṇa there was a play of the Self with the Self, an enjoyment and delight of the Self in the Self through the complete absorption and harmony of the two sundered parts. But here the parts not only unite to become the whole but they are realized as the sole reality. This unity is achieved not through a destruction of being, for the Ātman is eternal (*avināśī*) and indestructible by nature, (*anucchittidharmā*) as Yājñavalkya assures Maitreyī. It is brought about by a 'transcendence' i.e., by passing beyond all forms (*upādhis*). Hence it must be clearly borne in mind that 'the being is in no wise "absorbed" on obtaining "Deliverance" although it may seem so from the point of view of manifestation, whence the "transformation" appears as a "destruction"; viewed from the standpoint of absolute reality, which alone remains for it, the being is, on the contrary, dilated beyond all limit, if one may use such an expresion, since it has effectively realized the fullness of its possibilities'[76].

Two aspects of Upaniṣadic Liberation

We have said that the same one Reality is viewed now as Prāṇa and now as Ātman from two aspects by the Upaniṣads, and so, in the attainment, too, the completeness comes only when both these are known. Reality as Prāṇa represents the aspect that is immanent in all existence and hence to know it means to become identified with the whole of existence, to become all. Reality as Ātman stands for the transcendent aspect, the true significance of which we have tried to comprehend already, and so, to know it means to become one with even that which overtops all existence and does not exclude all existence. On knowing this second aspect of Reality as Ātman, one does not cease to know all, as is commonly supposed, but the two realizations, of identification with all and with that which is beyond all, go together. There is a significant passage in the *Praśna Upaniṣad* which speaks of the simultaneous realization of both the aspects of Reality: 'He who comes to know the shadowless, bodiless, colourless, the pure and the immutable, attains that Supreme immutable one and he, the knower of all, becomes all'[77]. The description of Reality purely in negative terms points to its transcendent aspect, but the effect that follows from its knowledge is not merely an attainment of that transcendence but also of the immanence. This proves, once again, that the transcendence is not an exclusion but something more than the deepest inclusion.

The general law, however, of the attainment is to pass to the transcendence through the immanence, to reach the Ātman through the Prāṇa. The limit of Prāṇa, which is the creative principle or energy is in the Creator or Īśvara or Prajāpati. Hence the highest attainment of Prāṇa means the attainment of the status of Īśvara. Beyond it is the status of Brahman. We know that many modern Vedāntins do not admit the possibility or necessity of the attainment of *Īśvaratva,* though they advocate the attainment of *Brahmatva.* But this is quite contrary to the views of the Upaniṣads and also of the great Ācarya Śaṅkara, as well as of the *Vedānta Sūtra.* The *Bṛhadāraṇyaka* specifically states that he who realizes the Ātman becomes 'the maker of the world, the maker of all, his are the worlds, he himself is verily the world'[78]. The author of '*Siddhāntaleśa',* at the end of his work, emphatically states that the liberated soul truly becomes one with Īśvara too. The *Vedānta-Sūtra,* which speaks of the absence of any power over the world (*jagadvyāpāravarjam*)[79] is not concerned with the supremely liberated soul, but only applies to those aspirants (*saguṇa upāsakāḥ*) who due to the lack of the complete unison, remain still in ignorance. But the truly liberated souls, having unquestionably attained the status of Īśvara, automatically have all the powers inherent in Him[80]. The Upaniṣads are replete with the ringing words of the seers, who having gained the supreme realization, felt their identity with the whole of creation. 'Having realized this, the sage Vāmadeva stated, "I became Manu as also Sūrya", and the Upaniṣad adds that 'whoever even today thus realizes that "I am Brahman", he, too, becomes all this'[81].

Thus the highest realization of *'Aham Brāhmā' smi'* carries with it, as a natural sequence, the consciousness of identification with all things whatsoever. The true inclusion of all within oneself comes only when one exceeds or transcends all, and hence, the attainment of *Īśvaratva* follows automatically from the attainment of *Brahmattva,* for the latter does not exclude the former, though it undoubtedly exceeds that. Similarly, another great seer, like Vāmadeva, named Triśanku cries out in an outburst of joy after the supreme attainment thus: 'I am the mover of the tree (of the world), my glory (rises) like the peak of a mountain, I am pure because high, I am the immortal essence of the Sun, I am the shining wealth, I am the pure Knowledge, immortal as well as undecaying'[82]. It seems that the seer finds all words inadequate to fully express the glory of his realization. Do such soul-stirring statements leave any further doubt about the unfathomable richness and infinite grandeur of the final realization of the Upaniṣads?

Bhartṛprapañca's view

It will be interesting here to refer to the view of the great old Vedāntin, Bhartṛprapañca, about liberation. Bhartṛpraprapañca is emphatic that the attainment of the status of Hiraṇyagarbha or the Sūtra is indispensably necessary for one who seeks to attain final liberation. As Hiriyanna puts his views: 'According to all Vedāntins, *virakti* or detachment is necessary before one qualifies for *mokṣa*....... Nobody, according to Bhartṛprapañca, can acquire genuine *virakti* who has not reached this state. Hence the first aim of a person that is desirous of liberation is to strive to reach this stage, by identifying himself, through *upāsanā* as taught in the Upaniṣads, with the Sūtra or Hiraṇyagarbha and carrying on simultaneously the *nitya-karmas* enjoined in the scripture........ It leads to *'apavarga'* or escape from *saṁsāra,* which Bhartṛpṛapañca viewed as distinct from *mokṣa,* though on the way to it (*apavargākhyām antarālāvasthām*—ŚB on BU, 3.2.13). The soul that has so far succeeded will not be born again, for it has given up all narrow attachment and its condition then is described as *antarālāvasthā* (i.e., a condition intermediate between *saṁsāra* and *mokṣa*). It is there free from all the ills of life. Though the baleful influences of attachment (*āsanga*), one of its two limiting factors, have then been overcome, the jiva has not yet realized its true nature, for *avidyā,* the other factor, persists separating it from Brahman. The *jīva* has so far identified itself with only Hiraṇyagarbha, a part of Brahman; and it has now to realize it as a part thereof. In other words, the oneness of the *jīva* with Brahman—not merely with Hiraṇyagarbha—is to be known, as taught in *Aham Brahma Asmi*'[83].

Bhartṛprapañca beautifully distinguishes between the two stages in liberation, one of which he calls *'apavarga'* and the other *'mokṣa'*. We have pointed out in our introductory remarks that the term *'mṛtyu'* is used in different senses in different contexts in the Upaniṣads. The freedom from '*mṛtyu*', which the Mukhya Prāṇa or the attainment of Hiraṇyagarbha brings, is merely a freedom from the grips of attachment or desire (*āsanga*), as we have shown in the chapter on contemplation. It is merely a relative freedom and hence Bhartṛprapañca rightly calls it an intermediate stage (*antarālāvasthā*). The true freedom comes only with the removal of *avidyā* or ignorance, which is the original *mṛtyu.*

Bhartṛprapañca only errs in this that he thinks that this *avidyā* will be removed through a synthesis (*samuccaya*) of *jñāna* and *karman.* The previous state of attainment of the status of *Sūtra,* no doubt, needs a synthesis, and the freedom from desire follows because of the very fact of coalescence (*mithuna*) of the two sundered parts, of which we have spoken. As the removal of *āsanga* necessarily involves a *samuccaya,* so the removal of *avidyā* necessarily precludes a *samuccaya,* for in the latter case there are no two things to be joined together, which has already been done, but only the last film of ignorance needs to be removed solely through the pure light of knowledge. However, we need not concern ourselves with the method of approach here. We should here only take note of the important fact that the Upaniṣads always refer to two distinct levels of realization and no liberation is complete without the gaining of both of them.

Comprehensive Conception of the Upaniṣadic Liberation

The Upaniṣads contain such a rich and varied expression about the attainment that it is possible to trace almost all the different conceptions about liberation to them. 'As a passage like the one from the *Chāndogya,* which tells us that the worshipper is lifted up to the region of the deity whom he has worshipped in life, support the doctrine of Madhva that absolution, consists not in being merged in the Absolute, nor even in being assimilated to Him, but in coming near his presence and participating in his glory'[84].

'Another passage from the *Maṇḍaka Upaniṣad* tells us that the best kind of eternal life should be regarded rather as the "companionship" of the highest God with whom the soul should be liberated at the time of the end. Not satisfied with a mere companionship, another passage declares that eternal life consists in attaining to an absolute "likeness" to God and enjoying life of personal immortality, a view which plays so large a part in the theology of Rāmānuja'.[85] Similarly one may trace the conception of immortalising the body itself, which is advocated by the school of Raseśvara Darśana, to a passage in the *Śvetāśvatara,* where it is said that the Yogi has neither sickness, nor death, he having attained a body full of the Yogic fire[86]. Even the art of prolonging life indefinitely was not unknown. We hear of one Mahīdāsa Aitareya, who lived for sixteen hundred years by completely defying the call of death[87]. All these varied descriptions are nothing but the intimations of realization at different levels of Reality as Prāṇa.

Gradual & Immediate Liberation

Prāṇa being a graded reality, the attainment of it, too, essentially becomes graded and thus numerous levels of attainment can be traced and studied here. But as the Ātman has no levels or grades in it, being single and indivisble by nature, its attainment, too, knows no variety or degree, less and more. If the attainment comes, it comes all at once, total and complete, and not by *stages* or degrees. Either the Ātman is known or it is not known. There is no intermediate stage between knowing and not-knowing.

The first variety of attainment is technically known as *kramamukti* or gradual liberation, while the second is called *sadyomukti* or immediate liberation. We have said that, according to the Upaniṣads, nothing but ignorance constitutes bondage, but it does not become possible to remove the ignorance all at once and that is why a long period of preparation and subsequent period of contemplation was found necessary to make one gradually fit to lift the veil of ignorance. It is not possible to complete the whole process within the brief span of one life alone. Some may stop with the preparation, others with a part of contemplation and so on, and hence, according to the Upaniṣads, one attains after death a status equal to his achievement in life, and the evolution may be carried on even there. Of course, a highly proficient seeker needs nothing but a single word of enlightenment from an illumined teacher for the removal of the last film of his ignorance, and immediately he attains the final realization. For him there can be no question of any posthumous evolution.

Concerning such a man of direct realization the Upaniṣad says 'Of him who is without desires, who is free from desires, the objects of whose desire have been attained, and to whom all objects of desire are but the Self—the vital airs do not depart. Being Brahman itself, he is united with Brahman'[88]. It is only in the case of the majority of human beings who fail to free themselves totally from ignorance while in life that an after-death journey or posthumous evolution is envisaged. It must, however, be always borne in mind that 'as concerns the being regarded in itself and in its totality, there can never be any question either of "evolution" or of "involution" in any sense whatever, its essential identity being in no wise altered by particular and contingent modifications of any sort, which can only affect one or other of its conditioned states'[89].

The Two Paths

The evolution is always of the Prāṇa, and the Prāṇa's evolution has always got a double movement, the one dark and the other bright, the one negative and the other positive. and even after death, the movement of Prana takes either of the two forms. These are technically called the *'pitryāna'* and the *'devayāna,'* the way of the fathers and the way of the gods or the *'dhūmamārga'* and the *'arcirmārga'*, the smoky way and the lighted way. The earliest reference to these two paths we find in the *Bṛhadāranyaka,* one of the oldest Upaniṣads, where it is said : 'I have heard of two ways about men, viz, of the fathers and of the gods and by them move all that are in the world'[90]. The Upaniṣad also speaks of a third way (*trtīya gatiḥ*) by which move the evil souls. About the destiny of such souls the Upaniṣad, in many places, says that they move to the 'sunless region covered by darkness' (*asūryā nāma te lokā andhena tamasā' vṛtāḥ*)[91] or the joyless regions (*anandā nāma te lokāḥ*)[92]. We, however, need not concern ourselves with this third way but must deal with the two ways briefly, the *dhūma* and the *arcira,* the dark and the bright.

The darkness and brightness of the way is made by *karman* and *jñāna* respectively. The first is dark because of the absence of enlightenment and hence is not the path of release but only of enjoyment and a subsequent return, while the second is bright because of the illumination of knowledge which gradually takes one towards the final liberation. The two paths are described in detail by both the *Bṛhadāraṇyaka* and the *Chāndogya*. The *Bṛhadāraṇyaka,* in connexion with the *Pañcāgnividyā,* describes the first path thus:, 'Those who thus know this, as well as those who worship in the forest faith and truth, attain the light, and move from light to day, from day to the bright half of the month, from the bright half of the month to the six months during which the Sun moves to the north, from the months to the sphere of the gods, from the sphere of the gods to the Sun, from the Sun to the lightning, and then a non-human person comes to those in the sphere of lightning and takes them to the spheres of Brahman and there, in those *brahmalokas,* they reside for an infinite length of time and theirs is no return'[93]. The *Chāndogya* account slightly differs from the above in this that it mentions also the moon after the Sun and then refers to the lightning.[94]

The second path is described thus : 'Those who conquer regions through sacrifice, gift and austerity, attain the smoke and move from the smoke to the night, from the night to the dark half of the month, from the dark half of the month to the six months during which the Sun moves to the south, from the months to the world of the fathers, from the world of the fathers to the moon'[95]. The *Chāndogya,* again, adds one in this path too, viz, the sky (*ākāśa*), between the world of the fathers and the moon[96]. The *Kauṣītakī,* however, makes a significant statement when it says that 'all those who depart from this world invariably go to the moon ... this is verily the door of heaven, this moon'[97]. Thus it seems that the moon was considered something as a junction-place, where all invariably went, some passing further upward and others again coming downward.

The *Kauṣītaki,* also, further develops the conception of the path of the gods. It describes it thus : 'He, having attained the path of the gods, comes to the world of fire, then to the world of wind, then to the world of Varuṇa, then to the world of the Sun, then to the world of Indra, then to the world of Prajāpati and finally to the world of Brahman'[98]. Then it proceeds further by saying that 'when such a soul has reached the world of Brahman, Brahman directs his attendants to run towards that soul and receive him with all the glory which is due to Brahman himself. He says that as the soul has reached the ageless river, he can never become old. He comes to the ageless river which he crosses merely by the movement of the mind. He then shakes off his good deeds as well as his bad deeds. ...And as a man driving fast in a chariot looks down on the revolving wheels, so does the soul look at day and night, good and bad and all the contrary pairs.

Being free from good and from evil, knowing Brahman, he moves towards Brahman'[99].

The Gītā also refers to the two paths thus : 'Fire, light, day-time, waxing moon, the half-year when the Sun ascends towards the north, then depart those who go to Brahman, knowing Brahman. Smoke, night, waning moon, the half-year when the Sun descends towards the south, there the Yogin attaining the light of the moon returns again. These are the two eternal paths of the world, the one bright and the other dark; by the one they go to return no more, by the other they go to return again'.[100]

Brahmaloka as the highest end

From all these detailed descriptions one thing comes out clearly, viz., that the highest plane to which graduated liberation (*kramamukti*) leads is, according to all accounts, the Brahmaloka. But it must be noted that mere attainment of the Brahmaloka does not necessarily give a complete guarantee against rebirth. It is true that the Upaniṣads say that theirs is no return who reach the Brahmaloka, but as Ānandagiri points out in his commentary, the Upaniṣads use two significant adjectives, viz., '*imam*' and '*iha*' which show that there is no return only in that particular cycle and so there is always a possibility of a return in the next cycle. Hence it turns out to be only relative and does not signify an absolute cessation of return[101]. The Gītā also specifically states that 'all the spheres (*lokas*), beginning with the Brahmaloka, come and go'[102]. Nīlakaṇṭha and Madhusūdana, in their commentaries, make it clear that there are two classes of men who attain the Brahmaloka: some reach there through such *upāsanās* or *vidyās* as the *Dahara-vidyā,* which lead to gradual liberation and so they get their final enlightenment there and become liberated along with Brahman, while others reach there through other *vidyās* like the *Pañcāgnividyā* which have no connexion with knowledge as such, and hence their return is inevitable[103].

Thus there are two distinct destinies for those who reach the Brahmaloka: some are destined to return, while others without returning are destined to be finally liberated at the proper time. It is concerning the latter that the *Muṇḍaka* says that 'those who have a sure comprehension through the knowledge of the Vedānta, the saints who are pure in being through renunciation, they are all liberated, in the

Brahmaloka, at the end of the cycle, being supremely immortal'[104]. Śrīdhara, in his commentary on the *Bhāgavata,* however, mentions the possibility of three forms of destiny for those who reach the Brahmaloka. Those who reach there through excellence of virtues become the *adhikārins,* in the next cycle, according to their degrees of virtue. Those, again, who go there on the strength of their worship of Hiraṇyagarbha and others are liberated along with Brahmā. But those who are the worshippers of Bhagavān or Īśvara willingly pass beyond the cosmos and rise up to the supreme status of Viṣṇu[105]. Thus of the three classes, one comes down at the end of a cycle, the other, though not destined to return, yet has to wait indefinitely there for the final liberation, while the third has no binding at all and simply passes through the region at will.

Conception of Brahmaloka

The conception of the Brahmaloka is, however, not very clear from the Upaniṣads. It seems that the term does not always signify the same sphere or world, and its use in the plural, in many places, also suggests that there are many grades of the same sphere, if not distinct worlds known by the same common name. The *Muṇḍaka,* for example, after describing the worship of the Fire, states that one, who so worships, is carried by the rays of the Sun to the holy Brahmaloka (*punyaḥ sukṛto brahmalokaḥ*), where all greet him with sweet words, and honours him[106]. It then goes to condemn the cult of fire or sacrifice, pointing out that it leads to birth and death, again and again. Finally, it speaks of the way of the enlightened and there does not speak of Brahmaloka or any *loka* but simply states that they depart there by the door of the Sun, where is the immortal Puruṣa, the immutable Ātman. Thus, evidently, the *Muṇḍaka* takes the Brahmaloka as a sphere which is attained only by the *karmins* or men of action or worshippers of the Fire and does not take it as a sphere for gradual liberation at all.

In the *Kaṭha,* the *śevadhi* or the treasure-house, referred to by Yama, is also nothing else but this Brahmaloka, as Sri Krishna Prem rightly points out. He says that in fact, it refers here to the great Treasure-house of the Universe, the world of Brahmā, the plane of Mahat or Cosmic Imagining'[107]. But Yama calls this *śevadhi* as impermanent (*'anityam'*) and as he speaks about it just after teaching the science of Fire to Naciketas, it becomes evident that it is won through the worship of the Fire and hence its impermanence becomes inevitable.

But the Brahmaloka, which is referred to in connexion with the *Dahara-vidyā* in the *Chāndogya,* appears to be of a totally different character. It appears almost identical with Brahman itself, as the descriptions show, and even Śaṅkara is constrained to explain the term as 'Brahman itself the sphere' (*brahma* eva *lokaḥ*), because it cannot be conceived as a sphere of Brahman and as such separate from it. Thus it is clear that in the former cases, the Brahmaloka denotes the world of Brahmā and not Brahman, while in the latter case it stands for Brahman, which is itself the sphere.

However, a distinction is generally drawn between Brahmaloka and Brahman, the transcendent Reality, by saying that 'while the brahmaloka, the sphere of unity, the *amūrta puruṣa,* is pure *nāman* existence, the attainment of the transcendent sphere implies the utter abandonment of both *rūpa* and *nāman*'[108]. The *nāman* stands for the first Creative Idea and hence Brahmaloka may be viewed as the supreme World of Ideas, which projects the world of forms (*rūpa*) down below. Hence it is significantly called the *'sakṛdbibhātaḥ',* the eternally shining sphere, because it is not a world of shadows, like the world of *rūpa,* but a world of light, being the world of *vāc* or *nāman*. In the gradual ascent from the world of *rūpa,* one must first pass to the world of pure *nāman* and only thence move further towards the complete transcendence. Thus in the scheme of *kramamukti*, Brahmaloka occupies a supremely important place and from one point of view, may be taken as the final limit of attainment.

Kramamukti and the Last Moment

In the conception of *Kramamukti,* the moment of departure from this world occupies a very important place and in fact, determines the whole nature of the future evolution and life. There is a natural indrawing of all the faculties of the senses and the mind at the hour of death, and hence the object of one's predominant passion in life spontaneously comes up at the moment and is seized with the whole being. It is clearly visualized now, all the distractions having ceased. That is why in *upāsanā* so much stress is laid on the last thought (*antyabhāvanā*), and in the Gītā, the Lord rightly asks Arjuna to constantly meditate on Him so that, at the end, he may attain to Him.[109]

Madhusūdana, in his commentary thereon, points out that this applies only to the worshippers (*upāsakas*) because they have to depend on the last thought. But those who realize the transcendent Reality get their liberation at the very moment of the dawning of knowledge, which dispels ignorance altogether and hence they do not stand in need of the final thought.[110]

The process of meditation, however, must be carried on unremittingly throughout life so that the object of meditation may, spontaneously, spring up in the mind at the moment of death. The Upaniṣads give a very vivid description of the process of death : 'When the vital airs are gathered around him, the soul, collecting together all the portions of life, moves down into the heart; and when the 'person in the eye' has turned away, then he ceases to know any form. He becomes concentrated in himself, that is the reason why, they say, he is not able to see; he is at one with himself, that is the reason why, they say, he is not able to speak or hear or know. Then the tip of the heart is filled with light and through that light the soul moves out, either by the way of the eye or the head or any other part of the body'.[111]

Importance of the Heart-centre

Now the most important centre in the whole process is the heart, where all the faculties are finally focussed or where the light of consciousncss contracts or withdraws itself from the whole body. The light gets out of the body through different channels and the particular channel that is taken for the exit determines the postmortem evolution. As the *Kaṭha* and the *Chāndogya* say: 'A hundred and one are the subtle channels of the heart: of them, one extends upwards to the head. Having gone up by that, one attains immortality; the others are for going forth differently'[112]. The one channel going upward is generally taken by the Yogin as the *suṣumnā,* and the passing out through the crown of the head (*brahmarandhra*) is generally taken as signifying a movement for liberation. In plain words, the one upward channel signifies the course of the straight motion of liberation, which follows only from the cessation of desire. The other innumerable channels are the diverse courses of the crooked movements of desire, which bring back the soul, again and again, to the world. The way of release is straight and one, while the ways of bondage are crooked and many.

The Sun & the Moon

Again, the two ways are closely connected with the two great symbols of the Sun and the Moon. The straight motion is connected with the Sun and the curve motion with the Moon, for it is only by piercing through the Sun that one secures total liberation, while from the Moon a return is inevitable. The Sun is called the 'door of the world', (*'lokadvāram'*)[113] by the *Chāndogya,* and Śaṅkara, in his commentary, makes clear that the *'loka'* here stands for the supreme Brahmaloka, of which the famous door is the Āditya or the Sun[114].

The Upaniṣad adds that it is the refuge or way of approach for the enlightened, while it is an obstruction or a bar to the unenlightened, for the enlightened pass through it upward, while the ignorant find it an insurmountable barrier that blocks further movement[115]. Śaṅkara explains why it proves to be a *'nirodha'* or obstruction for the ignorant. It is because the light of the Sun, in their case, remains diffused, and they are overpowered by the light and are kept confined within the body and hence cannot get hold of the upward channel towards the crown of the head[116].

This also makes clear the prayer to the Sun, in the *Īśa,* for contracting its rays, because that alone makes possible the passage towards liberation and final union. We have also seen that the *Muṇḍaka* speaks of the departure of the enlightened through the door of the Sun (*sūryadvāreṇa te virajāḥ prayānti*)[117]. All these show how important a place the Sun occupies in the conception of graded liberation. The Sun, we have mentioned, stands for the Sabda Brahman or the principle that is active in creation, and hence, to pass out of creation, one must pierce through it. The passing out through the head signifies this piercing through the Sun.

The different bodies of the Self

It is generally supposed that after one pierces through the Sun, his subtle body (*sūkṣma śarīra*) is burnt or dropped. But the causal body (*kāraṇa śarīra*) still persists and moves towards the Brahmaloka. According to the Vedāntic conception, the dropping of all the three bodies constitutes liberation. Hence *'aśarīratva'* or bodilessness is a term sometimes used as synonymous with liberation. According to the Vedānta, to have a body is to have a separate individuality and so long as separateness exists, utter liberation cannot be said to have been gained. But the Vaiṣṇava Vedāntists like Rāmānuja, who take the individual soul as an eternal portion of Brahman, do not recognize that in liberation one loses all forms or bodies. They explain the Upaniṣadic text which says that 'so long as one has a body there is no escape from likes and dislikes, only on becoming bodiless likes and dislikes do not touch', as meaning merely the absence of the body of nature constituted by *karman* and not of the *aprākṛta* or divine form[118]. Hence they conceive that when the soul drops the subtle body after crossing the Virajā river,—which is probably the same as the ageless river, referred to in the Kauṣītaki as Vijarā, a later name formed perhaps by a metathesis of the earlier one—it is endowed with a celestial form which has a further evolution towards the Brahmaloka[119].

There is no evolution without a body, and hence the Vaiṣṇavas, who give an account of the posthumous evolution in richer details, naturally have to conceive of subtler and subtler bodies fit for higher evolution. The conception of infinite varieties of body has been worked out probably in the richest detail by the school of the medieval Indian saint, Kabir. According to them, the highest form of body is technically called *Haṁsadeha,* which is *tattvātīta* or beyond all categories. Then comes the *tattvamaya* body, which has two varieties, viz., one of *cit tattva* and the other of *acit tattva.* The latter, again, has two forms, viz., of pure *acit,* and of impure *acit.* The latter, again, has two sub-divisions, viz., one, the *kāraṇa* and the other, the *kārya.* The latter finally, splits into two, viz., the *sūkṣma* and the *sthūla.* Such accounts are very interesting from the standpoint of *kramamukti,* for no final limit can be drawn to the evolution of Prāṇa and consequently to the evolution of the body or the form.

The Problem of Jīvanmukti

The question of the body finally brings us to the most important problem connected with liberation, which is allied to or rather rises out of the two conceptions we have been just discussing, viz., *sadyomukti* (immediate liberation) and *kramamukti* (gradual liberation). *Sadyomukti,* we have seen, signifies immediate liberation, and so the question comes : Is liberation possible while in life, here and now? This is the age-old problem of *Jīvanmukti,* which has baffled many, and has given rise to innumerable points of view.

We have seen that it is the removal of ignorance that constitutes liberation, according to the Upaniṣads. If ignorance is removed all at once, it becomes possible to achieve liberation immediately, and it is only for those who fail to remove it in life that a gradual evolution after death is envisaged. There is no difficulty with the second conception but about the first conception of *sadyomukti,* the problem is that if liberation is immediate and if it means the total removal of ignorance, then there must be an immediate separation from the body, too, which is a product of ignorance. 'The body and the actions performed by the body are due to ignorance, and when knowledge results ignorance must disappear, being very much opposed to the same. If the material cause disappears, the effect can no longer persist; and hence, if the body persists, that shows that ignorance still persists and liberation has not been attained. In other words, liberation conflicts with the presence of ignorance, and the movements of the body are evident indications of the persistence of ignorance'[120]. In the face of such a difficulty, some, like Rāmānuja, frankly deny the possibility of the attainment of liberation in life. They say that *jīvanmukti* is merely a name and to hold such a conception while tied to the *prārabdha karman* is merely to deceive others[121]. Hence according to them, the real liberation comes only after death, which is known as *videhamukti.* The Sāṅkhya, though recognizing *jīvanmukti,* places the *videhamukti* on a higher grade by calling it absolute and final, and, as such, takes the former not as real and absolute liberation but only as a relative one. It, however, accounts for the persistence of the body, even after *viveka-jñāna* has been gained, by saying that it goes on existing for some time, like the potter's wheel, through the momentum of the previous potencies (*saṁskāra*)[122]. This is evidently a very poor and disappointing solution; rather, the Sāṅkhya has no genuine conception of *jīvanmukti* at all.

Vedantic theories about Prārabdha

The teachers of the Vedāntic school have tried to explain away the difficulty by devising numerous theories. Some try to explain it almost in the Sāṅkhya way, by saying that though knowledge dispels ignorance immediately, yet it does not destroy the effects of ignorance directly and hence the body and its movements continue for some time. Another common explanation is that knowledge does not destroy all actions but only the *sañcita* or the 'stored' and the *āgāmin* or the 'future'. The *prārabdha,* i.e., that which has already commenced bearing fruit, must run its usual course and can only be exhausted through experience (*bhoga*). Hence, even after *tattvajñāna* has dawned, the body continues to exist so long as the *prārabdha* is not completely exhausted. There are, again, some who think that knowledge only removes the sense of *truth* or *reality* that is attached to the world, and so even after one has gained knowledge one goes on existing in the world till the end of his *prārabdha*[123]. 'According to others, *avidyā* (ignorance) has two aspects—the veiling (*āvaraṇa*) aspect and the projective or creative aspect (*vikṣepa*). Knowledge or revelation is opposed to the veiling aspect of ignorance and hence it is the veiling aspect only that is removed by knowledge. The creative aspect, however, persists even after knowledge, and it is this residual portion of ignorance (*avidyāleśa*) that explains the persistence of the body and the actions of the liberated individual (*jīvanmukta*).'[121] There are numerous other views on the problem but we refrain from discussing them in details here.[125]

Vidyāraṅya's View examined

The problem, to our view, is purely a creation of our ignorance or misunderstanding of the true nature of the Upaniṣadic knowledge. We have pointed out, in the prolegomena, the lamentable confusion that has crept in the later Vedāntic thought regarding the actual nature of the Upaniṣadic knowledge. This becomes all the more evident from the conception about liberation propounded by the later Vedāntins. Vidyāranya, in his *Jīvanmuktiviveka,* refers to the two types of liberation, viz., *jivanmukti* and *videhamukti.*[126] But, according to him, *jīvanmukti* is not gained through knowledge nor does *videhamukti* mean liberation after death. He gives a new connotation to the latter term and takes it as meaning merely the absence of the generation of future bodies. Hence, according to him, with the dawning of knowledge one gets *videhamukti,* which he also calls *kaivalya,* but for *jivanmukti* one has to achieve the extinction of the mind (*manonāśa*) and the exhaustion of the desires (*vāsanākṣaya*). He says that most people describe *videhamukti* as that which follows after the dropping off of the present body, and take by the term *'deha'* all the bodies, present as well as future, but he takes it as meaning merely the future body (*'bhāvideha'*) and so *'videha'*, according to him, means merely the separation from future bodies, which is guaranteed by *jñāna,* and not from the present body too. So long as the present body persists, there is bound to be the action of the mind and the desires, and to inhibit them one has to practise *manonāśa* and *vāsanākṣaya,* and acquire the divine treasure of noble desires to overcome the evil tendencies of the mind and the base desires. Thus evidently, according to Vidyāraṇya, *jñāna* has to be supplemented by *yoga* for the achievement of *jīvanmukti*, for *jñāna* has no power whatsoever over the mind and the desires which must have their play despite the dawn of knowledge. This reduces *jñāna* to a mere intellectual apprehension, but the Upaniṣadic knowledge (*jñāna*), we have shown, is of a totally different category. That knowledge dawns only to one who is full of the divine qualities (*'daivī sampat'*) and whose mind is already tranquil. Therefore *manonāśa* and *vāsanākṣaya* do not follow that knowledge but precede it. After the knowledge is gained, nothing more remains to be done to supplement it, for the fulfilment is complete and instantaneous.

Solution of the Problem

To the Upaniṣads the whole problem is inadmissible, because the Reality, the attainment of which brings liberation, is not an excluding principle that has something in opposition to it, whether it be the world or the body. The supreme consciousness is gained not by going out of the body but here and now (*atra brahma samaśnute*).[127] 'He tears up the knots of ignorance *here'* (*so' avidyāgranthīn vikiratī' ha somya*).[128] Nor is it a fact that it has no power over the *prārabdha karman,* for, declares the Upaniṣad, 'torn are the knots of the heart, dispelled are all the doubts, extinguished are the actions on that Supreme being seen'. Echoing this, the Gitā says that the fire of knowledge burns *all* actions. Neither the Upaniṣads nor the Gītā make any reservations with regard to the extinction of actions. 'The body cannot constitute an obstacle to Deliverance any more than any other type of contingency; nothing can enter into opposition with absolute totality, in the presence of which all particular things are as if they were not. In relation to the supreme goal there is perfect equivalence between all the states of existence, so that no distinction any longer holds good between the living and the dead man (taking these expressions in the earthly sense)'.[129] In this conception of *jīvanmuktī,* 'we note a further essential difference between Deliverance and "Salvation" : the latter, as the Western religions conceive it, cannot be effectually obtained, nor even be assured (that is to say obtained virtually), before death'.[130] Again, the Vedantic view of liberation is very different from the Stoic conception of freedom. Liberation does not mean an withdrawal from a *real* universe, as the Stoics conceive it'[131], for here there is no real world separate from Brahman, as nothing exists apart from that one Supreme Reality. Accordingly, 'it would be a mistake to suppose that liberation acquired when the being is quit of bodily form (*videhamukti*) is more complete than liberation "during life" (*jīvanmukti*)'.[132]

Objections answered

It may, however, be asked : Are there not certain passages in the Upaniṣads which virtually deny *jīvanmukti and* say that liberation is truly gained only after death? One such text runs thus: 'There is no escape from likes and dislikes so long as one is in the body; only on becoming bodiless, likes and dislikes do not touch' Those who are not conversant with the true Upaniṣadic spirit merely misinterpret this text, and especially the term *'aśarīram'*, and thus get into a confusion. Śaṅkara raises the question in his commentary on the *Brahmasūtras* and gives the most effective answer to those who misinterpret the above text. He puts the question thus: 'The *Śruti* says that only on becoming free from the body, the good or bad do not touch'. Does it mean that the freedom from the body will come after the fall of the body and not while living?' and he answers with an emphatic 'no', and continues: 'Because, relation with the body is purely due to false knowledge; and it is not possible to imagine any other form of connexion with the body save the false knowledge characterised by identification in the form that the body is the Self. We have said that its freedom from the body is eternal because it is not due to any action. It is also not to say that the relation with the body is due to the *dharma* and *adharma* done by it, because the relation with the body being not proved, it is also not proved that *dharma* and *adharma* are done by the Self........ Therefore, relation with the body being due to false cognition, it becomes established that an enlightened man may have freedom from body even while alive. Therefore, the *Śruti* says about the knower of Brahman: 'As the slough of the snake cast on an ant-hill lies dead, thus does this body lie. Now is he without body, immortal, essence, Prāṇa, Brahman and the Light itself'. 'He is with an eye yet, as if, without an eye, with an ear yet, as if, without an ear, with the power of speech yet, as it were, without speech, with a mind yet, as if, without a mind, with life and yet, as if, without life and so on'[134].

Śaṅkara, thus, makes perfectly clear that the *'aśarīratva'* does not mean a quitting of the body but merely the forsaking of the false sense of selfhood attached to the body. The text from the *Bṛhadāraṇyaka,* which he quotes, aptly illustrates how utterly separated from the body does the enlightened soul become, even while alive. All the particular functions of the body and the senses, of the mind and life are still there, yet they are all, as it were, not there. This is the mystery of the transcendent freedom of the Ātman, which does not exclude anything, but allows everything to have its full play while itself remaining untouched by them all.

Similarly, the other famous text which is very often quoted in support of *videhamukti,* viz. *'tasya tāvad eva ciram yāvan no vimoksye atha sampatsye'*[135] is also grossly misunderstood and also misinterpreted. If one takes the particular context where the statement occurs then it is found that there is no justification of connecting it with something after death. There the Upaniṣad gives the beautiful illustration of a man who loses the track of his original home or country being left with closed eyes in a place far away from it, and narrates how he again gets instruction from an experienced man and moving accordingly from village to village finally reaches back to his native place. After this it is stated, 'similarly, here a man who has an instructor, knows' (*ācāryavān puruṣo veda*). Immediately after it, comes the above statement, which has since become famous. Hence, we think, what is really meant to be conveyed by the statement and especially by the term *'vimokṣye'* is nothing but the release from ignorance and not release from the body, which is absolutely out of the context. The release from ignorance comes immediately with the hearing of the instruction from the *Ācārya,* as in the case of the man from Gāndhāra. Therefore, it is said : 'He has only this much delay. As soon as he becomes freed from ignorance he attains (his true nature)'. The gaining of one's nature (*sampatsye*) follows immediately with the release from ignorance (*vimoksye*). It is thus evident, beyond doubt, that those who have a bias for *videhamukti* twist the meaning of the text.

Conclusion

Thus it is clear that the Upaniṣad nowhere states that complete liberation is not possible while in the body, but rather, on the contrary, warn the seeker that unless he knows the Reality while in life, *here and now,* a supreme disaster awaits him and thereby tries to convey that the true liberation must be achieved while in life and not after death[136]. Of course, the Upaniṣadic conception is so rich and comprehensive that it also gives scope to those who fail to realize it in life by opening out the alternative path of *kramamukti.* But the stress is always on *jīvanmukti,* because that is the true liberation achieved through a realization of the transcendent aspect of the Ātman.

Thus the problem of bliss (*ānanda*) is finally solved. There is no need of getting out of the world or quitting the body for obtaining that bliss or immortality. There is no particular place where it is to be had nor any particular time when it is to be enjoyed. It can be had, here and now, immediately with the dispelling of ignorance. 'Having attained this, the seers become content with their knowledge, their purpose accomplished, free from all desire and full of composure. Having attained the all-pervading Ātman on all sides, ever concentrating their minds, they enter into all.'[137] This is the end of the road (*so' adhvanaḥ pāram ucyate*),[138] the supreme status of the all-pervading Viṣṇu (*tad viṣṇoḥ paramaṁ padam*),[139] and as the *Ṛgveda* declares, there, 'in the supreme status of Viṣṇu, is the fount of honey' (*viṣṇoḥ pade parame madhva utsaḥ*).[140] Here is the eternal bliss, the absolute fulfilment, the final attainment and here is the end of all instruction (*etāvad anuśāsanam*).[141]

References

1. KU, 12.
2. nā'vagatabrahmātmabhāvasya yathāpūrvaṁ saṁsāritvam. yasya tu yathāpūrvaṁ saṁsāritvaṁ nā 'sāv avagatabrahmātmabhāva ity anavadyam. ŚB. on VS, 1.1.4.
3. tat savitur vareṇyaṁ madhu vātā ṛtāyate. BU, 6.3.6.
4. CU, 1.1.3.
5. MU, 2.2.7.
6. bhūmai 'va sukhaṁ nā 'lpe sukham asti......yo vai bhūmā tad amṛtam atha yad alpaṁ tan martyam. CU, 7.24.1.
8. SDS, p. . 6.
9. kāmārthāv eva puruṣārthau, muktir nā 'sty eve 'ti cārvākāḥ. PPB, Setu ṭikā p. 25.
10. PPB, p. 25.
11. labdhānantacatuṣkasya lokāgūḍhasya cā 'tmanaḥ./ kṣīṇāṣṭakarmaṇo muktir nirvyāvṛttir jinoditā.// SDS, p. 88.
12. idam eva ca svātantryaṁ mokṣa iti siddham. VKL, p. 3.
13. navānām ātmaviśeṣaguṇānām atyantocchittir niśśreyasam. PPB, Vyomavati Vṛtti. p. 20.
14. vādhalakṣaṇasyai 'kaviṁśatiprabhedaduḥkhasyā 'tyantavimokṣo 'parvargaḥ.

sakalakarmocchedalakṣaṇam apavargam āhuḥ. VKL, p. 4.

15. trividhaduḥkhātyantanivṛttir atyantapuruṣārthaḥ. SS, 1.1.

16. saṁyogābhāvo hānaṁ tad dṛśeḥ kaivalyam. YS, 2.25.

guṇānāṁ pratiprasavaḥ kaivalyaṁ svarūpapratiṣṭhā vā citiśakter iti. Ibid, 4.34.

17. Prābhākarā api...dehendriyādisambandhasya dharmā dharmaparīkṣayā 'nimittam ātyantikocchedalakṣaṇaṁ manyante. Bhāṭṭās tu....nityajñānena nityasukhābhivyaktir muktir ity āhuḥ. duḥkhābhāvamātram eva vā muktir ity api tadīyāḥ kecit. VKL, p. 4.

18. Ibid. p. 5.

*Vātsāyana, in his commentary on the *Nyāyasūtras,* refers to the view of a school of Naiyāyikas who held that liberation consists in the manifestation of eternal bliss. This old Naiyāyika view possibly later came to pass as the view of the Mimāṁsakas. For a detailed discussion of this interesting point reference may be made to Dr. G.N. Śāstri's *Kiraṇāvali* (Bengali ed.) pp. 93-94.

19. anāgatadehendriyabuddhyanutpādaḥ brahmaprāptiḥ, tadrūpapariṇāmalakṣanā vā muktir iti, BS, p. 119.

20. rāgāpakarṣaṇena svarūpaprāptilkṣaṇā. Ibid.

21. VKL, p. 5.

22. Ibid.

23. liṅgaśarīrāpagamo muktir ity eke. PPB, Setu ṭīkā p. 25.

24. viśiṣṭapradeśe akṣayaśarīrādilābho niśśreyasam. ātmaikatavijñānāt paramātmani layaḥ. Maheśvaraprasādād aśuddhaiśvaryavināśe tadguṇasaṅkrāntim. Ibid. Vyomavatī Vṛttī p. 20.

25. surāsurasevanaṁ muktir iti pāṣaṇḍāḥ. Ibid.

26. ātyantikasukhaprāptiduḥkhavicchedakāṅkṣiṇaḥ/
arthato muktim evā 'mī kāmayante 'khilā janāḥ.// VRS. 2.41.

27. CU, 8.3.2.

28. BU, 1.4.8.

29. PU, p. 344.

30. Ibid. p. 345.

31. MBV, pp. 166-7.

32. nityaś ca mokṣaḥ sarvair mokṣavādibhir abhyupagamyate. ŚB on VS, 1.1.4.

33. PU, p. 346.

34. VS, 1.1.4.

35. vidyodayo nā 'sti prativandhakṣayaṁ vinā./
adhītavedavedārtho 'py ata eva na mucyate.// VRS, 2.3.

36. CU, 8.13.1.

37. UL, p. 22.

38. Ibid.

39. PVU, p. 587.

40. BU, 2.5.19.

41. BU, 1.4.3.

42. Ibid, 1.4.2.

43. Ibid. 1.4.3.

44. KTU, 1.2.7.

45. TU, 2.7.

46. Ibid. 2.9.
47. KTU, 2.5.12.
48. Ibid. 1.2.13.
49. MU, 3.1.10.
50. Ibid, 3.2.2.
51. Mā. 9.
52. ātmany atiśayaḥ kaś cen na ko'pī' ty etad uttaram./ citte vā 'tiśayaḥ kaś ced bodha eve' ti biddhi bhoḥ. VRS, 2.15.
53. YS, 2.15.
54. Ibid. VB.
55. KM, p. 64.
56. Cf. muktaye yaḥ śilātvāya śāstram ūce mahāmuniḥ.
57. duḥkhatrayābhighātāj jijñāsā. SK, 1.
58. duḥkhajanmapravṛttidoṣa-mithyājñānānām uttarottarāpāye tadanantarāpāyād apavargaḥ. NS, 2.
59. BU, 1.4.3.
60. IU, 11.
61. KTU, 2.6.8.
62. CU, 8.12.3.
63. CU, 3.16.10.
64. Sa vā eṣa evaṁ paśyan evaṁ manvāna evaṁ vijānan ātmaratir ātmakrīḍa ātmamithuna ātmānandaḥ sa svarāḍ bhavati tasya sarveṣu lokeṣu kāmacāro bhavati. CU. 7.25.2.

    mṛtyuṁ jayati. BU, 1.2.7.

    taṁ taṁ lokaṁ jayate tāṅs ca kāmān. PRU, 3.1.10.
65. sa sarvajñaḥ sarvam evā' viveśa. PRU, 4.11.
66. te sarvagaṁ sarvataḥ prāpya dhīrāḥ yuktātmānaḥ sarvam evā' viśanti. MU, 3.2.5.

    ya evaṁ vedā 'ham brahmā 'smī 'ti sa idaṁ sarvam bhavati. BU, 1.4.10.
67. CU, 8.12.3.
68. CU, 7.25.2.
69. MU, 3.1.4.
70. paśyaty acakṣuḥ sa śṛṇoty akarṇaḥ. ŚU, 3.19.
71. KU, 4-8.
72. MU, 3.2.8.
73. BU, 2.4.12.
74. RPU, p. 115.
75. BU, 2.4.13-14.
76. MBV, p. 140.
77. PRU, 4.10.
78. yasyā 'nuvittaḥ pratibuddha ātmā' smin sandehye gahane praviṣṭaḥ/ sa viśvakṛt sa hi sarvasya kartā tasya lokāḥ sa u loka eva./ BU, 4.4.13.
79. VS, 4.4.17.
80. saguṇopāsakānām akhaṇḍasākṣātkārābhāvād nā' vidyānivṛttiḥ......teṣām na niravagraham aiśvaryam. nissandhibandham īśvarabhāvam prāptānāṁ tat sarvam iti mahato viśeṣasya sadbhāvāt. SLS, pp. 516-17.
81. BU, 1.4.10.
82. TU, 1.10.
83. IA, Vol. LIII. pp. 77-86.
84. CSU, p. 209.
85. CSU, p. 165.
86. na tasya rogo na jarā na mṛtyuḥ./ prāpto hi yogāgnimayaṁ śarīram.// ŚU, 2.12.
87. CU, 3.16.7.
88. BU, 4.4.6.

89. MBV, p. 124.
90. BU, 6.2.2.
91. ĪU, 3.
92. BU, 4.4.11. KTU, 1.1.3.
93. BU, 6.2.15.
94. CU, 4.15.5-6.
95. BU, 6.2.16.
96. CU, 5.10.1-6.
97. KSU, 1.2.
98. KSU, 1.4.
99. Ibid.
100. Gītā, 8.24-26.
101. imam iti viśeṣaṇād anāvṛttir asmin kalpe, kalpāntare tv āvṛttir iti sūcyate. Ānandagiri on CU, 4.15.5.
102. Gītā. 8.16.
103. ye kramamuktiphalābhir daharādividyābhir brahmalokaṁ gatās te tatraī'va jñānam prāpya brahmaṇā saha mucyante. ye tu pañcāgnividyābhir brahmalokaṁ gatās te' anupāsitaparameśvarāḥ punar āvartante iti. Nīlakaṇṭha's Comm. on Gītā. 8.16.
104. MU, 3.2.6.
105. tatra ca brahmalokagatānām prāṇināṁ trividhā gatiḥ. ye puṇyotkarṣeṇas gatās te kalpāntare puṇyatāratamenā' dhikāriṇo bhavanti. ye tu hiranyagarbhādyupāsanabalena gatās te brahmaṇā saha mucyante. ye tu bhagavadupāsakāsa te tu svecchayā brahmāṇḍam bhitvā vaiṣṇavam padam ārohanti. Śrīdhara's Comm. on BH, 2.2.27.
106. MU, 1.2.5-6.
107. YK, p. 77.
108. NRDR, p. 40.
109. Gītā, 8.7.
110. idaṁ ca saguṇabrahmacintanam upāsakānām uktaṁ teṣām antyabhāvanāsāpekṣatvāt. nirguṇabrahmajñāninām tu jñānasamakālam evā' jñānanivṛttilakṣaṇāyā mukteḥ siddhatvān nāsty antyabhāvanāpekṣe' ti draṣṭavyam. Madhusūdana's Comm. on Gītā 8.7.
111. BU, 4.4.1-2.
112. KTU, 2.3.16; CU, 8.6.6.
113. CU, 8.6.5.
114. etad vai khalu prasiddham brahmalokasya dvāram ya ādityaḥ. Ibid. ŚB.
115. etad vai khalu lokadvāraṁ viduṣāṁ prapadanaṁ nirodho aviduṣām. Ibid.
116. soureṇa tejasā deha eva niruddhāḥ santo mūrdhanyayā nāḍyā no' tkrāmanta eve' ty arthaḥ, Ibid, ŚB.
117. MU, 1.2.11.
118. uktaśruteḥ karmajanyaprākṛtaśarīraviṣayakatvāt aprākṛtaśarīrasya śrutipramāṇasiddhatvāt. PPGV, p. 610.
119. ....virajāṁ tīrtvā sūkṣmaśariīraṁ vihāyā 'mānavakarasparśād aprākṛtadivyavigrahayuktaḥ. YMD p. 77.
120. PHS, p. 182.
121. Jīvanmuktir iti paribhāṣāmatrai' va .... prārabdhena karmaṇā nibaddhamānānāṁ .... satāṁ

muktā vayam ity ajñajanavañcakatāmātratvāc ca. PPGV, p. 603.

122. tiṣṭhati saṃskāravaśād cakrabhramivad dhṛtaśarīraḥ. SK, 67.

123. pāramārthikaprapañcopadarśakāṁśasyai' va vidyayā virodhāt, prātibhāsikamātrāṁśeṇā' virodhāt. ARR, p. 45.

124. PHS, pp, 183-84.

125. PHS, p. 182 ff.

126. JMV, p. 210 ff.

127. KTU, 2.3.14.

128. MU, 2.1.10.

129. MBV, p. 170.

130. Ibid.

131. PHS, p. 191.

132. MBV, p. 172.

133. na ha vai saśarīrasya sataḥ priyāpriyayor apahatir asty aśarīram vāva santaṁ na priyāpriye spṛśataḥ. CU, 8.12.1.

134. śarīre patite' aśarīratvaṁ syān na jīvata iti cen na. saśarīratvasya mithyājñānanimittatvāt. na hy ātmanaḥ śarīrātmābhimānalakṣaṇaṁ mithyājñānaṁ muktvā anyataḥ saśarīratvaṁ śakyaṁ kalpayitum. ....tasmān mithyāpratyayanimittatvāt saśarīratvasya siddhaṁ jīvato 'pi viduṣo aśarīratvam. ŚB on VS, 1.1.4.

135. CU, 6.14.2.

136. iha ced avedīd atha satyam asti/ no ced ihā' vedīn mahatī vinaṣṭiḥ.// KU, 13.

137. MU, 3.2.5.

138. KTU, 1.3.9.

139. KTU, 1.3.9.

140. RV, 1.154.5.

141. KTU, 2.3.15.

INDEX

Abhaya 268
Abheda 92
Abhinavagupta 112
Abhitāpa 198, 199, 200
Abhyāroha 24
Ācārya 130, 141, 293
Adhikāra 32
Adhikārin 32, 284
Adhyayana 138, 139, 140
Adhyāpana 140
Adhyāsa 172-173
Āditya 8, 178, 192, 195, 196, 210, 287
Āditya Puruṣa 207
Agni 8-9, 11, 13-14, 195
Agni-vidyā 9, 23
Aham Brahma Asmi 267, 277-78
Ahaṁgraha 172-73
Āhāraśuddhi 132, 153
" meaning of the term 159
Aitareya Upaniṣad 22, 178-79, 186
Ajātaśatru 29, 30, 207
Ajñāna 265
Ākāśa 184, 198
Akṣara 69
Ālambana 129, 165
Alexander 88-89, 217, 222
Alokākāśa 261
Amṛta 259, 261, 273
Amūrta Purṣa 285
Analytic Way 22, 206-229
Ānanda 15, 139, 222-23, 228, 259-60, 267-68, 270, 294
Ānandagiri 283
Ānandamaya 22, 173, 223-28
Anāśaka 161
Āṇavamala 66
Angiras 27
Āngirasa 164
Anirvacanīya 75
Anna-Annāda 218
Annamaya 143, 217-18, 223
Anṛta 51
Antaḥkaraṇa 72
Antevāsin 130
Anugraha 66
Anupāya 112
Anupraveśa 48
Aparokṣa 104
Apavarga 278-79
Aprākṛta 288
Āpya 264-65
Ārambhavāda 49
Arcirā 262, 281
Arcirmārga 281
Aristotle 103
Arjuna 285
Āropa 172-73
Arthāpatti 107
Arthavāda 208
Āruṇi 142
Aśabda 44-45
Āsana 176
Āsanga 279-80
Aśarīram 292
Aśarīratva 287, 293
Asat 52, 76, 78
Asura 151-53, 159-61, 162-63
Aśvamedha 24-25
Aśvapati 29, 31, 34
Atharvan 27
Atharvā 28